PRAISE FOR: ***President Who -- Forgotten Founders.***

This is a brilliant and most enjoyable book which helps us to rediscover our rich history and heritage. Stan Klos clearly establishes that Virginia -- not Delaware -- became the first State in the Perpetual Union of the United States America ... because it was the first to ratify the Articles of Confederation (1779). You too will want to read his documentation complete with photographs and facsimiles of primary source documents of our lively and enlightening Americana history.

-- G. William Thomas, Jr., President,
James Monroe Memorial Foundation
http://www.MonroeFoundation.org

A well-written and extremely thought provoking piece of historical scholarship. By using extensive primary source materials, Stan Klos effectively proves his point that from 1781 to 1789 ten men served as President of the United States in Congress Assembled. Mr. Klos does not wish to displace George Washington as "Father of Our Country." Rather, Mr. Klos is seeking recognition for Washington's predecessors. A must read for anyone interested in American Presidential history.

-- Greg Priore
Archivist, William R. Oliver Special Collections Room
Carnegie Library of Pittsburgh

It is a masterpiece in defining presidential history. Stanley Klos clearly presents the historic path of the presidency beginning with the first President of the United States in Congress Assembled Samuel Huntington, to the eleventh President, George Washington. It is a must read for any serious student of American History.

- Senator Bill Stanley
President of the Norwich Historical Society

... a thought provoking argument for "righting" our history books about the very early years of our democracy. Samuel Huntington, His Excellency the President of the United States in Congress Assembled, indeed!

- Lee Langston-Harrison, Curator
James Madison's Montpelier

Quick – who was the first U.S. President? Wrong! At least, so this site tells us – documenting, as it does, no fewer than 10 possible holders of the office between 1774 and 1778. These ten men were the leaders of the Confederation Congress and Continental Congress, which (as you know if you read clear through that John Adams biography like you said you did) preceded Mr. Washington's inauguration in 1789. Deep historical truth? Trivial anomaly? Read all about it and decide for yourself on this absorbing corner of the great Virtualology.com site. –

-- Hot Sites Support Staff
USA TODAY

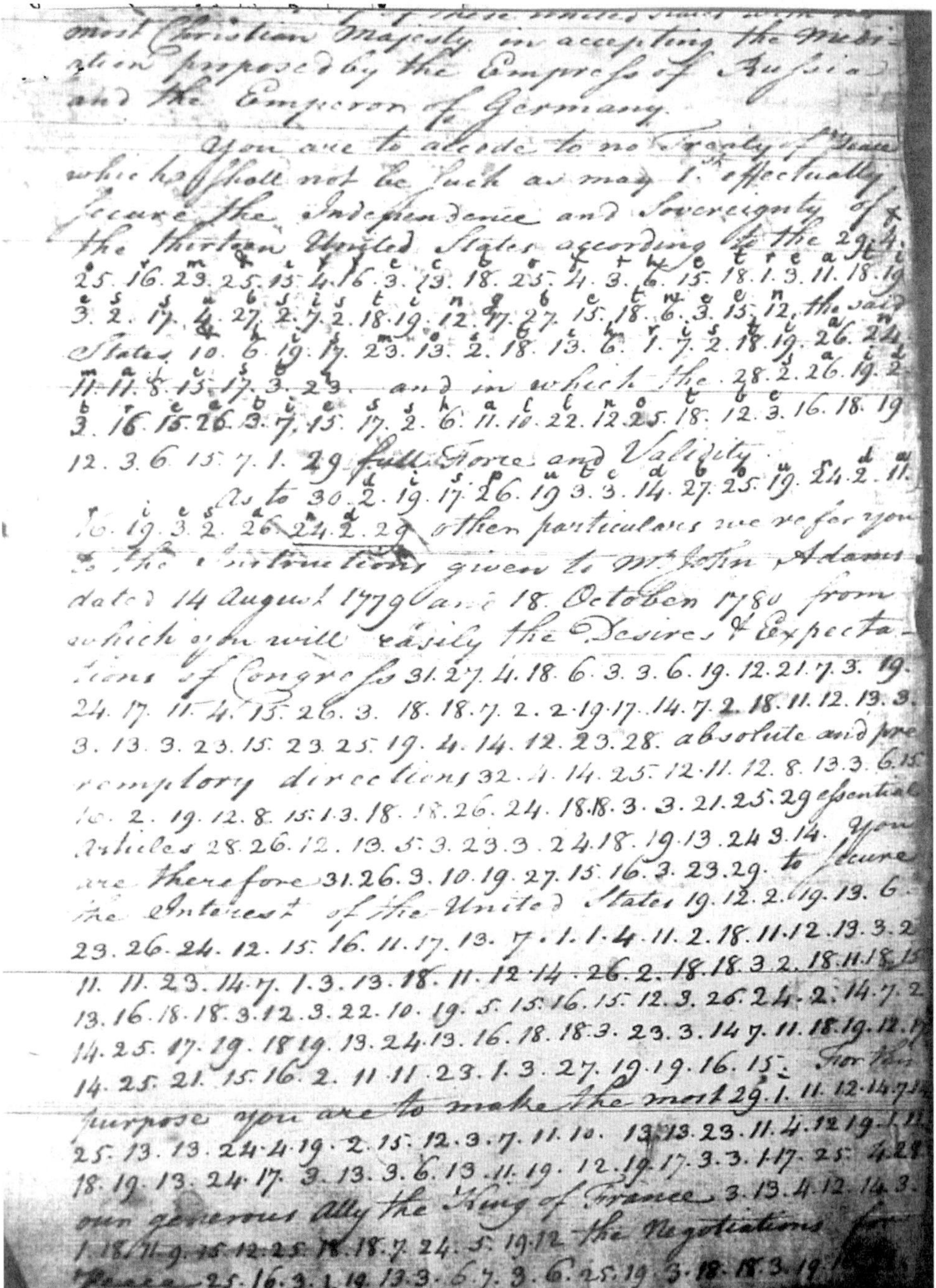

most Christian Majesty in accepting the Mediation proposed by the Empress of Russia and the Emperor of Germany.

You are to accede to no Treaty of Peace which shall not be such as may 1st effectually secure the Independence and Sovereignty of the thirteen United States according to the 29. 4. 25. 16. 23. 25. 15. 4. 16. 3. 13. 18. 23. 4. 3. 6. 15. 18. 1. 3. 11. 18. 19. 3. 2. 17. 4. 27. 2. 7. 2. 18. 19. 12. 17. 27. 15. 18. 6. 3. 15. 12. the said States 10. 6. 19. 17. 23. 13. 2. 18. 13. 6. 1. 7. 2. 18. 19. 26. 24. 11. 11. 8. 15. 17. 3. 23. and in which the 28. 2. 26. 19. 2. 3. 16. 15. 26. 3. 7. 15. 17. 2. 6. 11. 10. 22. 12. 25. 18. 12. 3. 16. 18. 19. 12. 3. 6. 15. 7. 1. 29 full Force and Validity.

As to 30. 2. 19. 17. 26. 19. 3. 3. 14. 27. 25. 19. 24. 2. 11. 16. 19. 3. 2. 26. 24. 2. 29 other particulars we refer you to the Instructions given to Mr. John Adams dated 14 August 1779 and 18 October 1780 from which you will easily the Desires & Expectations of Congress 31. 27. 4. 18. 6. 3. 3. 6. 19. 12. 21. 7. 3. 19. 24. 17. 11. 4. 15. 26. 3. 18. 18. 7. 2. 2. 19. 17. 14. 7. 2. 18. 11. 12. 13. 3. 3. 13. 3. 23. 15. 23. 25. 19. 4. 14. 12. 23. 28. absolute and peremptory directions 32. 4. 14. 25. 12. 11. 12. 8. 13. 3. 6. 15. 10. 2. 19. 12. 8. 15. 1. 3. 18. 18. 26. 24. 18. 18. 3. 3. 21. 25. 29 essential Articles 28. 26. 12. 13. 5. 3. 23. 3. 24. 18. 19. 13. 24. 3. 14. You are therefore 31. 26. 3. 10. 19. 27. 15. 16. 3. 23. 29. to secure the Interest of the United States 19. 12. 2. 19. 13. 6. 23. 26. 24. 12. 15. 16. 11. 17. 13. 7. 1. 1. 4. 11. 2. 18. 11. 12. 13. 3. 2 11. 11. 23. 14. 7. 1. 3. 13. 18. 11. 12. 14. 26. 2. 18. 18. 3. 2. 18. 11. 18. 15 13. 16. 18. 18. 3. 12. 3. 22. 10. 19. 5. 15. 16. 15. 12. 3. 26. 24. 2. 14. 7. 2 14. 25. 17. 19. 18 19. 13. 24. 13. 16. 18. 18. 3. 23. 3. 14 7. 11. 18. 19. 12. 1[illegible] 14. 25. 21. 15. 16. 2. 11. 11. 23. 1. 3. 27. 19. 19. 16. 15. For this purpose you are to make the most 29. 1. 11. 12. 14. 7 [illegible] 25. 13. 13. 24. 4. 19. 2. 15. 12. 3. 7. 11. 10. 13. 13. 23. 11. 4. 12 19. 1. [illegible] 18. 19. 13. 24. 17. 3. 13. 3. 6. 13. 11. 19. 12. 19. 17. 3. 3. 1. 17. 25. 4. 28 our generous Ally the King of France 3. 13. 4. 12. 14. 3. 1. 18. 11. 9. 15. 12. 25. 18. 18. 7. 24. 5. 19. 12 the Negotiations for Peace 25. 16. 3. 1. 19. 13. 3. 6. 7. 3. 6. 25. 19. 3. 18. 18. 3. 19. [illegible]

July 1781 letter to Thomas Jefferson, Benjamin Franklin and John Adams in code instructing on treaty negotiations from President of the United States in Congress Assembled Samuel Huntington -- *Courtesy of the Library of Congress*

PRESIDENT WHO?

FORGOTTEN FOUNDERS

BY: STANLEY L. KLOS

A KLOS FAMILY BOOK

PUBLISHED BY ESTORIC.COM

CARNEGIE, PENNSYLVANIA

For our children

Louis, Eilleen, Christopher, Nicholas, Alexandra, Mariesha, Zachary & Kathleen

Thank you Marie!

Estoric.com

"Pushing the Envelope"

428 Washington Avenue
Carnegie, PA 15106

Edited by: Beth Klein Ellis

Designed by: Diana Welch & Joseph Paonessa

Manufactured in the United States of America

ISBN 0-9752627-5-0

CONTENTS

Introduction

The First Chapter of this book gives a brief history of the American Presidency from 1774 to 1789 making the case that 10 men served as President of the United States in Congress Assembled before George Washington. Please understand that I am only advocating these men be recognized for what they are, Presidents of the United States in Congress Assembled and not displace George Washington as "The Father of Our Country". I am trying not to re-write history but right it.

The following chapters in this work are brief biographies on each of the Continental Congress and United States in Congress Assembled Presidents with autographs, letters and key Historical Documents from their Presidency. A dictator once maintained

> *"One is able to win people far more by the spoken than the written word, as the greatest changes in this world have never been brought about by the goose quill!"*

Wrong! It has been the written word (Bible, Koran, Magna Carte, Declaration of Independence, US Constitution, etc.) that has changed and continues to revolutionize the world. It was prudent, therefore, to include photographs of the actual primary letters and documents that formed the foundation of the United States of America throughout this book.

In 1999 these biographies were just edits of *Appleton's Cyclopedia of American Biography* to compliment the historic ephemera in my *Rebels With A Vision -- Historical Documents of Freedom* touring exhibit. Since 1999 the research on each of the Patriots has expanded and in most cases the biographies have been entirely re-written after conscientious research. The Chapter on Arthur St. Clair is particularly extensive as I reside in Upper St. Clair, Pennsylvania and thought it prudent to thoroughly educate my eight children on the accomplishments of their hometown's namesake with an expanded biography.

Recently, more time and research was spent on Samuel Huntington's Chapter as I was given the distinct honor to keynote his re-entombment on November 24, 2003. All chapters have been written to stand alone, so there is some redundancy in the verbiage. For instance, Elias Boudinot and Arthur St. Clair share several paragraphs on the Military Mutiny that held Congress hostage at Independence Hall. In July 1783, Boudinot was President of the United States in Congress Assembled and St. Clair was the General who negotiated their release; hence the duplication of the account in their biographies.

The Presidents stories are colorful, patriotic and quite moving. Most importantly these chapters on the Early Republic of the United States will provide readers with a vast insight into the workings of our 21st century political System.

George Santayana, a notable philosopher, once wrote, *"Those who do not learn from history are doomed to repeat it."* This view of history, as astute as it may be, is the classic example of seeing the glass half empty. Words like DOOMED and NOT LEARNED have echoed through the classrooms long enough, enveloping HISTORY with a negative aura.

A new approach to the historical adventure is blossoming and I am proud to be a small part of the metamorphosis.

At the signing of the 1787 US Constitution, Benjamin Franklin pointed to the President's Chair, which had a sun carved on it and said:

> *"I have often...in the course of this session...looked at that...without being able to tell whether it was rising or setting; but now at length I have the happiness to know that it is a rising and not a setting sun."*

This positive *"Rising Sun"* philosophy is something we all should embrace in life. So in this adventure into the lives of the forgotten presidents of the United States please keep your mind open and remember that *"History is the Crystal Ball to the Future; all you have to do is examine it."*

It is my sincere wish that you will discover, in *President Who?*, bursts of historical light that will clarify your vision and enrich your journey as a citizen of this bold and wonderful 21st Century World.

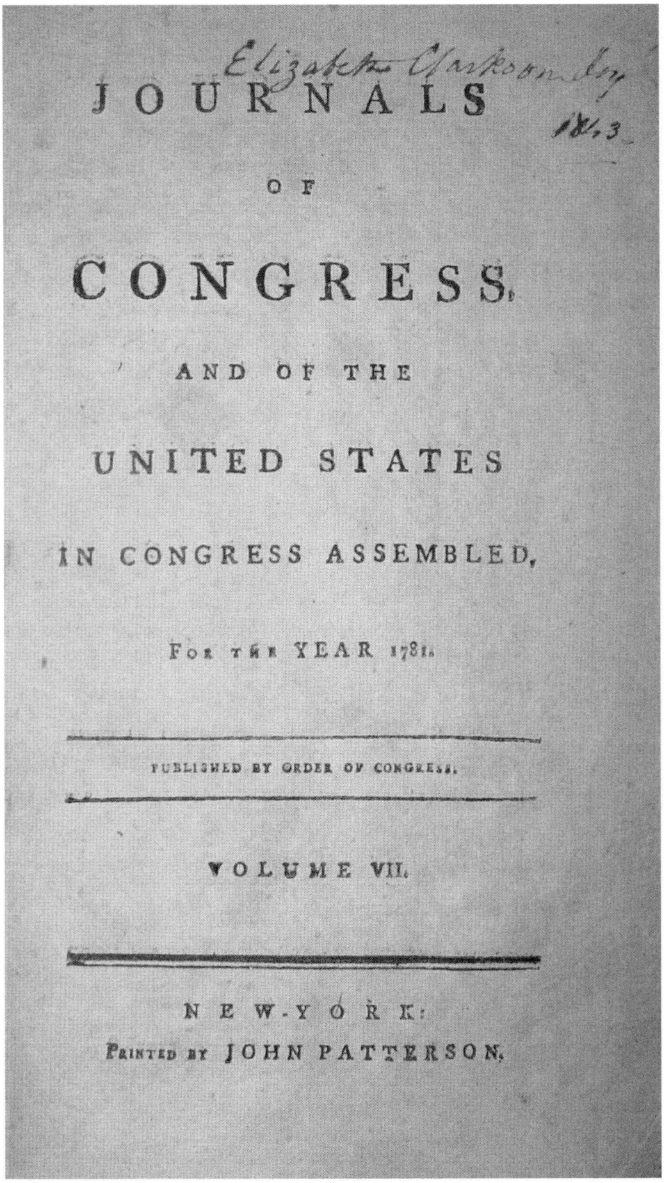

JOURNALS

OF

CONGRESS,

AND OF THE

UNITED STATES

IN CONGRESS ASSEMBLED,

FOR THE YEAR 1781.

PUBLISHED BY ORDER OF CONGRESS.

VOLUME VII.

NEW-YORK:

PRINTED BY JOHN PATTERSON.

Journal of Congress and United States in Congress Assembled used by the author to corroborate the Library of Congress Online Journals. This Journal was published by John Patterson of New York in 1787 by order of the United States in Congress Assembled – *Courtesy of the Klos Family*

A Brief chronology of late 18th Century Colonial America

1763 – The French and Indian War for Empire ends with a Paris Treaty. King George III signs a Proclamation prohibiting English settlement west of the Appalachians. Parliament, in desperate need of money, passes The Sugar Act, increasing duties on imported sugar, textiles, coffee, wines and indigo dye.

1765 – The British Stamp Act passes Parliament and imposes a direct tax on the American colonies to be paid directly to King George III. The Stamp Act Congress convenes in New York City and passes a resolution calling on King George III to repeal the act. One year later that act is repealed.

1766 – English Parliament passes the Declaratory Act declaring the British government's absolute authority over the American colonies.

1767 – The Townshend Revenue Acts are passed by Parliament taxing imported paper, tea, glass, lead and paints.

1768 – John Hancock and other Selectman call for a town meeting at Faneuil Hall from September 23 to September 28, 1768 and 96 towns answered Hancock's call to address taxation and self government grievances. On the final day of the meeting, warships arrived in Boston with the first British reinforcements, and on October 1 two regiments arrived from Halifax, effectively beginning British occupation of its own colony. British troops stayed in Boston until forced to evacuate in March 1776.

1770 – John Adams successfully defends the soldiers who open fire on a Massachusetts crowd of colonists who had been harassing them. Five are killed and six are wounded and the event goes down in history as The Boston Massacre. That same year, the Townshend Acts are repealed and taxes are removed from all items but tea.

1773 – The Tea Act gives the British East India Company a monopoly on tea by allowing it to bypass the British Crown Tax. Colonists masquerading as Mohawk Indians, board British ships and dump 342 containers of tea into Boston harbor in an event now known as "The Boston Tea Party."

1774 – Coercive Acts passed by Parliament to rebuke Massachusetts for its continuing resistance to parliamentary rule. These four laws effectively end self-rule in Massachusetts.

1774 – The First Continental Congress organizes in Philadelphia's City Tavern and formally meets in Carpenter Hall with every colony represented but Georgia. In attendance are George Washington, Patrick Henry and John Hancock. Declaration of Resolves is passed, asserting the rights of colonists and rejecting absolute British authority over colonies.

1775 – England Declares Massachusetts to be in a state of rebellion. The New England

Restraining Act is also passed, requiring the Colonies to trade only with Britain. Patrick Henry gives a speech in which he declares, "give me liberty or give me death."

Later that same year, British troops headed to destroy a weapons depot at Concord are confronted by Massachusetts militiamen and the "shot heard round the world" begins the American Revolution. The Second Continental Congress convenes and unanimously appoints George Washington as General of the Continental Army.

1776– On July 2, 1776 The United Colonies of America declare themselves to be free and Independent States at the Pennsylvania Colonial Statehouse in Philadelphia. On July 4th, 1776 The Declaration of Independence is passed. Thomas Paine writes "Common Sense." After losses in New York and New Jersey Washington, on Christmas Eve, attacks the British and wins victory at the Battle of Trenton.

1777 – Articles of Confederation are finally passed by the Continental Congress of the United States, but require unanimous ratification by all thirteen States. The Continental Congress continues to conduct the war under the resolutions and laws of the United Colonies of America while they await ratification. First American flag commissioned by Congress. Virginia becomes the first state by ratifying the Articles on December 16, 1777.

1778 – After success at Saratoga Benjamin Franklin signs treaties with France, formally allying the US to France against Britain. South Carolina on February 5th, New York, February 6th, Rhode Island, February 16th, Georgia, February 26th, Connecticut, February 27th, New Hampshire March 4th, Pennsylvania, March 5th, Massachusetts, March 10th, North Carolina, April 24th, and New Jersey, November 20th, ratify the Articles of Confederation.

1779 – Delaware, the 12th State, ratifies the Articles of Confederation February 1st.

1780 – British effectively capture the Southern States when Charleston, South Carolina falls. Former President of the Continental Congress, Henry Middleton of South Carolina, pledges allegiance to the British Crown. General Benedict Arnold found to be a spy and accepts a commission in the British Army.

1781 - On February 2, 1781 Maryland final ratifies the Articles of Confederation. On March 1, Maryland's ratification is presented to the Continental Congress. With all thirteen States present the Continental Congress declares the Articles ratified, forming the Perpetual Union of the United States of America. On March 2, 1781 Congress changes their name as prescribed by the new Constitution to the United States in Congress Assembled. Continental Congress President Samuel Huntington is retained and becomes the President of the United States in Congress Assembled. Cornwallis surrenders to Washington in September 1781 after the siege of Yorktown. The British Parliament votes to end the war and authorizes the King to negotiate the peace with the Americans.

1782 –An initial peace treaty is signed in Paris recognizing American independence and agreeing to the British withdrawal from American soil.

1783 – Military mutinies and holds Congress, who is in session in Independence Hall, hostage.

1784 – The Treaty of Paris is ratified by the Congress. Thomas Mifflin signs as the President of the United States of America.

1786 – Shays Rebellion breaks out in New England over protests of unfair taxing laws, and corrupt judges. The Articles of Confederation Government is weak and failing. The States call for a revision of the Articles of Confederation in Annapolis, Maryland but only 5 States show. They recommend Congress call for a second convention to revise the Articles in May 1787. Congress does not adopt the resolution.

1787 – General Arthur St. Clair, the man who negotiated Congress' release in 1783, is elected President of the United States in Congress Assembled. He immediately supports the committee's recommendation to revise the Articles of Confederation. The Convention convenes in May. In July St. Clair's Congress passes the Northwest Ordinance. On September 17th the Convention in Philadelphia signs, not a document revising the Articles of Confederation, but a new Constitution. President Arthur St. Clair and Congress receive the New Plan for The Federal Government and decide not to alter one word, voting to send it on to the states for ratification.

1788 – The Constitution is ratified and elections are scheduled under the new articles of the 1787 document.

1789 – The United States in Congress Assembled disbands and the new House of Representatives, Senate, Supreme Court and President assume the offices prescribed to them under the US Constitution. George Washington is sworn in as the 1st President of the United States under the 1787 Constitution.

CHAPTER ONE

Portrait of George Washington from
Appleton Cyclopedia of American Biography

GEORGE WASHINGTON

11th President of the United States
1st Under the US Constitution

The following historical documentation lends proof to the thesis that 10 men held the office of US President in Congress Assembled prior to the inauguration of George Washington in 1789. The official correspondence and the Journals of the Continental Congress and the United States in Congress Assembled clearly give testament to the existence of a Pre-Constitutional US Presidency. The Founders' legislative actions and resolutions also confirm such. Additionally, the recognition of the US Presidency by foreign leaders and the unanimous ratification of the Articles of Confederation in 1781 are irrefutable proof that the office of President of the United States in Congress Assembled was more then just the presiding arm of the unicameral US Government.

Important accomplishments by these early leaders and facts about them have all been forgotten due to the popular belief that the US Presidency began with George Washington. Even most history teachers and professors would be hard pressed to answer key US foundational questions as they have been rendered indistinguishable by the Constitutional Presidency and the extraordinary accomplishments of George Washington. For instance:

> Which Continental Congress President did George Washington call the "*Father of our Country*"?
>
> Which US President wrote and introduced the resolution that declared US Independence on July 2, 1776?
>
> Which Continental Congress President signed George Washington's Commander-in-Chief's Commission?
>
> Which US President conspired in the Conway Cabal to replace George Washington as Commander-in-Chief with General Horatio Gates?
>
> Which US President persuaded holdout Maryland to ratify the Articles of Confederation thereby creating the "*Perpetual Union*" known as the United States of America in 1781?
>
> Which Continental Congress President was imprisoned in the Tower of London and later exchanged for General Cornwallis?
>
> Which Continental Congress President persuaded John Adams and Benjamin Franklin to ignore the direct order of the United States in Congress Assembled demanding France be included in the negotiations of the Treaty of Paris?
>
> Which US President, in the summer of 1783, negotiated the peaceful release of President Elias Boudinot and the entire Confederation Congress from Independence Hall?
>
> Which US President's signature ratified the Treaty that ended the war with England?
>
> Which US President sponsored the legislation to hold the 1787 Constitutional Convention in Philadelphia after the Annapolis Convention failed to reach a quorum in 1786?

How did you do on answering these questions? 90%? 80%? 70% ? If you scored 2 correct answers or 20% you are on par with the thousands of listeners who have attended our nationally renowned exhibits. This book includes chapters on each of the Presidents and their accomplishments in the Continental Congress and/or the United States in Congress Assembled.

Both presidents of the United States and Continental Congress Presidents who presided over the 1774 - 1788 unicameral US Government *(there was only one component with Congress serving as the executive, legislative, and judicial branches)* throughout the War of Independence are virtually unknown to the US public. The fact that Samuel Huntington is not recognized as the first President of the United States is primarily due to the reality that our first set of national laws, the Articles of Confederation, failed to provide our founding fathers with a constitution capable of governing the United States. This, coupled with the 1774 Continental Congress' *"Oath of Secrecy"* on congressional debates, has all but muted the founding legislative discourse and consequently thwarted the official recognition of these 10 men as Presidents of The United States in Congress Assembled as well as with their four Confederation Congress President predecessors.

To make the founding US Presidential History even more perplexing some historians maintain incorrectly that John Hanson was the first President of the United States. In fact on January 29th, 2004 I received a rather frantic call from David Halaas, the Chief Historian of the Heinz History Center, a branch of the Smithsonian Institute. I had consigned Presidential letters of John Hancock, Thomas McKean, Thomas Mifflin, Elias Boudinot and Arthur St. Clair as well as the first public printing of the US Constitution to the Smithsonian's traveling exhibit *"A Glorious Burden, The American Presidency,"* which was due to open two days later in Pittsburgh. The exhibit's part on the Continental Congress and United States in Congress Assembled had just arrived at the museum. The Smithsonian had no account of the United States in Congress Assembled and had John Hanson as the first President of the Continental Congress. They were incorrect on both accounts. David said, "... *either you are all wrong or this Smithsonian Exhibit* (which had already has been half way around the Country) is wrong." I assured him I was right. David said, *"I knew you must have been right but needed to hear it again before I call the Smithsonian."* I showed up with the original 1781 Journal of the Continental Congress and 1782 Journal of the United States in Congress Assembled the following evening. He said he would notify the Smithsonian on the 31st and pull the *"Hanson"* sign and verbiage.
I decided to send the Smithsonian Senior Educator this letter on February 2nd, the 217 anniversary of President St. Clair's election to office:

Julia Forbes, Senior Educator
Smithsonian's "American Presidency, A Glorious Burden"

Dear Dr. Forbes,

Just a heads-up from one fellow educator to another. Your exceptional traveling exhibit "American Presidency, A Glorious Burden" starts off with John Hanson as the first President of The Continental Congress. The source of this myth is primarily the responsibility of author Seymour Wemyss Smith's book "John Hanson Our First President." In this 1932 book he incorrectly makes the case that John Hanson was the first elected President of the United States in Congress Assembled. This is inaccurate as Samuel Huntington assumed the office when the Articles of Confederation were ratified March 1, 1781 transforming the Continental Congress to United States in Congress Assembled.

Additionally, the first President elected under the Articles of Confederation was Samuel Johnson on July 9, 1781 and he turned the position down. On July 10, 1781 Thomas McKean was elected and accepted becoming the 2nd President of the United States in Congress Assembled.

John Hanson was the 3rd President of the United States in Congress Assembled and not the 1st of the Continental Congress as your display indicates. In fact Hanson was never a member of the Continental Congress. The first President of the Continental Congress of the United Colonies of America was Peyton Randolph. The first President of the Continental Congress of the United States of America was John Hancock. The first President of the United States in Congress Assembled was Samuel Huntington. The first President of the United States under the 1787 Constitution was, of course, George Washington who unlike his predecessors was not "a presiding officer" as the title indicates.

Another reason why this fallacious reasoning is perpetuated is that Hanson was the first President to serve the prescribed full one-year term (1781–82) under the newly ratified Articles of Confederation. Additionally, he was the first President to win the office by delegates elected by their respective states under the ratified Articles of Confederation. Be that as it may, Samuel Huntington became the First President of the United States in Congress Assembled upon the Articles ratification on March 1, 1781, an undisputable FACT.

Historical inaccuracies aside, it is essential to cry out that these pre-1789 Presidents were great American heroes, leaders and visionaries. For instance, it was then Continental Congress and later US President John Hancock's signature along with Secretary Charles Thomson's that that appeared on the Declaration of Independence Broadside presented to King George III and his generals in 1776. The bulls-eye remained on their backs for many months, as the names of the other signers were not published until 1777.

Continental Congress President Henry Laurens' Congress succeeded in passing the Articles of Confederation in 1777, the ratification in 1781 created the "*Perpetual Union*" of the United States. Later, as a US Diplomat, Laurens' mission to the Netherlands for monetary support ended with his capture and imprisonment in the Tower of London. He was freed only after the Battle of Yorktown as a prisoner exchange with British General Cornwallis.

The newly elected delegates of November 1786 were not able to form a quorum until January 17th, 1787 and failed to elect a President. Arthur St. Clair, a true forgotten hero of the revolution, was elected President of the United States in Congress Assembled in the shadows of Shay's Rebellion and the near collapse of the Articles of Confederation Government on February 2, 1787. St. Clair's Congress successfully enacted the necessary legislation to convene the Constitutional Convention in Philadelphia after its failure to reach a quorum in 1786 at Annapolis under President Nathaniel Gorham. St. Clair's 1787 administration also passed the Northwest Ordinance, which had lingered in Congress since 1784 and was herald by Daniel Webster many years later,

"We are accustomed to praise lawgivers of antiquity ... but I doubt whether one single law of any lawgiver, ancient or modern, has produced the effects of more distinct, marked, and lasting character than the Ordinance of 1787."

Finally, President Arthur St. Clair received and signed the order that sent the new US Constitution to the 13 original states for deliberation despite a new provision prohibiting future foreign born citizens *(like him)* to hold the Presidency, should it be ratified.

These and many other events, accomplishments and laws form the monumental foundation that lies beneath the current US Presidency. These colossal footers have been hidden so long that this book will do little to awaken the vast US Citizenry to rediscover and embrace their nation's remarkable roots of sheer courage, unquestionable sacrifice and unending patriotism. What these Lost Presidents require to be reborn in the consciousness of all American Citizens is nothing short of an Act of Congress or at the very least an amendment to include them in the Presidential Order that honors each Constitutional President with a gravesite wreath laying ceremony on their respective birthdays. As long as the US Government officially recognizes George Washington as the first President of the United States these men, their sacrifices and the remarkable accomplishments of their unicameral office will never receive the acknowledgment they rightfully deserve.

The foundational proofs supporting official recognition of a pre-1789 US Presidency by both the 21st Century US Congress and US President are summarized as follows:

1. The Journals of Congress clearly indicate that there were six Presidents of the Continental Congress and ten Presidents of the United States in Congress Assembled before George Washington's Inauguration in 1789. Two of the Presidents, John Hancock and Samuel Huntington served in both offices.

2. These fourteen Presidents, aside from Secretary Charles Thomson, were the only members of the confederation freely elected by Congress to represent the United Colonies/States in their entirety.

3. The First State to ratify The *"Perpetual Union"* of the United States was Virginia *(not Delaware)* on December 16 1777. However, it wasn't until March 1, 1781 when Maryland agreed to the mandatory unanimous ratification of the Articles of Confederation, that first *"Constitution"* of the United States legally bound the 13 States into one united country.

4. The President of the United States in Congress Assembled on March 1, 1781 was Samuel Huntington of Connecticut who by virtue of the Articles' ratification became the 1st President of the United States in Congress Assembled.

5. Nine more Presidents of the United States in Congress Assembled under the Articles of Confederation were duly elected after Samuel Huntington. The Presidents on many occasions used their office to exercise much influence on United States public affairs and legislation.

6. These 10 US Presidents in Congress Assembled presided over the unicameral government of the United States of America from 1781 to 1788 under the Articles of Confederation. The word *"President"* is derived from *"to preside"* which was just one function of the US Presidency under the Articles of the Confederation.

7. The Presidents signed congressional laws, treaties, and military orders. They called for Congressional assembly and adjournment. Presidents signed military commissions including George Washington's commander-in-chief appointment, received foreign dignitaries, received, read, answered, and at their own discretion held or disseminated the official mail addressed to Congress and the President of the United States in Congress Assembled. The Presidents each had one vote in the Unicameral Congress. The Presidents presided, much like the Chief Justice of the Supreme Court, over judicial Congressional Cases. The current US President conducts many of the same duties today but is not permitted, under the 1787 Constitution, to vote, act as a presiding judge or to receive, open, and hold Congress' mail or serve as a judiciary official of the United States.

8. The government of the United States provided for the President's expenses, servants, clerks, housing, and transportation. Their home state was expected to provide for their salary.

9. In 1788 the President of the United States in Congress Assembled official duties were replaced by President George Washington (executive branch), Chief Justice John Jay (judicial branch), President of the US Senate John Adams and Speaker of the US House of Representatives Frederick A.C. Muhlenberg (legislative branch) under the new US Constitution.

10. In 1861 President Abraham Lincoln refused to recognize the secession of South Carolina and the other Southern States claiming they were legally bound to the United States not by the US Constitution but by the "*Perpetual Union*" they ratified under the Articles of Confederation in 1781.

"*The express plighting of faith by each and all of the original thirteen in the Articles of Confederation, two years later, that the Union shall be perpetual is most conclusive.*" – *(Abraham Lincoln's Address to Congress in Special Session 4 July 1861.)*

A "*Perpetual Union*" of the United States that was first governed by President Samuel Huntington.

Clearly these 10 points make a "*stars and stripes*" foundational case that George Washington was not the 1st President of the United States nor is George Walker Bush the 43rd. They are the 11th and 53rd, respectively. The order or should we say the proper order of US Presidency is as follows:

Samuel Huntington
1st President of the United States in Congress Assembled
March 1, 1781 to July 6, 1781

Thomas McKean
2nd President of the United States in Congress Assembled
July 10, 1781 to November 5, 1781

John Hanson
3rd President of the United States in Congress Assembled
November 5, 1781 to November 4, 1782

Elias Boudinot
4th President of the United States in Congress Assembled
November 4, 1782 to November 3, 1783

Thomas Mifflin
5th President of the United States in Congress Assembled
November 3, 1783 to June 3, 1784

Richard Henry Lee
6th President of the United States in Congress Assembled
November 30, 1784 to November 23, 1785

John Hancock
7th President of the United States in Congress Assembled
November 23, 1785 to June 6, 1786

Nathaniel Gorham
8th President of the United States in Congress Assembled
June 1786 - November 13, 1786

Arthur St. Clair
9th President of the United States in Congress Assembled
February 2, 1787 to October 29, 1787

Cyrus Griffin
10th President of the United States in Congress Assembled
January 22, 1788 to March 4, 1789

George Washington
11th President of the United States
US Constitution
1789 to 1797

Presidents of the Continental Congress as The United Colonies of America

The Continental Congress was officially formed on September 5, 1774 in Philadelphia's Carpenters Hall to petition King George III after England passed the Intolerable Acts. The first *unofficial* meeting of delegates actually took place the day before in *The City Tavern* just down the street *(yes the true birthplace of the Continental Congress was in a Philadelphia tavern).* The debates at the tavern meeting were significant as the decision was made to hold the First Continental Congress in a private, rather than public hall. When Congress convened the next day South Carolina delegate Thomas Lynch nominated Peyton Randolph to be chairman. Randolph was elected by unanimous vote. Connecticut Delegate Silas Deane wrote of Randolph to Mrs. Deane:

> " ... *Designed by nature for the business, of an affable, open and majestic deportment, large in size, though not out of proportion, he commands respect and esteem by his very aspect, independent of the high character he sustains* ..."

So began the road to the current US Presidency!

By May 10, 1775, when the Second Continental Congress met, armed conflict had begun. Despite this, the delegates moved slowly toward independence waiting until July 2, 1776 to adopt Richard Henry Lee's resolution to declare independence from Great Britain:

> *"Resolved, That these United Colonies are, and of right ought to be, free and independent states, that they are absolved from all allegiance to the British Crown, and that all political connection between them and the state of Great Britain is, and ought to be, totally dissolved."*

The 1774-76 leaders of the continental legislature of the Thirteen Colonies were:

Peyton Randolph

September 5, 1774 to October 22, 1774
and May 20 to May 24, 1775

Henry Middleton

October 22, 1774 to October 26, 1774

John Hancock

October 27, 1775 to July 1, 1776

Presidents of the Continental Congress United States of America

After Independence, the United Colonies, now called the United States, needed a formal confederation to govern and conduct the war against England. The Confederation Congress took 17 months after Independence to pass the Articles of Confederation. The delegates signed the Articles on November 15, 1777 under their new President Henry Laurens. Unlike the Constitution of 1787 this confederation charter required the ratification of all 13 states before becoming the first "*Constitution*" of the United States of America.

Fortunately it took a long time to ratify the Articles of Confederation. This enabled Congress to pass crucial wartime legislation with only a majority vote versus the 9 to 4 State margin mandated by the pending Articles of Confederation. Most historians agree that under a 1777 "*ratified*" Articles of Confederation this new government would have fallen apart. The pressures of a difficult war did result in many crucial seven state congressional quorums. On several occasions, a fleeing Congress passed crucial legislation with only 7 states voting four to three. These resolutions would have failed the constitutional test under the Articles of Confederation.

The Presidents who served under the "*Declaration of Independence's Confederation Congress*" during this difficult period of American History and ratification consideration were:

John Hancock
July 2, 1776 to October 29, 1777;

Henry Laurens
November 1, 1777 to December 9, 1778

John Jay
December 10, 1778 to September 28, 1779

Samuel Huntington
September 28, 1779 to February 28, 1781

Presidents of the United States in Congress Assembled

Ratification of the Articles of Confederation was delayed until March 1, 1781 by Maryland due to border disputes. On March 1, 1781 with this 13th state's ratification the Continental Congress ceased to exist and "*The United States in Congress Assembled*" was placed at the head of each page of the Official Journal of Congress. The New United States in Congress Assembled Journal reported on March 2, 1781:

> *The ratification of the Articles of Confederation being yesterday completed by the accession of the State of Maryland: The United States met in Congress, when the following members appeared: His Excellency Samuel Huntington, delegate for Connecticut, President ...*

Another important fact with regards to the unanimous Articles of Confederation approval is the *State Order of Ratification.* This order of ratification is the absolute proof of which State has the bragging rights of being "*FIRST*" as it was the Articles of Confederation that formed the

> "*Perpetual Union between the states of New Hampshire, Massachusetts-bay, Rhode Island and Providence Plantations, Connecticut, New York, New Jersey, Pennsylvania, Delaware, Maryland, Virginia, North Carolina, South Carolina and Georgia*"

providing President Lincoln, some 80 years later, with the foundation of his legal authority to stop the secession of the southern states in 1861.

On January 1, 1999, in a related blunder in American History, the United States Mint proudly unveiled its first George Washington State Quarter with the mark of Delaware on its reverse. This State's Quarter was released first because, by virtue of a poorly researched Act of Congress, the US Mint was forced to recognize Delaware as the first state. Delaware was chosen because it was the first State to ratify the US Constitution on December 7, 1787. If Congress, the President or their staff did their historical homework this erroneous legislation would never have memorialized Delaware as the First State on the Washington Quarter. Delaware actually joined the United States of America when it ratified the Articles of Confederation on February 1, 1779. The first state to actually adopt statehood was Virginia, which ratified the "Perpetual Union" on December 16, 1777. Delaware was actually the 12th state to join the Union.

Moreover, it is a sin of history that the US Mint currently serves as the official government agency to perpetuate Delaware's First State Myth as their third Director, Elias Boudinot, was the 4th President of the United States in Congress Assembled under the Articles of Confederation. One would think that a Government Institution once headed by a US President under the Articles would be more "in tune" with the historical facts behind US Statehood and object to such erroneous legislation. When I confronted the US Mint on this error they agreed and rightfully passed the buck to the US Congress.

The correct order of US State ratification and entrance into the Union can be found below:

US Statehood Order

Articles of Confederation - 1 to 13 States
US Constitution - 37 to 50 States

	State	State Passes Ratification	Reported to Congress	Delegates Sign
1	Virginia	16 December 1777	25 June 1778	9 July 1778
2	South Carolina	5 February 1778	25 June 1778	9 July 1778
3	New York	6 February 1778	23 June 1778	9 July 1778
4	Rhode Island	16 February 1778	23 June 1778	9 July 1778
5	Georgia	26 February 1778	25 June 1778	9 July 1778
6	Connecticut	27 February 1778	23 June 1778	9 July 1778
7	New Hampshire	4 March 1778	23 June 1778	9 Jul 1778-8 Aug 1778
8	Pennsylvania	5 March 1778	25 June 1778	9 Jul 1778-22 Jul 1778
9	Massachusetts	10 March 1778	23 June 1778	9 July 1778
10	North Carolina	24 April 1778	25 June 1778	21 July 1778
11	New Jersey	20 November 1778	25-26 Nov. 1778	26 Nov 1778
12	Delaware	1 February 1779	16 February 1779	22 Feb 1779-5 May 1779
13	Maryland	2 February 1781	12 February 1781	1 March 1781

Sources: *The Documentary History of the Ratification of the Constitution: Vol. 1: Constitutional Documents and Records, 1776-1787,* ed. Merrill Jensen, Madison, Wis.: State Historical Society of Wisconsin, 1976; *Encyclopedia of American History: Bicentennial Edition,* ed. Richard Morris, New York; Harper & Row, 1976; *Documents of American History,* ed. Henry Steele Commanger, Englewood Cliffs, NJ; Prentice-Hall, 1973.

To reiterate, the First State was Virginia and the First US President was Mr. Samuel Huntington of Connecticut who was leading the Confederation Government in 1781. Huntington's term commenced in 1779 and he had served well beyond the one-year term limitation now mandated by the March 1, 1781 ratification of the Articles of Confederation. Despite this the former Confederation Congress President was recognized as President of the United States in Congress Assembled during the ratification celebration of March 1, 1781 at the Capitol. The "*The United States in Congress Assembled*" was placed at the head of each page of the Official Journal of Congress. Huntington by virtue of this ratification became President of the United States and served as *President of the United States in Congress Assembled* until July 6, 1781 when he tendered his resignation:

> "*The President having informed the United States in Congress assembled, that his ill state of health*" ... *not permit him to continue longer in the exercise of the duties of that office*".

The presidency was not filled until July 10th when Thomas McKean of Delaware was elected President after North Carolina's Samuel Johnston declined his July 9th nomination. Yes that is correct, someone actually refused after the ballots were cast to serve as President of the United States.

The War effectively ended with Cornwallis' surrender in Yorktown, October 19, 1781 only 6 months after the Articles' ratification and formal establishment of President of the United States in Congress Assembled. It was during this period that Congress and its Foreign Commissioners sought favorable terms in a Peace Treaty with Great Britain. Peace Commissioner John Jay, a former President of the Confederation Congress took it upon himself to ignore Congress' instructions mandating the inclusion of France in the treaty negotiations with Great Britain. Peace Commissioners John Adams and Benjamin Franklin heeded this "*presidential wisdom*" and followed Jay's lead keeping France in the dark until treaty negotiations were completed with England. The Treaty of Paris officially ended the War with Great Britain and the United States gained a vast amount of land that now comprises the states of Ohio, Indiana, Illinois, Michigan, and Wisconsin. This land was known as the Northwest Territory. Many founders believed that the sale of Northwest Territory real estate to settlers and speculators would pay the mountain of debt incurred during the War for Independence and fund the United States Government for many generations.

The Historical Record Case for The First US Presidency

The Articles of Confederation's Presidency was held in high esteem by most *US Founding Fathers.* It is essential to note that our National Archives, museums, libraries and historical societies are filled with many letters and manuscripts attesting to this esteem by the founders including the first three US Constitutional Presidents, Washington, Adams, and Jefferson. For example, Washington writes Secretary Charles Thompson on being informed of the election of a new President

Headquarters near Dobbs Ferry 21st of July 1781

> *Sir,*
>
> *I have been honored by your letter of the 10th that Congrefs, upon the retiring of the late President Huntington elected the honorable Thomas McKean, Esq. to preside in their respectable body, I shall for the future conduct my correspondence agreeable to this information.*
>
> *I have the Honor sir your most obedient servant -- George Washington*

In another letter, dated the same day to the new President, Washington conveys to McKean the importance of Presidential communication to the Commander-in-Chief:

> Headquarters near Dobbs Ferry 21st of July 1781
>
> *Sir,*
>
> *I have been honored by your Excellency's three Letters of the 14th and 17th of this Month, with the several Resolutions of Congress, and the Extracts from intercepted Letters, inclosed (sic).*
>
> *I am much obliged by your Attention in the Communication of the Extracts, although I had been favored with them thro' another Channel, previous to the Receipt of your Favor; the Intelligence to be collected from them, if properly improved, I think may turn greatly to our Advantage.*
>
> *I take this Opportunity most sincerely to congratulate you Sir, on the Honor conferred on you by Congress, in being elected to preside in that most respectable Body; happy, as I expect to be in your Correspondence, I dare say I shall have no Reason to complain of the Mode of your conducting it; as from a knowledge of your Character I flatter myself it will ever be performed with great Propriety.*
>
> *I take the Liberty however to request as a particular Favor, that you will be so good as to convey to me, as you have Opportunity, any interesting Intelligence which you may receive, either from Europe or respecting our Continental Affairs; your Situation will put it particularly in your Power to oblige me in this Request, <u>and be assured Sir! that a greater Obligation cannot be conferred, since for Want of Communication in this Way, I have often been left in the Dark in Matters which essentially concern the public Welfare; and which, if known, might be very influential in the Government of my Conduct in the Military Line.</u> I am happy to be informed by Accounts from all Parts of the Continent, of the agreeable Prospect of a very plentiful Supply of almost all the Productions of the Earth. Blessed as we are with the Bounties of Providence, necessary for our support and Defence (sic), the Fault must surely be our own (and great indeed will it be), if we do not, by a proper Use of them, attain the noble Prize for which we have so long been contending, the Establishment of Peace, Liberty and Independence.*
>
> *I have the Honor sir your most obedient servant -- George Washington*

This letter in particular from Washington to President John Hanson is a good example of the high esteem held for this office:

Philadelphia, November 30, 1781.

> *Sir:*
>
> *Your Excellency's several Favors of the 10th. 13th. and 24th. instant with their Inclosures were handed me while on the Road to this Town, which has prevented my Reply before the present Moment. While I Congratulate your Excellency on your Appointment to fill the most important Seat in the United States, I take the same opportunity to thank you with great Sincerity for the very polite Manner in which you are pleased to tender me the Advantages of your Correspondence. As a mutual free Communication cannot fail to be attended with great Satisfaction to me, and will undoubtedly be productive of very useful Consequences to the public Cause, your Excellency may be assured I shall pay very particular Attention to this Correspondence.*
>
> *I sincerely Accord to your Excellency's Sentiment that Our public Affairs at present assume a promising Aspect; but suffer me to begin the Freedom of our Correspondence, by Observing to your Excellency, that upon our future vigorous Improvement of the present favorable Moment, depend the happy Consequences which we now promise ourselves as the Result of all the successful Events of the last Campaign.*

Letters alone didn't establish the former President of the Continental Congress as President of the United States. Acts, laws, and resolutions of Congress conducted official US business with these leaders signing their names as Presidents of the United States in Congress Assembled. Here are four examples from the Official US Journals of The United States in Congress Assembled:

> *Example #1: The United States in Congress assembled --To all who shall see these presents, send greeting.*
>
> *It having been represented to Congress by their minister plenipotentiary at the Court of Versailles, that the king of Sweden has signified by his ambassador at that Court to our said minister his desire to enter into a treaty with the United States in Congress assembled; and we being willing to promote the same for establishing harmony and good intercourse between the citizens of the United States and the subjects of the said king:--Know ye, therefore, That we, confiding in the integrity, prudence and ability of the honourable Benjamin Franklin, esquire, have nominated, constituted and appointed, and by these presents do nominate, constitute and appoint the said Benjamin Franklin, our minister plenipotentiary, giving him full powers, general and special, to act in that quality, to confer, treat, agree and conclude with the person or persons vested with equal powers by the said king, of and concerning a treaty of amity and commerce between the United States in Congress assembled, and the king of Sweden; and whatever shall be so agreed and concluded for us and in our name to sign and thereupon to make such treaty, conventions and agreements as he shall judge conformable to the ends we have in view, hereby promising in good faith that we will accept, ratify and execute whatever shall be agreed, concluded and signed by our said minister. And whereas it may so happen*

that our aforesaid minister may die, or be otherwise incapacitated to execute this commission: We do, in that case, by these presents constitute and appoint the honourable John Adams our minister plenipotentiary for the purpose aforesaid; and in case of his death or incapacity, we appoint the honourable John Jay our minister plenipotentiary for the purpose aforesaid; and in case of his death or incapacity also, we do appoint the honourable Henry Laurens our minister plenipotentiary for the purpose aforesaid, with all the powers herein before delegated to the honourable Benjamin Franklin.

In witness whereof we have caused these to be sealed with our seal. Done at Philadelphia this 28th day of September in the year of our Lord 1782 and in the year of our Independence, by the United States in Congress assembled.

In testimony whereof, we have caused the seal of the United States of America to be affixed to these presents.

Witness His Excellency John Hanson, Esq. President of the United States in Congress assembled, the twenty-eighth day of September, in the year of our Lord, one thousand seven hundred and eighty-two, and of our sovereignty and Independence the seventh.

Example #2: The United States In Congress Assembled,

To Oliver Pollock Esquire Greeting:

We reposing special trust and confidence in your abilities and integrity have constituted and appointed, and by these presents do constitute and appoint you our commercial agent during our pleasure, at the city and port of Havannah, to manage the occasional concerns of Congress, to assist; the American traders with your advice, and to solicit their affairs with the Spanish Government, and to govern yourself according to the orders you may from time to time receive from the United States in Congress assembled. And that you may effectually execute the office to which you are appointed, we request the Governor, Judges and all other officers of his Catholic Majesty to afford you all countenance and assistance.

In Testimony whereof we have caused the Seal of the United States of America to be hereunto affixed. Witness his Excellency Elias Boudinot, President of the United States in Congress assembled, the second day of June in the Year of our Lord one thousand seven hundred and eighty three, and of our Sovereignty and Independence the seventh

Example #3: The United States in Congress Assembled

To all who shall see these presents send Greeting:

Whereas, we have judged it proper that one or more convention or conventions be held with the Native Americans residing within the boundaries of the United States of America in the northern and middle departments comprehending the whole of the Native Americans known by the name of the Six Nations and all to the northward and westward of them and as far south as the Cherokees exclusive, for the purposes of receiving them into the favour and protection of the United States and of establishing boundary lines of property for separating and dividing the settlements of the citizens of the United States of America from the Native American villages and hunting grounds and thereby extinguishing as far as possible all occasion of future animosities, disquiet and vexation;

Now, therefore, Know Ye that we reposing special trust and confidence in the integrity, prudence and ability of our trusty and beloved George Rogers Clarke, Oliver Wolcot, Nathaniel Greene, Richard Butler and Stephen Higgenson, have nominated, constituted and appointed and by these presents do nominate constitute and appoint them the said George Rogers Clarke, Oliver Wolcot, Nathaniel Greene, Richard Butler and Stephen Higgenson our commissioners giving and granting to them and to any three of them full power and authority for us and in our name to confer, treat, agree and conclude with the said Native Americans or with any nation or tribe of Native Americans within the boundaries of the United States or bordering thereon in the northern and middle departments aforesaid, of and concerning the establishment of peace with the said Native Americans, extinguishing their claims and settling boundaries between them and the citizens of the United States, in as ample form and with the same effect as if we were personally present and acted therein, hereby promising to hold valid and to fulfil and execute whatever shall be agreed upon, concluded and signed by our said commissioners or any three of them.

In testimony whereof we have caused the seal of the United States of America to be hereunto affixed, witness his Excellency Thomas Mifflin, president of the United States in Congress assembled this twelfth day of March in the year of our Lord one thousand seven hundred and eighty-four and of our Sovereignty and independence the eighth.

Example #4: Resolved, That the resolutions of the 23d. of April, 1784, in the words following Viz: "That so much of the Territory ceded or to be ceded by individual States to the United States as is already purchased or shall be purchased of the Native American Inhabitants, and offered for sale by Congress, shall be divided into distinct States in the following manner, as nearly as such Cessions will admit; that is to say, by parallels of latitude, so that each State shall comprehend from North to South two degrees of latitude beginning to count from the completion of forty five degrees North of the equator; and by Meridians of longitude, one of which shall pass through the lowest point of the rapids of Ohio, and the other through the western Cape of the mouth of the great Kanhaway: but the Territory eastward of this last Meridian, between the Ohio, lake Erie and Pennsylvania, shall be one State whatsoever may be its comprehension of Latitude. That which may lie beyond the Completion of the 45th degree between the said Meridians shall make part of the State adjoining it on the South; and that part of the Ohio, which is between the same Meridians coinciding nearly with the parallel of 39° shall be substituted so far in lieu of that parallel on a boundary line"; And "That the preceding articles shall be formed into a charter of Compact; shall be duly executed by the President of the United States in Congress Assembled under his hand

and the seal of the United States; shall be promulgated; and shall stand as fundamental Constitutions between the thirteen original States and each of the several States now newly described, unalterable from and after the sale of any part of the Territory of such State, pursuant to this resolve, but by the joint consent of the United States in Congress assembled, and of the particular State within which such alteration is proposed to be made" be and they are hereby repealed

Clearly these, along with many other laws and resolutions in the Journals of the Unicameral Congress, prove the existence of the Office, President of The United States, some eight years before George Washington.

Speaking of George Washington Our 11th US President

One of the most remarkable events of United States history occurred on December 23, 1783 with President Thomas Mifflin. In November of 1783 the British finally evacuated New York and Congress made the momentous decision to place the Continental Army on a "*Peace Footing* ". It was in Annapolis, where the US Government convened, that the last great act of the Revolutionary War occurred in 1783. Congress formally received George Washington, and instead of declaring himself King resigned his commission as Commander-in-Chief to the President of the United States.

What made this action especially remarkable was that George Washington, at his pinnacle of his power and popularity, surrendered the commission to President Thomas Mifflin. It was Mifflin who, as a Major General and a member of the Board of War, conspired to replace Washington as Commander-in-Chief with Horatio Gates in 1777. What follows is The United States in Congress Assembled Journal's account of George Washington's December 23, 1783 resignation.

According to order, his Excellency the Commander-in-Chief was admitted to a public audience. Being seated, and silence ordered, the President, after a pause, informed him that the United States in Congress assembled, were prepared to receive his communications; Washington arose and addressed Congress as follows:

'Mr. President:

The great events on which my resignation depended, having at length taken place, I have now the honor of offering my sincere congratulations to Congress, and of presenting myself before them, to surrender into their hands the trust committed to me, and to claim the indulgence of retiring from the service of my country.

Happy in the confirmation of our independence and sovereignty, and pleased with the opportunity afforded the United States, of becoming a respectable nation, I resign with satisfaction the appointment I accepted with diffidence; a diffidence in my abilities to accomplish so arduous a task; which however was superseded by a confidence in the rectitude of our cause, the support of the supreme power of the Union, and the patronage of Heaven.

The successful termination of the war has verified the most sanguine expectations; and my gratitude for the interposition of Providence, and the assistance I have received from my countrymen, increases with every review of the momentous contest.

While I repeat my obligations to the army in general, I should do injustice to my own feelings not to acknowledge, in this place, the peculiar services and distinguished merits of the gentlemen who have been attached to my person during the war. It was impossible the choice of confidential officers to compose my family should have been more fortunate. Permit me, sir, to recommend in particular, those who have continued in the service to the present moment, as worthy of the favorable notice and patronage of Congress.

I consider it an indispensable duty to close this last act of my official life by commending the interests of our dearest country to the protection of Almighty God, and those who have the superintendence of them to his holy keeping. Having now finished the work assigned me, I retire from the great theatre of action, and bidding an affectionate farewell to this august body, under whose orders I have so long acted, I here offer my commission, and take my leave of all the employments of public life'

He then advanced and delivered to President Mifflin his commission, with a copy of his address, and returned to having resumed his place, whereupon the President Thomas Mifflin returned him the following answer:

Sir,

The United States in Congress assembled receive with emotions, too affecting for utterance, the solemn deposit resignation of the authorities under which you have led their troops with safety and triumph success through a long a perilous and a doubtful war. When called upon by your country to defend its invaded rights, you accepted the sacred charge, before they it had formed alliances, and whilst they were it was without funds or a government to support you. You have conducted the great military contest with wisdom and fortitude, through invariably regarding the fights of the civil government power through all disasters and changes. You have, by the love and confidence of your fellow-citizens, enabled them to display their martial genius, and transmit their fame to posterity. You have persevered, till these United States, aided by a magnanimous king and nation, have been enabled, under a just Providence, to close the war in freedom, safety and independence; on which happy event we sincerely join you in congratulations.

Having planted defended the standard of liberty in this new world: having taught an useful lesson a lesson useful to those who inflict and to those who feel oppression, you retire from the great theatre of action, loaded with the blessings of your fellow-citizens, but your fame the glory of your virtues will not terminate with your official life the glory of your many virtues will military command, it will continue to animate remotest posterity ages and this last act will not be among the least conspicuous

We feel with you our obligations to the army in general; and will particularly charge ourselves with the interests of those confidential officers, who have attended your person to this interesting affecting moment.

We join you in commending the interests of our dearest country to the protection of Almighty God, beseeching him to dispose the hearts and minds of its citizens, to improve the opportunity afforded them, of becoming a happy and respectable nation. And for you we address to him our earnest prayers, that a life so beloved may be fostered with all his care; that your days may be happy, as they have been illustrious; and that he will finally give you that reward which this world cannot give.

President Thomas Mifflin's third month in office was equally eventful. On January 14, 1784 Congress finally assembled enough States to ratify the Definitive Treaty of Peace, which half-ended the War with Great Britain (King George III did not ratify the treaty for Britain until April 9, 1784, officially ending the War). On January 21st the following proclamation was published and appeared in the Pennsylvania Gazette:

PHILADELPHIA, January 21.
By the UNITED STATES in CONGRESS assembled.
A PROCLAMATION.

WHEREAS Definitive Articles of peace and friendship, between the United States of America and his Britannic Majesty, were concluded and signed at Paris on the 3d day of September, 1783, by the Plenipotentiaries of the said United States and of His said Britannic Majesty, duly and respectively authorized for that purpose, which definitive articles are in the words following:

And we, the United States in Congress assembled, having seen and duly considered the definitive articles aforesaid, did, by a certain article, under the seal of the United States, bearing date this 14th day of January, 1784, approve, ratify and confirm the same, and every part and clause thereof, engaging and promising that we would sincerely and faithfully perform and observe the same, and never to suffer them to be violated by any one, or transgressed in any manner, as far as should be in our power.

And being sincerely disposed to carry the said articles into execution, truly, honestly and with good faith, according to the intent and meaning thereof, We have thought proper, by these presents, to notify the premises to all the good citizens of these States, hereby enjoining all bodies of magistracy, legislative, executive and judiciary, all persons bearing office, civil or military, of whatever rank, degree or powers, and all others, the good citizens of these states, of every vocation and condition, that, reverencing those stipulations entered into on their behalf, under the authority of that federal bond, by which their existence as an independent people is bound up together, and is known and acknowledged by the nations of the world, and with that good faith, which is every man's surest guide, within their several offices, jurisdictions and vocations, they carry into effect the said definitive articles, and every clause and sentence thereof, strictly and completely.

> *Given under the seal of the United States. Witness his Excellency THOMAS MIFFLIN, our President, at Annapolis, this 14th day of January 1784, and of the sovereignty and independence of the United States of America, the eighth.*

Did you note the "*our President,*" yes the "*our President,*" under "*the Great Seal of the United States*" on the official resolution that ended the War with Great Britain.

So revered was this office by second President of the United States, Thomas McKean *(Signer of the Declaration of Independence),* that the Presidency was used to turn down his party's 1804 nomination for Vice President under Thomas Jefferson saying:

> "*... President of the United States in Congress Assembled in the year of 1781 (a proud year for Americans) equaled any merit or pretensions of mine and cannot now be increased by the office of Vice President.*"

Of course 1781 was also the year of Washington's great triumph over Lord Cornwallis. President Boudinot later exchanged General Cornwallis for the imprisoned Henry Laurens in the Tower of London but that is another forgotten US President story to be re-told in a future publication.

In closing one could flood this chapter with hundreds of examples to prove the official existence of ten US Presidents before George Washington under the Articles of Confederation. Additionally, Peyton Randolph, Henry Middleton, and John Hancock should also be recognized as Presidents of the Continental Congress in the United Colonies of America while John Hancock again, along with John Jay, Henry Laurens, and Samuel Huntington should be honored as The Presidents of the Continental Congress in the United States of America. All of these men presided over our great nation at its most perilous time.

For over four years now I have sought Congressional action to properly honor the ten men who served as President of the United States in Congress Assembled under the ratified Articles of Confederation with the renumbering of George Washington and George W. Bush to 11th and 53rd, respectively. Aside from the usual letters and political contacts, I have loaned my personal collection "*Rebels With A Vision - Founding Documents of Freedom*" to various museums, libraries, universities, and even the Republican 2000 National Convention hoping to shine a national spotlight on these flagrant flaws in US History. I also purchased each of the names of the Founders in a .com, .net or .org format and posted historical documents at each site along with brief biographies.

In addition to Congressional recognition, I have written President George Bush numerous letters supported by venerable Institutions such as the *James Monroe Foundation* and *James Madison's Montpelier,* requesting that at the very least these Presidents, along with their four Continental Congress predecessors - *Peyton Randolph, Henry Middleton, John Jay and Henry Laurens* -- be included in the Presidential Order, mandating an official wreath of commemoration be laid at their tombs on the anniversary of their birthdays. This is nothing new as it is a standing Presidential Order, each year, for all deceased US Presidents under the Constitution.

All letters, emails, personal calls, web sites, and exhibits have resulted in no formal Congressional legislation or amendment to the Presidential Order.

Therefore in September 2003, *(just after agreeing to loan several key founding documents to the Smithsonian's a Glorious Burden Exhibit The Presidency)* I decided to explore help from the third branch of government. To date, I have successfully conferred with lawyers in four states to discuss filing for a declaratory judgment in Federal Court on "*Who was the First President of the United States in Congress Assembled*" and "*Which State was the first to join the 'Perpetual Union' of the United States of America*". I know the legal facts point clearly to President Samuel Huntington and the Commonwealth of Virginia respectively.

The Virginia attorneys suggested we file in Alexandria, due to the Commonwealth's #1 claim on statehood while my local attorneys have counseled that Pennsylvania is a more appropriate venue, as three of the ten Confederation US Presidents were Pennsylvanians. Personally, I prefer the State of Connecticut, as it is the home and resting place of the First President of the United States, Samuel Huntington.

In a final attempt to win over Presidential or Congressional support I am waiting to see if the Smithsonian's Exhibit, *The American Presidency, A Glorious Burden* turns some heads toward this historic cause. I am determined, however, that if President Bush or Congress does not act soon my only course will be the Federal Court System. I am certain the facts are irrefutable and that the Federal Court of Virginia, Pennsylvania or Connecticut will surely see the merit in correcting the historical record. I am determined to insure that the proper recognition of President of the United States in Congress Assembled be recognized and correct the State order on the Washington Quarter be corrected in 2004.

I intend to prove beyond a shadow of a doubt by the end of 2004 that "*Samuel Huntington was the First President of the United States in Congress Assembled*", *Samuel Huntington, Thomas McKean, John Hanson, Elias Boudinot, Thomas Mifflin, Richard Henry Lee, John Hancock, Nathaniel Gorham, Arthur St. Clair and Cyrus Griffin were elected as President of the United States in Congress Assembled, and "Virginia was the first to join the 'Perpetual Union' of the United States of America"*.

MARCH, 1781.

According to the order of the day, the honourable John Hanſon and Daniel Carroll, twoof the delegates for the ſtate of Maryland, in purſuance of the act of the legiſlature of that ſtate, entitled, " An act to empower the delegates of this ſtate in Congreſs to ſubſcribe and ratify the articles of confederation, " which was read in Congreſs on the 12th of February laſt, and a copy thereof entered on the minutes, did, in behalf of the ſaid ſtate of Maryland, ſign and ratify the ſaid articles, by which act the confederation of the United States of America was compleated, each and every of the Thirteen United States, from New-Hampſhire to Georgia, both included, having adopted and confirmed, and by their delegates in Congreſs ratified the ſame, as follows.

TO ALL TO WHOM theſe preſents ſhall come, we the underſigned delegates of the ſtates affixed to our names, ſend greeting:

WHEREAS the delegates of the United States of America in Congreſs aſſembled, did on the fifteenth day of November, in the year of our Lord one thouſand ſeven hundred and ſeventy-ſeven, and in the ſecond year of the independence of America, agree to certain articles of confederation and perpetual union between the ſtates of New-Hampſhire, Maſſachuſetts-Bay, Rhode Iſland and Providence Plantations, Connecticut, New York, New-Jerſey, Pennſylvania, Delaware, Maryland, Virginia, North-Carolina, South-Carolina, and Georgia, in the words following, viz.

ARTICLES OF CONFEDERATION AND PERPETUAL UNION between the ſtates of New-Hampſhire, Maſſachuſetts-Bay, Rhode-Iſland and Providence Plantations, Connecticut, New-York, New-Jerſey, Pennſylvania, Delaware, Maryland, Virginia, North-Carolina, South-Carolina, and Georgia.

Article 1. The ſtile of this confederacy ſhall be *The United States of America.*

Article 2. Each ſtate retains its ſovereignty, freedom, and independence, and every power juriſdiction. and right, which is not by this confederation expreſsly delegated to the United States in Congreſs aſſembled.

Article 3. The ſaid ſtates hereby ſeverally enter into a firm league of friendſhip with each other for their common defence, the ſecurity of their liberties, and their mutual and general wellfare; binding themſelves to aſſiſt each other againſt all force offered to or attacks made upon them or

G any

Articles of Confederation March 1, 1781 Official Printing -- Journals of Congress and Journals of the United States in Congress Assembled for the years 1781 and 1782 -- *Courtesy of the Klos Family*

MARCH, 1781. 49

The UNITED STATES in CONGRESS Aſſembled,

March 2, 1781,

The ratification of the articles of confederation being yeſterday compleated by the acceſſion of the ſtate of Maryland :

The United States met in Congreſs, when the following members appeared :

His excellency Samuel Huntington, delegate for Connecticut, preſident.

New-Hampſhire,	Mr. John Sullivan,
Maſſachuſetts,	Mr. Samuel Adams,
	Mr. James Lovell,
	Mr. Artemas Ward.
Rhode-Iſland and Providence Plantations,	Mr. James Mitchel Varnum,
Connecticut,	Mr. Jeſſe Root,
	Mr. Oliver Wolcott,
New-York,	Mr. James Duane,
	Mr. William Floyd.
New-Jerſey,	Mr. John Witherſpoon,
	Mr. Abraham Clark.
Pennſylvania,	Mr. Samuel J. Atlee,
	Mr. Henry Wynkoop,
	Mr. Thomas Smith,
Delaware,	Mr. Thomas Rodney,
	Mr. Thomas M'Kean,
Maryland,	Mr. John Hanſon,
	Mr. Carroll,
Virginia,	Mr. Joſeph Jones,
	Mr. James Madiſon,
	Mr. Theodorick Bland,
	Mr. Meriwether Smith,
North Carolina,	Mr. Thomas Burk,
	Mr. William Sharpe,
	Mr. Samuel Johnſton,
South-Carolina,	Mr. John Mathews,
	Mr. Thomas Bee,
	Mr. Iſaac Motte,

Georgia,

March 2nd, 1781 Official Printing -- Journals of Congress and Journals of the United States in Congress Assembled for the years 1781 and 1782 -- *Courtesy of the Klos Family*

DEPARTMENT OF THE TREASURY
UNITED STATES MINT
WASHINGTON, D.C. 20220

May 13, 2002

Mr. Stanley L. Klos
P.O. Box 623
Carnegie, PA 15106

Dear Mr. Klos:

This is in response to your letter to the Director of the United States Mint, Henrietta Holsman Fore, dated April 16, 2002, regarding the United States Mint 50 State Quarters® Program (hereinafter "Program"). Specifically, you raised the following questions regarding the Program:

1. Did your management team discuss the Articles of Confederation State ratification order when finalizing the quarters' release date?
2. If yes; why did the Mint decide to use the US Constitution order over the Articles of Confederation and who made the final decision?
3. If no; could your office provide me with a reason why the Articles of Confederation were not considered?

The "50 States Commemorative Coin Program Act" (Public Law 105-124, as codified at 31 U.S.C. § 5112(l)) directs the Secretary of the Treasury to issue quarter dollar coins that shall have designs on the reverse side that are emblematic of the 50 States. The Act also states:

> **(3) Issuance of coins commemorating 5 states during each of the 10 years. ---**
>
> **(A) In general.** – The designs for the quarter dollar coins issued during each year of the 10-year period …shall be emblematic of 5 States selected in the order in which such *States ratified the Constitution of the United States or were admitted into the Union, as the case may be*.

31 U.S.C. § 5112(l)(3)(A)(emphasis added).

Therefore, the United States Mint followed the specific mandate of Congress in its use of the ratification order of the U.S. Constitution to honor the 50 States for this Program. As such, there was no discussion by United States Mint officials regarding the Articles of Confederation.

Treasury letter dated May 13, 2002 explaining the *"US Mint followed the specific mandate of Congress"* ıoring Delaware as "the First State" completely ignoring the fact the Perpetual Union of the ited States was formed by the Articles of Confederation and first ratified by Virginia.

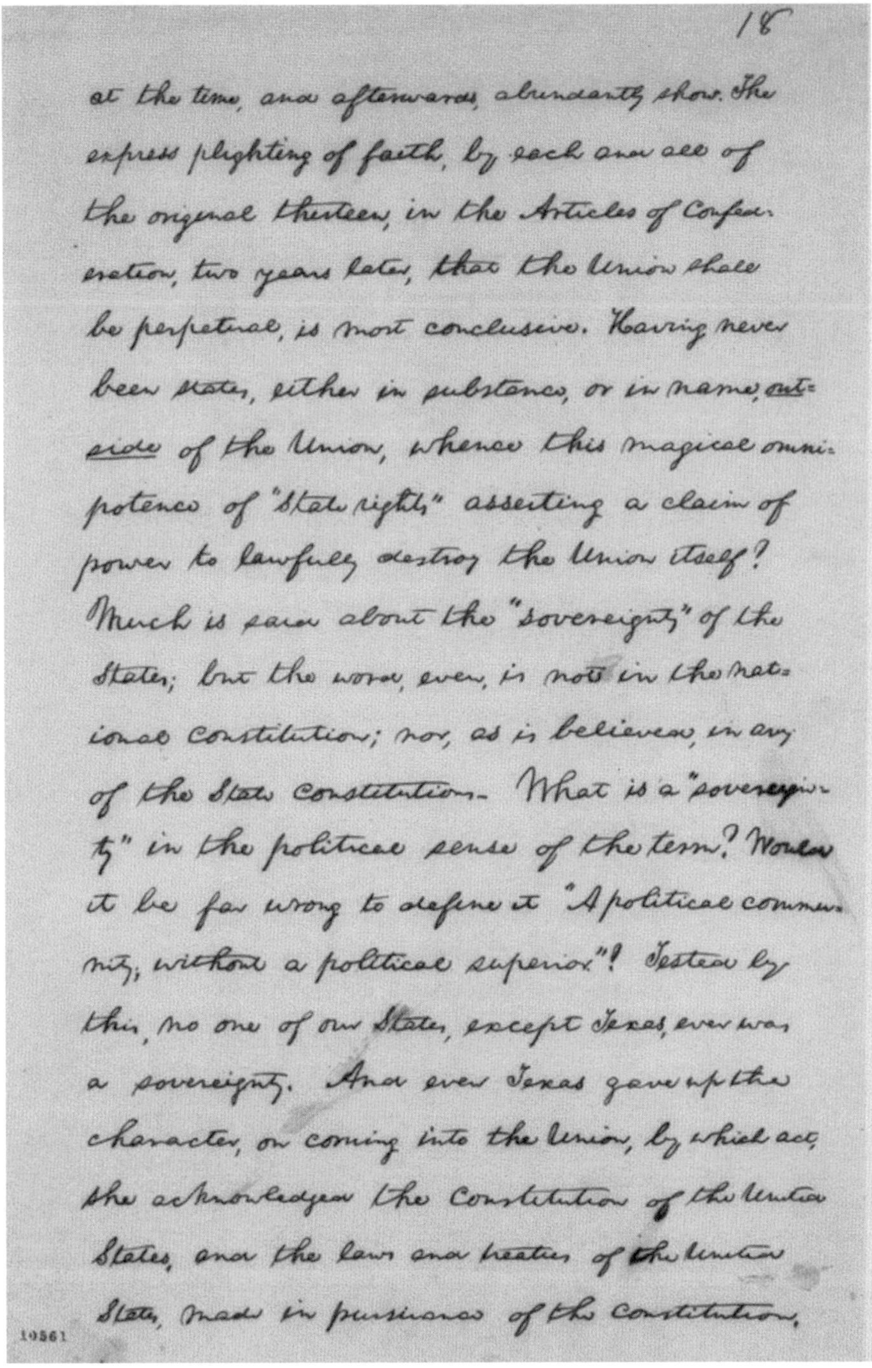
18

at the time, and afterwards, abundantly show. The
express plighting of faith, by each and all of
the original thirteen, in the Articles of Confederation, two years later, that the Union shall
be perpetual, is most conclusive. Having never
been States, either in substance, or in name, outside of the Union, whence this magical omni-
potence of "State rights," asserting a claim of
power to lawfully destroy the Union itself?
Much is said about the "sovereignty" of the
States; but the word, even, is not in the national Constitution; nor, as is believed, in any
of the State constitutions. What is a "sovereignty" in the political sense of the term? Would
it be far wrong to define it "A political commu-
nity, without a political superior"! Tested by
this, no one of our States, except Texas, ever was
a sovereignty. And even Texas gave up the
character, on coming into the Union, by which act,
she acknowledged the Constitution of the United
States, and the laws and treaties of the United
States, made in pursuance of the Constitution,

10561

Abraham Lincoln Message to Congress, July 4, 1861, First Printed Draft, with Changes in Lincoln's Hand – T – *Courtesy of The Abraham Lincoln Papers at the Library of Congress*

Smithsonian Traveling Exhibit *"The American Presidency A Glorious Burden"* at the Heinz History Center in Pittsburgh. This February 1, 2004 Photo shows the beginning of the exhibit explaining, incorrectly, that John Hanson was the First President of the Continental Congress. In the background are the 1783 Printing of the Articles of Confederation, John Hancock 1777 letter signed as President ordering General St. Clair to defend Fort Ticonderoga, President Boudinot's 1783 letter thanking General St. Clair for freeing Congress from the Military Mutineers, A Thomas McKean 1781 letter signed as President, A Thomas Mifflin 1787 document signed as Speaker of the Pennsylvania Constitutional Convention, and the September 18, 1787 First Public Printing of the US Constitution all on loan from the Klos Family.

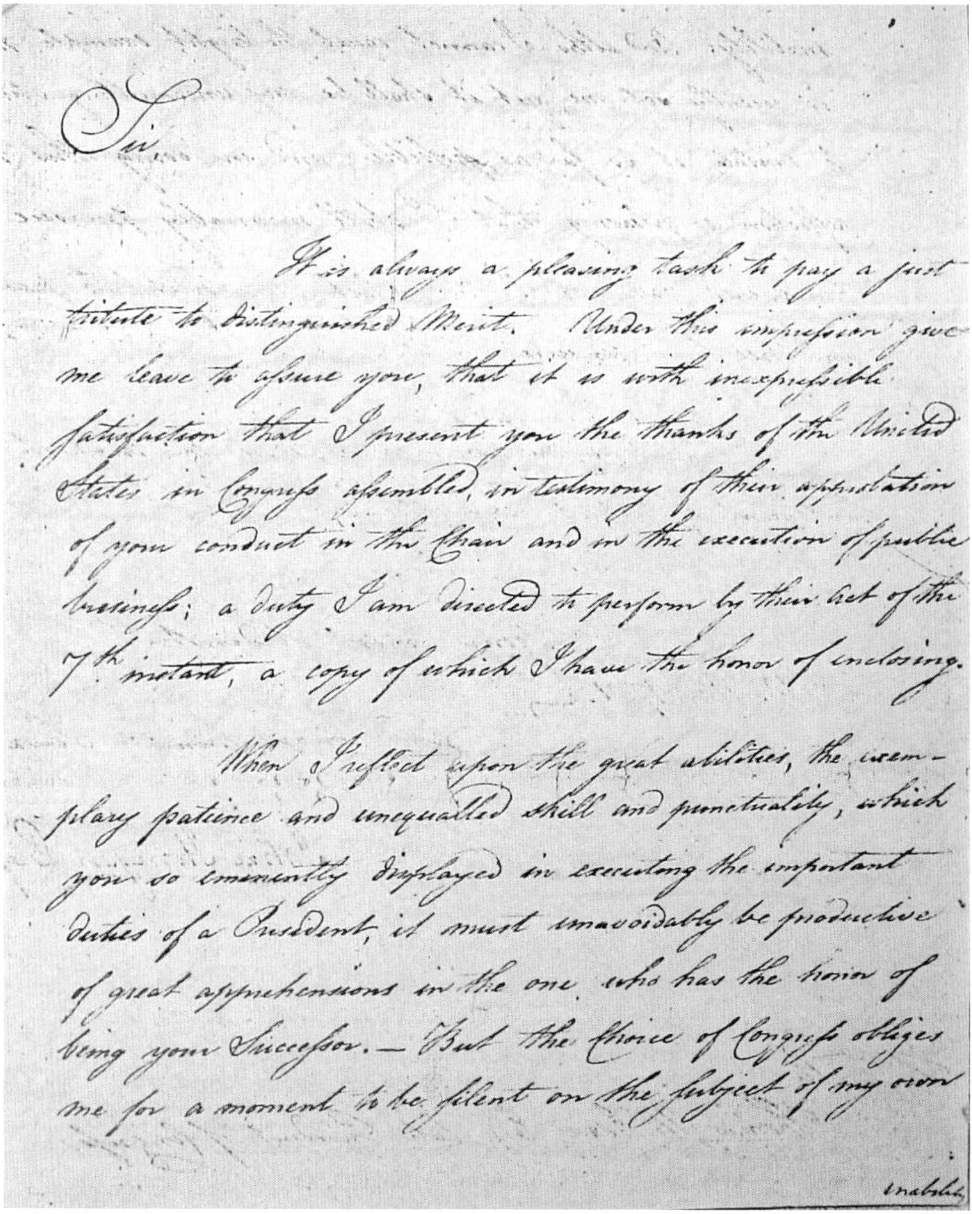

Sir,

It is always a pleasing task to pay a just tribute to Distinguished Merit. Under this impression give me leave to assure you, that it is with inexpressible satisfaction that I present you the thanks of the United States in Congress assembled, in testimony of their approbation of your conduct in the Chair and in the execution of public business; a duty I am directed to perform by their Act of the 7th instant, a copy of which I have the honor of inclosing.

When I reflect upon the great abilities, the exemplary patience and unequalled skill and punctuality, which you so eminently displayed in executing the important duties of a President, it must unavoidably be productive of great apprehensions in the one who has the honor of being your Successor. — But the Choice of Congress obliges me for a moment to be silent on the subject of my own

inability

Page 1 of a November 1781 letter by John Hanson 3rd President of the United States in Congress Assembled to Thomas McKean 2nd President of the United States in Congress Assembled giving the official thanks of Congress – *Courtesy of the Library of Congress*

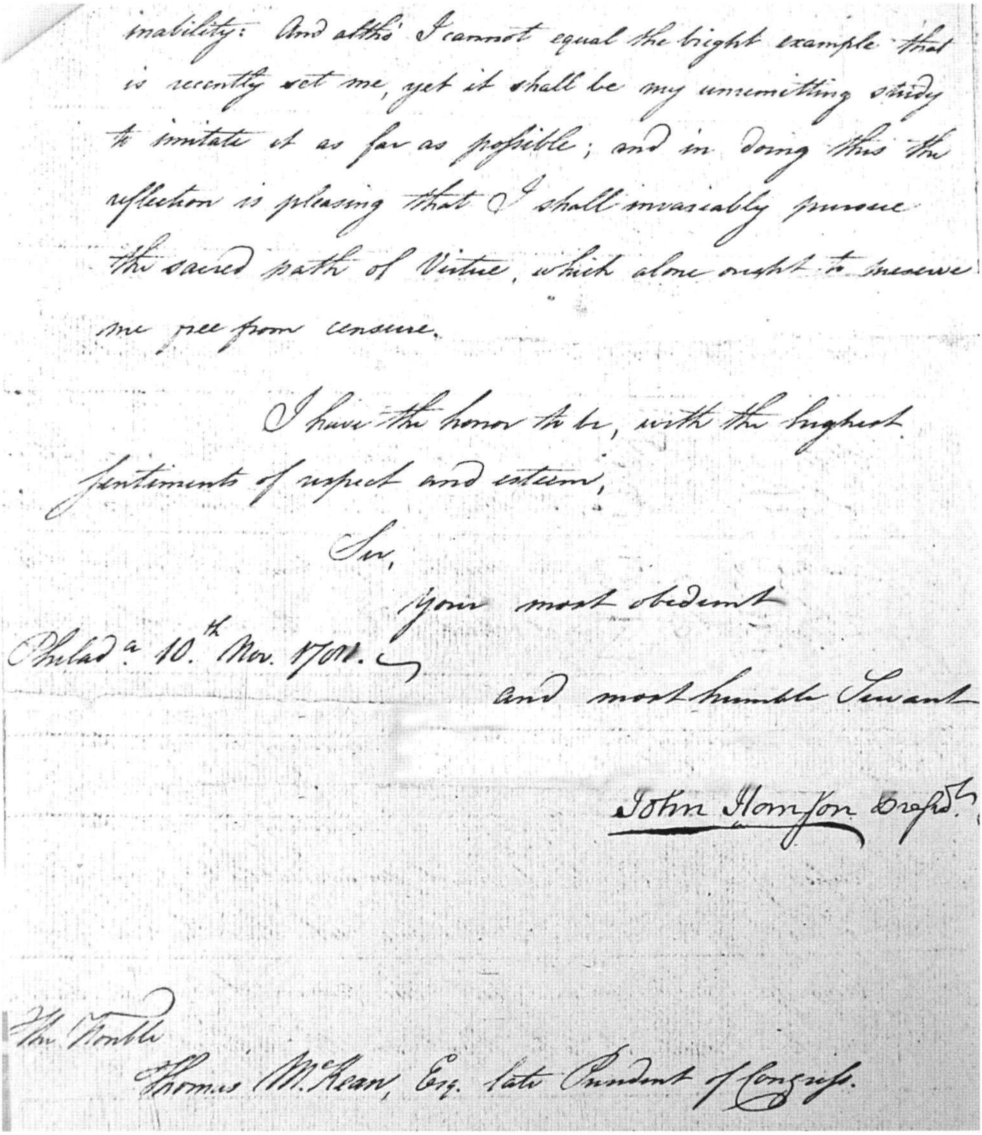

inability: And altho' I cannot equal the bright example that is recently set me, yet it shall be my unremitting study to imitate it as far as possible; and in doing this the reflection is pleasing that I shall invariably pursue the sacred path of Virtue, which alone ought to preserve me free from censure.

I have the honor to be, with the highest sentiments of respect and esteem,

Sir,

Your most obedient

Philada. 10th Nov. 1781.

and most humble Servant

John Hanson Presdt.

The Honble

Thomas McKean, Esq. late President of Congress.

Page 2 of a November 1781 letter by John Hanson 3rd President of the United States in Congress Assembled to Thomas McKean 2nd President of the United States in Congress Assembled giving the official thanks of Congress – *Courtesy of the Library of Congress*

CHAPTER TWO

Portrait of Peyton Randolph from
Appleton Cyclopedia of American Biography

PEYTON RANDOLPH

First President of the Continental Congress
United Colonies of America
September 5, 1774 to October 22, 1774
and May 20 to May 24, 1775

Peyton Randolph was born in Tazewell Hall, Williamsburg, Virginia, in 1721 and died in Philadelphia, Pennsylvania, 22 October 1775. After graduation from William and Mary he was fortunate enough to study law at the Inner Temple, London due to his father's influence. Sir John Randolph's standing in Virginia was the primary force behind his son's appointment as king's attorney for Virginia in 1748, when fellow knight, Sir William Gooch was governor.

Peyton was also chosen representative of Williamsburg in the House of Burgesses in the same year. At the opening of his career as law officer he was brought in opposition to the apostle of Presbyterianism, the Reverend Samuel Davies. Peyton, having questioned whether the Toleration Act extended to Virginia, was told by Davies, that if not, neither did the Act of Uniformity. Some prominence was bestowed on the young lawyer when this position was sustained by the Attorney General in England. In 1751, the newly appointed governor Dinwiddie and his family were guests of Peyton Randolph, but the latter held his ground and resisted the royal demand of a pistole fee on every land-patent.

In 1754 the burgesses commissioned the king's attorney to repair to London to impress on the English ministry the unconstitutionality of the exaction. There he encountered the crown lawyers, Campbell and Murray (afterward Lord Mansfield), with marked ability. The pistole fee was removed from all lands less in extent than one hundred acres, and presently ceased altogether. Governor Dinwiddie was naturally angry that the king's attorney should have left the colony without his consent and on a mission hostile to his demand. A petition of the burgesses that the office of attorney should remain open until Peyton Randolph's return pointed the governor to his revenge; he suspended the absent attorney, and in his place appointed George Wythe. Wythe accepted the place, only to retain it until his friend's return. Randolph's promised compensation for the London mission, £2,500, caused a long struggle between the governor and the burgesses, who made the sum a rider to one of £20,000 voted for the Native American war. The conflict led to a prorogation of the house. Meanwhile the lords of trade ordered reduction of the pistole fee, and requested the reinstatement of Randolph.

> *"You must think y't some w't absurd," answered Dinwiddie (23 October, 1754), "from the bad Treatm't I have met with. However, if he answers properly w't I have to say to him, I am not inflexible ; and he must confess, before this happened he had greater share of my Favs, and Counten'ce than any other in the Gov't."*

The attorney acknowledged the irregularities and was reinstated. There was a compromise with the new house about the money. When tidings of Major General Edward Braddock's *French and Native American War* defeat near present day Pittsburgh reached Williamsburg, an association of lawyers was formed by the king's attorney which was joined by other gentlemen, altogether one hundred, who marched under Randolph to the front and placed themselves under command of Colonel William Byrd. They were led against the Native Americans, who retreated to Fort Duquesne. During the next few years Peyton Randolph was occupied with a revision of the laws, being chairman of a committee for that purpose. He also gave attention to the affairs of William and Mary College, of which he was appointed a visitor in 1758. In 1760 he and his brother John, both law-examiners, signed the license of Patrick Henry, Wythe and Pendleton having refused. *"The two Randolphs," says Jefferson, "acknowledged he was very ignorant of law, but that they perceived that he was a man of genius, and did not doubt he would soon qualify himself."*

Peyton Randolph was one of the few intimate friends of George Washington. In politics, Randolph was Washington's mentor. Thomas Jefferson was also an admirer; in a letter to his grandson, the author of the Declaration of Independence declares that in early life, amid difficulties and temptations, he used to ask himself how Peyton Randolph would act in such a situation, and what course would meet with his approbation.

Peyton Randolph was a political conservative in the cause of independence. In 1764 Randolph drew up the remonstrance of the burgesses against the threatened stamp-act, but when it was passed, and Patrick Henry, then a burgess, had carried, by the smallest majority, his "*treasonable*" resolutions, the attorney was alarmed; Jefferson heard Randolph saying in going out, "*By God, I would have given five hundred guineas for a single vote!*" In 1766 Randolph was appointed speaker and resigned his office as king's attorney, devoting his attention to the increasing troubles of the country. The burgesses recognized in his legal knowledge and judicial calmness a ballast for the sometimes tempestuous patriotism of Patrick Henry, and Randolph was placed at the head of all important committees.

He was Chairman of the Committee of Correspondence between the colonies in May 1773, presided over the Virginia convention of 1 August 1774, and was the first of seven deputies appointed by it to the proposed congress at Philadelphia. On August 10th, 1773 he summoned the citizens of Williamsburg to assemble at their court-house, where the proceedings of the State convention were ratified and instructions to their delegates given the unconstitutionality of binding American colonies by British statutes and aid subscribed for the Boston sufferers. For his presidency at this meeting his name was placed on the roll of those to be attainted by parliament, but the bill was never passed.

Peyton Randolph traveled to Pennsylvania and Continental Congress was officially formed on September 5, 1774 in Philadelphia's Carpenters Hall to petition King George III after England passed the Intolerable Acts. The first *unofficial* meeting of delegates actually took place the day before in *The City Tavern* just down the street *(yes the true birthplace of the Continental Congress was in a Philadelphia tavern).* The debates at this tavern meeting were significant as the decision was made to hold the First Continental Congress in a private, rather than public hall. When Congress convened the next day, South Carolina delegate Thomas Lynch nominated Peyton Randolph to be chairman. Peyton was elected by unanimous vote. Connecticut Delegate Silas Deane wrote of Peyton to Mrs. Deane:

" ... *Designed by nature for the business, of an affable, open and majestic deportment, large in size, though not out of proportion, he commands respect and esteem by his very aspect, independent of the high character he sustains* ... "

The Journals of the Continental Congress under his presidency report:

> **1774 - September 5** Congress convenes at Carpenters' Hall- elects Peyton Randolph president, Charles Thomson secretary. September 17 Endorses Suffolk Resolves from Massachusetts. **September 27** Adopts non-importation agreement, to begin December 1. **September 28** Orders Joseph Galloway's plan of union to lie on the table. **September 30** Resolves to halt exports to Great Britain, Ireland, and the West Indies effective September 10, 1775.
>
> **1774 - October 1** Resolves to prepare an address to the king. **October 14** Adopts declaration of grievances and rights. **October 18** Approves the Association. **October 21** Approves an address to the people of Great Britain and one to the inhabitants of the colonies. **October 22** Agrees to reconvene on **May 10, 1775**, "unless the redress of grievances, which we have desired, be obtained before that time." Elects Henry Middleton president. **October 26** Approves an address to the king and a letter to Quebec. Congress dissolves itself.*
>
> *Citation for this Chronology in Congress as well as the other Presidential Chapters and many have been edited but taken directly from: Smith, Paul H., et al., eds. LETTERS OF DELEGATES TO CONGRESS, 1774-1789. 25 volumes, Washington, D.C.: Library of Congress, 1976-2000).

He was but fifty-three years of age in 1774, but was described by a fellow-member as *"a venerable man,"* to which is added *"an honest man; has knowledge, temper, experience, judgment, above all, integrity--a true Roman spirit."* His noble presence, gracious manners, and imperturbable self-possession won the confidence of all. He was constantly relied on for his parliamentary experience and judicial wisdom.

Returning to Virginia, he remained active in colonial politics. On 20 January, 1775, he issued a call to the counties and corporations of Virginia, requesting them to elect delegates to a convention to be held at Richmond, 21 March, the call being signed *"Peyton Randolph, moderator."* He was elected to that convention on 4 February.

On the night of 20 April 1775, the gunpowder was clandestinely removed from the public magazine at Williamsburg by order of Lord Dunmore, governor of Virginia. Randolph persuaded the enraged citizens not to assault the governor's residence. To 700 armed men assembled at Fredericksburg, who offered their services, he wrote a reply assuring them that the wrong would be redressed if menace did not compel Dunmore to obstinacy. Through his negotiations with Lord Dunmore, assisted by the approach of Henry's men, £300 was paid for the powder, and hostilities were delayed. Randolph resumed his duties as speaker of the burgesses in May 1775, and after their adjournment he returned to the Congress at Philadelphia and was re-elected President. The Journals record:

> **1775 - May 10th** Second Continental Congress convenes at Pennsylvania State House reelects President Peyton Randolph and Secretary Charles Thomson. **May 17** Resolves to ban exports to British colonies failing to join the Association. **May 18** Receives news of the capture of Ticonderoga and Crown Point. **May 24th** The Congress met according to adjournment, but Peyton

Randolph, President, being under a necessity of returning home and having set out this Morning early, the chair was vacant. Upon motion, John Hancock was unanimously chosen President.

Peyton was forced once again to abandon his office of President because Lord Dunmore of Virginia had called a session of the Assembly, in which Randolph was the Speaker. On June 25, 1775 Thomas Jefferson presented his credentials as a replacement for Peyton Randolph.

Peyton Randolph returned to the Continental Congress after serving as Speaker of the Virginia Assembly in October 1775. He was placed on a Committee *"to take into consideration the state of the trade of America, and report their opinion"*. On October 23rd, however, Peyton Randolph suddenly died. The Journals of the Continental Congress reported:

> *Information being given to Congress that yesterday the Honorable Peyton Randolph suddenly departed this life, Resolved, That this Congress will attend his funeral as mourners, with a crape round their left arm, ∥ according to the association & par; That the Congress continue in Mourning for the space of one month. That a Committee of three be appointed to the superintend the funeral.*
>
> *The members chosen, Mr. Henry Middleton, Mr. Stephen Hopkins, and Mr. Samuel Chase. That the Committee waits on the Reverend Mr. Jacob Duché, and requests him to prepare a proper discourse to be delivered at the funeral.*
>
> *On Tuesday afternoon his remains were removed from Mr. Benjamin Randolph's, to Christ Church, where an excellent sermon on the mournful occasion was preached by the Rev. Mr. Duché, after which, the corpse was carried to the burial ground and deposited in a vault till it can be conveyed to Virginia.*
>
> *The Funeral was conducted in the following order:*
>
> *The Three Battalions, Artillery; Companies And Rifle-Men Of This City; The Clergy; The Body With Pall Supported By Six Magistrates; Hon. John Hancock, Esq; The Members Of Assembly; Committee Of Safety; Mayor And Corporation Committee Of City And Liberties; Vestry Of Christ And St. Peter's Churches.*
>
> *Citizens.*

From the Pennsylvania Packet, Oct. 30, 1775.

> *"On the day his Remains were interred there was a greater collection of People that I had ever seen. The three Battalions were under Arms. Their Standards and Colors were furled with black Gauze: their Drums muffled, and covered with Gauze. The Bells at Christ Church were muffled. There, Mr. Duché preached a most excellent sermon:--thence the Corpse was carried to the Burying-yard, the way being lined on each side by the Battalions, leaning on their arms reversed."*

John Adams wrote the following account of his death to James Warren on October 24, 1775:

Dear Sir, I have only Time to acquaint you that Yesterday, that eminent American, and most worthy Man The Honorable Peyton Randolph Esq. our first venerable President, departed this Life in an Apoplectic Fit. He was seized at Table having but a few Moments. before set down with a good deal of Company to dinner. He died in the Evening, without ever recovering his senses after the first Stroke.

As this Gentleman Sustained very deservedly One of the first American Characters, as he was the first President of the united Colonies, and as he was universally esteemed for his great Virtues and shining Abilities, the Congress have determined to shew his Memory and Remains all possible Demonstrations of Respect.(1) The whole Body is to attend the Funeral, in as much Mourning as our Laws will admit. The Funeral is to be tomorrow. I am the more pleased with this Respect on Account of an Impropriety, which you know was unfelt.

This venerable Sage, I assure you, since he has stood upon the same Floor with the rest of Us has rose in the Esteem of all. He was attentive, judicious and his Knowledge, Eloquence, and classical Correctness shewed Us the able and experienced Statesman and Senator, whereas his former station had in a great Measure concealed these and shewed Us chiefly the upright and impartial Moderator of Debate.

You would have wondered more at the Want of [Sensi] bility which you remarked if you have [been] here and seen, the Difference.

Mr Randolph was as firm, stable and consistent a Patriot as any here-the Loss must be very great to Virginia in Particular and the Continent in general.

His death is alluded to with sorrow in one of Washington's dispatches to Congress. His body was conveyed from Philadelphia in the following year by his nephew, Edmund Randolph, and buried in the chapel of William and Mary College.

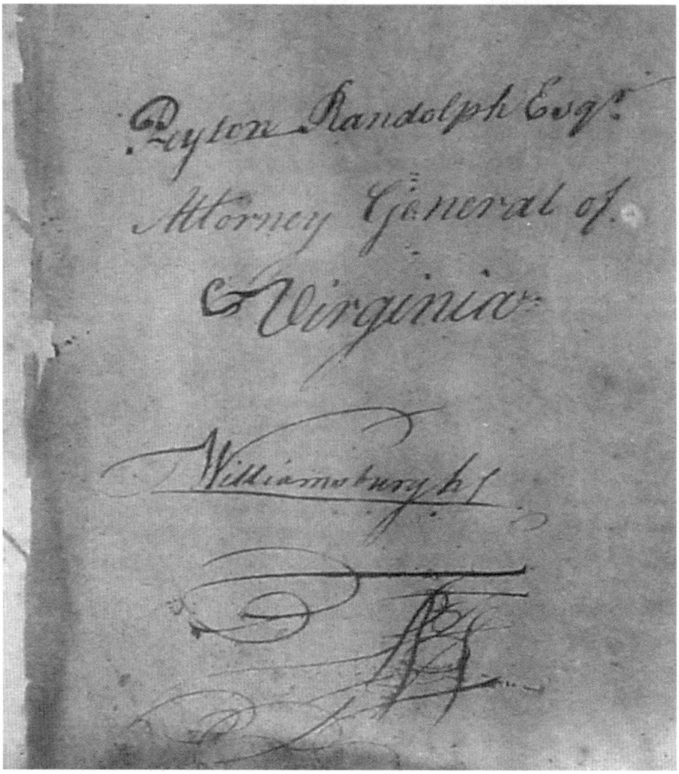

Peyton Randolph signed law book as Attorney General of the Virginia Colony – *Courtesy of the Klos Family*

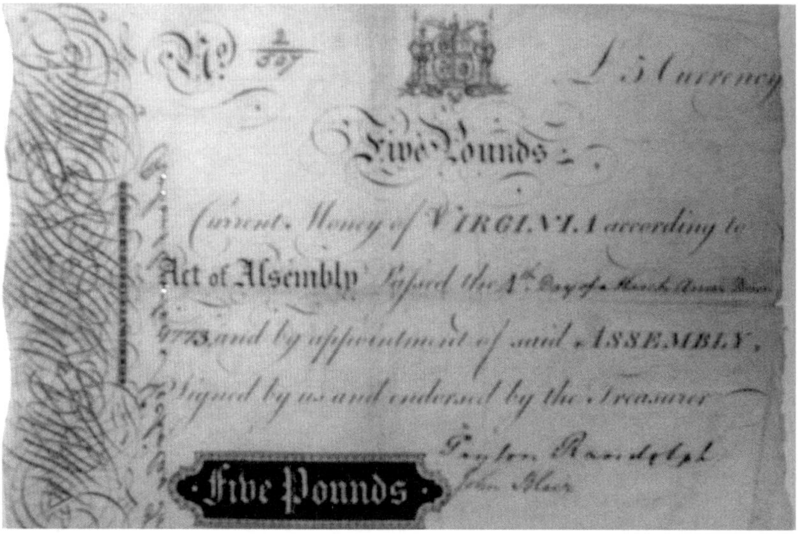

Peyton Randolph signed Colonial Note date 1773 a year before his Presidency of the Continental Congress of the United Colonies – *Courtesy of the Klos Family*

CHAPTER THREE

Portrait of Henry Middleton by Benjamin West
Courtesy of Middleton Place Plantation

HENRY MIDDLETON

2nd President of the Continental Congress
United Colonies of America
October 22, 1774 to October 26, 1774

Henry Middleton was born in South Carolina in 1717 and died in Charleston, South Carolina on June 13, 1784. In 1745 he was elected to the commons, and was speaker of that body from 1745 -1747, and represented St. George's in 1754 -1755. In 1755 he was commissioner of Native American affairs and was appointed to the South Carolina Colonial Council, of which body he was a member until 1770, when he resigned.

In 1774 he was sent as a delegate to the Continental Congress and was one of the most conservative members of the entire delegation. For that reason, among others, he was elected President of the Continental Congress in October 1774 according to the Journals.

1774 - October 22 Agrees to reconvene on May 10, 1775, "*unless the redress of grievances, which we have desired, be obtained before that time.*" Elects Henry Middleton President. **October 26** Approves an address to the king and a letter to Quebec. Congress dissolves itself.

Although Middleton's tenure as President was only four days and Peyton Randolph was re-elected in 1775, the following Petition of Congress to King George III passed during his Presidency and was unanimously approved and sent to Great Britain:

To the Kings most excellent majesty, Most gracious Sovereign

We your majestys faithful subjects of the colonies of Newhampshire, Massachusetts-bay, Rhode-island and Providence Plantations, Connecticut, New-York, New-Jersey, Pennsylvania, the counties of New-Castle Kent and Sussex on Delaware, Maryland, Virginia, North-Carolina, and South Carolina, in behalf of ourselves and the inhabitants of these colonies who have deputed us to represent them in General Congress, by this our humble petition, beg leave to lay our grievances before the throne.

A standing army has been kept in these colonies, ever since the conclusion of the late war, without the consent of our assemblies; and this army with a considerable naval armament has been employed to enforce the collection of taxes.

The Authority of the commander in chief, and, under him, of the brigadiers general has in time of peace, been rendered supreme in all the civil governments in America.

The commander in chief of all your majesty's forces in North-America has, in time of peace, been appointed governor of a colony.

The charges of usual offices have been greatly increased; and, new, expensive and oppressive offices have been multiplied.

The judges of admiralty and vice-admiralty courts are empowered to receive their salaries and fees from the effects condemned by themselves. The officers of the customs are empowered to break open and enter houses without the authority of any civil magistrate founded on legal information.

The judges of courts of common law have been made entirely dependant on one part of the legislature for their salaries, as well as for the duration of their commissions.

Councellors holding their commissions, during pleasure, exercise legislative authority.

Humble and reasonable petitions from the representatives of the people have been fruitless.

The agents of the people have been discountenanced and governors have been instructed to prevent the payment of their salaries.

Assemblies have been repeatedly and injuriously dissolved.

Commerce has been burthened with many useless and oppressive restrictions.

By several acts of parliament made in the fourth, fifth, sixth, seventh, and eighth years of your majesty's reign, duties are imposed on us, for the purpose of raising a revenue, and the powers of admiralty and vice-admiralty courts are extended beyond their ancient limits, whereby our property is taken from us without our consent, the trial by jury in many civil cases is abolished, enormous forfeitures are incurred for slight offences, vexatious informers are exempted from paying damages, to which they are justly liable, and oppressive security is required from owners before they are allowed to defend their right.

Both houses of parliament have resolved that colonists may be tried in England, for offences alleged to have been committed in America, by virtue of a statute passed in the thirty fifth year of Henry the eighth; and in consequence thereof, attempts have been made to enforce that statute. A statute was passed in the twelfth year of your majesty's reign, directing, that persons charged with committing any offence therein described, in any place out of the realm, may be indicted and tried for the same, in any shire or county within the realm, whereby inhabitants of these colonies may, in sundry cases by that statute made capital, be deprived of a trial by their peers of the vicinage.

In the last sessions of parliament, an act was passed for blocking up the harbor of Boston; another, empowering the governor of the Massachusetts-bay to send persons indicted for murder in that province to another colony or even to Great Britain for trial whereby such offenders may escape legal punishment; a third, for altering the chartered constitution of government in that province; and a fourth for extending the limits of Quebec, abolishing the English and restoring the French laws, whereby great numbers of British freemen are subjected to the latter, and establishing an absolute government and the Roman Catholic religion throughout those vast regions, that border on the westerly and northerly boundaries of the free protestant English settlements; and a fifth for the better providing suitable quarters for officers and soldiers in his majesty's service in North America.

To a sovereign, who "glories in the name of Briton" the bare recital of these acts must we presume, justify the loyal subjects, who fly to the foot of his throne and implore his clemency for protection against them.

From this destructive system of colony administration adopted since the conclusion of the last war, have flowed those distresses, dangers, fears and jealousies, that overwhelm your majesty's dutiful colonists with affliction; and we defy our most subtle and inveterate enemies, to trace the unhappy differences between Great-Britain and these colonies, from an earlier period or from other causes than we have assigned. Had they proceeded on our part from a restless levity of temper, unjust impulses of ambition, or artful suggestions of seditious persons, we should merit the opprobrious terms frequently bestowed upon us, by those we revere. But so far from promoting innovations, we have only opposed them; and can be charged with no offence, unless it be one, to receive injuries and be sensible of them.

Had our creator been pleased to give us existence in a land of slavery, the sense of our condition might have been mitigated by ignorance and habit. But thanks be to his adorable goodness, we were born the heirs of freedom, and ever enjoyed our right under the auspices of your royal ancestors, whose family was seated on the British throne, to rescue and secure a pious and gallant nation from the popery and despotism of a superstitious and inexorable tyrant. Your majesty, we are confident, justly rejoices, that your title to the crown is thus founded on the title of your people to liberty; and therefore we doubt not, but your royal wisdom must approve the sensibility, that teaches your subjects anxiously to guard the blessings, they received from divine providence, and thereby to prove the performance of that compact, which elevated the illustrious house of Brunswick to the imperial dignity it now possesses.

The apprehension of being degraded into a state of servitude from the pre-eminent rank of English freemen, while our minds retain the strongest love of liberty, and clearly foresee the miseries preparing for us and our posterity, excites emotions in our breasts, which though we cannot describe, we should not wish to conceal. Feeling as men, and thinking as subjects, in the manner we do, silence would be disloyalty. By giving this faithful information, we do all in our power, to promote the great objects of your royal cares, the tranquility of your government, and the welfare of your people.

Duty to your majesty and regard for the preservation of ourselves and our posterity, the primary obligations of nature and society command us to entreat your royal attention; and as your majesty enjoys the signal distinction of reigning over freemen, we apprehend the language of freemen can not be displeasing. Your royal indignation, we hope, will rather fall on those designing and dangerous men, who daringly interposing themselves between your royal person and your faithful subjects, and for several years past incessantly employed to dissolve the bonds of society, by abusing your majesty's authority, misrepresenting your American subjects and prosecuting the most desperate and irritating projects of oppression, have at length compelled us, by the force of accumulated injuries too severe to be any longer tolerable, to disturb your majesty's repose by our complaints.

These sentiments are extorted from hearts, that much more willingly would bleed in your majesty's service. Yet so greatly have we been misrepresented, that a necessity has been alleged of taking our property from us without our consent "to defray the charge of the administration of justice, the support of civil government, and the defense protection and security of the colonies." But we beg leave to assure your majesty, that such provision has been and will be made for defraying the two first articles, as has been and shall be judged, by the legislatures of the several colonies, just and suitable to their respective circumstances: And for the defense protection and security of the colonies, their militias, if properly regulated, as they earnestly desire may immediately be done, would be fully sufficient, at least in times of peace; and in case of war, your faithful colonists will be ready and willing, as they ever have been when constitutionally required, to demonstrate their loyalty to your majesty, by exerting their most strenuous efforts in granting supplies and raising forces. Yielding to no British subjects, in affectionate attachment to your majesty's person, family and government, we too dearly prize the privilege of expressing that attachment by those proofs, that are honorable to the prince who receives them, and to the people who give them, ever to resign it to any body of men upon earth.

Had we been permitted to enjoy in quiet the inheritance left us by our forefathers, we should at this time have been peaceably, cheerfully and usefully employed in recommending ourselves by every testimony of devotion to your majesty, and of veneration to the state, from which we derive our origin. But though now exposed to unexpected and unnatural scenes of distress by a contention with that nation, in whose parental guidance on all important affairs we have hitherto with filial reverence constantly trusted, and therefore can derive no instruction in our present unhappy and perplexing circumstances from any former experience, yet we doubt not, the purity of our intention and the integrity of our conduct will justify us at that grand tribunal, before which all mankind must submit to judgment.

We ask but for peace, liberty, and safety. We wish not a diminution of the prerogative, nor do we solicit the grant of any new right in our favor. Your royal authority over us and our connexion with Great-Britain, we shall always carefully and zealously endeavor to support and maintain.

Filled with sentiments of duty to your majesty, and of affection to our parent state, deeply impressed by our education and strongly confirmed by our reason, and anxious to evince the sincerity of these dispositions, we present this petition only to obtain redress of grievances and relief from fears and jealousies occasioned by the system of statutes and regulations adopted since the close of the late war, for raising a revenue in America--extending the powers of courts of admiralty and vice-admiralty--trying persons in Great Britain for offences alleged to be committed in America--affecting the province of Massachusetts-bay, and altering the government and extending the limits of Quebec; by the abolition of which system, the harmony between Great-Britain and these colonies so necessary to the happiness of both and so ardently desired by the latter, and the usual intercourses will be immediately restored. In the magnanimity and justice of your majesty and parliament we confide, for a redress of our other grievances, trusting, that when the causes of our apprehensions are removed, our future conduct will prove us not unworthy of the regard, we have been accustomed, in our happier days, to enjoy. For appealing to that being who searches thoroughly the hearts of his creatures, we solemnly profess, that our councils have been influenced by no other motive, than a dread of impending destruction.

Permit us then, most gracious sovereign, in the name of all your faithful people in America, with the utmost humility to implore you, for the honor of Almighty God, whose pure religion our enemies are undermining; for your glory, which can be advanced only by rendering your subjects happy and keeping them united; for the interests of your family depending on an adherence to the principles that enthroned it; for the safety and welfare of your kingdoms and dominions threatened with almost unavoidable dangers and distresses; that your majesty, as the loving father of your whole people, connected by the same bands of law, loyalty, faith and blood, though dwelling in various countries, will not suffer the transcendent relation formed by these ties to be farther violated, in uncertain expectation of effects, that, if attained, never can compensate for the calamities, through which they must be gained.

We therefore most earnestly beseech your majesty, that your royal authority and interposition may be used for our relief; and that a gracious answer may be given to this petition.

That your majesty may enjoy every felicity through a long and glorious reign over loyal and happy subjects and that your descendants may inherit your prosperity and dominions 'til time shall be no more, is and always will be our sincere and fervent prayer.

SIGNED: Henry Middleton, Jno Sullivan, Nathl Folsom, Thomas Cushing, Samuel Adams, John Adams, Robt. Treat Paine, tep Hopkins, Sam: Ward, Elipht Dyer, Roger Sherman, Silas Deane, Phil. Livingston, John Alsop, Isaac Low, Jas. Duane, John Jay, Wm. Floyd, Henry Wisner, S: Boerum, Wil: Livingston, John De Hart, Stepn. Crane, Richd. Smith, E Biddle, J: Galloway, John Dickinson, John Morton, Thomas Mifflin, George Ross, Chas Humphreys, Cæsar Rodney, Thos M: Kean, Geo: Read, Mat. Tilghman , Ths. Johnson Junr, Wm. Paca, Samuel Chase, Richard Henry Lee, Patrick Henry, Go. Washington, Edmund Pendleton, Richd. Bland, Benjn Harrison, Will Hooper, Joseph Hewes, Rd. Caswell, Tho Lynch, Christ Gadsden, J. Rutledge, Edward Rutledge.

Agents to whom the Address to King is to be sent for New Hampshire, Paul Wentworth Esqr. Massachusetts Bay,William Bollan Esqr, Doctr. Benj: Franklin Doctr. Arthur Lee, Rhode Island, none Connecticut, Thomas Life, Esqr. New Jersey, Doctr Benj. Franklin, Pensylvania, Doctr Benj. Franklin, New York, Edmund Burke, Delaware, Maryland, Virginia, N. Carolina, none, South Carolina, Charles Garth, Esqr.

In 1775 Middleton was elected President of the Provincial Congress of South Carolina and received the public thanks of that body, which at that time was considered a high honor. In 1775 Middleton was re-elected by the Provincial Congress of South Carolina as delegate to the Continental Congress. He was a member of the council of safety, and by his position, wealth, and powerful family connection did much to turn the balance in Carolina in favor of the Congress's direction towards colonial self-government.

In 1776 Henry Middleton was prevented by ill health from returning to Congress. His delegate slot was filled by his eldest son, Arthur Middleton, who voted for Independence on July 2, 1776 and signed the Declaration of Independence on August 2, 1776.

Henry Middleton's health rebounded and he joined the South Carolina legislative council in 1777 where he was a reluctant supporter of Independence. In 1778 he was elected to the South Carolina State Senate and served to 1780. On May 12, 1780 the British General Charles Cornwallis captured Charleston, South Carolina. Then State Senator Henry Middleton pledged his allegiance to the crown and urged his fellow countrymen to do the same. This came as a great blow to then Continental Congress President Samuel Huntington who was desperately trying to get Maryland to ratify the Articles Of Confederation forming the Perpetual Union of the United States.

Henry Middleton, despite his flip-flop on Independence was forgiven. After the war he prospered in South Carolina. Middleton was a large and successful planter, owning about 50,000 acres and 800 slaves, and he was constant in his efforts to improve the agriculture and commerce of the colony. Henry twice remarried, but his five sons and seven daughters were all children of his first wife, who died in 1761.

CHAPTER FOUR

Portrait of John Hancock from
Appleton Cyclopedia of American Biography

JOHN HANCOCK

1776 President of the Continental Congress
7th President of the United States
in Congress Assembled
November 23, 1785 to June 6, 1786

John Hancock was born in Quincy, Massachusetts, on January 12, 1737 and died there on October 8, 1793. John Hancock received a strong childhood education and graduated from Harvard in 1754. Upon the death of his father he was adopted by his uncle, Thomas, who took him into his counting-house and left him a large fortune, as well as the business.

In 1765 as an effort to recoup large losses of gold during the French and Indian War the British Stamp Act passes Parliament and imposes a direct tax on the American colonies to be paid directly to King George III. The Stamp Act Congress convenes in New York City and passes a resolution calling on King George III to repeal the Act. One year later that act is repealed. In 1766 Parliament passes the Declaratory Act declaring the British government's absolute authority over the American colonies. In that same year Hancock In 1766 was chosen to represent Boston in the Massachusetts House of Representatives with James Otis, Thomas Cushing, and Samuel Adams, "*where,*" says Eliot, "*he blazed a Whig of the first magnitude*" defying the taxes of the British Empire. The seizure of Hancock's sloop, the "*Liberty,*" for an alleged evasion of the laws of trade, caused a riot, the royal commissioners of customs barely escaping with their lives.

In 1767, in another attempt to obtain revenue from the colonies, the Townshend Revenue Acts were passed by Parliament, taxing imported paper, tea, glass, lead and paints. In February of 1768, Samuel Adams and James Otis drafted – and the Massachusetts Assembly adopted – a circular letter to the other American Assemblies protesting these taxes. They expressed the hope that redress could be obtained through petitions to King George III, and called for a convention to discuss the problem and draft petitions to the Crown. The British government, however, provoked a confrontation by ordering the Massachusetts Assembly to rescind the letter and ordered Governor Bernard to dismiss the assembly if they refused.

In protest to this and other British laws, John Hancock and other Selectman called for a town meeting at Faneuil Hall on September 23, 1768. On September 28th 96 towns answering Hancock's call to address taxation and self-government grievances against the British Crown. The circular read:

> *"YOU are already too well acquainted with the _hreatenin [sic] and very alarming Circumstances to which this Province, as well as America in general, is now reduced. Taxes equally detrimental to the Commercial interests of the Parent Country and her Colonies, are imposed upon the People, without their Consent; - Taxes designed for the Support of the Civil Government in the Colonies, in a Manner clearly unconstitutional, and contrary to that, in which 'till of late, Government has been supported, by the free Gift of the People in the American Assemblies or Parliaments; as also for the Maintenance of a large Standing Army; not for the Defence [sic] of the newly acquired Territories, but for the old Colonies, and in a Time of Peace. The decent, humble and truly loyal Applications and Petitions from the Representatives of this Province for the Redress of these heavy and very _hreatening [sic] Grievances, have hitherto been ineffectual…The only Effect…has been a Mandate…to Dissolve the General Assembly, merely because the late House of Representatives refused to Rescind a Resolution of a former House, which imply'd nothing more than a Right in the American Subjects to unite in humble and dutiful Petitions to their gracious Sovereign, when they found themselves aggrieved…*

"The Concern and Perplexity into which these Things have thrown the People, have been greatly aggravated, by a late Declaration of his Excellency Governor BERNARD, that one or more Regiments may soon be expected in this Province…

"Deprived of the Councils of a General Assembly in this dark and difficult Season, the loyal People of this Province, will, we are persuaded, immediately perceive the Propriety and Utility of the proposed Committee of Convention…".

Signed "John Hancock," also signed "Joseph Jackson," "John Ruddock," "John Rowe," and "Samuel Pemberton" as Selectmen of Boston

This particular Hancock document had a demonstrable effect - *it changed the world* - as the governor called for British reinforcements. Hancock's convention composed a list of grievances, passed several resolutions, and adjourned. Two days later, royal transports unloaded British troops at the Long Wharf and began a military occupation of Boston that would last until March 17, 1776. It was the beginning of the end of British Colonialism in America.

In response to the affray known as the "*Boston Massacre,"* on March 5th, 1770 Hancock, at the funeral of the slain Bostonians, delivered an address to the mourning citizens. So radiant and fearless was the speech in its reprobation of the conduct of the soldiery and their leaders that it greatly offended the Colonial Governor. This speech also gave him much notoriety throughout the colonies.

In 1774 he was elected, with Samuel Adams, to the Provincial congress at Concord, Massachusetts, and subsequently became its president. It was to secure these two patriots that the expedition to Concord in April, 1775, which led to the battle of Lexington, was undertaken by authorities. However it was futile, as they succeeded in making their escape. On 12 June, General Gage issued a proclamation offering pardons to all the rebels, excepting Samuel Adams and John Hancock, *"whose offences," it was declared, "are of too flagitious a nature to admit of any other consideration than that of condign punishment."*

Mr. Hancock was a delegate from Massachusetts to the Continental Congress from 1775 until 1780, and from 1785 until 1786, serving as president of that body from May 25, 1775 until October 1777. The Second Continental Congress opened on May 10, 1775 with Peyton Randolph serving as President of the Continental Congress of the United Colonies. Once again Randolph was called to Virginia for a Burgesses session. Henry Middleton declined the Presidency due to ill health. Samuel Adams and his cousin John Adams decided to champion the cause of their wealthy benefactor John Hancock and he was elected President on May 25th. The Adam's regretted their decision because John Hancock aligned himself with delegates who were, at best, tepid in the cause of independence. Additionally he used his office in an opulent fashion much to the disappointment of his Massachusetts Colleagues. When Randolph returned to Congress John Hancock, despite many delegates charging he was only elected to temporarily fill his absence, he made no overture to surrender the Presidency.

Despite his attempts to thwart revolution, John Hancock presided over the Continental Congress who supported the vote for Independence on July 2, 1776, declaring the Colonies free and independent states. The Declaration of Independence, which was passed on July 4th, as first published, bore only his and Charles Thomson's names as president and secretary. In 1776 he was also commissioned Major-General of the Massachusetts militia. In the autumn of 1776 congress gave Washington instructions to destroy Boston if necessary to dislodge the enemy. Mr. Hancock then wrote Washington that, although probably the largest property-owner in the city, *"he was anxious the thing should be done if it would benefit the cause."* John Adams said of Hancock's character: *"Nor were his talents or attainments inconsiderable. They were far superior to many who have been much more celebrated. He had a great deal of political sagacity and insight into men. He was by no means a contemptible scholar or orator. Compared with Washington, Lincoln, or Knox, he was learned."*

The president's style of living in Philadelphia was on par of his wealthy home in Boston. When Congress was forced to flee to Baltimore in December 1776, John Hancock was unable to find quarters to meet his usual life style. In a letter to Robert Morris dated January 14th, 1777 he writes:

> *I have got to House keeping, but really my Friend in a very poor house, and but just furniture enough to liver tolerably descent tho' when I tell you I give 25 pounds this currency Philadelphia you would judge it to be amply furnished. I have only two rooms and one of them I am obliged to let my servants occupy....*

Four weeks later Hancock found himself on the road again as the Congress moved back to Philadelphia. Congress moved again on September 28, 1777 to Lancaster Pennsylvania, then on to York September 30th to June 27th, 1778. On October 29th he resigned from the Presidency.

He took his leave of Congress on the 29th and decided to make a *"farewell address"* to his fellow delegates who were quite flattering of his Presidency. He explained that his duties required his unremitting attention, which had greatly impaired his health making his immediate retirement critical. These parting comments were not popular with his fellow delegates and the motion of thanks only passed six States to four with one divided. His own delegation, Massachusetts voted *"no"* against thanking Hancock. Samuel Adams believed that any thanks to any President was *"... unprecedented, impolitick, dangerous."* Despite this John Hancock requested an escort of horse guard to protect him from the Tories on his trip back to Boston. George Washington furnished the former President with twelve dragoons.

John Hancock's Continental Congress Chronology is remarkable and is summarized as follows:

> **1775 - May 24** Elects John Hancock President of the Continental Congress.
>
> **May 26** Resolves to send a second petition to the king and to put *"these colonies . . . into a state of defense."*

June 1 Resolves against an "expedition or incursion" into Canada. **June 2** Receives Massachusetts proposal to take up civil government. **June 7** Resolves to observe **July 20** as a Fast Day. **June 9** Endorses assumption of civil authority in Massachusetts by the provincial convention. **June 10** Resolves to organize a Continental Army. **June 15** Appoints George Washington Commander in Chief of the army. **June 22** Resolves to print $2 million in Continental currency. **June 27** Approves invasion of Canada.

July 5 Approves petition to the king. **July 6** Approves *"Declaration on Taking Arms."* **July 8** Approves address to inhabitants of Great Britain. **July 12** Organizes three departments for Native American affairs. **July 21** Ignores Benjamin Franklin's proposed Articles of Confederation. **July 27** Resolves to establish a system of military hospitals. **July 31** Adopts response to Lord North's Conciliatory Resolution.

August 2 Adjourns until September 5.

September 13 Archives quorum and reconvenes; Georgia fully represented for first time. **September 19** Appoints secret committee to purchase military supplies abroad. **September 22** Appoints committee to consider *"the state of the trade of America."* **September 27** Orders publication of corrected journals of Congress. **September 29** Appoints Committee of Conference to confer with General Washington and various New England executives.

October 3 Receives Rhode Island proposal for building an American fleet. **October 5** Recommends to General Washington a plan to intercept British supply ships. **October 6** Recommends that provincial governments arrest persons deemed a danger to *"the liberties of America."* **October 7** Adopts report on fortification of the Hudson River **October 13** Resolves to fit out armed vessels; appoints Naval Committee. **October 17** Appoints John Morgan Director General of hospitals, replacing Benjamin Church upon his arrest for correspondence with the enemy; appoints committee to estimate damages inflicted by British arms. **October 24** Adjourns to attend funeral of Peyton Randolph. **October 26** Publishes resolution authorizing exports in exchange for arms. **October 30** Increases naval authorization and expands Naval Committee.

November 1 Reaffirms general embargo on exports, extended to March 1, 1776; commends provincial authorities for ignoring parliamentary trade exemptions designed to undermine American unity. **November 2** Appoints Committee to the Northward to confer with General Schuyler; receives report of Committee of Conference. **November 3** Recommends formation of new provincial government in New Hampshire. **November 4** Adopts resolutions for reconstitution of General Washington's army in Massachusetts, and for defense of South Carolina and Georgia. **November 9** Adopts new oath of secrecy; publishes report of king's refusal to receive Olive Branch Petition.

November 10 Adopts plan for promoting manufacture of saltpeter; orders enlistment of first two battalions of marines. **November 13** Orders publication of new "*Rules and Regulations*" for Continental Army. **November 15** Receives account of capture of St. Johns. **November 16** Adopts resolution to improve delegates' attendance in Congress. **November 17** Adopts regulations pertaining to prisoners of war. **November 22** Authorizes exemptions to ban on exports to Bermuda. **November 23** Adopts resolves to improve peaceful relations with the Six Nations. **November 25** Adopts regulations pertaining to prize cases. **November 28** Adopts "*Rules for the Regulation of the Navy of the United Colonies*"; adopts measures for the defense of North Carolina. **November 29** Appoints Committee of Secret Correspondence; resolves to print $3,000,000 in Continental currency; receives account of capture of Montreal.

December 2 Sends Benjamin Harrison to Maryland to promote defense of the Chesapeake. **December 4** Recommends formation of new provincial government in Virginia; appoints committee to dissuade New Jersey Assembly from separately petitioning king. **December 6** Publishes response to king's August 23 proclamation declaring colonies in state of rebellion. **December 8** Resolves to confine John Connolly for plotting with Lord Dunmore against western Virginia. **December 13** Authorizes construction of 13 ships for Continental Navy. **December 14** Appoints Marine Committee. **December 15** Receives plan for creation of committee to sit during recess of Congress. **December 20** Recommends cessation of hostilities between Connecticut and Pennsylvania settlers in Wyoming Valley. **December 22** Authorizes an attack on Boston; appoints Esek Hopkins commander in chief of Continental Navy. December 26 Adopts plan for redemption of Continental bills of credit. **December 29** Adopts resolutions for importing and manufacturing salt. **December 30** Recommends Secret Committee negotiations with Pierre Penet and Emanuel de Pliarne for European arms and ammunition.

1776 - January 1 Recommends "the reduction of St. Augustine." **January** 3 Recommends a quarantine of Queens County, N.Y., for refusal to send deputies to the New York Convention. **January 6** Adopts regulations for the division of marine prizes. **January 8** Orders reinforcements to Canada; receives news of the king's speech from the throne (October 27, 1775) and of the destruction of Norfolk, Virginia **January 11** Resolves that any person refusing to accept Continental currency "*shall be. . . treated as an enemy of his country.*" January 16 Limits black recruitment to the reenlistment of "*free negroes who have served faithfully in the army at Cambridge.*" **January 17** Receives news of General Montgomery's defeat at Quebec; appoints a committee to prepare regulations for opening American ports on March 1, 1776. **January 19** Orders additional reinforcements to Canada in response to General Montgomery's defeat. **January 24** Orders publication of a public statement on the repulse at

Quebec and of a new "*Letter to the Inhabitants of the Province of Canada.*" **January 25** Orders preparation of a monument and delivery of a funeral oration in tribute to the memory of General Montgomery. **January 26** Appoints a committee "*to repair to New York, to consult and advise ... respecting the immediate defense of the said city.*" **January 27** Directs the Secret Committee to import goods for use of the commissioners of Native American affairs "*in order to preserve the friendship and confidence of the Indians.*" **January 31** Forbids enlistment of prisoners of war.

February 5 Recommends that additional efforts be made to instruct and convert the Native Americans. **February 13** Exempts inter-colonial trade in naval stores from general trade restrictions; tables draft "*address to the inhabitants of these Colonies.*" **February 15** Appoints a committee to proceed to Canada to promote support for the American cause. **February 17** Appoints the Treasury Committee; resolves to emit additional $4 million; appoints General Charles Lee to the Canadian command. **February 23** Appoints committees to promote the manufacture of firearms and the production of salt petre, sulphur, and powder. **February 26** Prohibits sailing of vessels loaded for Great Britain, Ireland, or the British West Indies. **February 27** Establishes separate military departments for the middle and southern colonies. **February 29** Receives General Washington's letter on Lord Drummond's peace mission.

March 1 Appoints General Charles Lee to command the southern department. **March 2** Committee of Secret Correspondence appoints Silas Deane as an agent to France to transact business "*commercial and political.*" **March 4** Removes the sailing ban on vessels loaded for Great Britain, Ireland or the British West Indies, and desiring to import arms and ammunition. **March 6** Appoints General John Thomas to the Canadian command. **March 9** Appoints a committee to study the "*state of the colonies in the southern department*"; denies military officers authority to impose test oaths. **March 14** Adopts resolves on defending New York and disarming the "*notoriously disaffected*" in all the colonies. **March 16** Declares May 17 "*a day of humiliation, fasting, and prayer.*" **March 20** Adopts instructions for the commissioners appointed to go to Canada. **March 23** Adopts a declaration and resolutions on privateering, subjecting British ships to seizure as lawful prizes. **March 25** Adopts a report on augmenting the defenses of the southern department. **March 27** Attends the funeral of Samuel Ward.

April 1 Establishes the Treasury Office. **April 2** Commends General Washington and his troops for conducting the successful siege and forcing the evacuation of Boston. **April 3** Adopts "*Instructions*" for privateers. **April 6** Opens the trade of the colonies "*to any parts of the world which are not under the dominion of the [King of Great Britain]*"; prohibits the importation of slaves. **April 11** Delivers a speech to Captain White Eyes of the Delaware Native Americans.

April 15 Urges cultivation of harmony between the Connecticut and Pennsylvania settlers in the Wyoming Valley. **April 16** Requests the Maryland Council of Safety to arrest Governor William Eden. **April 23** Appoints Continental *"agents for prizes in the several colonies"*; instructs the commissioners to Canada *"to publish an Address to the people of Canada."* **April 29** Instructs a committee *"to prepare a plan of an expedition against Fort Detroit."* **April 30** Appoints the Native American Affairs Committee.

May 6 Postpones prescribing procedures for receiving peace commissioners rumored to be en route to America; resolves to raise *$10 million "for the purpose of carrying on the war for the current year"* and appoints a ways and means committee. **May 9** Resolves to emit an additional $5 million. **May 10** Recommends that the colonies *"adopt such government as shall, in the opinion of the representatives of the people, best conduce to the happiness and safety of their constituents."* **May 15** Adopts a preamble to its resolution on establishing new governments, asserting the necessity of suppressing *"the exercise of every kind of authority"* under the British crown. **May 16** Requests General Washington's presence in Philadelphia to consult on forthcoming campaign. **May 17** Adjourns to observe Fast Day. **May 21** Receives news of George III's negotiations for nearly 17,000 German mercenaries to be sent to America. **May 22** Adopts measures to bolster American forces in Canada; resolves to emit additional $5 million in bills of credit. **May 24** Begins consultation with Generals Washington, Gates and Mifflin on forthcoming campaign. **May 25** Resolves "that it is highly expedient to engage the Native Americans in the service of the United Colonies." **May 27** Holds audience with deputies of the Six Nations; receives instructions directed to the North Carolina and Virginia delegates pertaining to independence.

June 1 Requests 6,000 militia reinforcements for Canada. **June 3** Requests nearly 24,000 militia reinforcements for General Washington at New York. June 7 Receives Richard Henry Lee's resolution respecting independence, foreign alliances and confederation. **June 10** Postpones debate on independence resolution; appoints committee to prepare a declaration of independence. **June 11** Receives Native American delegation; receives report from commissioners to Canada. **June 12** Appoints committees to prepare *"the form of a confederation"* and *"a plan of treaties to be proposed to foreign powers"*; creates Board of War and Ordinance. **June 14** Recommends *"detecting, restraining, and punishing disaffected and dangerous persons"* in New York; embargoes salt beef and pork. **June 17** Adopts general reform of the forces in Canada. June 19 Recommends seizure and confinement of Governor William Franklin. **June 21** Orders inquiry into the causes of miscarriages in Canada. **June 24** Adopts resolves on allegiance and treason and recommends legislation for punishing counterfeiters in several colonies; suspends enlistment of Mohegan and Stockbridge Native Americans. **June 26** Adopts bounty for three-year enlistments. **June 28** Reads draft declaration of independence.

July 2 United Colonies declare independence from Great Britain. **July 4** Adopts the Declaration of Independence; prepares mobilization for the defense of New York, New Jersey and Pennsylvania. **July 8** Clarifies jurisdictions of Northern Commanders Gates and Schuyler; augments Washington's discretionary powers and commissary general's authority. **July 10** Denounces British treatment of prisoners captured at the Cedars in Canada. **July 12** Reads and orders printing of the draft of the Articles of Confederation. **July 17** Adopts "*rules and orders for the government of this house.*" **July 18** Reads draft "*plan of treaties to be entered into with foreign states.*" **July 19** Orders publication of Lord Howe's commission and correspondence to expose false expectations for a negotiated peace. **July 20** Commends commanders of the American victory at Charleston. **July 22** Adopts procedures for negotiating prisoner exchange; authorizes emission of additional $5 million in bills of credit; opens debate on articles of confederation. **July 24** Broadens regulations for confiscating British goods on the high seas. **July 26** Orders publication of an account of a conference between General Washington and a representative of Lord Howe. **July 30** Recommends southern expedition against Cherokees; adopts sundry resolves in response to report on the miscarriages in Canada.

August 2 Delegates sign engrossed Declaration of Independence; Congress authorizes employment of the Stockbridge Native Americans. **August 6** Proposes general prisoner-of-war exchange. August 8 Orders General Lee to return to Philadelphia from Charleston; concludes three-week debate on Articles of Confederation. **August 12** Holds inquiry into conduct of Commodore Esek Hopkins. **August 13** Opens debate on revision of Articles of War. **August 14** Adopts plan for encouraging desertion of foreign mercenaries. **August 15** Rebukes Commodore Esek Hopkins. **August 16** Censures Commodore Esek Hopkins. **August 19** Orders Commodore Hopkins to resume command of Continental fleet; adopts extensive new instructions for Native American commissioners in middle department. **August 20** Reads draft of the Articles of Confederation and orders them printed in preparation for debate in committee of the whole. **August 23** Authorizes additional troops on Continental establishment for frontier defense. **August 26** Adopts measures for relief of disabled soldiers and seamen. **August 27** Resolves to encourage foreign mercenaries to desert from British army. **August 30** Adopts plan to improve postal system.

September 3 Receives General John Sullivan's written report on Lord Howe's proposal for peace conference. September 6 Designates Benjamin Franklin, John Adams, and Edward Rutledge to meet with Lord Howe. **September 9** Revises style of Continental commissions, replacing "*United Colonies*" with "*United States.*" **September 11** Committee meets with Lord Howe on Staten Island. **September 16** Adopts new plan for a Continental Army of 88 battalions and system of bounties for recruitment of officers and soldiers.

September 17 Adopts Plan of Treaties; receives report of the committee appointed to confer with Lord Howe and orders it published. **September 20** Adopts Articles of War. **September 22** Sends committee to New York "*to inquire into the state of the army.*" **September 25** Resolves to send committee to Ticonderoga to improve administration of northern army. **September 26** Appoints Silas Deane, Benjamin Franklin, and Thomas Jefferson as commissioners at Paris. **September 28** Adopts "*letters of credence*" for commissioners at Paris and plan for their maintenance.

October 1 Appoints Thomas Mifflin as Quartermaster General to replace Stephen Moylan; appoints committee to bring in plan for military academy. **October 2** Refuses to accept General Philip Schuyler's resignation as Commander of Northern department. **October 3** Resolves to borrow $5 million and establishes system of loan offices to transact the business. **October 7** Receives General Charles Lee's personal report on southern department and advances $30,000 indemnity to him for loss of property in England. **October 9** Appoints John Morgan and William Shippen, Jr., Director of Military Hospitals "*on the east side of Hudson's river*" and in New Jersey, respectively. **October 14** Accepts the report of the committee on the appeal of the libel case Joshua Wentworth v. the Elizabeth from the maritime court of New Hampshire. **October 18** Appoints Thaddeus Kosciuszko colonel of engineers in Continental Army. **October 22** Appoints Arthur Lee to replace Jefferson as Commissioner at Paris; instructs commissioners to procure eight line-of-battle ships from France. **October 28** Appoints committee to conduct inquiry into monopolizing and engrossing of military supplies. **October 30** Rejects Maryland proposal to substitute money for land as an additional bounty; adopts new formula for division of prize money in Continental Navy.

November 2 Resolves to emit additional $5 million. **November 6** Resolves to appoint naval board in Philadelphia "*to execute the business of the navy, under the direction of the Marine Committee.*" **November 11** Directs Board of War to confer with Pennsylvania Council of Safety on defense of Philadelphia. **November 15** Adopts new pay plan for Continental Navy. **November 18** Adopts lottery system to raise Continental funds. **November 20** Resolves to enlarge navy by eight additional ships. **November 23** Receives news of evacuation of Fort Lee and British crossing of Hudson River. **November 25** Urges Pennsylvania to mobilize militia for six-week emergency.

December 1 Holds emergency Sunday session; authorizes General Washington to order troops from east side of Hudson River to west side. **December 5** Hears Address of Native American delegation. **December 8** Holds emergency Sunday session. **December 11** Proclaims day of fasting and humiliation; instructs General Washington to contradict report that Congress was preparing to adjourn from Philadelphia. **December 12** Adjourns to Baltimore; leaves General Israel Putnam to direct defense of Philadelphia. **December 20** Reconvenes in Baltimore; inquires into treatment of Gen. Charles Lee since his recent capture by the British. **December 21** Appoints George Clymer, Robert Morris and George Walton to executive committee of Congress at Philadelphia. **December 23** Authorizes commissioners at Paris to borrow *"two millions sterling,"* arm six vessels of war and seek information on Portugal's hostile actions toward American ships. **December 26** Appoints committee to prepare plan *"for the better conducting the executive business of Congress, by boards composed of persons, not members of Congress."* **December** 27 Confers extraordinary powers on General Washington for six months. **December 30** Approves new instructions for American commissioners abroad and votes to send commissioners to *"courts of Vienna, Spain, Prussia and the Grand Duke of Tuscany."* **December 31** Receives General Washington's announcement of his victory over Hessian garrison at Trenton.

1777 - January 1 Appoints Benjamin Franklin Commissioner to the Court of Spain. **January** 3 Directs General Washington to investigate and protest General Howe's treatment of Congressman Richard Stockton and other American prisoners. **January 6** Denounces Howe's treatment of General Charles Lee and threatens retaliation against prisoners falling into American hands. **January 8** Authorizes posting continental garrisons for the defense of western Virginia and financing Massachusetts' expedition against Fort Cumberland, Nova Scotia. **January 9** Dismisses John Morgan, Director General of Military Hospitals, and Samuel Stringer, Director of the Northern Department hospital. **January 14** Adopts proposals to bolster Continental money and recommends state taxation to meet state quotas. **January 16** Proposes appointment of a commissary for American prisoners held by the British; orders inquiry into British and Hessian depredations in New York and New Jersey. **January 18** Orders distribution of authenticated copies of the Declaration of Independence containing the names of signers. **January 24** Provides money for holding a Native American treaty at Easton, Pennsylvania. **January 28** Appoints committee to study the condition of Georgia. **January 29** Directs Joseph Trumbull to conduct an inquiry into activities of his deputy commissary Carpenter Wharton. **January 30** Creates standing committee on appeals from state admiralty courts.

February 1 Orders measures for suppressing insurrection in Worcester and Somerset counties, Maryland. **February 5** Orders measures for obtaining troops from the Carolinas; instructs Secret Committee on procuring supplies from France. **February 6** Directs measures for the defense of Georgia and for securing the friendship of the southern Native Americans. **February 10** Recommends temporary embargo in response to British naval *"infestation"* of

Chesapeake Bay. **February 12** Recommends inoculation of Continental troops for smallpox. **February 15** Endorses the substance of the recommendations adopted at the December-January New England Conference and recommends the convening of two similar conferences in the middle and southern states. **February 17** Endorses General Schuyler's efforts to retain the friend ship of the Six Nations. **February 18** Directs General Washington to conduct inquiry into military abilities of foreign officers. **February 19** Elects five major generals. **February 21** Rejects General Lee's request for a congressional delegation to meet with him to consider British peace overtures; elects 10 brigadier generals. **February 22** Resolves to borrow $13 million in loan office certificates. **February 25** Adopts measures to curb desertion. **February 26** Raises interest on loan office certificates from 4% to 6%. **February 27** Cautions Virginia on expeditions against the Indians: adjourns to Philadelphia, Pennsylvania to reconvene on March 5.

March 5-11 Fails to attain quorum. **March 11** urges Delaware and New York to dispatch delegates to Congress. **March 12** Reconvenes. **March 13** Cautions agents abroad against recruiting foreign officers with limited English language skills; appoints committee "*to confer with General Gates upon the general state of affairs.*" **March 15** Reprimands General Schuyler for comments "*highly derogatory to the honour of Congress.*" **March 17-18** Adjourns for lack of a quorum-only eight states represented. **March 19** Appoints committee on applications of foreign officers for military appointments; declines Baron de Kalb's offer of service. **March 21** Appoints committee to confer with General Nathanael Greene. **March 22** Establishes and specifies the organization and duties of the office of Secretary of Congress. **March 24** Informs General Washington that Congress never intended him to feel bound by a majority in a council of war contrary to his own judgment. **March 25** Urges Virginia to suspend operations planned against her western Indians; directs General Gates to take command of the army at Fort Ticonderoga; appoints William C. Houston Deputy secretary of Congress. **March 26** Suspends Esek Hopkins from his command of the Continental Navy. **March 29** Reaffirms decision not to send a delegation to confer with General Lee.

April 1 Adopts plan for "*better regulating the pay of the army.*" April 4 Adopts commissary reforms recommended by General Greene. **April 7** Adopts plan to reorganize the medical department. **April 8** Adopts proposals to honor the memory of Generals Joseph Warren and Hugh Mercer. **April 10** Orders measures for the defense of the western frontiers and appoints General Edward Hand to the command at Fort Pitt. **April 11** Appoints William Shippen, Jr., Director General of Military Hospitals and a new staff of physicians and surgeons general. **April 14** Adopts measures to improve recruiting; revises Articles of War. **April 16** Urges Rhode Island, Massachusetts and Connecticut to attack the British forces at Rhode Island. **April 18** Resolves to publish report on depredations; appoints committee to conduct inquiry into General Schuyler's command. **April 21** Resumes debate on Articles of Confederation. **April 22** Orders William Franklin into close confinement in retaliation for his urging Americans to seek royal pardons. **April 25** Orders measures for reinforcing and mobilizing General Washington's army. **April 29** Orders measures for the defense of Lake Champlain and Ticonderoga. **April 30** Appoints committee to evaluate the consequences of the British raid on Danbury; adopts quartermaster and commissary general reforms.

May 1 Considers possible hostilities against Portugal; appoints Arthur Lee commissioner to Spain. **May 3** Exonerates General Philip Schuyler from charges of misusing public funds. **May 5** Debates Articles of Confederation. **May 7** Appoints Ralph Izard commissioner to Tuscany. **May 9** Appoints William Lee commissioner to Berlin and Vienna. **May 14** Debates reorganization of the quartermaster department. May 20 Resolves to emit an additional $5 million. **May 22** Appoints Gen. Philip Schuyler to command of the northern department. **May 29** Considers draft of Address to the Inhabitants of the United States.

June 3 Appoints committee to oversee the defense of Pennsylvania. **June 4** Empowers General Washington to offer rewards to encourage British desertions. **June 6** Directs Secret Committee and Marine Committee to make an accounting of their proceedings and expenditures. **June 10** Reorganizes the commissary department. **June 11** Receives committee report on "*ways and means for defraying the expense of the current year.*" **June 14** Adopts the United States flag; disciplines Deputy Muster Master Gunning Bedford for issuing a challenge to delegate Jonathan Dickinson Sergeant for remarks made in Congress. **June 17** Memorializes General David Wooster for bravery during the defense of Danbury, Connecticut. **June 18** Orders George Morgan to convene an Native American conference at Fort Pitt. **June 23** Resumes debate on Articles of Confederation; hears New York complaint against inhabitants of "*the New Hampshire Grants.*" **June 30** Rebuffs movement to establish Vermont statehood.

July 1 Adopts instructions for commissioners to Vienna, Berlin and Tuscany. **July 3** Adopts instructions for the commissioner to the United Provinces; dispatches troops to suppress Delaware and Maryland loyalists. **July 5** Creates Committee of Commerce to replace the Secret Committee. **July 7** Condemns Generals Greene, Knox, and Sullivan for an "*attempt to influence*" Congress. **July 11** Appoints committee to proceed to camp "*to make a diligent enquiry into the state of the army.*" **July 14** Receives news of the retreat from Ticonderoga and Mount Independence. **July 16** Appoints committee to confer with the French officer du Coudray on his "*agreement*" with Commissioner Silas Deane.

July 23 Dismisses 12 naval officers to make an "*example*" of "*combinations of officers to extort increase of pay and allowances.*" **July 25** Appoints committee to study the defense of the southern frontier; commends Colonels Barton and Meigs for "*enterprize and valour*" in capturing General Prescott and conducting an expedition on Long Island. **July 29** Orders an inquiry into the evacuation of Ticonderoga and Mount Independence. **July 31** Commissions the Marquis de Lafayette a major general.

August 1 Begins inquiry into Commissioner Silas Deane's contracts with foreign officers. **August 4** Appoints General Horatio Gates to replace General Philip Schuyler as Commander of the Northern Department. **August 5** Begins consideration of Committee to Camp report on the "*state of the army.*" **August 7** Directs General Washington "*to negotiate an exchange of prisoners with the enemy.*" **August 8** Records first roll call vote-on motion to promote Brigadier General Benedict Arnold. **August 11** Directs implementation of General Washington's proposals for defense of the Delaware. **August 15** Agrees to accept parole of prominent Pennsylvania dissidents seeking to avoid exile to Virginia. **August 20** Directs mustering of the Pennsylvania militia; dispatches New Jersey militia to New York to relieve troops for frontier defense. **August 21** Endorses General Washington's proposal to march his main army toward the Hudson River; receives news of American victory at Bennington, Vermont. **August 22** Learns of British invasion of the Chesapeake; alerts Washington to the British threat to Philadelphia and issues call for the Pennsylvania, Delaware, Maryland, and Virginia militia. **August 26** Requests Pennsylvania and Delaware to apprehend and disarm the "*notoriously disaffected*" within their states. **August 28** Reverses decision to parole prominent Pennsylvania dissidents and orders their removal from the state.

September 1 Orders inquiry into the failure of General John Sullivan's expedition against Staten Island. **September 4** Orders further call-up of Pennsylvania and New Jersey militia. **September 6** Directs Clothier General to provide clothing bounties to troops. **September 8** Rebukes Silas Deane for exceeding his authority in negotiating agreements with foreign officers in France. **September 9** Orders General Washington to write Congress at least twice daily "*advising the position and movements of the armies.*" **September 10** Adopts ways and means motion to pay interest accruing on loan office certificates in bills of exchange on the commissioners at Paris. **September 11** Learns of the American defeat at Brandywine Creek. **September 12** Directs General Israel Putnam to reinforce Washington's army. **September 14** Orders General Sullivan's recall until the inquiry ordered into his conduct is completed; resolves to convene in Lancaster, Pennsylvania if the evacuation of Philadelphia becomes necessary. **September 15** Orders investigation of a conspiracy rumored to be impending in Pennsylvania.

September 16 Grants General Washington broad powers to punish military officers and to impress supplies for the army; orders removal of supplies from Philadelphia **September 18** Evacuates Philadelphia **September 19-26** Delegates in flight to Lancaster, Pennsylvania **September 27** Convenes at Lancaster; adjourns to York. **September 30** Convenes at York.

October 1 Resolves to meet twice daily. **October 2** Authorizes delegates to draw provisions from Continental commissaries. **October 4** Commends sundry officers for bravery in defense against General Burgoyne's northern invasion. **October 7** Debates *"mode of voting"* under draft Articles of Confederation. **October 8** Adopts penalties for *"communicating"* with the enemy; commends Washington for the *"brave exertions"* of his army at Germantown. **October 9-14** Debates taxation proposals under draft of Articles of Confederation. **October 15** Debates powers of Congress under draft of Articles of Confederation. **October 17** Reorganizes the Board of War. **October 20** Exonerates General John Sullivan for failure of Staten Island expedition; learns informally of General Gates' capture of General Burgoyne's army at Saratoga. **October 22** Orders inquiry into the conduct of Native American Commissioner George Morgan. **October 23-30** Debates and revises draft of Articles of Confederation. **October 29** President Hancock takes leave of Congress.

He was a member of the Massachusetts constitutional convention of 1780, and was governor of the state from 1780 until 1785. On January 29, 1785 John Hancock resigned as Governor of Massachusetts. As in 1778, Hancock assigned ill health as the cause for retirement. On June 16th, 1785 he was elected as delegate to the United States in Congress Assembled. Young John Quincy Adams wrote his father on August 3rd *"It is generally supposed here that Mr. Hancock will next year be seated in the Chair of Congress."* John Hancock wrote his sister on July 17th:

> *Mr. Hancock, being too infirm to act as Governor of Massachusetts, is chosen a member of Congress ... and will probably take his rest in the President's seat next November. This is escaping Scylla to fall into Charybdis.*

On June 16th, 1785 Hancock was elected to the United States in Congress Assembled, but could not attend the session of Congress in November 1785 due to his illness. However, he was elected President of the United States in Congress Assembled on the 23rd of November 1785. His presidential duties were performed by the two chairmen – David Ramsay (23 November, 1785 - 12 May, 1786) and Nathaniel Gorham (15 May - 5 June, 1786). John Jay, Secretary of Foreign Affairs wrote John Adams on May 4th 1786:

> *Mr. Hancock is still at Boston, and it is not certain when he may be expected; this is not a pleasant circumstance, for though the chair is well filled by a chairman, yet the President of Congress should be absent as little and seldom as possible.*

On 29 May 1786, Hancock, who held on to this office for six months, had his letter of resignation written. On 29 May 1786, Hancock, who was unable to write himself, had his letter of resignation written. It was presented to the Congress on 5 June 1786 and the resignation was accepted. The Chronology of John Hancock's Congress is as follows:

1785 - November 23 Achieves quorum, seven states represented; elects John Hancock president (in absentia), David Ramsay, chairman. **November 24** Elects two congressional chaplains. **November 25** Receives report on British Consul John Temple. **November 28-29** Fails to achieve quorum.

December 2 Recognizes John Temple as British Consul. **December 5-26** Fails to achieve quorum. **December 27** Receives Secretary at War reports.

1786 – January 2 Receives British complaint on treatment of loyalists. **January 4** Receives reports on states' response to appeals to grant Congress authority to raise revenue and regulate trade. **January 5** Receives report on Algerian capture of American seamen. **January 12** Receives report on settlement of Continental accounts. **January 18** Refers Connecticut cession to committee. **January 19** Orders report on 1786 fiscal estimates. **January 27** Elects Samuel Shaw consul to Canton, China. **January 30** Appeals to six un-represented states to send delegates.

February 1 Removes injunction of secrecy on correspondence concerning "*the appointment of Commissioners to treat with the Barbary powers.*" **February 3** Debates states' response to congressional fiscal appeals. **February 8** Receives report on French loan interest requirements. **February 9** Justifies abolishing salaries of court of appeals judges. **February 16-24** Fails to achieve quorum. **February 25** Receives reports on Franco-American postal plan and on 1786 fiscal estimates.

March 3 Repeats call to the states for authority to regulate trade. **March 7** Appoints committee to confer with New Jersey Assembly on its refusal to comply with 1786 Continental Requisition. **March 10** Rejects New York appeal for an extension of time for receiving Continental claims from citizens of the state. **March 14** Clarifies form of oaths required for Continental officeholders. **March 17-18** Fails to achieve quorum. **March 21** Receives report on capital punishment in military courts martial. **March 22** Receives report of New Jersey's reversal of opposition to 1786 Continental Requisition. **March 24** Appoints single commissioner to consolidate settlement of accounts of the five great departments (clothier, commissary, hospital, marine and quartermaster). **March 27** Orders arrest of Major John Wylles for execution of army deserters. **March 29** Directs secretary for foreign affairs to report on negotiations for British evacuation of frontier posts.

April 5 Receives report on "*negotiations, and other measures to be taken with the Barbary powers.*" **April 10** Receives report on Connecticut land cession. **April 12** Receives board of treasury report on coinage.

April 19 Rejects Massachusetts request for Continental ordnance **April 27** Receives translations of French decree on fisheries bounties.

May 2 Holds audience with Cornplanter and other Seneca chiefs. **May 5** Holds audience with Cornplanter and other Seneca chiefs. **May 6** Fails to achieve quorum. **May 8** Appoints second commissioner for settlement of accounts of the five great departments. **May 9** Directs Continental Geographer to proceed with survey of western territory. **May 11** Debates Connecticut cession. **May 12** Declares navigable waters in the territories forever free to their inhabitants and to the citizens of the United States. **May 15** Elects Nathaniel Gorham chairman of Congress to succeed David Ransay. **May 17** Ratifies Prussian-American Treaty of Commerce. **May 18** Postpones until September meeting of agents for Georgia-South Carolina boundary dispute. **May 22-25** Debates Connecticut cession. **May 26** Declares conditional acceptance of Connecticut cession. **May 29** Fails to achieve quorum. **May 31** Amends Rules to War; receives John Jay request for a committee to confer with him on negotiations with Diego de Gardoqui.

June 5 Receives resignation of President John Hancock; receives report on military establishment.

John Hancock recovered and was elected Governor again in 1787. He was a strong supporter of the US Constitution and its ratification process. In the presidential election of 1789, Governor Hancock received four electoral votes for US President under the new United States Constitution against George Washington and John Adams. He was re-elected annually as Governor of Massachusetts and served in that capacity until his death in 1793.

John Hancock was described by his supporters as:

> *"a man of strong common sense and decision of character, of polished manners, easy address, affable, liberal, and charitable. In his public speeches he displayed a high degree of eloquence. As a presiding officer he was dignified, impartial, quick of apprehension, and always commanded the respect of congress."*

He employed his large fortune for useful and benevolent purposes, and was a liberal donor to Harvard College. When the best method of driving the British from Boston was under discussion at a patriotic club in that town, he is said to have declared, "*Burn Boston, and make John Hancock a beggar, if the public good requires it.*" He received the degree of A.M. from Yale and Princeton in 1769, and that of L.L.D. from Brown in 1788 and from Harvard in 1792.

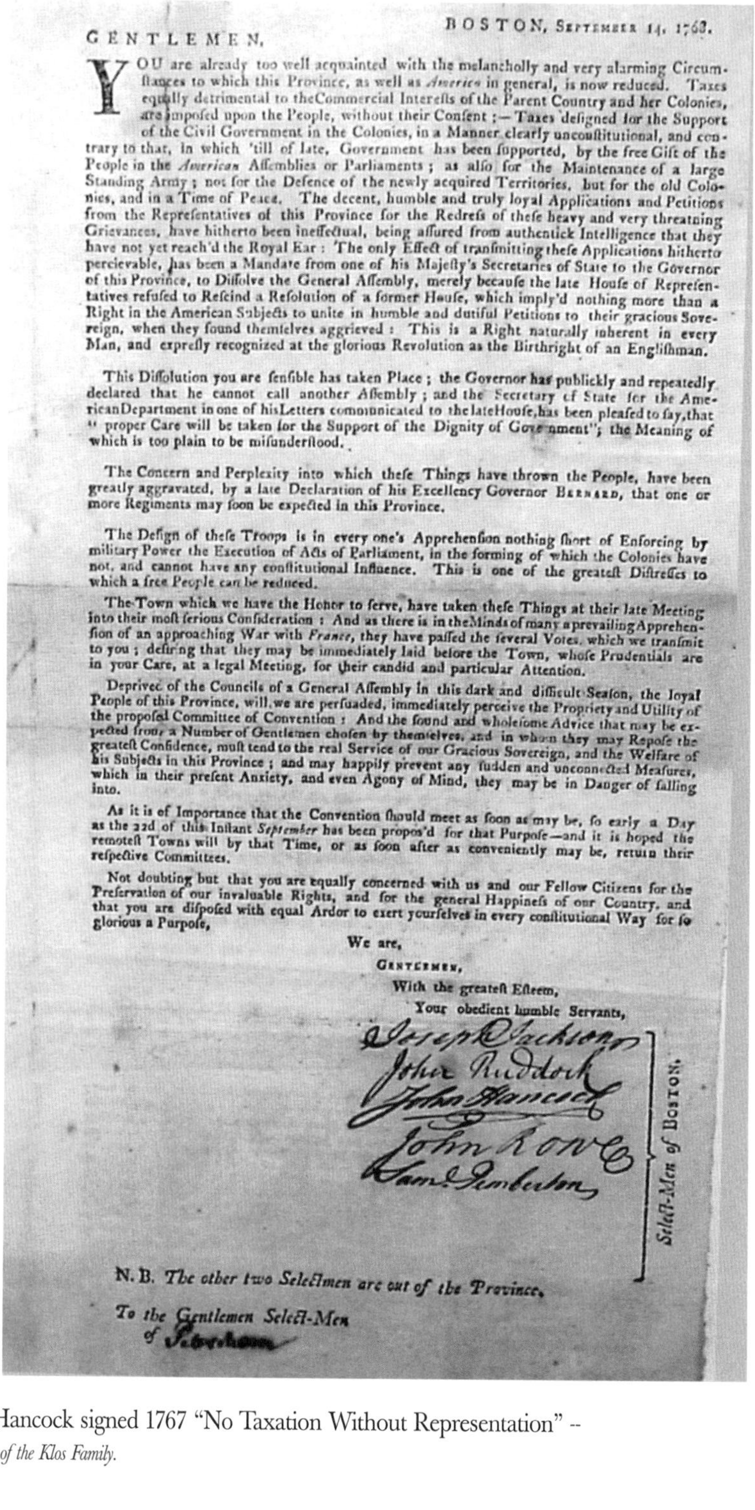

BOSTON, SEPTEMBER 14, 1768.

GENTLEMEN,

YOU are already too well acquainted with the melancholly and very alarming Circumstances to which this Province, as well as *America* in general, is now reduced. Taxes equally detrimental to the Commercial Interests of the Parent Country and her Colonies, are imposed upon the People, without their Consent ;— Taxes designed for the Support of the Civil Government in the Colonies, in a Manner clearly unconstitutional, and contrary to that, in which 'till of late, Government has been supported, by the free Gift of the People in the *American* Assemblies or Parliaments ; as also for the Maintenance of a large Standing Army ; not for the Defence of the newly acquired Territories, but for the old Colonies, and in a Time of Peace. The decent, humble and truly loyal Applications and Petitions from the Representatives of this Province for the Redress of these heavy and very threatning Grievances, have hitherto been ineffectual, being assured from authentick Intelligence that they have not yet reach'd the Royal Ear : The only Effect of transmitting these Applications hitherto percievable, has been a Mandate from one of his Majesty's Secretaries of State to the Governor of this Province, to Dissolve the General Assembly, merely because the late House of Representatives refused to Rescind a Resolution of a former House, which imply'd nothing more than a Right in the American Subjects to unite in humble and dutiful Petitions to their gracious Sovereign, when they found themselves aggrieved : This is a Right naturally inherent in every Man, and expresly recognized at the glorious Revolution as the Birthright of an Englishman.

This Dissolution you are sensible has taken Place ; the Governor has publickly and repeatedly declared that he cannot call another Assembly ; and the Secretary of State for the American Department in one of his Letters communicated to the late House, has been pleased to say, that "proper Care will be taken for the Support of the Dignity of Government"; the Meaning of which is too plain to be misunderstood.

The Concern and Perplexity into which these Things have thrown the People, have been greatly aggravated, by a late Declaration of his Excellency Governor BERNARD, that one or more Regiments may soon be expected in this Province.

The Design of these Troops is in every one's Apprehension nothing short of Enforcing by military Power the Execution of Acts of Parliament, in the forming of which the Colonies have not, and cannot have any constitutional Influence. This is one of the greatest Distresses to which a free People can be reduced.

The Town which we have the Honor to serve, have taken these Things at their late Meeting into their most serious Consideration : And as there is in the Minds of many a prevailing Apprehension of an approaching War with *France*, they have passed the several Votes, which we transmit to you ; desiring that they may be immediately laid before the Town, whose Prudentials are in your Care, at a legal Meeting, for their candid and particular Attention.

Deprived of the Councils of a General Assembly in this dark and difficult Season, the loyal People of this Province, will, we are persuaded, immediately perceive the Propriety and Utility of the proposed Committee of Convention : And the sound and wholesome Advice that may be expected from a Number of Gentlemen chosen by themselves, and in whom they may Repose the greatest Confidence, must tend to the real Service of our Gracious Sovereign, and the Welfare of his Subjects in this Province ; and may happily prevent any sudden and unconnected Measures, which in their present Anxiety, and even Agony of Mind, they may be in Danger of falling into.

As it is of Importance that the Convention should meet as soon as may be, so early a Day as the 22d of this Instant *September* has been propos'd for that Purpose—and it is hoped the remotest Towns will by that Time, or as soon after as conveniently may be, return their respective Committees.

Not doubting but that you are equally concerned with us and our Fellow Citizens for the Preservation of our invaluable Rights, and for the general Happiness of our Country, and that you are disposed with equal Ardor to exert yourselves in every constitutional Way for so glorious a Purpose,

We are,

GENTLEMEN,

With the greatest Esteem,

Your obedient humble Servants,

Joseph Jackson
John Ruddock
John Hancock
John Rowe
Saml Pemberton

Select-Men of BOSTON.

N.B. *The other two Selectmen are out of the Province.*

To the Gentlemen Select-Men
of [illegible]

John Hancock signed 1767 "No Taxation Without Representation" --

Courtesy of the Klos Family.

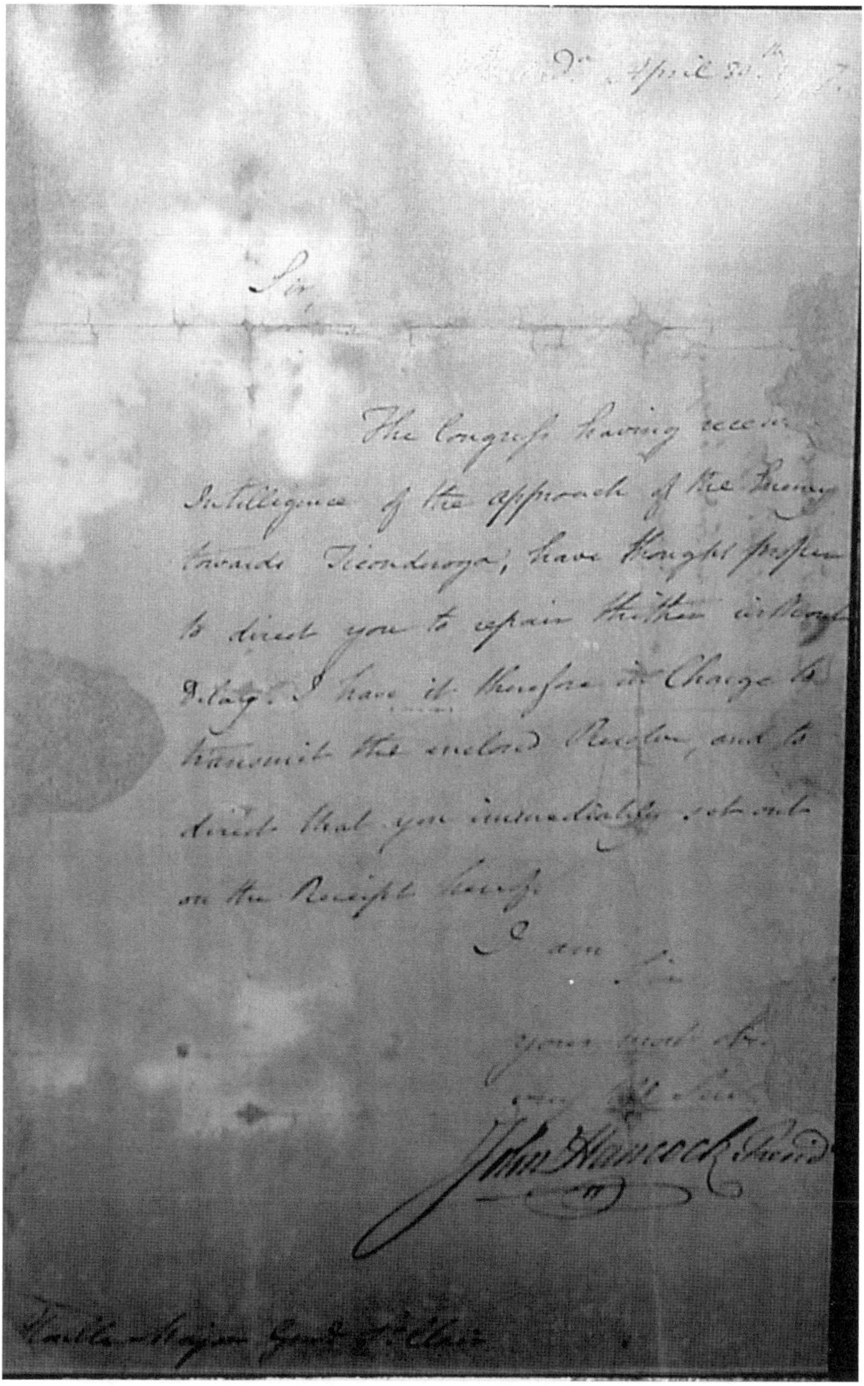
Sir

The Congress having recd Intelligence of the approach of the Enemy towards Ticonderoga; have thought proper to direct you to repair thither without Delay. I have it therefore in Charge to transmit the enclosed Resolve, and to direct that you immediately set out on the Receipt hereof.

I am Sir
your most obedt
humble Servt
John Hancock Presidt

Honble Major Genl St. Clair

John Hancock 1777 letter ordering Major General Arthur St. Clair to defend Fort Ticonderoga -- *Courtesy of the Klos Family.*

CHAPTER FIVE

Portrait of Henry Laurens from
Appleton Cyclopedia of American Biography

HENRY LAURENS

Second President of the Continental Congress
Served November 1, 1777 to December 9, 1778

Henry Laurens was born March 6, 1724 in Charleston, South Carolina and died there on December 8, 1792. His ancestors were Huguenots, who had left France at the revocation of the edict of Nantes. He was educated in Charleston and became a clerk in a counting-house there; he was then transferred to a similar house in London in order to obtain a systematic business education. Upon his return, he engaged in mercantile pursuits and earned a fortune. Laurens, as a businessman, was conspicuous in his opposition of British aggression, and had frequent contests with the crown judges, especially in respect to their decisions in marine law and in the courts of admiralty. The pamphlets that he published in opposition to these measures give evidence to his great legal ability.

Laurens also served in a military campaign against the Cherokees, about which he left a diary in manuscript form. Retiring from business, in 1771 he sailed to England to oversee the education of his sons. During this period he traveled through Great Britain and on the European continent. While in London he was one of the thirty-eight Americans who signed a petition in 1774 to dissuade parliament from passing the Boston Port Bill. He returned to Charleston in 1774 and was elected a member of the first Provincial congress there in 1775. Laurens drew up a form of association to be signed by all the Friends of Liberty and also became President of the Council of Safety.

In 1776, he was made vice president of South Carolina under the new constitution and was elected delegate to the Continental Congress. To John Lewis Gervais on September 5, 1777 he wrote, *"Congress is not the respectable body which I have expected to have found ..."* In another letter the Southern Gentlemen wrote that *"venality, peculation and fraud"* were the order of the day.

Upon the resignation of John Hancock, Laurens moved that Congress solicit Hancock to remain, but he was only seconded and no more. Henry Laurens was elected President of the Continental Congress on November 1, 1777. He was an active participant in debate especially, when he the sole delegate represented by South Carolina. His Presidency drew criticism by his fellow delegates, as he was not hesitant to use his chair to make timely and uncomplimentary remarks about his colleagues. As President Laurens opposed any expeditions against Florida urging Congress instead to defend Georgia and South Carolina from Native Americans and Tory resistance.

In his book the President of the Continental Congress 1774 – 1789 Jennings B. Sanders writes:

> *Laurens is unique among the ... Presidents ... His letters give an insight into the workings of Congress and the Presidential office ... As President, he was intimately acquainted with all Congressional affairs; indeed, many matters were necessarily known only to him until their presentation from the chair. Congressional leadership must not be construed to mean merely the activities of members on the floor of that body. One gains the impression from a perusal of the correspondence of the day, that important matters were discussed informally outside Congress by coteries, fractions, and cliques as they ate their meals together or visited their rooming places. Action in Congress, therefore, might at times be little more than formal recognition of what had already been agreed upon outside. Through this type of leadership a President might exercise great influence, and yet never participate in debate from the chair.*

Henry Laurens wrote to Louis Fleury on April 28, 1778 *"...these I say are private Sentiments drawn from friends among my Coadjutors in Congress."* On April 7, 1778 to James Duane Laurens writes *"... The Letter has not yet been presented to Congress, but has undergone severe strictures from knot of our friends who call here late at night and conned it over."* The fact that the President, for the most part, received all official correspondence and choose when and if it should be brought before Congress wielded his office the power to accelerate or impede the consideration of all official business.

Henry Laurens tenure as President was during one of most stormy periods in the Revolutionary War. He seemed to align himself against John Jay, Robert Morris and Silas Deane (conservatives) but kept his distance from the republicans. It the power struggle between George Washington and Horatio Gates known as the Conway Cabal, Henry Laurens walked the middle ground. Laurens was anxious to play the role of "peacemaker" between Gates and Washington but sided with the later when the support counted. The summary of the Journals of the Continental Congress during Lauren's Presidency is as follows:

> **1777 - November 1** Elects Henry Laurens president of Congress. **November 4** Commends General Gates and his army for their defense against Burgoyne's invasion as well as recognizing various other officers and units for their defense of the Delaware. **November 7** Names new appointees to reorganized Board of War. **November 10-14** Conducts final debates on Articles of Confederation. **November 15** Adopts the Articles of Confederation. **November 17** Transmits Articles of Confederation to states for their consideration. **November 19** Directs General Washington to inquire into the treatment of American prisoners. **November 20** Adopts report on pacification of the western frontier. **November 21** Recalls Commissioner Silas Deane from the court of France. **November 22** Adopts economic program asking the states to levy taxes, call in paper money and regulate prices. **November 24** Adopts measures for improving the provisioning of the army. **November 27** Recommends confiscation of loyalist property in the states; completes reconstitution of the Board of War, Horatio Gates named president. **November 28** Appoints committee to confer with General Washington; orders inquiry into the failures of the Rhode Island expedition and the Delaware River defenses; appoints John Adams Commissioner to France. **November 29** Appoints committee to obtain a French translation of the Articles of Confederation and to invite Canada "*to accede to the union of these states.*"
>
> **December 1** Rejects alteration of the Saratoga Convention to permit embarkation of Burgoyne's army from Rhode Island. **December 3** Resolves to seek $2 million loan from France and Spain; directs suppression of Delaware loyalists; adopts instructions for retaining continued neutrality of the Six Nations; endorses proposal for a surprise attack against Lake Champlain. **December 8** Orders Silas Deane's immediate return to Congress. **December 10** Denounces General William Howe's treatment of American prisoners; authorizes General Washington to impress supplies in Pennsylvania. **December 13** Appoints General Thomas Conway to newly constituted post of Inspector General of the Army. **December 16** Receives report of the committee at head quarters. **December 19** Questions General Washington's plans for a winter cantonment. **December 26** Debates implementation of the Saratoga Convention. **December 30** Grants navy boards increased authority over naval officers; extends General Washington's powers to impress supplies, discipline officers, and punish spies.

1778 -- January 2 Dismisses Esek Hopkins from the Continental Navy. **January 8** Detains Convention Army in America until properly notified of Britain's "*explicit ratification of the convention of Saratoga.*" **January 11** Appoints committee to repair to headquarters to concert with General Washington on the reform of the army. **January 12** Examines John Folger on the theft of dispatches from the commissioners in France. **January 14** Accepts Baron Steuben's tender of services as a volunteer in the Continental Army. **January 15** Orders creation of additional magazines for supply of the army in Pennsylvania. **January 16** Instructs Committee at Camp to evaluate an attack on Philadelphia. **January 17** Resolves to issue an additional $10 million in loan office certificates. **January 20** Appoints Charles Carroll and Gouverneur Morris to the Committee at Camp to replace members named from the Board of War. **January 21** Adopts measures to secure improved British treatment of American prisoners of war. **January 23** Names General Lafayette to command an invasion of Canada. **January 27** Appoints committee to confer on the reform of the hospital department. **January 30-31** Studies proposals for reform of the quartermaster department and for retaining the neutrality of the Native Americans in the northern department.

February 2 Appoints officers for Canadian expedition. **February 3** Prescribes oath required of all officers of the United States Military. **February 4** Directs Commissioner to the court of Tuscany to seek $1 million loan; receives Committee at Camp recommendation that Jeremiah Wadsworth be appointed Commissary General of Purchases. **February 6** Reforms medical department; appoints middle department physician general. **February 11** Adopts regulations for Commissary General of military stores. **February 13** Requests North Carolina beef and pork embargo. **February 16** Resolves to emit additional $2 million in bills of credit. **February 17** Suspends Board of War's special purchasing agents. **February 19** Relocates Convention Army for security purposes. **February 23** Appoints committee to reexamine feasibility of Canadian expedition. **February 26** Adopts resolves for arranging a prisoner exchange; adopts new Continental Army quotas and recruiting regulations. **February 27** Prescribes death penalty for persons convicted of aiding the enemy.

March 2 Appoints Nathanael Greene Quartermaster General and adopts new quartermaster regulations; urges cavalry recruitment; suspends Canadian expedition. **March 3** Authorizes General Burgoyne's return to England. **March 4** Authorizes Washington to employ Native Americans with the army. **March 5** Resolves to emit additional $2 million in bills of credit. **March 7** Designates **April 22** a day of fasting and prayer. **March 12** Urges states to keep three delegates in constant attendance. **March 13** Adopts new commissary regulations; reassigns Generals Lafayette and de Kalb. **March 16** Orders return of Pennsylvania pacifists exiled to Virginia; orders study of state compliance with recommendations of Congress. **March 18** Increases Washington's authority to negotiate prisoner exchanges. **March 21** Adopts measures for defense of the northern department. **March 24** Resolves to resume once daily sessions. **March 26** Orders arrest of Delaware loyalists to thwart invasion threat. **March 28** Appoints Casimir Pulaski to command independent cavalry corps. **March 30** Adopts revised prisoner exchange instructions.

April 4 Resolves to emit additional $1 million in bills of credit; empowers Washington to call New Jersey, Pennsylvania and Maryland Militia. **April 7** Adopts contract terms for Commerce Committee to execute with Roderique Hortalez & Co. **April 9** Sets pay and allowances for commissary officers and appoints Jeremiah Wadsworth commissary general of purchases. **April 10** Holds acrimonious debate on letter criticizing Washington, sparking walkout of Thomas Burke and Edward Langworthy. **April 11** Orders Thomas Burke to answer charges of disrupting proceedings of Congress; resolves to emit additional $5 million in bills of credit. **April 14** Adopts regulations for commissary general of purchases. April 15 Responds to Delaware protest that General Smallwood's seizure of loyalists infringed on the internal police of the state; directs General Gates to take command of the northern department. **April 16** Rejects motion to refer issue of Continental officers' pensions to the states. **April 18** Orders inquiry into the loss of the Virginia. **April 22** Orders publication of statement on North Ministry's peace proposals. **April 23** Urges states to pardon and forgive penitent loyalists; requests Maryland to send troops to suppress Delaware uprising. **April 25** Resolves that Thomas Burke's withdrawal from Congress was "*disorderly and contemptuous.*" **April 26** Holds Sunday debate on half-pay proposal for Continental officers. **April 28** Accepts General Conway's resignation. **April 29** Adopts plan to encourage desertion of British mercenaries seeking land and citizenship in the United States.

May 3 Holds Sunday session to consider treaties of commerce and alliance negotiated with France. **May 4** Ratifies the treaties with France. **May 5** Instructs commissioners to secure revocation of two treaty of commerce articles. **May 8** Adopts an Address to the Inhabitants of the United States. **May 9** Issues proclamation denouncing seizures of neutral shipping by American armed vessels. **May 11** Instructs Massachusetts on safeguarding the rights of the owners of an illegally seized Portuguese vessel. **May 13** Rejects motion to refer proposed officer pension plan to the states. **May 15** Adopts plan to provide half pay for officers for seven years after the conclusion of the war. **May 18** Receives "*plan for regulating the army*" from the Committee at Camp. **May 19** Orders emission of $6.3 million in bills of credit to pay interest on loan office certificates. **May 21** Authorizes Massachusetts to assist Nova Scotia revolutionaries at Continental expense; adopts principles for governing prisoner exchanges. **May 22** Resolves to emit additional $5 million in bills of credit.

May 26 Adopts revised "*rules*" of Congress. **May 27** Adopts new "*Establishment of the American Army.*" **May 28** Revises commissions of the American commissioners to Vienna, Berlin, and Tuscany. May 30 Resumes twice daily sessions "*for the space of one month.*"

June 1 Debates instructions for the American commissioners in Europe. **June 4** Recommends suspension of state price regulations; directs Washington to "*proceed in arranging*" the army. June 6 Rejects peace proposals submitted by Lord Howe and Sir Henry Clinton. **June 8** Embargoes provisions *(effective June 10-November 15, 1778)*. **June 11** Receives notice of the arrival of the Carlisle Peace Commission at Philadelphia; orders expedition against Fort Detroit; orders quartermaster department inquiry. **June 13** Receives letter from the Carlisle Peace Commission. **June 17** Adopts reply to the Carlisle Peace Commission orders; halt to personal "*correspondence with the enemy.*" **June 20** Receives notice of the British evacuation of Philadelphia; resolves to emit additional $5 million in Continental currency. **June 22-25** Debates proposed state amendments to the Articles of Confederation. **June 25** Orders reinforcements for Rhode Island. **June 26** Orders Articles of Confederation to be engrossed for signing. **June 27** Adjourns from York, "*to Thursday next, to meet at the State House in Philadelphia.*"

July 2-6 Convenes in Philadelphia, but adjourns "*from day to day*" for lack of a quorum. **July 7** Achieves quorum; thanks Washington for "*gaining the important victory of Monmouth.*" **July 9** Corrects engrossed Articles of Confederation and begins the signing; directs committee of arrangement to repair to headquarters. **July 11** Receives news of the arrival in Delaware Bay of the French fleet carrying Conrad Alexandre Gerard and Silas Deane; directs Washington to prepare for a joint Franco-American offensive. **July 14** Appoints committee to arrange public reception for the French minister Gerard. **July 18** Rejects renewed overtures from the Carlisle Peace Commission. **July 20** Endorses Ebenezer Hazard's plan to collect "*various state papers relative to the origin and progress of the several European settlements in North America.*" **July 23** Orders inventory of goods left in Philadelphia at the time of the British evacuation; receives Jean Holker's commissions as French marine agent and consul in Philadelphia. **July 25** Defers attack on Fort Detroit; adopts measures for Pennsylvania and New York frontier defense. **July 30** Emits additional $5 million in Continental currency. July 31 Appoints committee to "*superintend an entertainment*" for the French minister

August 1 Consigns tobacco for payment of Beaumarchais' contract claims. **August 3** Investigates commissaries Benjamin Flower and Cornelius Sweers for fraud. **August 6** Holds formal audience with French Minister Gerard. **August 7** Debates proposal to discipline Board of War members for disregarding an order of Congress. **August 10** Postpones proposal to exchange former

New Jersey governor William Franklin for Delaware president John McKinly. **August 11** Adopts declaration denouncing Peace Commissioner George Johnstone for attempted bribery of American leaders. **August 13** Curtails issuance of passes for travel to British occupied New York; orders Silas Deane to attend Congress. **August 15** Orders Silas Deane to prepare an oral report on his mission to France; adopts resolution for maintaining the secrecy of correspondence of the committee for foreign affairs. **August 17** Hears Silas Deane's testimony; receives resignation of Major General Thomas Mifflin. **August 20** Refers report on the inspector general's department to Washington; rejects motion to exchange William Franklin for John McKinly. **August 21** Orders printing of the proceedings of General Charles Lee's court-martial; hears Silas Deane conclude "the general account" of his mission to France. **August 24** Orders the release of commissary Benjamin Flowers and the prosecution of deputy commissary Cornelius Sweers. **August 28** Receives news of failure of the Franco-American attack on Newport. **August 31** Adopts measures to improve recruitment of the Continental Army.

September 1 Refers passport application of British Secret Agent John Temple to the state of Pennsylvania. **September 2** Recommends granting exemptions to the provisions embargo. **September 3** Resolves to permit recruitment of German mercenary deserters; postpones expedition planned against Seneca Native Americans. **September 5** Ignores appeal of secret British agent Dr. John Berkenhout for release from Pennsylvania jail; prints additional $5 million in continental currency. **September 9** Votes thanks to General John Sullivan for the conduct of his forces at Rhode Island; ordered Rhode Island expedition inquiry **September 11** Authorizes dispersal of Gen. John Burgoyne's Convention Army for its more convenient subsistence; urges Maryland to curb evasions of the embargo. **September 14** Appoints Benjamin Franklin Minister Plenipotentiary to France; approves exchange of William Franklin for John McKinly. **September 19** Reads Committee of Finance report; orders finance report printed. **September 22** Orders examination of William Carmichael on the activities of Silas Deane in France. **September 25** Appeals to Virginia and North Carolina to aid South Carolina and Georgia; appoints Benjamin Lincoln to command the southern department. **September 26** Reorganizes the offices of the treasury; emits an additional $10 million in Continental currency. **September 28** Conducts examination of William Carmichael. **September 30** Conducts examination of William Carmichael; reassigns Casimir Pulaski's legion.

October 2 Extends embargo to January 31, 1779; requests states to seize provisions to prevent engrossing and speculation. **October 3** Informs Casimir Pulaski *"that it is the duty of every military officer in the service of these states, to yield obedience"* to the laws of the states. **October 5** Conducts examination of William Carmichael on the activities of Silas Deane in France.

October 6 Invites Dr. Richard Price to become a citizen and move to the United States to assist "*in regulating their finances.*" **October 8** Lifts limitations on the price of silver and gold. **October 12** Adopts resolves to suppress "*theatrical entertainments, horse racing, gaming, and such other diversions as are productive of idleness, [and] dissipation.*" **October 13** Orders Washington to take measures for frontier defense. **October 14** Receives documents from Silas Deane and schedules continuation of inquiry into charges made against him. **October 15** Receives intelligence of the distribution of a "*Manifesto and Proclamation*" from the British peace commissioners. **October 16** Orders seizure of persons attempting to distribute "*manifestoes*" of the British commissioners; orders removal of the Convention Army to Charlottesville, Va. **October 17** Commends Comte d'Estaing for his attempts to assist the forces of the United States. **October 21** Orders arrest of British commissary of prisoners in Philadelphia; declares opposition to "*partial and parole exchanges*" of prisoners of war in favor of "*a general exchange*"; commends the Marquis de Lafayette and declares thanks to the king of France. **October 22** Assigns Horatio Gates to command of the eastern department; adopts instructions for the American minister to France and a "*Plan of an Attack upon Quebec.*" **October 26** Appoints a committee to prepare a publication on "*matters relating to*" negotiations with the British peace commissioners. **October 27** Responds to the Governor of Havana for his introduction of Juan de Miralles, unofficial Spanish agent to the United States. **October 29** Reorganizes the Board of War. **October 30** Adopts a "*Manifesto*" vowing to take "*exemplary vengeance*" against future acts of enemy barbarity. **October 31** Rejects proposal from the Spanish Governor of New Orleans for an attack on West Florida.

November 2 Authorizes an attack on East Florida. **November 3** Appoints a comptroller, auditor, treasurer and commissioners of accounts for the reorganized treasury office. **November 4** Orders printing of the Franco-American treaties; resolves to emit additional $10,000,000 in Continental currency. **November 7** Orders December 30 set apart as "a day of general thanksgiving"; reaches compromise in dispute over provisioning prisoners of war. **November 10** Augments plans for an expedition against East Florida. **November 11** Exempts embargoed flour purchased in Virginia for the French navy. **November 12** Denies John Connolly's plea to be treated as a prisoner of war because of parole violations. **November 14** Adopts incentives for naval enlistments. **November 17** Orders closer confinement of John Connolly; adopts Thanksgiving Day resolve. **November 19** Authorizes Washington to appoint commissioners to negotiate a prisoner exchange; receives Thomas McKean's charges against General William Thompson. **November 20** Hears General Thompson's denial of Thomas McKean's charges. **November 23** Examines witnesses in McKean-Thompson dispute. **November 24** Adopts rules for settling rank and seniority disputes in the Continental Army;

authorizes Board of War *"to finish the arrangements of the army agreeably to the resolutions of Congress."* **November 26** Receives New Jersey's ratification of Articles of Confederation. **November 27** Rejects petition for exempting grain for Bermuda from the embargo. **November 28** Responds to Admiral James Gambier's threat to retaliate against American prisoners of war.

December 3 Confirms General Philip Schuyler's court-martial acquittal; receives letters recommending British Secret Agent John Temple. **December 5** Endorses Washington's recommendations for suspending preparations for a Canadian invasion; confirms General Charles Lee's court-martial conviction. **December 7** Orders Silas Deane to report in writing on *"his agency . . . in Europe"*; hears testimony in McKean-Thompson dispute. **December 9** Receives Henry Laurens' resignation as president of Congress.

Laurens' resignation from the Presidency was quite dramatic, with Laurens hoping that his lengthy "farewell address" would inspire his fellow delegates to rise and demand he remain in office. Instead Congress elected John Jay, who Henry Laurens considered a political rival. It was a defeat that was sufficiently painful as evidence by a July 17, 1779 letter to John Laurens: *"... tell my friends they will find, that my resignation on the 9th of December was, as I then said to them, the greatest act of my life."*

In 1779 he was appointed minister to Holland to negotiate a treaty that had been unofficially proposed to William Lee by Van Berekel, Pensioner of Amsterdam. He sailed on the packet *"Mercury,"* which was captured by the British frigate *"Vestal,"* of twenty-eight guns, off Newfoundland. Mr. Laurens threw his papers overboard; but they were recovered, and gave evidence of his mission. The refusal of Holland to punish Van Berckel, at the dictation of Lord North's ministry, was instantly followed by war between Great Britain and Holland. Mr. Laurens was taken to London, examined before the privy-council, and imprisoned in the Tower of London, on October 6th, 1780, on *"suspicion of high treason"* for nearly fifteen months, during which his health was greatly impaired. He was ill when he entered, but no medical attendance was provided, and it was more than a year before he was granted pen and ink to draw a bill of exchange to provide for himself. But he obtained a pencil, and frequently communication was carried by a trusty person to the outside world; he even corresponded with American newspapers.

When his son John appeared in Paris in 1781 to negotiate a loan with France, Mr. Laurens was informed that his confinement would be the more rigorous because the young man had openly declared himself an enemy to the king and his country. It was suggested that if Mr. Laurens would advise his son to withdraw from his commission, such action would be received with favor at the British court; he replied that his son was a man who would never sacrifice honor, even to save his father's life. Laurens received attention from many friends, among whom, was Edmund Burke. Twice he refused offers of pardon if he would serve the British ministry. While a prisoner he learned of his son John's death in a skirmish in South Carolina, and on 1 December, 1781, he addressed a petition to the House of Commons, in which he said that he had striven to prevent a rupture between the crown and colonies, and asked for more liberty.

He was soon afterward exchanged for Lord Cornwallis and commissioned by Congress one of the ministers to negotiate peace. He then went to Paris, where, with John Jay and Benjamin Franklin, he signed the preliminaries of the Treaty of Paris, November 30th. 1782, and was instrumental in the insertion of a clause prohibiting the British evacuation, the "*carrying away any negroes or other property of the inhabitants.*"

On his return to Charleston he was welcomed with enthusiasm and offered many offices, which his impaired health forced him to decline. He retired to his plantation near Charleston and devoted his life to agriculture. His will concluded with this request:

> "*I solemnly enjoin it on my son, as an indispensable duty, that, as soon as he conveniently can, after my decease, he cause my body to be wrapped in twelve yards of tow-cloth and burned until it be entirely consumed, and then, collecting my bones, deposit them wherever he may think proper.*"

This was the first cremation in this country.

Some of Laurens's political papers have been published in the collections of the South Carolina historical society, and his rebus letter to Lord George Gordon is reprinted in the "*Magazine of American History*" (December, 1884).

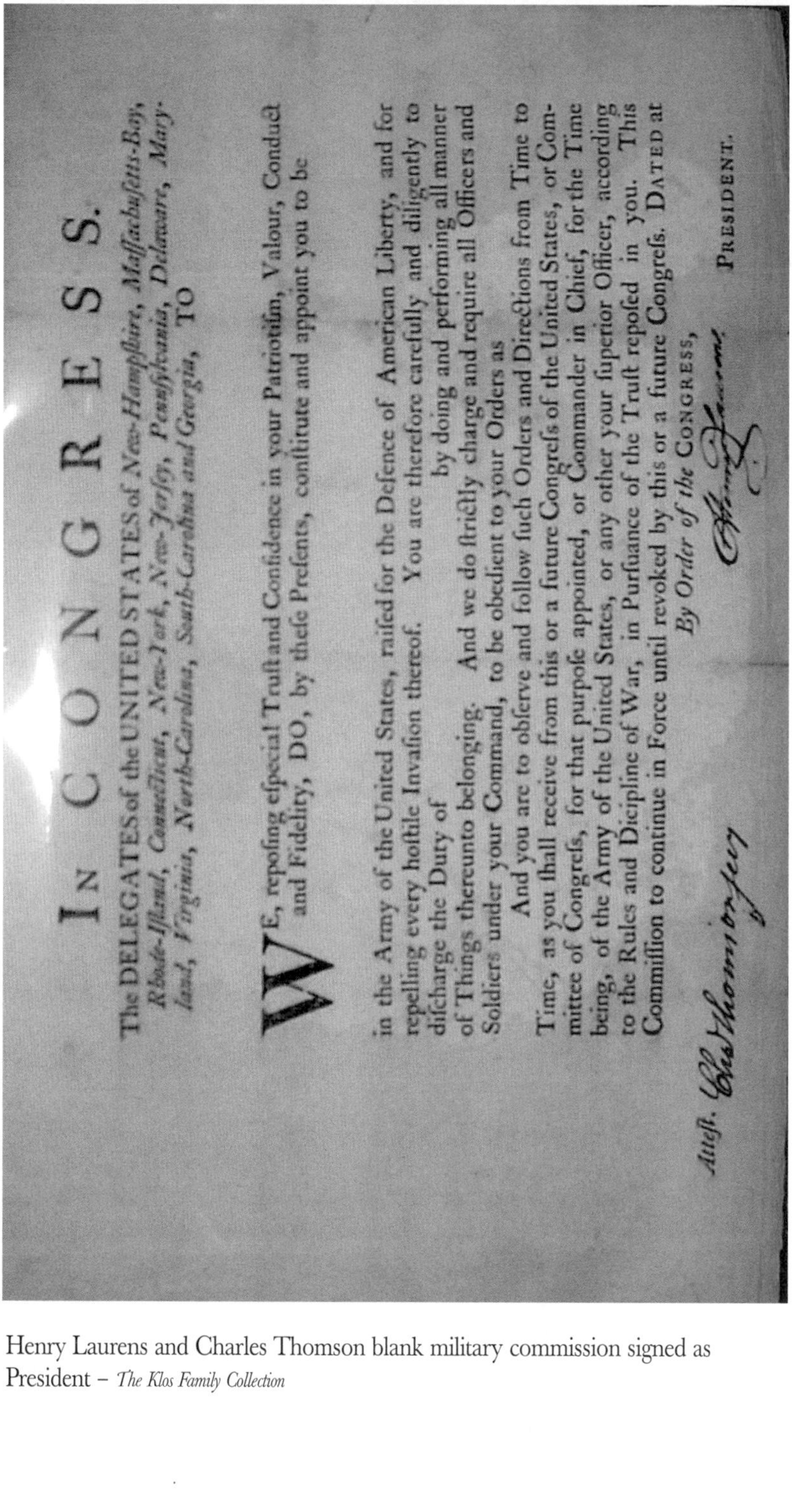

IN CONGRESS.

The DELEGATES of the UNITED STATES of *New-Hampshire*, *Massachusetts-Bay*, *Rhode-Island*, *Connecticut*, *New-York*, *New-Jersey*, *Pennsylvania*, *Delaware*, *Maryland*, *Virginia*, *North-Carolina*, *South-Carolina and Georgia*, TO

WE, reposing especial Trust and Confidence in your Patriotism, Valour, Conduct and Fidelity, DO, by these Presents, constitute and appoint you to be

in the Army of the United States, raised for the Defence of American Liberty, and for repelling every hostile Invasion thereof. You are therefore carefully and diligently to discharge the Duty of by doing and performing all manner of Things thereunto belonging. And we do strictly charge and require all Officers and Soldiers under your Command, to be obedient to your Orders as

And you are to observe and follow such Orders and Directions from Time to Time, as you shall receive from this or a future Congress of the United States, or Committee of Congress, for that purpose appointed, or Commander in Chief, for the Time being, of the Army of the United States, or any other your superior Officer, according to the Rules and Discipline of War, in Pursuance of the Trust reposed in you. This Commission to continue in Force until revoked by this or a future Congress. DATED at

By Order of the CONGRESS,

PRESIDENT.

Attest.

Henry Laurens and Charles Thomson blank military commission signed as President – *The Klos Family Collection*

CHAPTER SIX

Portrait of John Jay from
Appleton Cyclopedia of American Biography

JOHN JAY

5th President of the Continental Congress
December 10, 1778 to September 28, 1779

John Jay was born in New York City on December 12th, 1745 and died in Bedford, Westchester County, New York, on May 17th, 1829. He was of Huguenot descent, and was educated in part by Pastor Stoope, of the French church at New Rochelle. He attended Kings College (now Columbia University) in Manhattan, graduating in 1766.

Jay studied law with Benjamin Kissam, having Lindley Murray as his fellow student and was admitted to the bar in 1766. When news of the passage of the Boston port bill reached New York on May 16th, 1776, Jay was appointed a member of a Committee of Correspondence with the other colonies. Their reply to the Boston Committee, attributed to Jay, recommended, as of the utmost moment, "a congress of deputies from the colonies in general."

Jay was a delegate to the First Continental Congress, which met in Philadelphia on September 5, 1774. As one of a committee of three, he prepared the "*Address to the People of Great Britain,*" which Thomas Jefferson, while ignorant of the authorship, declared to be "*a production certainly of the finest pen in America.*" Jay was an active member of the committee of observation in New York, on whose recommendation the counties elected a provincial congress. He was also active on a committee of association of 100 members, invested by the city of New York with general undefined powers. He was a member of the second congress, which met in Philadelphia, 10 May 1775, and drafted the "*Address to the People of Canada and of Ireland*". During that period he carried against a strong opposition a petition to the king, which was signed by the members on July 8th. The rejection of this petition, leaving no alternative but submission or resistance opened the way for a general acquiescence in the Declaration of Independence.

Jay was a member of the secret committee appointed by Congress, 29 November 1775, after a confidential interview with a French officer, "*to correspond with the friends of America in Great Britain, Ireland, and other parts of the world.*" While he was attending congress at Philadelphia, Jay's presence was requested by the New York convention, which required his counsel. This convention met at White Plains, 9 July 1776, and on Jay's motion unanimously approved the Declaration of Independence, which on that day was received from Congress. The passage of a part of Lord Howe's fleet up the Hudson induced the appointment by the convention of a secret committee vested with extraordinary powers, of which Jay was made chairman. Another committee was formed to defeat conspiracies in the state against the liberties of America. The resolutions guiding this committee were drawn by Jay and its minutes, many of which are in his hand, show the energy with which it exercised its powers through arrests, imprisonments, and banishments, and the vigorous system demanded by the critical condition of the American cause. The successes of the British in New York; the retreat and needs of Washington's army, had induced a feeling of despondency, and Jay was the author of an earnest appeal to his countrymen, which by order of Congress was translated into German and widely circulated.

Jay drafted the state constitution adopted by the convention of New York, which met successively at Harlem, Kingsbridge, Philip's Manor, White Plains, Poughkeepsie and Kingston. He was appointed chief justice of the state, holding his first term at Kingston on 9 September 1777, and acting also on the council of safety, which directed the military occupation of the state and wielded an absolute sovereignty. He was visited at Fishkill, in the autumn of 1778, by General Washington for a confidential conversation on the invasion of Canada by the French and American forces, which they concurred in their disapproval, chiefly on the probability that if conquered it would be retained by France.

Jay was again sent to Congress on a special occasion, the withdrawal of Vermont from the jurisdiction of New York. New York was determined to hold the Presidency, and their choice was General Schuyler who was not present at the time. According to Sparks, editor *Writings of Washington: "On the account of his abscense, Mr. Jay was prevailed upon to take the chair, with a resolution on his part to resign in favor of General Schuyler as soon as he attends"* Only three days after taking his seat he was, elected president of the Continental Congress December 1, 1778 with eight states voting for him and four for Henry Laurens. John Jay was actually serving in a dual role of Chief Justice of New York and President of the Continental Congress. He did not resign the Chief Justice position until shortly before resigning the Presidency, in order to accept the position of Foreign Secretary to the United States.

During the Presidency John Jay aligned himself with the contingent that was against the Adams and Lees. According to Sanders, *"He wrote to Washington that the Marine and Commercial Committees did not and could not amount to much because they were mere tools of the 'Family Compact' who desired to keep them useless and impotent for their own purposes. And of course he was no friend of Gates and the Cabal Crowd."* Jay was is described by most Congressional Scholars as an elitist believing that the wealthy, socially connected and men of intellect should govern the country.

The Journals of the Continental Congress of Jay's Presidency are summarized as follows:

> **1778 - December 10** Elects John Jay president of Congress; endorses Gerard's proposal for encouraging privateering. **December 14** Resolves to emit additional $10,000,000 in Continental currency. **December 16** Resolves to contract the supply of Continental currency, to accept presidential expenses as a public charge and to ask the states to raise $15,000,000 in taxes; confirms General Arthur St. Clair's court martial acquittal. **December 18** Directs Washington to attend Congress in keeping with his suggestion for "*a personal conference.*" **December 22** Hears Silas Deane "*read his written information*" concerning his agency in Europe. **December 23** Continues Silas Deane hearing; continues hearing into McKean-Thompson dispute. **December 24** Receives General Washington; continues hearing into McKean-Thompson dispute; accepts General Thompson's "*apology.* " **December 25** Observes Christmas. **December 26** Adopts loan office regulations for exchanging Continental bills. **December 29** Adopts Gerard's proposal for protecting American grown masts; appoints three additional Continental Brigadiers. **December 31** Continues Silas Deane hearing; adopts additional fiscal resolves. January 1
>
> **1779 – January 1** Defers planned Franco-American attack on Canada. **January 2** Adopts additional fiscal resolves to curb depreciation. **January 5** Receives Gerard's protest against Thomas Paine's published letters concealing supplies from France. **January 6** Conducts inquiry into Gerard's charges against Thomas Paine. **January 7** Adopts Gerard's charges against Thomas Paine; dismisses Paine from his position as Secretary to the Committee for Foreign Affairs. **January 8** Receives Henry Laurens' admission that he had informed Thomas Paine of Congress' confidential proceedings against him. **January 9** Orders Henry Laurens to submit written statement of his "*suspicion*

of fraudulent proceedings" by Robert Morris. **January 11** Receives Henry Laurens' charges against Robert Morris. **January 12** Disavows charges published by Thomas Paine concerning supplies received from France. **January 14** Resolves to reassure France that the United States "*will not conclude either truce or peace . . . with out [her] formal consent.*" **January 15** Receives Francis Lewis' statement on Henry Laurens' charges against Robert Morris. January 19 Hears Henry Laurens' explanation concerning his charges against Robert Morris. **January 20** Appoints committee to conduct foreign affairs inquiry. **January 21** Appoints committee to "*examine into principles of the powers of the . . . Committee on Appeals*" and the refusal of Pennsylvania to honor the committee's decree in the case of the Active. **January 22** Resolves to request Virginia, North Carolina and the Comte d'Estaing to provide assistance for Georgia and South Carolina. **January 23** Adopts resolves to improve recruitment of Continental troops and to augment the authority of the commander in chief. **January 26** Appoints committee to investigate Pennsylvania's charges against General Benedict Arnold, Continental Commander of Philadelphia. **January 28** Debates Gerard's contention that Congress should compensate France for aid rendered by d'Estaing to the southern states, in accordance with article four of the Treaty of Alliance. **January 30** Approves General Washington's request for leave to return to camp.

February 1 Debates Pennsylvania complaint against Matthew Clarkson. **February 2** Orders reinforcements for South Carolina and Georgia. **February 3** Confers with Gerard on supplying French fleet; resolves to emit additional $5 million in Continental currency; resolves to borrow $20 million in loan office certificates. **February 5** Resolves to request French aid for South Carolina defense. **February 8** Recommends embargo exemptions for relief of Rhode Island and Massachusetts; withdraws request for French aid for South Carolina; discourages French request for provisions for Martinique. **February 9** Recommends relief for owners of Portuguese vessel illegally seized by American privateer; augments treasury staff to speed settlement of army accounts. **February 11** Exonerates Robert Morris of accusations made by Henry Laurens. **February 15** Meets with Gerard on Spanish offer to mediate peace and need to formulate American negotiating demands. **February 16** Orders inquiry into Pennsylvania's charges against Benedict Arnold. **February 18** Reorganizes Inspector General's Department and Ordnance Department. **February 19** Resolves to emit additional $5 million in Continental currency. **February 22** Receives William Lee's proposal for a commercial treaty with the United Provinces; Delaware ratifies Articles of Confederation. **February 23** Debates negotiating instructions should Spain arrange peace talks with Great Britain. **February 25** Accepts resignation of Major General Thomas Mifflin; augments defense of the northern frontiers. **February 26** Authorizes embargo exemptions for the relief of Rhode Island and Massachusetts.

March 1 Debates peace terms (boundaries). **March 4** Debates peace terms (boundaries). **March 5** Authorizes Washington to negotiate a cartel for a general exchange of prisoners. **March 6** Adopts Declaration on Continental Authority over Admiralty Appeals. **March 9** Urges states to accelerate recruitment and revises bounty provisions. **March 10** Debates peace terms (boundaries). **March 11** Debates peace terms (status of Nova Scotia); creates corps of engineers. **March 15** Debates peace terms (boundaries). **March 16** Debates peace terms (boundaries); authorizes reorganization of the corps of waggoners. **March 17** Debates peace terms (boundaries). **March 19** Adopts peace terms concerning boundaries. **March 20** Adopts Fast Day proclamation. **March 22** Debates peace terms (fisheries). **March 23** Reorganizes clothing department. **March 24** Reprimands Matthew Clarkson for affronts to the civil authorities of Pennsylvania; debates peace terms (fisheries and navigation of the Mississippi). **March 27** Resolves to report the yeas and nays in the published journals. **March 29** Adopts measures for the defense of South Carolina and Georgia. **March 30** Debates peace terms (fisheries). **March 31** Resolves to publish the journals of Congress weekly.

April 1 Endorses New York's plan for reprisals against the Seneca Indians; resolves to emit additional $5 million in Continental currency. **April 2** Adjourns for Good Friday. **April 3** Adopts resolutions for restoring harmony with Pennsylvania officials incensed over Congressional response to their prosecution of Benedict Arnold. **April 6** Opens debate on the recall of American commissioners abroad. **April 7** Adopts plan to encourage rebellion in Nova Scotia; debates recall of American commissioners abroad. **April 8** Authorizes prisoner exchange in the southern department. **April 9** Debates recall of American commissioners abroad. **April 13** Endorses plan for creation of a corps of French volunteers in South Carolina. **April 14** Reaffirms authority of state officials to issue safe conduct passes. **April 15** Debates recall of American commissioners abroad. **April 19** Accepts resignation of Major General Philip Schuyler; authorizes additional brigade for Rhode Island defense. **April 20** Debates recall of American commissioners abroad. **April 21** Debates recall of American commissioners abroad. **April 22** Rejects motion to recall Benjamin Franklin. **April 26** Debates recall of American commissioners abroad. **April 27** Appropriates 2,000 guineas in specie for Washington's secret service. **April 30** Debates recall of Arthur Lee.

May 1 Debates recall of Arthur Lee. **May 3** Rejects motion to recall Arthur Lee (tie vote). **May 4** Appoints committee to meet with Delaware Native American delegation. **May 5** Resolves to emit additional $10 million in Continental currency. **May 6** Observes day of fast. **May 7** Denies Bermuda petition for provisions embargo exemption; orders Virginia and North Carolina reinforcements to South Carolina. **May 8** Debates peace terms (fisheries). **May 10** Authorizes Washington to concert combined Franco-American operations. **May 11** Appoints General Duportail commandant of the corps of engineers. **May 12** Debates peace terms (fisheries). **May 13** Debates peace terms (fisheries). **May 14** Meriwether Smith charges Henry Laurens with injuring the honor of Congress. **May 15** Henry Laurens denounces attack by Meriwether Smith. **May 17** Directs Native American affairs commissioners (northern department) to consult with Washington on all Native American treaty negotiations. **May 18** Authorizes embargo exemption for provisions for Bermuda. **May 19** Increases states' 1779 quotas an additional $45 million. **May 20** Receives Virginia proposal for ratifying Articles of Confederation by less than unanimous consent; debates recall of Ralph Izard. **May 21** Receives Maryland delegate instructions on Articles of Confederation; receives Connecticut delegate instructions on ratifying confederation without the state of Maryland. **May 24** Debates Deane-Lee controversy; authorizes retaliation for cruelties committed by British forces against French subjects in Virginia. **May 25-26** Confers (by committee) with Delaware Native American delegation. **May 26** Allows Pennsylvania President Reed to address Congress on American fiscal crisis; adopts address to the inhabitants of America on meeting finance and manpower quotas. **May 27** Debates peace terms (fisheries). **May 29** Debates New York proposals for settlement of Vermont issue.

June 1 Resolves to send a committee to Vermont. **June 3** Debates peace terms (fisheries). June 4 Resolves to emit additional $10 million. **June 5** Adopts plan to fund Beaumarchais' claims. **June 7** Adopts vote of confidence in quartermaster and commissary generals (refuses to accept Commissary Jeremiah Wadsworth's resignation); appoints committee to consider powers of foreign consuls. **June 8** Recalls Ralph Izard and William Lee, American commissioners abroad. **June 10** Debates Arthur Lee's recall. **June 11** Resolves to borrow $20 million domestically at 6 percent interest. **June 12** Exonerates Dr. John Morgan. **June 14** Debates price regulation proposals. **June 15** Directs Washington to investigate charges against Dr. William Shippen, Jr.; prepares request for supplies from king of France. **June 16** Denounces seizure of New York officials by inhabitants of the New Hampshire Grants. **June 17** Debates peace terms; reaffirms French alliance provisions prohibiting negotiation of separate peace. **June 19** Debates peace terms (fisheries). **June 21** Reverses plan to enlist German deserters; de bates financial reform. **June 23** Debates financial reform. **June 24** Debates peace terms (fisheries). **June 25** Debates financial reform. **June 28** Rejects quartermaster appeal for relief from state taxes.

July 1 Debates peace terms (fisheries). **July 2** Sets procedures for exchanging withdrawn emissions of Continental currency. **July 6** Approves export of provisions for French fleet; debates peace terms (fisheries). **July 7** Debates financial reform. **July 9** Orders investigation of commissary and quartermaster purchasing practices. **July 12** Confers with French Minister Gerard; receives report from two members of Vermont Committee. **July 13** Receives report from other two members of Vermont Committee. **July 14** Debates substance of conference with French minister. **July 15** Orders retaliation for British mistreatment of naval prisoners. **July 16** Receives Arthur Lee's response to charges by Silas Deane. **July 17** Resolves to emit additional $15 million; threatens retaliation for British mistreatment of Captain Gustavus Conyngham; debates peace terms (fisheries). **July 19** Directs Marine Committee to prepare plan of retaliation for recent raids on Connecticut. **July 21** Recommends compensation for Portuguese vessel illegally seized by American privateer. **July 22** Debates peace terms (fisheries). **July 23** Adopts plan for the protection of Continental property within the states. **July 24** Debates peace terms (fisheries). **July 26** Commends victors for capture of British post at Stony Point. **July 27** Orders Virginia reinforcements to South Carolina. **July 28** Debates financial reform. **July 29** Debates peace terms (fisheries). **July 30** Adopts ordinance for reorganizing the treasury. **July 31** Debates peace terms (fisheries).

August 2 Exonerates Jean Holker on charges of profiteering and reaffirms Continental protection for French consuls and other officials. **August 3** Debates peace terms (French alliance provision against separate peace). **August 5** Debates peace terms (re. Spanish subsidy, Florida and navigation of the Mississippi). **August 6** Authorizes payment of Silas Deane's expenses and releases him from obligation to remain in America. **August 7** Debates peace terms (re. Spanish interests in North America). **August 10** Requests North Carolina reinforcements for South Carolina. **August 13** Debates instructions for minister plenipotentiary to negotiate peace. **August 14** Debates instructions for minister plenipotentiary to negotiate peace. **August 17** Urges states to provide half pay for Continental officers. **August 18** Augments pay and allowances for Continental officers. **August 21** Requests states to extend provisions embargo to January 1, 1780. **August 25** Urges states to lift restrictions on interstate inland trade. **August 26** Appoints committee for creating a supreme court for admiralty appeals. **August 28** Debates financial reform. **August 31** Receives Henry Laurens' complaint against Secretary Thomson for disrespectful behavior.

September 1 Resolves that *"on no account whatever"* will Congress emit more than $200 million Continental currency. **September 3** Receives notice that Minister Gerard will return to France. **September 4** Observes death of William Henry Drayton. **September 7** Receives notification of Spanish entry into the war against Britain; adopts farewell response to Gerard. **September 9** Adopts letter of thanks to king of France; debates terms of prospective alliance with Spain. **September 10** Issues appeal to states for clothing; debates relations with Spain. **September 11** Debates relations with Spain.

September 14 Reads memorials of Indiana and Vandalia land companies. **September 16** Debates ways and means proposals. **September 17** Conducts farewell audience for Gerard; resolves to emit additional $15 million; debates relations with Spain; debates ways and means proposals. **September 18** Debates relations with Spain. **September 20** Orders military and naval reinforcements for southern department; debates relations with Spain. **September 21** Debates ways and means proposals. **September 22** Debates New Hampshire Grants claims. **September 23** Debates New Hampshire Grants claims, de bates relations with Spain. **September 24** Requests authorization from Massachusetts, New Hampshire and New York to mediate New Hampshire Grants claims; commends victors for attack on Paulus Hook; debates relations with Spain. **September 25** Debates relations with Spain and conduct of peace negotiations. **September 26** Nominates minister plenipotentiary to negotiate treaties of peace and of alliance with Spain. **September 27** Elects John Jay Minister to Spain and John Adams to negotiate peace.

On 27 September 1778, Jay resigned his office as President and was appointed Minister to Spain. He was later appointed as one of the commissioners to negotiate a peace. He sailed with Mrs. Jay, on 20 October, in the American frigate "*Confederacy,*" which, disabled by a storm, put into Martinico. From there they proceeded in the French frigate "*Aurora,*" which brought them to Cadiz, 22 January 1780. Jay, while received with personal courtesy, found no disposition to recognize American independence; Congress added to the embarrassing position of the minister at a reluctant court by drawing bills upon him for half a million dollars, assuming that he would have obtained a subsidy from Spain before they should have become due. Jay accepted the bills, some of which were afterward protested. The Spanish court advanced money for only a few of them and the rest were later paid with money borrowed by Franklin from France.

While in Spain, Jay was added by Congress to the peace commissioners, headed by John Adams, and at the request of Benjamin Franklin, on 23 June 1782, went to Paris, where Franklin was alone. The position of the two commissioners was complicated by the fact that Congress, under the persistent urgency of Luzerne, the French minister at Philadelphia, had materially modified the instructions originally given to Mr. Adams. On 15 June, 1781, Congress instructed its commissioners

> " *to make the most candid and confidential communications upon all subjects to the ministers of our generous ally, the king of France; to undertake nothing in their negotiations for peace and truce without their knowledge and concurrence, and ultimately to govern yourselves by their advice and opinion.*"

Two arguments were used in support of this instruction: First, the king was explicitly pledged by his minister to support the United States "*in all points relating to their prosperity*", *and second, that* "*nothing*" would be yielded by Great Britain which was not extorted by the address of France. "*An interesting memoir* " in the French archives, among the papers under the head of "*Angleterre,*" shows that the interests of France required that the ambition of the American colonies "*should be checked and held down to fixed limits through the union of the three nations,*" England, France and Spain. Before the arrival of Jay, Franklin had an informal conversation, first with Grenville, and then with Mr. Oswald, who had been sent by the cabinet of Rockingham. On 6 August, Oswald presented Jay and Franklin with a commission prescribing the terms of the Enabling Act, and authorizing him

> "*to treat with the colonies and with any or either of them, and any part of them, and with any description of men in them, and with any person whatsoever, of and concerning peace,*" etc.

This document led to a new complication in the American commission by developing a material difference of opinion between Jay and Franklin.

When the commission was submitted to Vergennes, he held that it was sufficient, and advised Fitzherbert to that effect. Franklin believed it "*would do.*" Jay declined to treat under the description of "*colonies*" refusing anything other than an equal footing. Oswald adopted Jay's view, but the British cabinet did not. Jay's refusal to proceed soon stayed the peace negotiations of the other powers, which Vergennes had arranged should proceed together, each nation negotiating for itself.

During Jay's residence in Spain he had learned much of the aims and methods of the Bourbon policy. He learned of this through a memoir submitted to him by Rayneval, as his "*personal views*" against our right to the boundaries as well as an intercepted letter of Marbois, secretary of legation at Philadelphia, against our claim to the fisheries. The secretive departure for England of Rayneval, the most skilful and trusted agent of Vergennes, convinced him that one object of Rayneval's mission was to prejudice Shelburne against the American claims. As a prudent counter-move to this secret mission, Jay promptly dispatched Benjamin Vaughan, an intimate friend and agent of Shelburne, to counteract Rayneval's adverse influence on American interests. This was done without consultation with Franklin, who did not concur with Jay regarding to Rayneval's journey. Franklin retained his confidence in the French court and was embarrassed and constrained by his instructions. It appears from "*Shelburne's*" *Life*" that Rayneval, in his interview with Shelburne and Grantham, after discussing other questions, proceeded to speak about America; and

> "*here Rayneval played into the hands of the English ministers, expressing a strong opinion against the American claims to the fisheries and the valleys of the Mississippi and the Ohio*";

Vaughan arrived almost simultaneously, bringing the "*considerations*" prepared by Jay. They enforced these points:

1. That, as Britain could not conquer the United States, it was for he interest to conciliate;
2. That the United States would not treat except on an equal footing;
3. That it was the interest of France, but not of England, to postpone the acknowledgment of independence to a general peace;

4. That a hope of dividing the fisheries with France would be futile, as America would not make peace without them;
5. That any attempt to deprive the United States of the navigation of the Mississippi, or of that river as a boundary, would irritate America;
6. That such an attempt, if successful, would sow the seeds of war in the very treaty of peace.

The disclosure of the grave difference between the Americans and their allies on the terms of peace, with the opportunity it afforded to England, consistent with the pride, interest, and justice of Great Britain and with the national jealousy of France, seems to have come to the cabinet with the force of a revelation. Its effect upon their policy was instantaneous and complete. A new commission in the form drafted by Jay, authorizing Oswald to treat with " *the United States*" el America, was at once ordered, and Lord Shelburne wrote to Oswald that they had said and done "*everything which had been desired,*" and that they had put the greatest confidence ever placed in man in the American commissioners. Vaughan returned "*joyfully*" with the new commission on September 27th, and on October 5th Jay handed to Oswald the plan of a treaty including the clauses relating to independence, the boundaries and the fisheries. Oswald, in enclosing the plan to his government, wrote: "*I look upon the treaty as now closed.*"

While the great success of the English at Gibraltar determined the ministry to resist the demands of France and Spain, it also induced them to attempt some modification of the concessions to the Americans, even though they had been made by Oswald with the approval of the cabinet. Strachey and Fitzherbert were therefore ordered to assist Oswald, and on 25 October John Adams arrived from Holland, where he had negotiated a treaty. He expressed to Franklin his entire approval of Jay's views and action, and at their next meeting with Oswald, Franklin said to Jay: "*I am of your opinion, and will go on with these gentlemen without consulting the court*". In writing to Livingston, Jay spoke of their perfect unanimity and specially acknowledged Mr. Adams's services on the eastern boundaries and Franklin's on the subject of the Tories. The provisional articles to take effect on a peace between France and England were signed 30 November 1782. When communicated to Vergennes, he wrote to Rayneval in England that the concessions of the English exceeded all that he had believed possible; Rayneval replied: "*The treaty seems to me like a dream.*" A new loan from France to America marked the continuance of their good understanding, Hamilton wrote to Jay that the terms of the treaty exceeded the anticipations of the most sanguine.

The violation of the instructions of Congress displeased a part of that body. Mr. Madison, who voted for the instruction, wrote: "*In this business Jay has taken the lead, and proceeded to a length of which you can form little idea. Adams has followed with cordiality. Franklin has been dragged into it.*" By contrast, Mr. Sparks, in his "*Life of Franklin,*" contends that the violation of their instructions by the American commissioners in concluding and signing their treaty without the concurrence of the French government was "*unjustifiable.*" By some error still unexplained, He represented the correspondence of Vergennes in the French archives as disproving the suspicions, which it authoritatively confirms. A map of North America, given in the *"Life of Shelburne,"* showing *"the boundaries of the United States, O Canada, and the Spanish possessions, according to the proposals of the court of France,"* shows that obedience by the American commissioners to the instruction to govern themselves by the opinion of Vergennes, would have shut out the United States from the Mississippi and the Gulf, and would have deprived them of nearly the whole of the states of Alabama and Mississippi, the greater part of Kentucky and Tennessee, the whole of Ohio, Michigan, Indiana, Illinois, Wisconsin and part of Minnesota, and the navigation of the Mississippi.

The definitive treaty, a simple embodiment of the provisional articles, for nothing more could be procured from the cabinet of Fox and North, was signed 3 September, 1783 and Jay returned to New York in July, 1784, having been elected by congress Secretary for Foreign Affairs. At the time this was the most important appointed post in the United States and he held the post until the establishment of the Federal government in 1789. His interest in foreign affairs is evident in his correspondence with Washington and Jefferson. Upon the formation of the National constitution he joined Alexander Hamilton and James Madison in contributing to the *"Federalist,"* and published an address to the inhabitants of New York in favor of the constitution.

John Jay was an active member of the New York convention, which, after a long struggle, adopted the constitution *"in full confidence"* that certain amendments would be adopted, and Jay was appointed to write the circular letter that secured the unanimous assent of the convention. Upon the organization of the Federal government, President Washington asked Jay to accept whatever place he might prefer, and Jay took the office of the First Chief Justice of the Supreme Court while resigning the post of president of the Abolition society.

In 1792 he consented to be a candidate for the governorship of New York, but the canvassers declined on technical grounds to count certain votes given for Jay, which would have made a majority in his favor, and Governor Clinton was declared elected. Jay was nominated by Washington in 1794 as special envoy to Great Britain, with whom our relations were then strained. He concluded his meetings with Lord Grenville on November 19th, 1794, the convention known in American history as *"Jay's Treaty,"* which was assailed with furious denunciations by the Democratic party, whose tactics severely tested the firmness of Washington's character and the strength of his administration. The treaty and its ratification against an unexampled opposition avoided a war with Great Britain. An English opinion of the treaty, in which America was denounced as a complete surrender to England, was expressed by Lord Sheffield where on the occurrence of the rupture with America, he wrote, *"We have now a complete opportunity of getting rid of that most impolitic treaty of 1794, when Lord Grenville was so perfectly duped by Jay."*

Five days before his return from England, Jay was elected governor of New York, an office to which he was re-elected in April 1798. At the close of his second term, in 1801, Jay declined a reappointment to the position of Chief Justice of the Supreme Court by President Adams.

John Jay passed the remainder of his life on his estate its Westchester County, New York, a property which had descended to Mr. Jay through his mother, Mary Van Cortlandt. It is situated some forty-five miles north of New York City about midway between the Hudson river and Long Island sound. The Bedford house, as the mansion is called, is placed on an eminence overlooking the whole beautiful rolling region between the two great bodies of water.

John Jay married on 28 April 1774, Sarah Vail Brugh Livingston, eldest daughter of Governor William Livingston. She accompanied her husband to Spain, and later was with him in Paris, where she was a great favorite in society. John Adams's daughter says of her at this time"

> *"Every person who knew her here bestows many encomiums on Mrs. Jay. Madame de Lafayette said she was well acquainted with her, and very fond of her, adding that Mrs. Jay and she thought alike, that pleasure might be found abroad, but happiness only at home in the society of one's family anal friends.* "

During the week of Washington's inauguration he dined with the Jays, and a few days later Mrs. Washington was entertained at Liberty Hall by Governor Livingston, Mrs. Livingston, and Mrs. Jay During the following season hospitalities were frequently exchanged between the president and the Jays. Daniel Webster said of Jay *"When the spotless ermine of the judicial robe fell on John Jay, it touched nothing less spotless than itself."* The life of John Jay has been written by his son and told also by Henry B. Renwick (New York, 1841). See *"The Life and Times of John Jay,"* by William Whitlock (New York, 1887)

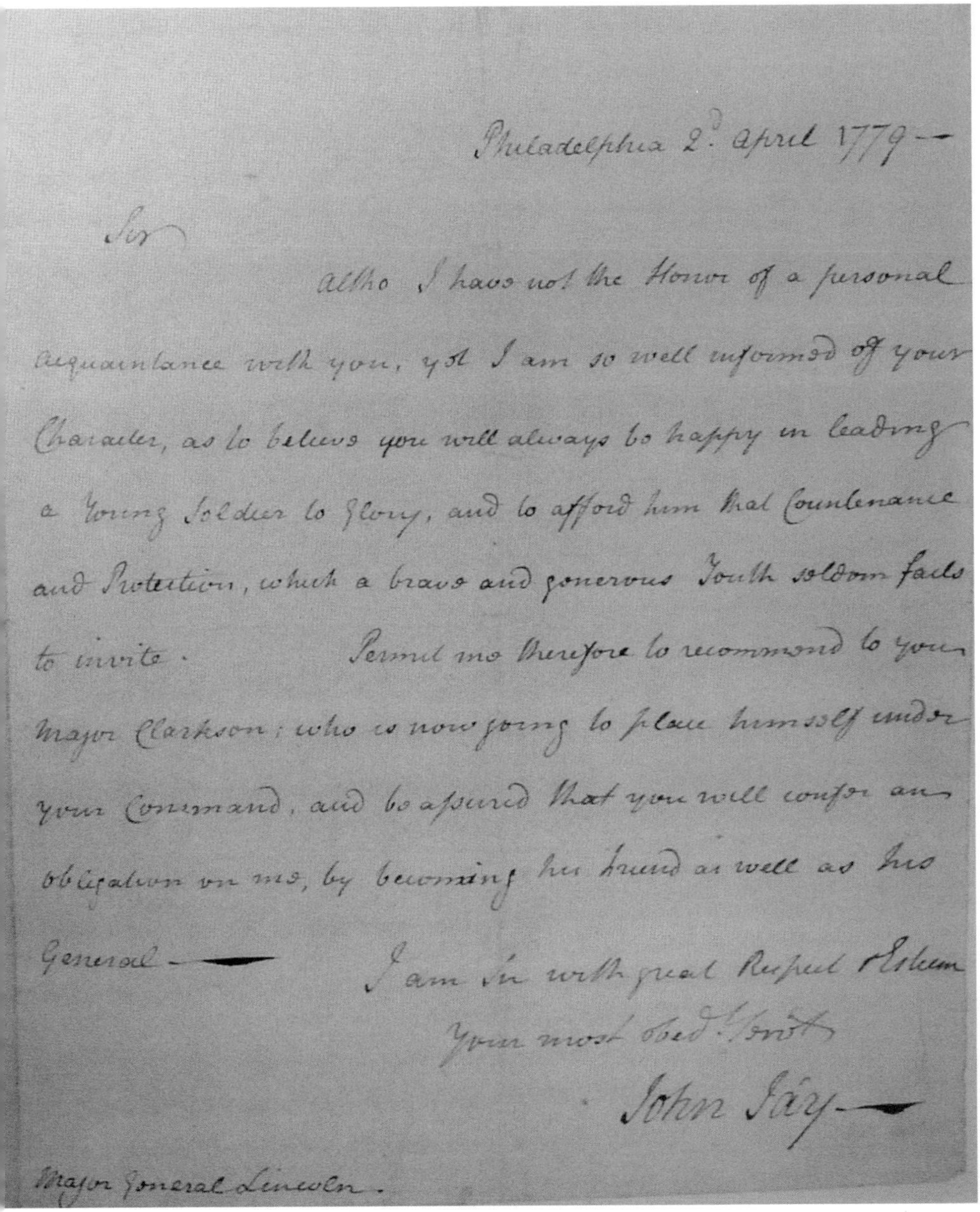
Philadelphia 2d. April 1779 —

Sir

Altho I have not the Honor of a personal Acquaintance with you, yet I am so well informed of your Character, as to believe you will always be happy in leading a Young Soldier to Glory, and to afford him that Countenance and Protection, which a brave and generous Youth seldom fails to invite. Permit me therefore to recommend to you Major Clarkson; who is now going to place himself under your Command, and be assured that you will confer an obligation on me, by becoming his friend as well as his General —

I am Sir with great Respect & Esteem

Your most obed.t Serv.t

John Jay —

Major General Lincoln.

John Jay, April 2, 1779 letter as President of the Continental Congress to Major General Benjamin Lincoln requesting he place Major Clarkson "under your command." Notice unlike the 1777 Hancock orders to St. Clair he doesn't use his title. I found this to be quite common in the letters of the Presidents in correspondence of "requests" to the Generals. – *Courtesy of the Klos Family Collection.*

CHAPTER SEVEN

Portrait of Samuel Huntington from
Appleton Cyclopedia of American Biography

SAMUEL HUNTINGTON

1st President of the United States in Congress Assembled March 1, 1781 to July 6, 1781
Signer of the Declaration of Independence
President of the Continental Congress September 28, 1779 to February 28, 1781

Samuel Huntington was born on July 16, 1731 in Scotland, Connecticut the son of a Puritan farmer. This date differs from the official Congressional Biography as during the restoration of the tomb a 207 year-old plaque was discovered with the bodies stating:

His Excellency Samuel Huntington Esq.
Governor of the State of Connecticut
was born July 16th AD 1731
and died January 5th AD 1796
aged 64 years

Both Martha and Samuel Huntington were re-interred on November 24, 2003 Old Norwichtown Cemetery, Norwich, New London County, Connecticut *(see editorial at end of section)*.

President Huntington was a self-educated man who, at age sixteen, was apprenticed to a cooper. He taught himself Latin at night and devoured every book on law he could find. At twenty-seven he was admitted to the bar, then moved to Norwich, a larger town offering more opportunity. After a year, however, he married Martha Devotion the local minister's daughter, and set up what would eventually become a most lucrative law practice.

In 1764, Huntington was elected to the provincial assembly and in quick succession became a justice of the peace, the king's attorney for Connecticut, and a member of the colony's council. He was elected to and served in the second Continental Congress of the United Colonies of America representing Connecticut at Independence Hall in Philadelphia.

Huntington worked hard and long for independence, however quietly. A fellow delegate wrote:

> *He is a man of mild, steady, and firm conduct and of sound methodical judgment, tho' not a man of many words or very shining abilities. But upon the whole is better suited to preside than any other member now in Congress.*

After signing the Declaration of Independence, Huntington served in the Continental Congress for three more years. Huntington, who was skeptical of entrusting large powers to individual or groups, was elected President and consequently he could be aligned with the Adams-Lee faction in the Continental Congress. Sanders notes,

> *"He cast his vote against half pay for seven years for officers of the army; was not in favor of recalling Izard from abroad, but voted for the recall of William and Arthur Lee, and did not believe that Jay should be instructed to abandon the free navigation of the Mississippi, if he deemed it necessary."*

He was elected President of the Continental Congress on September 28, 1779 as a replacement to John Jay who accepted the position of Foreign Secretary. In a September 29th in a letter from Jay to Clinton the former President approved of the election clearly indicating he did not alienate the Conservation Faction of Congress. Arthur Lee wrote to Elbridge Gerry a year later that, *"Toryism is triumphant here. They have displaced every Whig but the President".* Clearly the son of a Connecticut farmer made a miraculous transformation from the Plow to the Presidency.

Huntington presided over the Confederation Congress during a critical period in the War for Independence. His commitment to Independence and his Presidency is renowned among scholars as his unwavering leadership held our nation together during a succession of military losses, sedition and defections:

October 10th, 1779 - American attempt to recapture Savannah, Georgia fails. Winter of 1779-80 - the coldest of the war and provisions for Washington and his army were scarce in Morristown, New Jersey, causing a mutiny. May 12, 1780 - British capture Charleston, South Carolina May 1780 - Former Continental Congress President Henry Middleton pledges his allegiance to the crown after the Fall of Charleston. May 29, 1780 - British crush American troops at Waxhaw Creek. August 16, 1780 - British rout Americans at Camden, South Carolina September 25, 1780 - Major General Benedict Arnold's plans to cede West Point to the British discovered. January 1, 1781 - Mutiny of unpaid Pennsylvania soldiers. January 14, 1781 - Benedict Arnold burns Richmond. March 15, 1781 - British win costly victory at Guilford Courthouse, North Carolina April 25, 1781 - General Greene defeated at Hobkirk's Hill, South Carolina May 15, 1781 - Cornwallis clashes with Greene at Guilford Courthouse, North Carolina June 6, 1781 - British hold off Americans at Ninety Six, South Carolina July 6, 1781 - General Anthony Wayne repulsed at Green Springs Farm, Virginia

By the fall of 1780 three years had elapsed since Burgoyne's surrender at Saratoga. The fortunes of the Americans, instead of improving, had grown worse to the point of desperation. France's aid had thus far proved to be quite minor. In addition, the southern army had been annihilated, US paper money, the "Continental" had become worthless and US credit abroad hinged on the dwindling fortunes of patriots like Robert Morris and Haym Salomon. After four years, the founding Articles of Confederation, which were to form the Perpetual Union of the United States of America, had yet to be ratified. Legally, the nation that sought foreign recognition and aid was not united, as its own "*constitution*" was not ratified by all 13 states. Prospects of the United States' survival were far past bleak, as the country had never been formed!

The army, clothed in rags, half-starved and not paid, was ripe for mutiny; desertions to the British lines averaged more than 100 a month. Samuel Huntington's Presidential Predecessor, former Continental Congress President Henry Middleton betrayed his fellow patriots and declared a renewed loyalty to King George III. Even George Washington wrote "*he had almost ceased to hope.*"

In the summer of 1780 the spirit of desertion now seized Washington's greatest General, Benedict Arnold, with whom the British commander had for some time tampered with through the mediation of John Andre and an American loyalist, Beverley Robinson. Stung by the injustice he suffered, and influenced by his surroundings, Arnold made up his mind to play a part like that which General Monk had played in the restoration of Charles II to the British throne. By putting the British in possession of the Hudson River at West Point, Arnold would deliver the British all that they had sought to obtain in the campaigns of 1776-'77. Once West Point was secured the American cause would thus become so hopeless that an occasion would be offered for negotiation.

In July 1780, General Arnold, who like President Huntington was a Norwich, Connecticut son, obtained command of West Point from George Washington in order to surrender it to the enemy. In September, when his scheme was detected by the timely capture of Andre, Arnold fled to the British at New York, a disgraced and hated traitor. As the winter of 1781 approached and the British advanced northward towards Virginia, desperation seized Washington's troops and resulted in a mutiny on January 1, 1781. Benedict Arnold conducted a plundering expedition into Virginia even burning Richmond on January 14, 1781.

Despite this, through painstaking diplomacy, encouragement and a firm commitment to independence, Huntington was successful in persuading the 13 states to meet their quotas of men, dollars and provisions, enabling Washington and his Generals to conduct what most 18th Century Americans believed to be a lost war for freedom. On September 10, 1780 Samuel Huntington, determined to achieve the ratification necessary to form the United States, brokered this legislation and sent this circular letter to each of the states:

> *Your Excellency will receive herewith enclosed an Act of Congress of the 6 Instant, adopting the report of a Committee; together with Copies of the several Papers referred to in the report.*
>
> *I am directed to transmit Copies of this report and the several Papers therein mentioned to the Legislatures of the several States, (1) that they may all be informed of the Desires & Endeavours of Congress on so important a Subject, and those particular States which have Claims to the Western Territory, & the State of Maryland may adopt the Measures recommended by Congress in Order to obtain a final ratification of the Articles of Confederation.*
>
> *Congress, impressed with a Sense of the vast Importance of the Subject, have maturely considered the same, and the result of their Deliberation is contained in the enclosed report, which being full & expressive of their Sentiments upon the Subject; without any additional Obervations: it is to be hoped, and most earnestly desired, that the Wisdom, Generosity & Candour of the Legislatures of the several States, which have it in their Power on the one Hand to remove the Obstacles, and on the other to complete the Confederation, may direct them to such Measures, in Compliance ...*
>
> *Samuel Huntington, President*

On the 30th of January, 1781, succumbing to Samuel Huntington's proofs that the enemies of the United States were taking advantage of the circumstance to propagate opinions of an inevitable dissolution of the Union, the Maryland legislature passed an act to empower their delegates to subscribe and ratify the Articles of Confederation. Finally on March 1, 1781, amidst all this Revolutionary War chaos, President Huntington accomplished what Continental Congress Presidents John Hancock, Henry Laurens and John Jay failed to do; he achieved the unanimous ratification of the Articles of Confederation. After four long years of ratification consideration, from 1778 to 1781, the Perpetual Union known as the United States of America became a legal reality:

> *"Articles of Confederation and perpetual Union between the states of New Hampshire, Massachusetts-bay Rhode Island and Providence Plantations, Connecticut, New York, New Jersey, Pennsylvania, Delaware, Maryland, Virginia, North Carolina, South Carolina and Georgia."*

I. The Stile of this Confederacy shall be "The United States of America".

II. Each state retains its sovereignty, freedom, and independence, and every power, jurisdiction, and right, which is not by this Confederation expressly delegated to the United States, in Congress assembled.

III. The said States hereby severally enter into a firm league of friendship with each other, for their common defense, the security of their liberties, and their mutual and general welfare, binding themselves to assist each other, against all force offered to, or attacks made upon them, or any of them, on account of religion, sovereignty, trade, or any other pretense whatever ..." (for the entire text please visit ArticlesofConfederation.com)

By virtue of this ratification, the ever fluid Continental Congress ceased to exist and on March 2nd "The United States in Congress Assembled" was placed at the head of each page of the Official Journal of Congress. The United States of America, which was conceived on July 2, 1776, had finally been born in 1781 under the watch of President Samuel Huntington.

The New Journal of the United States in Congress Assembled reported on March 2, 1781:

The ratification of the Articles of Confederation being yesterday completed by the accession of the State of Maryland: The United States met in Congress, when the following members appeared: His Excellency Samuel Huntington, delegate for Connecticut, President ...

The March 2, 1781 circular letter that President Samuel Huntington sent to each of the states stated:

By the Act of Congress herewith enclosed your Excellency will be informed that the Articles of Confederation & perpetual Union between the thirteen United States are formally & finally ratified by all the States.

We are happy to congratulate our Constituents on this important Event, desired by our Friends but dreaded by our Enemies.

Samuel Huntington, President

The office President of the United States in Congress Assembled, was now established by the Articles; the term was limited to one year by the appointment (election) of the delegates:

to appoint one of their members to preside, provided that no person be allowed to serve in the office of president more than one year in any term of three years;

A form of this method of election was later incorporated into the US Constitution of 1787, with the people of each state voting for electors (delegates). The Electors, in turn, vote for the President of the United States, which in 2000 resulted in George W. Bush winning the US Presidency despite loosing the popular vote.

In 1781 Samuel Huntington, had already served as President of the Continental Congress for 17 months. The Articles, the first US Constitution, limited all presidencies to a term of one year. Since there was no operating constitution prior to 1781,

Huntington was eligible to serve one year as President under the Articles. Upon the urging of his fellow delegates he agreed to accept the new office of President of the United States in Congress Assembled.

The first use of the title President of the United States in the Journals of Congress was by the Treasury Department:

> *Treasury Office March 12th. 1781. The Board of Treasury to whom was referred the letter from the Honble. the Minister of France to Samuel Huntington his Excellency the President of the United States in Congress assembled on the subject of the affairs of the late Monsieur De Coudray dated the 4th. instant beg leave to report as follows ....*

For a full report see Journals of the United States in Congress Assembled THURSDAY, AUGUST 23, 1781.

Eighty years later, on July 4, 1861, President Abraham Lincoln would use the Articles of Confederation's language against South Carolina, North Carolina, Georgia and Virginia regarding their attempt to secede from the United States. It was the unanimous "Perpetual Union" verbiage in the Articles that provided President Lincoln with the legal authority, not granted in the US Constitution, to Preserve the Union.

> *"The express plighting of faith by each and all of the original thirteen in the Articles of Confederation, two years later, that the Union shall be perpetual is most conclusive."* - *Abraham Lincoln's Address to Congress in Special Session 4 July 1861.*

Lincoln, a student of history, must have gained great strength during the dark days of the Civil War from President Samuel Huntington's perseverance. One can only imagine the embarrassment and pressure Huntington endured from his Presidential predecessor, Henry Middleton, declaring his loyalty to King George III after the fall of Charleston. One can only imagine the pressures that were placed upon President Huntington when his fellow Norwich Revolutionary sold out to the British after the fall of the Southern States in 1781. In September of the same year Benedict Arnold was actually sent to attack New London, in order to divert Washington from his southward march against Cornwallis. One can only imagine the overtures that must have been made by the British through Arnold's Norwich Family, of amnesty, rank, land and money, if President Huntington would declare allegiance to the crown. President Huntington remained true to independence, presiding over the ratification ceremonies, and like Abraham Lincoln, preserved the Perpetual Union of the United States of America.

Sara (Huntington) Abbott writes of this period in President Huntington's life:

> *How true to this hazardous declaration, of his principles, Mr. Huntington subsequently proved; how intelligently and fearlessly he met all the responsibilities involved in it; how, step by step, he showed himself more and more indispensable to its efficient maintenance; how he won for himself, from the leaders of that day, the place and honor of leadership over even themselves, is abundantly attested by their vote of September 28,1779, in which he is chosen their PRESIDENT, with a unanimity as honorable to them as to him. Nor did he fail in*

this trying office, an office which called for the highest qualities both of the jurist and statesman. From the date of his election, until his resignation, July 6, 1781, he was most incessantly and acceptably engaged in the engrossing cares of his office. Perhaps no one of those honored men who were called to that eminent post during the formative period of our government, occupied it with more credit than he. Certainly never did congress show sincerer reluctance than when, from utter exhaustion of his strength, he was forced to ask either for a temporary, or a final retirement from the office. For two months they delayed seeking for a successor, hoping that meanwhile he might so far recover as to justify his continuance. But such had been the tax upon his strength that be was compelled to insist upon his resignation, about a month before the close of his second year. The resignation was accepted, and a hearty vote of thanks testified to the confidence which congress reposed in him as the chief executive of the nation, and their gratitude for his impartial and able administration.

An example of one daunting challenge Huntington faced can be found in this letter to Caesar Rodney. The letter is dated Philadelphia, Pennsylvania 13 November, 1780 only 6 months after General Benjamin Lincoln surrendered to British Forces in Charleston, South Carolina. The British, who now effectively controlled the Carolinas and Georgia, were making liberal use of papers and clearances that they took from this great southern "prize." In this letter, a beleaguered President Huntington asks Caesar Rodney of Delaware to support his resolution, adopted at the urging of Minister of France, to deal with the problem of British Spies and their disruption of our trade with France and other allies.

Transcript:

Circular, Philadelphia November 13, 1780

Sir,

Congress having received Information from the Honorable the Minister of France, of Inconveniencies & Injuries received by our Allies, resulting from the Abuse the British make of Papers & Clearances they take in American Prizes, by personating the Officers & Commanders named in such Papers, being fully acquainted with the Language & Manners of our Officers & Seamen &c.

In Compliance with the request of the Minister of France, Congress have adopted the enclosed Resolution in Order to detect such Abuses in future; and I am to request your Excellency's Attention to the necessary Measures for carrying the same into effectual Execution.

I have the Honor to be with the highest Respect
your Excellency's most obedient and very humble Servant

Sam. Huntington President.

His Excellency

The President of Delaware State

Huntington's accomplishments as President didn't end with the Articles' ratification. On April 5, 1781 Huntington's Congress passed an ordinance, which declared Congress' "sole and exclusive right and power (inter alia) of appointing courts for the trial of piracies..." and empowered "the justices of the supreme or superior courts of judicature, and judge of the Court of Admiralty of the several and respective states, or any two or more of them" to hear and try offenders charged with such offences. Huntington sent this circular letter on April 19th, 1781 to all the states:

> *Your Excellency will receive herewith enclosed, an Ordinance for establishing Courts for the Trial of Piracies and Felonies committed upon the high Seas, passed in Conformity to Articles of Confederation.*
>
> *I have the Honor to be &c, &c,*
>
> *Samuel Huntington, President*

By May 1781 Samuel Huntington strongly supported Robert Morris's financial plan for the maintenance of the army, which was ready to disband by its own act. It was perceived by many states that Congress had no power to enforce taxation. Morris proposed the establishment of a Bank at Philadelphia with a capital of four hundred thousand dollars, the promissory notes of which should be a legal-tender currency to be received in payment of all taxes, duties and debts, due the United States. The plan was approved by Congress, as seen below:

> *Resolved, That Congress do approve of the plan for establishing a national bank in these United States, submitted to their consideration by Mr. R. Morris, the 17 day of May, 1781; and that they will promote and support the same by such ways and means, from time to time, as may appear necessary for the institution and consistent with the public good:*
>
> *That the subscribers to the said bank shall be incorporated agreeably to the principles and terms of the plan, under the name of The President, Directors and company of the bank of North-America, so soon as the subscription shall be filled, the directors and president chosen, and application for that purpose made to Congress by the president and directors elected.*
>
> *So it was resolved in the affirmative.*

With the able guidance of Mr. Morris, who was the Secretary of the Treasury, that corporation furnished the means for saving the Continental army from disbanding. He collected the taxes as well as using his private fortune freely for the public welfare.

Much about Samuel Huntington's accomplishments and the inner workings of the United States Government during this period of revolution is lost. The historical record is severely fragmented because the Congressional delegates, the Secretary of War, Secretary of State, Minister of Finance, Secretary of the United States, and President of the United States were all bound by an oath of secrecy not to publish or record the debates and intrigues of the new Confederation Government. The Journals of The United States in Congress Assembled record only resolution outcomes and a minuscule amount of official correspondence that were deemed necessary to enter into the official record. Only now, as institutions, libraries, foundations and private individuals upload their rare private and official Pre-Washington presidential letters to the Internet, is the full nature of the US President's office coming to light.

What we are learning from these letters and the official Journals of Congress is that Samuel Huntington and the other nine Presidents under the Articles of Confederation issued orders, ratified treaties, executed military commissions, received foreign dignitaries, called for Congressional sessions, held councils of War and signed foreign loans as both President of Congress and President of the United States depending on the situation. Treaties, for instance, were signed as President of the United States, while resolutions of Congress were signed as President of Congress

One only needs to search for the Journals of United States in Congress Assembled online. Here are a few examples of official documents issued as President of the United States in Congress Assembled found in the search:

> Journals of the United States in Congress Assembled -THURSDAY, AUGUST 23, 178;MONDAY, SEPTEMBER 16, 1782; SATURDAY, SEPTEMBER 28, 1782;MONDAY, JUNE 2, 1783;FRIDAY, MARCH 12, 1784;FRIDAY, APRIL 23, 1784; FRIDAY, MARCH 24, 1786.

The Chronology of Samuel Huntington's Presidency in both the Continental Congress and United States in Congress Assembled is as follows:

> **1779 - September 28** Elects Samuel Huntington president of Congress; adopts commissions and instructions for John Adams and John Jay.
>
> **October 1** Orders the preparation of a plan for reorganizing the conduct of naval affairs. **October 2** Requests Vermont claimants to authorize Congress to settle Vermont claims. **October 4** Adopts instructions for minister to Spain (John Jay). **October 6** Admonishes Benedict Arnold on treatment of Pennsylvania officials. **October 7** Calculates and apportions 1780 state fiscal quotas. **October 9** Adopts circular letter to the states on meeting fiscal quotas. **October 13** Authorizes Arthur Lee to return to America. **October 14** Commends John Sullivan on conduct of expedition against the Indians; resolves to emit an additional $5 million; sets day of thanksgiving. **October 15** Adopts instructions for minister to Spain; resolves to seek a loan in Holland. **October 20** Adopts thanksgiving day proclamation. **October 21** Appoints Henry Laurens to negotiate Dutch loan. **October 22** Rejects appeal for Continental intervention against state taxation of Continental quartermasters. **October 26** Adopts instructions for negotiation of Dutch loan and treaty of amity and commerce. **October 28** Creates Board of Admiralty, ending management of naval affairs by congressional committee. **October 30** Urges Virginia to reconsider decision to open land office for sale of unappropriated lands.

November 1 Appoints Henry Laurens to negotiate Dutch treaty of amity and commerce. **November 2-3** Adjourns because of expiration of President Huntington's credentials as Connecticut delegate. **November 5** Notified of evacuation of Rhode Island; appoints committee to plan an executive board to supervise Continental officials. **November 8** Requests correspondence files of former presidents of Congress. **November 9** Elects Treasury officers. **November 10** Orders deployment of three frigates to South Carolina. **November 11** Orders reinforcement of southern department; observes funeral of Joseph Hewes. **November 13** Rejects resignation of General John Sullivan; approves parole of Generals William Phillips and Baron Riedesel of the Convention Army. **November 16** Undertakes care of Spanish prisoners held at New York; rejects Massachusetts' appeal to retain Continental taxes to defray Penobscot expedition costs; recommends that states compel persons to give testimony at Continental courts-martial. **November 17** Holds audience with the newly arrived French minister, the Chevalier de La Luzerne; resolves to emit an additional $10 million. **November 18** Gives General Washington free hand to coordinate operations with the French armed forces. **November 19** Recommends state adoption of price regulations. **November 23** Resolves to draw bills of exchange to £100,000 sterling each on John Jay and Henry Laurens. **November 25** Adopts new regulations for clothing Continental Army; discharges committee for superintending the commissary and quartermaster departments. **November 26** Appoints Admiralty commissioners. **November 29** Commemorates General Pulaski's death- resolves to emit an additional $10 million; accepts resignation of Commissary General Jeremiah Wadsworth. **November 30** Appoints committee to confer with Washington at headquarters; accepts resignation of General John Sullivan.

December 2 Receives notification of Spanish declaration of war against Britain; appoints Ephraim Blaine commissary general of purchases. **December 3** Resolves to move Congress from Philadelphia at the end of April 1780; appoints Admiralty commissioners. **December 6** Reinforces armed forces in southern department. **December 9** Observes ay of thanksgiving. **December 15** Recommends that states extend provisions embargo to April 1780. **December 16** Authorizes Gen. Benjamin Lincoln to coordinate southern operations with Spanish officers at Havana. **December 20-24** Debates proposal to borrow $20 million abroad. **December 24** Authorizes use of depositions of witnesses at courts martial in non-capital cases. **December 27** Recommends moratorium on granting lands in region of Pennsylvania-Virginia boundary dispute; orders Post Office to institute twice-weekly deliveries in place of weekly deliveries. **December 28** Authorizes Continental reimbursement of militia expenses incurred defending Connecticut against invasion. **December 31** Endorses Board of War plan to employ greater secrecy to reduce procurement expenses.

1780 - January 3 Postpones decision on selecting a new site for Congress. **January 4-8** Debates plan for creating a court of appeals. **January 8** Reorganizes Georgia's Continental regiments. **January 10** Dismisses Charles Lee, second ranking Continental general; debates plan for reducing the army to curtail expenses. **January 12** Sends emergency appeal to the states for provisioning the army; abolishes mustermaster's department. **January 13** Adopts new regulations for negotiation of prisoner exchanges. **January 14** Recommends that states make provision for guaranteeing the privileges and immunities of French citizens recognized in the Franco-American treaty of amity and commerce. **January 15** Creates Court of Appeals in admiralty cases. **January 17** Endorses export of grain to French forces by the French agent of marine. **January 18** Resolves to print the journals of Congress monthly, but ends practice of printing the yeas and nays. **January 20** Orders investigation into the expenses of the staff departments; abolishes barrackmaster's department. **January 22** Elects judges to Court of Appeals. **January 24** Adopts new measures for recruitment of Continental troops. **January 25** Halts pay of inactive naval officers. **January 26** Appoints committee to confer with the French minister on joint Franco-American operations. **January 27** Authorizes inflation adjustment in the salaries of Continental officials. **January 31** Pledges to wage a vigorous campaign in conjunction with French forces during 1780.

February 4-5 Debates Continental Army quotas for 1780. **February 9** Sets state quotas and adopts recruitment measures for an army of 35,000 by April 1, 1780. **February 11** Affirms commitment to the re-conquest of Georgia. **February 12** Confirms sentence in the court-martial of General Benedict Arnold. **February 16-24** Debates proposals for a system of in-kind requisitions from the states. **February 22** Debates congressional privilege issue arising from the complaint of Elbridge Gerry. **February 25** Adopts system of in-kind requisitions from the states. **February 28** Postpones decision on selecting a new site for Congress.

March 2 Postpones debate on Vermont controversy. **March 3** Sets *"day of fasting, humiliation and prayer."* **March 4** Commends John Paul Jones and crew of Bonhomme Richard for victory over Serapis. **March 8** Orders reinforcements for the southern department. **March 13-18** Debates proposals for fiscal reform. **March 18** Repudiates Continental dollar, adopting measures for redeeming bills in circulation at the ratio of 40 to 1. **March 20** Recommends state revision of legal tender laws. **March 21** Postpones debate on Vermont controversy. **March 24** Observes Good Friday. **March 26** Observes funeral of James Forbes. **March 27** Rejects proposals for a new site for Congress; receives plan for reorganizing quartermaster department. **March 29-31** Debates proposals for adjusting Continental loan office certificates for inflation.

April 1 Debates plan for reorganizing quartermaster department. **April 3** Rejects motion to hear Elbridge Gerry appeal. **April 4** Authorizes defense of New York frontier at Continental expense. **April 6** Resolves to send a committee to confer with Washington at headquarters. **April 8** Authorizes partial reimbursement to Massachusetts for Penobscot expedition expenses. **April 10** Authorizes depreciation allowances for Continental troops. **April 12** Adopts instructions for Committee at Head quarters.
April 13 Appoints committee at headquarters. **April 15** Appoints Joseph Ward commissary general of prisoners. **April 17** Rejects proposal to appoint a "*resident*" at the Court of Versailles. **April 18** Authorizes depreciation allowances for holders of Continental loan office certificates; authorizes issuance of commissions to Delaware Native Americans. **April 20** Resolves to draw bills of exchange on John Jay in Spain. **April 21** Adopts measures for the relief of prisoners of war. **April 24** Adopts appeal to the states to meet fiscal quotas. **April 28** Appoints Cyrus Griffin to Court of Appeals, William Denning to Board of Treasury.

May 2 Revises commissions, bonds and instructions for privateers. **May 5** Doubles rates of postage. **May 10** Adopts regulations for replacing destroyed loan office certificates. **May 15** Three Georgia delegates attend, representing the state for the first time in more than a year. **May 17** Considers Committee at Headquarters report presented by John Mathews. **May 18-20** Debates La Luzerne memorial on Franco- American cooperation. **May 19** Urges states to remit quota payments immediately. **May 20** Urges states to meet troop quotas immediately. **May 22** Urges Delaware to extend provisions embargo indefinitely. **May 23** Debates Vermont controversy. **May 26** Requests states to receive Continental certificates in payment of taxes. **May 29** Debates Vermont controversy. **May 30** Rescinds Committee at Headquarters instruction on the propriety of reducing the-Continental Army.

June 1 Adopts measures for defense of New York and New Hampshire frontiers. **June 2** Censures Vermont settlers and pledges final determination of the Vermont controversy whenever nine "**disinterested**" states are represented in Congress. **June 5** Adopts plans for cooperating with anticipated French forces. **June 6** Orders arms for southern defense. **June 9** Postpones Vermont inquiry to September 12. **June 12** Orders restrictions on the issuing of Continental rations; creates two extra chambers of accounts to facilitate settlement of staff department accounts. **June 13** Appoints Horatio Gates to southern command. **June 14** Adopts measures for the defense of the southern department. **June 15** Issues circular letter to the states to reinforce the appeals of the Committee at Headquarters. **June 19** Adopts measures to prevent and punish counterfeiting. **June 20** Empowers John Adams to seek Dutch loan. **June 21** Reaffirms commitment to Franco-American military cooperation; appoints an agent to transact US affairs in Portugal. **June 22** Endorses plan to establish a private bank for provisioning and supplying the Continental Army. **June 23** Orders inquiry into the fall of Charleston, South Carolina; reaffirms support for Georgia and South Carolina. **June 28** Adopts plan for paying depreciation allowances to holders of Continental loan office certificates.

July 3 Orders Admiralty Board to implement intelligence gathering plan. **July 5-6** Debates plan to reform quartermaster department. **July 7** Endorses La Luzerne's request to permit the shipment of provisions to Spanish forces in the West Indies. **July 11** Orders publication of Congress' May 1778 resolution requesting that Articles 11 and 12 of the Franco-American Treaty of Commerce be revoked. **July 13** Orders Washington to seek the exchange of General du Portail, chief of engineers. **July 15** Reorganizes quartermaster department; continues Nathanael Greene in office as Quarter-master general. **July 17** Receives announcement of arrival of French fleet at Rhode Island. **July 19** Opens debate on the court-martial of Dr. William Shippen, Jr., Director General of hospitals. **July 20** Suspends Deputy Quartermaster Henry Hollingsworth . **July 25** Appoints Charles Pettit Assistant Quartermaster General. **July 26** Orders deployment of Continental frigates to cooperate with French fleet; orders reforms in the department of military stores. **July 27** Transfers responsibility for issuing privateer commissions and bonds to the office of the secretary of Congress.

August 2 Lifts restrictions on Washington's operational authority; chides Committee at Headquarters. **August 3-4** Debates Quartermaster Greene's resignation request. **August 5** Appoints Timothy Pickering quartermaster general to succeed Nathanael Greene; orders Washington to confer with French officers to plan the expulsion of the enemy from Georgia and South Carolina. **August 7** Instructs Washington on exchanging prisoners of war and on reinforcing the southern department. **August 9** Authorizes drawing bills of exchange on Benjamin Franklin for the relief of the southern department. **August 11** Dismisses Committee at Headquarters. **August 12** Reforms department of military stores; responds to general officers' grievances. **August 17** Commends General Rochambeau and the conduct of the French forces. **August 18** Confirms court-martial acquittal of William Shippen, Jr. **August 22** Orders punishment of abuses in the staff departments. **August 23** Adopts regulations for the issuance of certificates in the commissary and quartermaster departments; authorizes drawing additional bills of exchange on Benjamin Franklin. **August 24-25** Extends additional benefits to general officers. **August 26** Exhorts states to implement Congress' March 18 resolves for exchanging Continental currency. **August 29** Appoints committee to plan a "*new arrangement of the civil executive departments.*" **August 31** Receives news of General Gates' defeat at Camden, **September 1** Receives informal invitation to trade with Morocco. September 5 Authorizes issuance of loan office certificates to

$1 million specie value at 6 percent interest. **September 6** Urges states to cede western land claims and Maryland to ratify Articles of Confederation. **September 8** Orders reinforcement of southern military department. **September 13** Sets salary schedule for the Continental establishment. **September 14** Reopens debate on Vermont dispute. **September 15** Appoints Abraham Skinner Commissary General of Prisoners; adopts plan to supply meat to Continental Army. September 19 Convenes evening session to continue Vermont dispute debate. September 21 Approves enlistment of troops for one year in absence of sufficient "*recruits enlisted for the war.* " **September 22** Authorizes drawing additional bills of exchange on Benjamin Franklin. **September 25** Adopts new plan for the inspecting department, consolidating mustering functions under the inspector general. **September 26** Resolves to instruct commanders of ships to observe principles conforming to the Russian Declaration on Neutral Rights. **September 27** Postpones Vermont dispute debate. **September 28** Resolves to limit presidential terms to one year. **September 30** Receives account of the treason of General Benedict Arnold; adopts new plan for the medical department.

October 2 Authorizes drawing additional bills of exchange on Franklin and John Jay. **October 3** Adopts new establishment for the Continental Army. **October 4** Adopts instructions for John Jay on navigation of the Mississippi River and southwestern boundaries. **October 6** Elects officers for hospital department. **October 10** Adopts Virginia proposal to reimburse state expenses related to cession of western lands and to require that ceded lands "*be disposed of for the common benefit of the United States.*" **October 13** Appoints Daniel Morgan brigadier general; creates third chamber of accounts. **October 14** Votes memorial for Baron de Kalb; commends various officers and troops for bravery at the Battle of Camden. **October 16** Receives proceedings of the Hartford convention of New England states. **October 17** Adopts letter of instruction for John Jay. **October 18** Instructs John Adams on peace negotiations; sets day of prayer and thanksgiving. **October 21** Endorses proposal to receive Cherokee delegation; revises Continental Army establishment. **October 23** Receives report on the victory at King's Mountain. **October 24** Sends urgent appeal to the states on the present distresses of the army. **October 25-31** Debates ways and means proposals. **October 30** Confirms Nathanael Greene's appointment to command of the southern department. **October 31** Orders cavalry reinforcement to southern department.

November 1 Authorizes drawing additional bills of exchange on Benjamin Franklin. **November 3** Rewards captors of Major John Andre. **November 4** Apportions $6 million specie tax, to be collected chiefly in-kind; appoints William Palfrey Consul to France. **November 7** Authorizes prisoner-of-war exchange. **November 9** Adopts letter of appeal to the states on present emergency. **November 10** Adopts measures to curtail enemy fraudulent use of American privateer commissions; directs steps for reducing forage expenses. **November 13** Commends troops engaged in the victory at King's Mountain **November 14** Authorizes capital punishment for persons supplying the enemy with provisions or military stores. **November 16** Receives Committee at Headquarters report; confers with Pennsylvania officials on provisions embargo. **November 17** Resolves to appeal to France for 25 million livres in aid. **November 22** Adopts appeal to the king of France; appoints William Geddes paymaster general. **November 23** Rescinds election of William Geddes as paymaster general. **November 24** Receives report on treasury inquiry. **November 27** Adopts measures for outfitting Continental ships; adopts additional privateer instructions. **November 28** Extends half-pay provisions to general officers; instructs Franklin on procuring aid from France and cultivating commerce with Morocco. **November 30** Adopts revised commissary regulations.

December 1 Adopts statement endorsing Arthur Lee's conduct abroad. **December 4** Prohibits unauthorized military purchases; appoints Simeon De Witt Geographer to the Continental Army. **December 6** Commends Benjamin Tallmadge's troops for Long Island raid; halts removal of Convention Army from Virginia. **December 7** Observes day of prayer and thanksgiving. **December 9** Adopts instructions for Consul to France, William Palfrey. **December 11** Appoints John Laurens "*envoy extraordinary*" to France. **December 15** Resolves to appoint a minister to Russia. **December 19** Appoints Francis Dana Minister to Russia. **December 21** Debates impact of John Laurens' appointment on Benjamin Franklin's mission in France; launches study of the conditions of Henry Laurens' imprisonment. **December 22** Appeals to the states to fulfill Continental troop quotas. **December 23** Adopts instructions for Special Envoy to France, John Laurens. **December 27** Instructs Benjamin Franklin on John Laurens' mission to France. **December 29** Commissions John Adams to negotiate a treaty of amity and commerce with the United Provinces.

1781 - January 3 Appoints committee to confer with Pennsylvania officials on the mutiny of the Pennsylvania Line. **January 5** Empowers the mutiny committee "to take such measures as may appear necessary to quiet the disturbances"; threatens retaliation for British mistreatment of American prisoners. **January 6** Revives committee for the reorganization of the executive departments. **January 8** Endorses proposal to receive Delaware Native American delegation. **January 9** Recommends prosecution of former clothier general, James Mease, for "*a high abuse of office.*" **January 10** Authorizes establishment of a permanent office for the Department of Foreign Affairs. **January 12** Endorses treasury inquiry report acquitting commissioners of the chambers of accounts. **January 15** Adopts new fiscal appeal to the states from New Hampshire to

Pennsylvania. **January 17** Appoints John Cochran Director of the Hospital Department and John Pierce Paymaster General. **January 19** Opens debate on fiscal crisis. **January 24** Receives report on the mutiny of the Pennsylvania Line. **January 31** Receives committee of the whole recommendation for a 5 percent impost.

February 2 Rejects Pennsylvania appeal for an emergency pay response for the Pennsylvania Line. **February 3** Recommends state action to empower Congress to levy a 5 percent impost. **February 5** Commends General Parsons' troops for the attack at Morrisania; defines alien property rights under the Franco-American treaties. **February 7** Adopts plan to create departments of finance, war, and marine. **February 8** Receives news of General Daniel Morgan's victory at Cowpens, South Carolina. **February 12** Receives Maryland act authorizing ratification of the Articles of Confederation. **February 15** Authorizes expenditures for the support of the eastern Native American department; authorizes John Jay to recede from previous instruction insisting on the free navigation of the Mississippi River. **February 19** Orders inquiry into the causes of the delay in the shipment of clothing and arms from France. **February 20** Orders the reinforcement and re-supply of the southern department; appoints Robert Morris superintendent of finance. **February 22** Assigns March 1 for completing and ratifying the confederation. **February 23** Debates and recommits report on the Hartford economic convention. **February 24** Doubles postage rates; adopts plan for ratifying ceremonies. **February 27** Commends John Paul Jones for "*distinguished bravery and military conduct, . . . particularly . . . over the British ship of war Serapis*"; elects Alexander McDougall secretary of marine. **February 28** Postpones election of secretary at war to October 1; imposes restrictions on ornate military uniforms and decorations; refers old business to the new Confederation Congress.

Chronology of the Journals of the United States in Congress Assembled:

March 1 Receives New York cession of western land claims; Maryland delegates sign and ratify Articles of Confederation; **celebrates completion of the Confederation**. **March 2** Debates rules for congressional representation; appoints committee to revise the rules of Congress. **March 3** Orders removal of Convention Army prisoners from Virginia. **March 6** Orders preparation of a plan for "*carrying into execution*" all congressional acts and resolutions. **March 7** Orders depreciation allowances for staff department officers. **March 9** Commends troops for victory at the battle of Cowpens. **March 10-14** Debates Continental finances. **March 15** Receives Connecticut Act authorizing Congress to levy imposts for a limited time. **March 16** Urges states to make Continental bills legal tender; appeals to states to meet fiscal quotas. **March 19** Authorizes bills of exchange drawn on Benjamin Franklin in France. **March 20**

Adopts Fast Day proclamation; accepts Robert Morris's conditions for serving as superintendent of finance. **March 22** Urges Connecticut to repeal time limitation from its approval of a Continental impost. **March 24** Receives pledge of continued French military support with warning of impending end to financial aid. **March 27** Adopts ordinance on the capture and condemnation of prizes. **March 28** Receives Board of Admiralty report on the delay of supplies from France. **March 30** Rejects Alexander McDougall's terms for accepting appointment as secretary of marine. **March 31** Rejects motion to grant Robert Morris removal authority in the office of finance.

April 2 Authorizes New York to raise two militia regiments at Continental expense. **April 3** Orders recall of General Burgoyne from his parole and preparation of a manifesto condemning British treatment of Henry Laurens. **April 4** Resolves against paying interest on bills of new emission. **April 5** Adopts ordinance for establishing courts of admiralty. **April 7** Adopts new instructions regulating privateers. **April 8** Convenes in rare Sunday session to prepare against threatened invasion of Delmarva Peninsula. **April 10** Orders limitation on bills of exchange drawn on ministers abroad. **April 11** Orders establishment of magazines for provisioning French forces to defray a credit of $400,000 drawn for Benjamin Franklin in France. **April 14** Commends John Paul Jones. **April 16** Reaffirms prohibition against Continental officers holding civil appointments. **April 18** Orders circulation to the states of a report on the public debt. **April 21** Grants Robert Morris removal authority in the office of finance. **April 23** Appoints committee to prepare impost ordinance. **April 27** Orders immediate steps against drawing bills of exchange on John Jay and Henry Laurens abroad.

May 1 Fails to convene quorum. **May 3** Observes Fast Day. May 4 Adopts revised congressional rules. **May 8** Receives report from "*committee of the week,*" inaugurating new procedure for expediting congressional business; refers visiting Catawba Native American delegation to Board of War. **May 14** Receives Robert Morris' acceptance as superintendent of finance; adopts "*ways and means*" measures for defraying costs "*of the ensuing campaign.*" **May 16** Authorizes John Jay to sell *America* (74-gun ship on the Portsmouth stocks) to Spain. **May 18** Authorizes General Wayne to impress provisions. **May 21** Receives Robert Morris proposal for establishing a bank. **May 26** Approves plan "*for establishing a national bank in these United States.*" **May 28** Authorizes John Jay to recede from demand for free navigation of the Mississippi River; considers report on conference with La Luzerne on Austro-Russian mediation offer. **May 31** Issues emergency call for troops for the southern department.

June 1 Appeals to the states to meet quotas. **June 4** Authorizes superintendent of finance to allocate French financial aid. **June 7-9** Adopts revised negotiating instructions for minister plenipotentiary; rejects motion to appoint additional peace commissioners. **June 11** Resolves to appoint two additional peace commissioners. **June 13** Elects John Jay additional commissioner to negotiate peace; adopts letter of thanks to King of France. **June 14** Authorizes exchange of John Burgoyne for Henry Laurens; resolves to appoint two additional peace commissioners; elects Benjamin Franklin, Henry Laurens and Thomas Jefferson to negotiate peace. **June 15** Adopts instructions for minister plenipotentiary. **June 16** Rejects motion for more severe corporal punishment for Continental troops. **June 18** Adopts regulations for clothier general's department. **June 19** Adopts instructions for Benjamin Franklin and rejects his request to resign. **June 23** Directs Robert Morris to expedite launching of *America.* **June 25** Rejects motion for appointing appeals judges "*during good behaviour.*" **June 26** Appoints John Paul Jones to command America; appoints Francis Dana Secretary to the Peace Commissioners. **June 27** Appoints Robert Smith, Agent at Havana.

July 2 Approves General Washington's request for 300 Pennsylvania riflemen. **July 4** Observes Independence Day. **July 6** Receives President Samuel Huntington's letter of resignation.

Samuel Huntington and his nine predecessors under the Articles of Confederation were without question Presidents of the United States before George Washington. Granted they did not serve as commander-in-chief but their office was in many ways much more complex and challenging then the Constitutional Presidency. One must understand that in 1789, US Unicameral President Cyrus Griffin was replaced by President George Washington (executive branch), Chief Justice John Jay (judicial branch), President of the US Senate John Adams and Speaker of the US House of Representatives Frederick A.C. Muhlenberg (legislative branch) under the new US Constitution. It is hard to imagine how any one person was able to cope with the duties and titles of all these offices. By May of 1781, President Huntington's health began to fail. Huntington, despite the pleadings of the delegates, tendered his resignation as President on July 6, 1781. The United States in Congress Assembled Journals reported:

> "*The President having informed the United States in Congress assembled, that his ill state of health*" ... *not permit him to continue longer in the exercise of the duties of that office*".

Congress held off electing a new President until July 10th in the hope that Huntington would recover and reconsider. On July 10th Delegate Thomas McKean was elected as the second President of the United States in Congress Assembled. On this day Congress also resolved:

> "*That the thanks of Congress be given to the hon. Samuel Huntington, late President of Congress, in testimony of their approbation of his conduct in the chair and in the execution of public business.*"

On October 19, 1781, three months after Huntington stepped down from the Presidency, George Washington and our French Allies trapped Cornwallis in Yorktown, effectively ending the Revolutionary War. During this three-month period Huntington recovered his health and served as an associate justice of the superior court in Connecticut. In 1785, he became lieutenant governor of Connecticut. A year later he was elected governor and was re-elected to that office for ten consecutive years. In 1788, as Connecticut's chief executive Huntington firmly advocated the ratification of the new Federal Constitution knowing full well the weaknesses of the Articles of Confederation. The Connecticut Society of the Sons of the American Revolution reports of Huntington's Governorship:

> *Aware of the need to diversify Connecticut's economy, he laid the foundations of Connecticut's future industrial expansion by espousing development of "useful Manufactures." The first manufacturing company to be incorporated in the United States was a silk manufacturing company in Mansfield in 1798. He labored actively for improvement of schools and roads, a more humane legal system, and fiscal reform. He advocated toleration of all religious sects and the abolition of slavery. During he governorship what is now the Old State House was authorized and built. A modest, industrious, independent-minded, and pious man throughout his distinguished career, he exemplified the ideal of the Puritan magistrate dedicated to the betterment of society.*

Huntington died on January 5, 1796 at the age of sixty-four and has just been re-interred at the Old Norwichtown Cemetery, Norwich, New London County, Connecticut, USA. Here is the account as reported by the Norwich Bulletin on Tuesday November 24, 2003:

> *The crack from the rifles of the First Company, Governors Foot Guard, sent a roll of thunder from the heart of the Old Cemetery to the rest of the nation: Here lies Samuel L. Huntington, the first president of the United States.*
>
> *Wearing their grenadier red uniforms topped with Busby caps, First Company guardsmen Malcolm Holland and Fred Modowski played "Taps" on their trumpets. A silence came over the 300 people gathered Monday afternoon for the Huntington's re-interment.*
>
> *Olive Buddington, chairwoman of the Norwich Historical Society's re-entombment committee, said she felt a lump in her throat as members of the Governor's Foot Guard lowered Huntington's coffin into his tomb.*
>
> *"He was the first president of the United States under the Articles of Confederation," U.S. Rep. Rob Simmons, R-2nd District, said before a ceremony reinterring Huntington and his wife, Martha, into their tomb.*
>
> *Simmons said he intends to pursue legislation to recognize Huntington as the first president and bestow upon him full honors given to any other president.*
>
> *Huntington, who was born in Scotland and lived most of his life in Norwich, brought the 13 states together to ratify the Articles of Confederation, said Stanley L. Klos, 49, a historian and collector of rare documents from Upper St. Clair, Pa.*

The articles were adopted by the Continental Congress in 1777, but it wasn't until March 1, 1781, when all the states had ratified the Articles that Huntington actually took office.

Klos argues the Declaration of Independence legalized the colonies' freedom from Great Britain and the Articles of Confederation legally founded the nation. Klos said George Washington was the first president under the Constitution, but 11th man overall to lead the fledgling nation.

Klos urged President George W. Bush to amend the presidential order and give Huntington and the other nine presidents under the Articles of Confederation the annual wreath laying on their graves on their birthdays.

Klos holds a doctorate from Pennsylvania State University and is the owner of a museum of rare documents, which include some signed by Huntington as president of the United States. He brought two documents to the funeral that show Huntington's signature as the governor of Connecticut and as president of the Congress.

"This was very overwhelming," said Channing Huntington of Canterbury, who represented the family. "It is a compilation of a dream. He has been my hero for so long."

The Huntingtons' bodies were exhumed Oct. 20 so the tomb, which was on the verge of collapse, could be rebuilt. Bill Stanley, president of the Norwich Historical Society, helped raise the $25,000 needed to rebuild it.

Church and Allen Funeral home donated the space for the Huntingtons' bodies while the tomb reconstruction took place.

The city's Department of Public Works donated 300 hours to the project worth about $10,000.

Director of Public Works Joseph Loyacano also put together a time capsule, which included newspaper articles, construction contracts, the schedule of the funeral, drawings of the tomb as it existed before the reconstruction, a picture of Huntington and thank-you letters sent to contributors of the Norwich Historical Society.

Stanley said he placed a personal note, stating "we have done our best and, if this tomb is reopened, we expect the same."

Stanley sealed the tomb by placing the last brick.

Huntington served as chief judge of the Superior Court, lieutenant governor and governor of Connecticut for 10 years. He died Jan. 5, 1796. He was 64.

Martha Huntington died June 3, 1794. She was 55.

"There is a great contrast between Huntington and (Benedict) Arnold," retired Norwich Free Academy teacher Pat Flahive said of Norwich's other famous Revolutionary War figure. "I hope (Huntington) gets the recognition he deserves."

The Rev. Stan White of the Preston City Congregational Church conducted the ceremony.

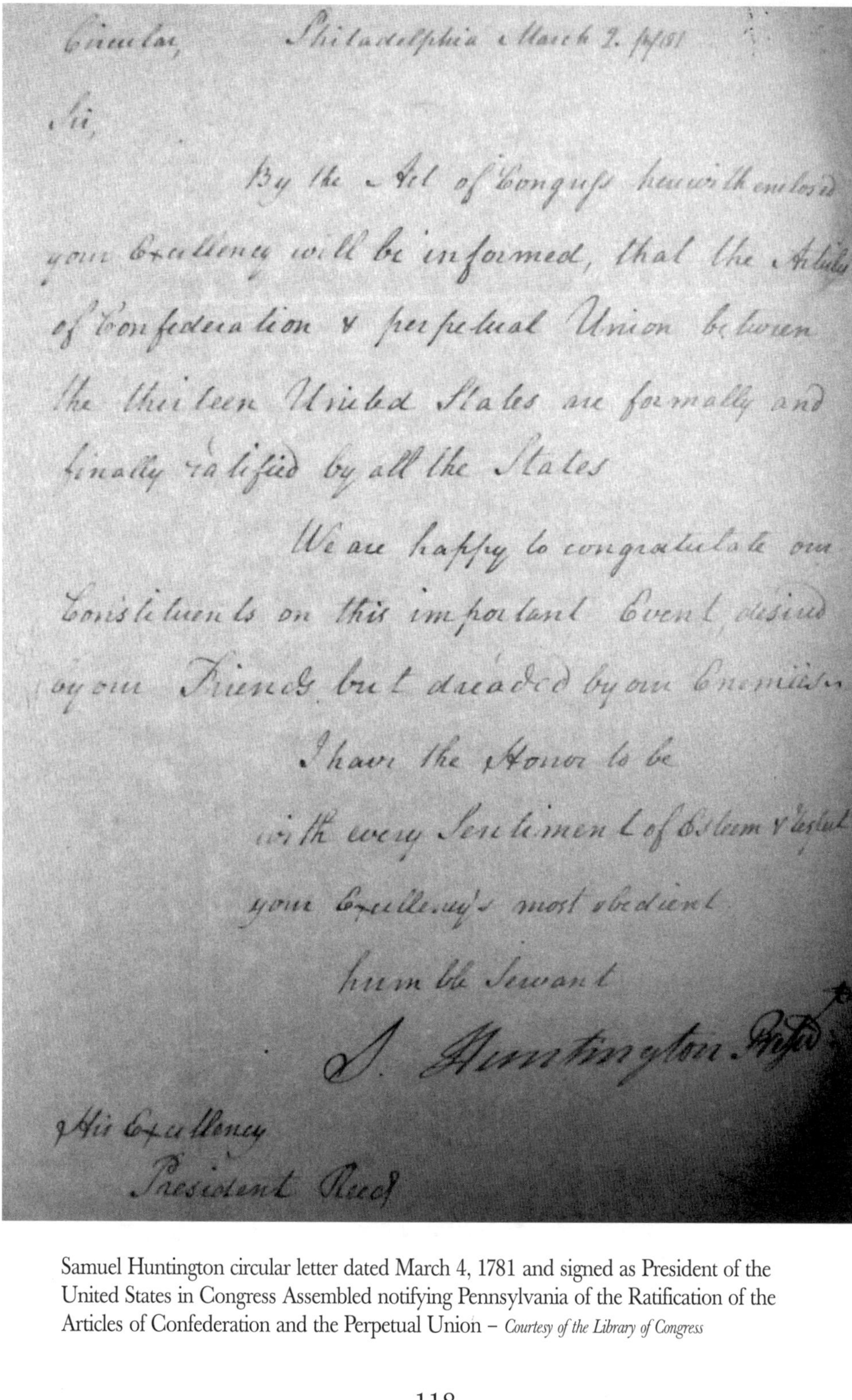

Circular, Philadelphia March 2. 1781

Sir,

By the Act of Congress herewith enclosed your Excellency will be informed, that the Articles of Confederation & perpetual Union between the thirteen United States are formally and finally ratified by all the States

We are happy to congratulate our Constituents on this important Event, desired by our Friends but dreaded by our Enemies.

I have the Honor to be
with every Sentiment of Esteem & respect
your Excellency's most obedient
humble Servant

S. Huntington Presid.

His Excellency
President Reed

Samuel Huntington circular letter dated March 4, 1781 and signed as President of the United States in Congress Assembled notifying Pennsylvania of the Ratification of the Articles of Confederation and the Perpetual Union – *Courtesy of the Library of Congress*

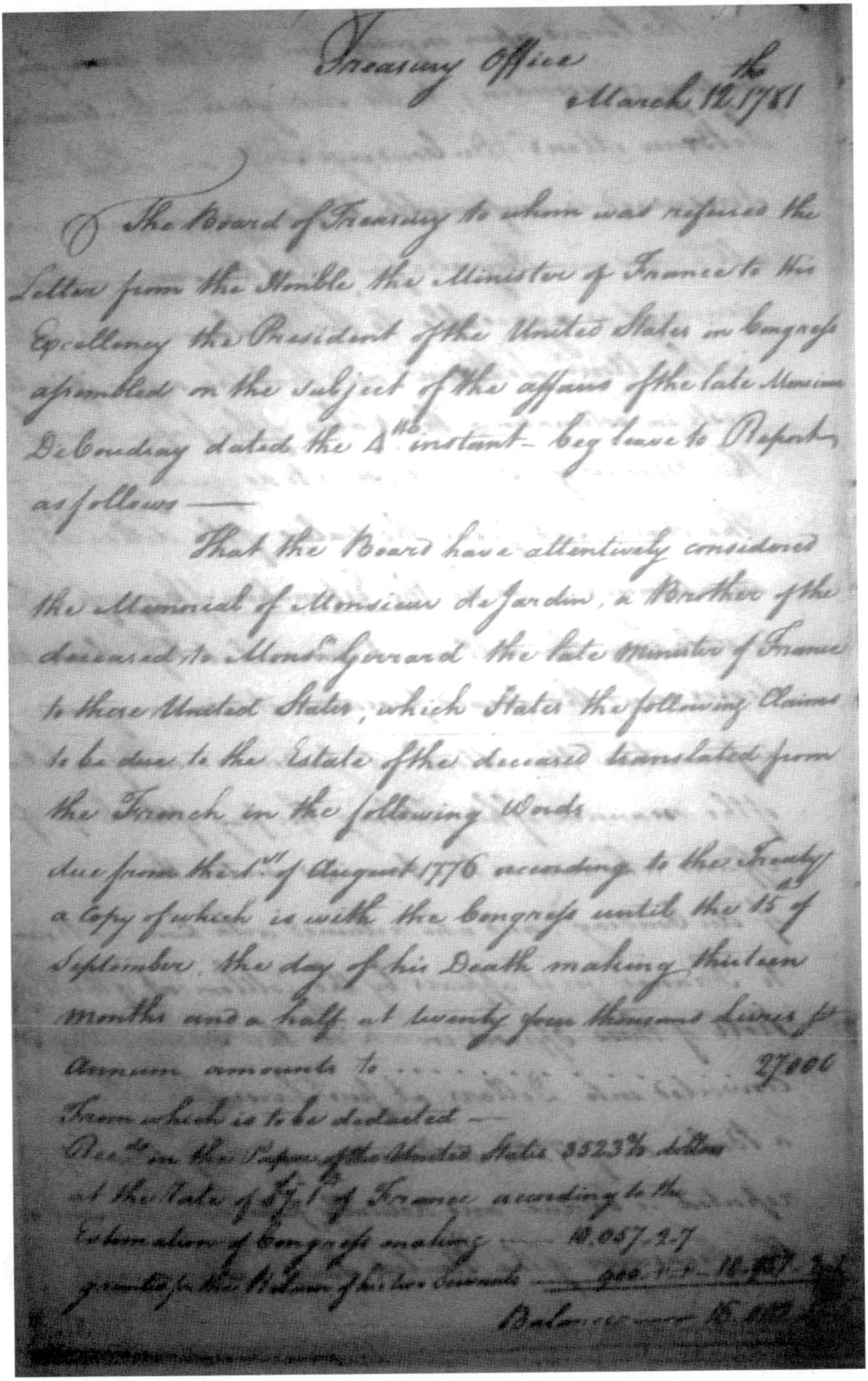
Treasury Office
March 12th 1781

The Board of Treasury to whom was referred the Letter from the Honble the Minister of France to his Excellency the President of the United States in Congress assembled on the subject of the affairs of the late Monsieur DeCoudray dated the 4th instant – beg leave to Report as follows —

That the Board have attentively considered the Memorial of Monsieur deJardin, a Brother of the deceased to Monsr Gerard the late Minister of France to these United States, which States the following Claims to be due to the Estate of the deceased translated from the French in the following Words ....

due from the 1st of August 1776 according to the Treaty a copy of which is with the Congress until the 15th of September the day of his Death making thirteen months and a half at twenty four thousand Livres pr Annum amounts to 27000

From which is to be deducted —

Recd in the Paper of the United States 3523 ⅓ dollars at the Rate of ... of France according to the Estimation of Congress making —— 10.057.2.7

March 12, 1781, only eleven days after the formation of the Perpetual Union, this US Treasury Report utilizes the title "President of the United States in Congress Assembled" for first time in the Journals of Congress. – *Courtesy of the Library of Congress*

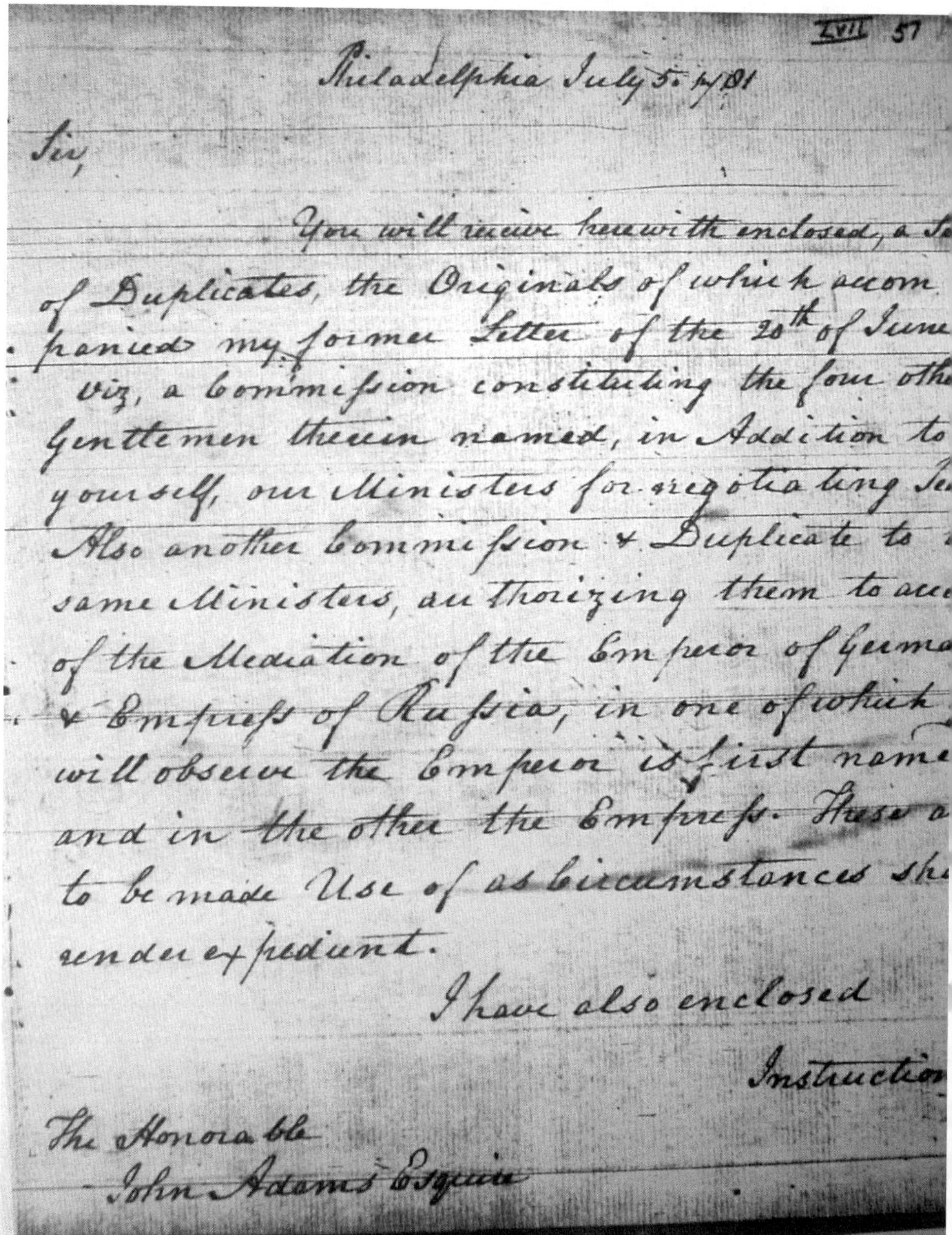

LVII 57

Philadelphia July 5. 1781

Sir,

You will receive herewith enclosed, a Se
of Duplicates, the Originals of which accompanied my former Letter of the 20th of June
viz, a Commission constituting the four othe
Gentlemen therein named, in Addition to
yourself, our Ministers for negotiating Pe
Also another Commission & Duplicate to
same Ministers, authorizing them to acc
of the Mediation of the Emperor of Germ
& Empress of Russia, in one of which
will observe the Emperor is first name
and in the other the Empress. These a
to be made Use of as circumstances sh
render expedient.

I have also enclosed

Instruction

The Honorable
John Adams Esquire

Page one - Samuel Huntington to John Adams dated July 5, 1781 just six days before his resignation with explicit instructions in "Cyphers" ordering the Foreign Minister " You will immediately communicate the receipt of these Dispatches to Dr. Franklin and Mr. Jay." – *Courtesy of the Library of Congress*

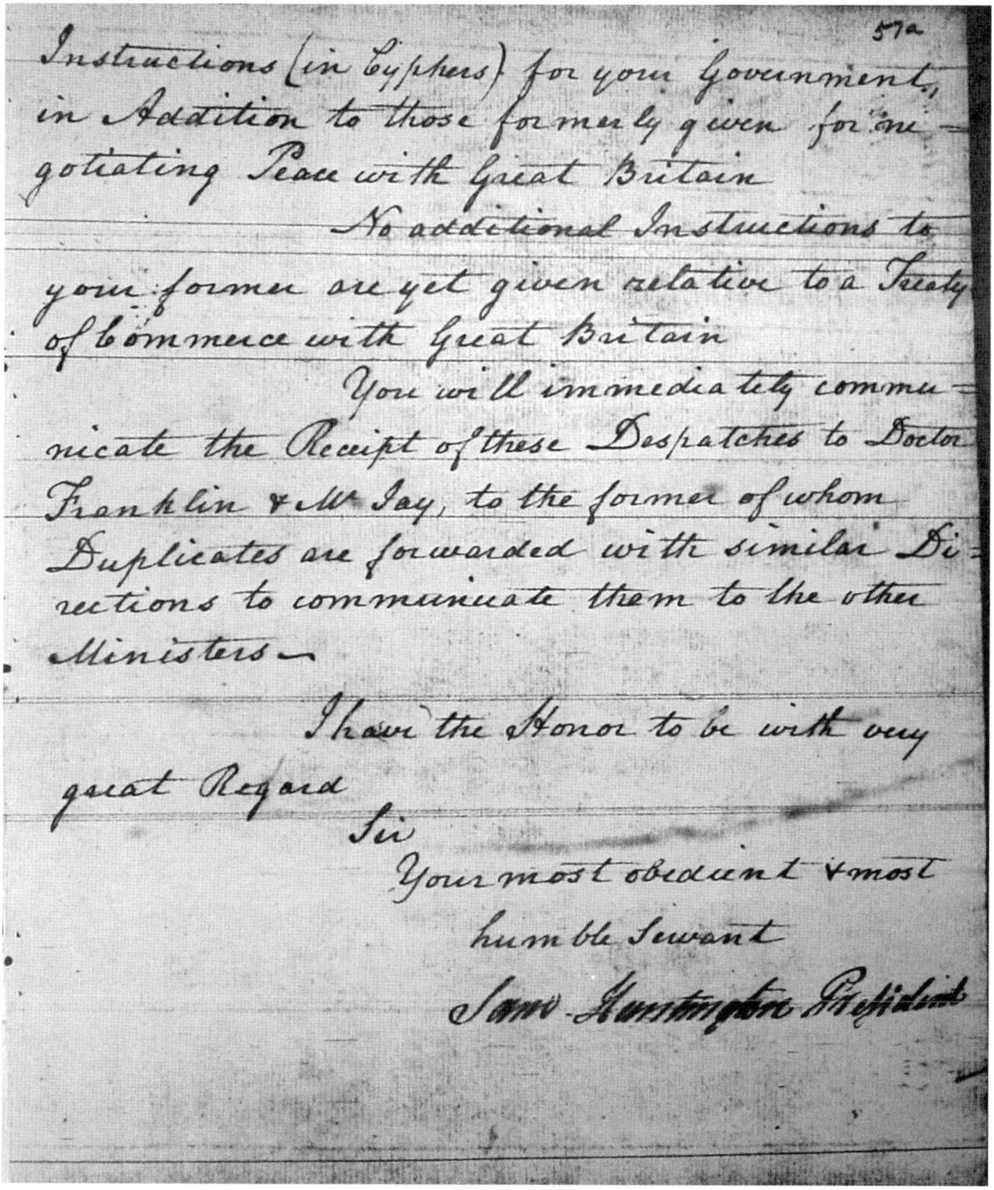

57a

Instructions (in Cyphers) for your Government, in Addition to those formerly given for negotiating Peace with Great Britain

No additional Instructions to your former are yet given relative to a Treaty of Commerce with Great Britain

You will immediately communicate the Receipt of these Despatches to Doctor Franklin & Mr Jay, to the former of whom Duplicates are forwarded with similar Directions to communicate them to the other Ministers—

I have the Honor to be with very great Regard

Sir

Your most obedient & most humble Servant

Saml Huntington President

Page two - Samuel Huntington to John Adams dated July 5, 1781 just six days before his resignation with explicit instructions in "Cyphers" ordering the Foreign Minister " You will immediately communicate the receipt of these Dispatches to Dr. Franklin and Mr. Jay." – *Courtesy of the Library of Congress*

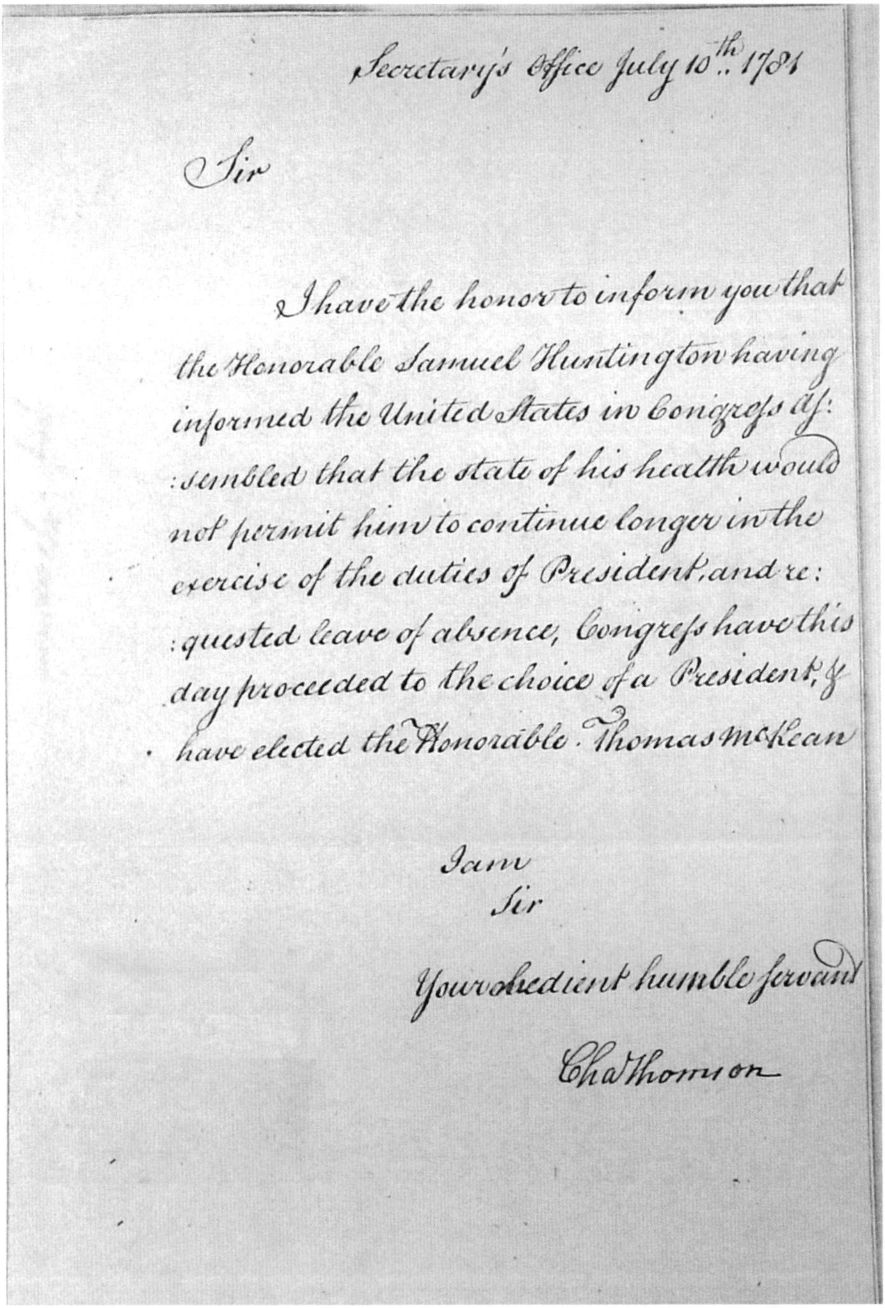

Secretary's Office July 10th. 1781

Sir

I have the honor to inform you that the Honorable Samuel Huntington having informed the United States in Congress assembled that the state of his health would not permit him to continue longer in the exercise of the duties of President, and requested leave of absence, Congress have this day proceeded to the choice of a President, & have elected the Honorable Thomas McKean

I am
Sir
Your obedient humble servant

Chas Thomson

Charles Thomson Secretary of the United States in Congress Assembled notifies Major General Greene on July 10th, 1781 of President Huntington's resignation –

Courtesy of the Library of Congress

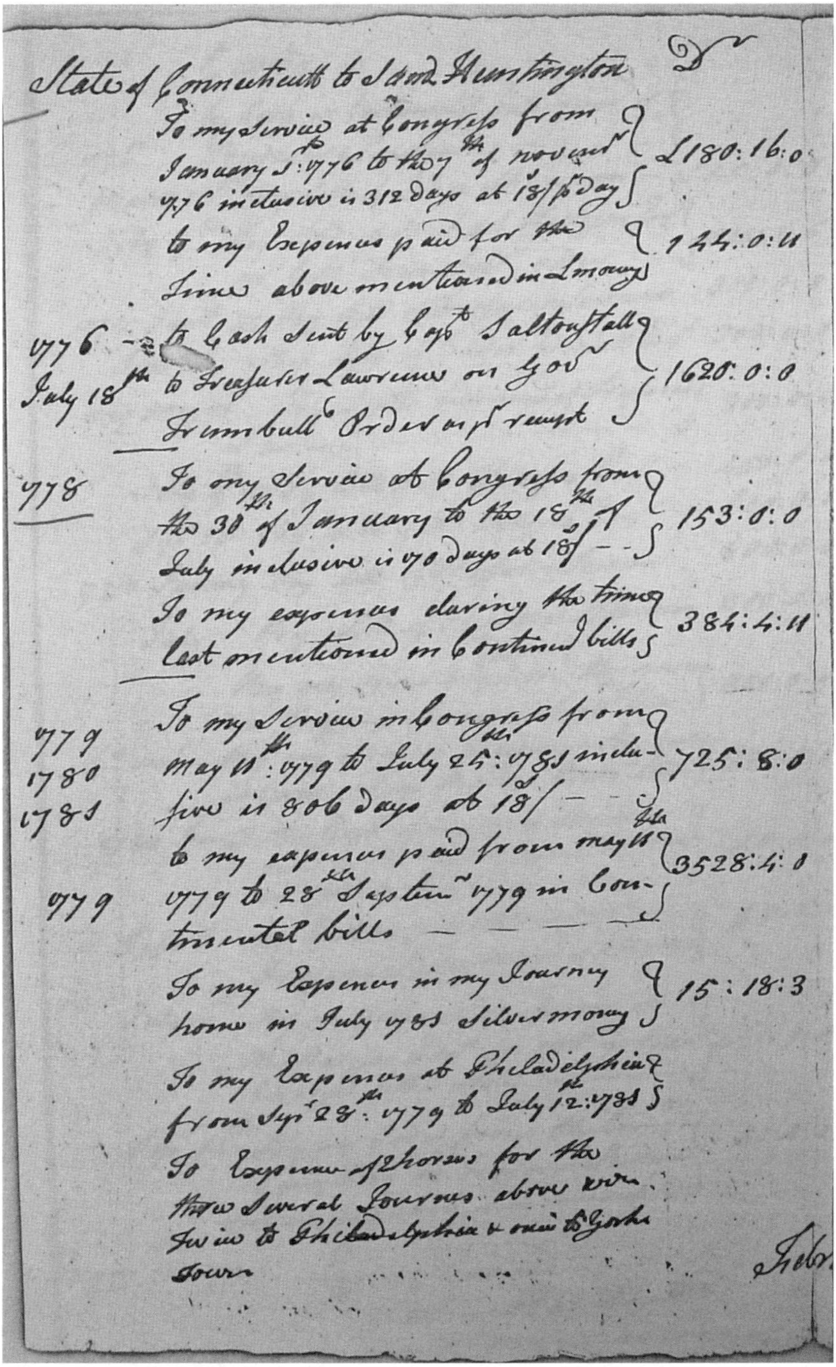
State of Connecticutt to Saml. Huntington Dr

	To my Service at Congress from January 1st 1776 to the 7th of Novemr 1776 inclusive is 312 days at 18/ pr day	£180:16:0
	to my Expences paid for the time above mentioned in L money	144:0:11
1776 July 18th	to Cash sent by Capt Saltonstall to Treasurer Lawrence on Govr Trumbull's Order as pr receipt	1620:0:0
1778	To my Service at Congress from the 30th of January to the 18th of July inclusive is 170 days at 18/	153:0:0
	To my expences during the time last mentioned in Continental bills	384:4:11
1779 1780 1781	To my Service in Congress from May 11th 1779 to July 25th 1781 inclusive in 806 days at 18/	725:8:0
1779	to my expences paid from May 11th 1779 to 28th Septemr 1779 in Continental bills	3528:4:0
	To my Expences in my Journey home in July 1781 Silver money	15:18:3
	To my Expences at Philadelphia from Sepr 28th 1779 to July 12th 1781	
	To Expence of 2 horses for the three Several Journies above viz. Twice to Philadelphia & once to York Town	

Febr

Page one - Samuel Huntington accounting as a Delegate from Connecticut –
Courtesy of the Library of Congress

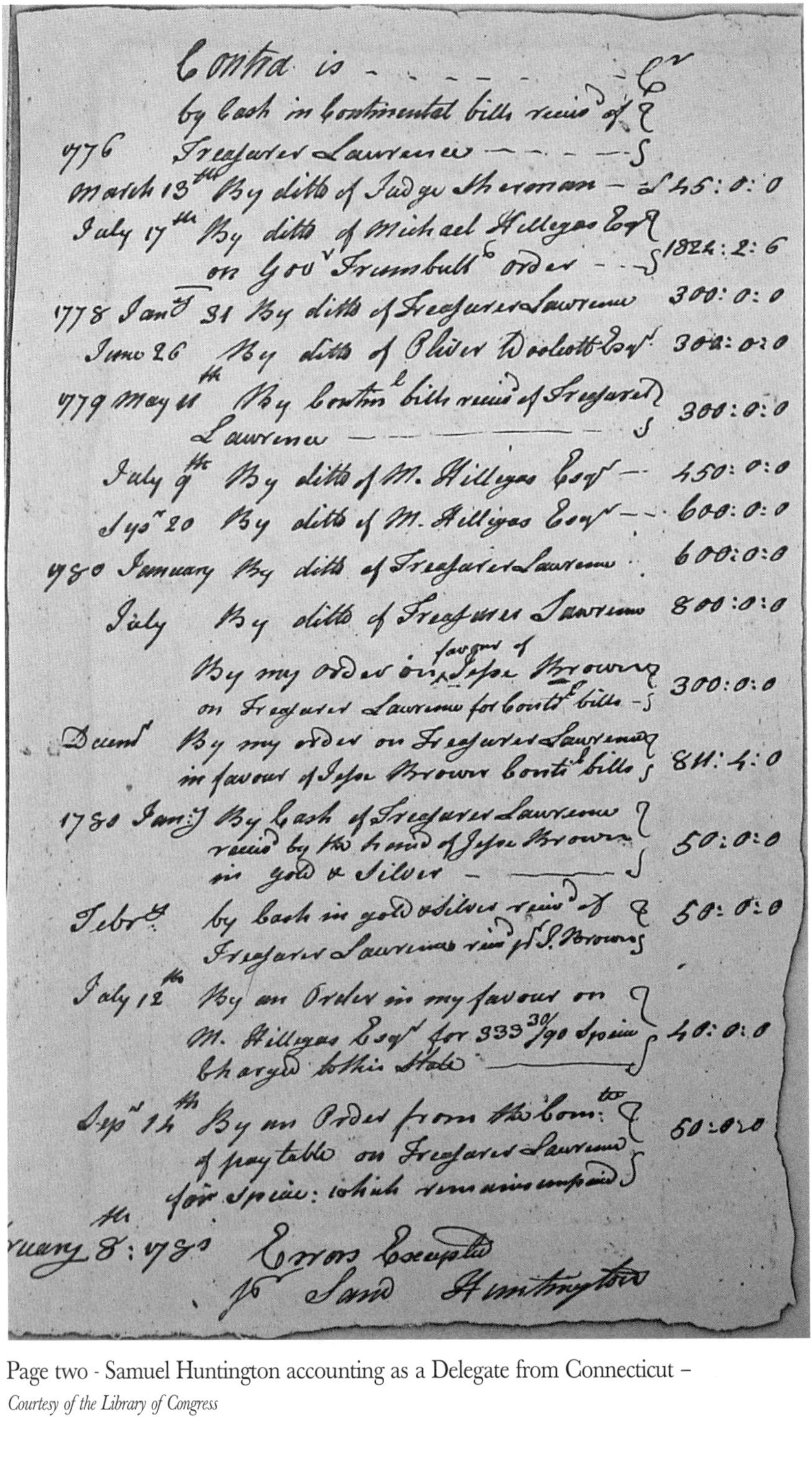
Contra is ------- Cr
by Cash in Continental bills recd of
776 Treasurer Lawrence ------
March 13th By ditto of Judge Sherman — £45:0:0
July 17th By ditto of Michael Hillegas Esqr on Govr Trumbulls order -- 1822:2:6
1778 Jany 31 By ditto of Treasurer Lawrence 300:0:0
June 26 By ditto of Oliver Wolcott Esqr 300:0:0
779 May 11th By Contin bills recd of Treasurer Lawrence ---- 300:0:0
July 9th By ditto of M. Hillegas Esqr — 450:0:0
Sepr 20 By ditto of M. Hillegas Esqr -- 600:0:0
780 January By ditto of Treasurer Lawrence 600:0:0
July By ditto of Treasurer Lawrence 800:0:0
By my order in favour of Jesse Brown on Treasurer Lawrence for Contl bills 300:0:0
Decemr By my order on Treasurer Lawrence in favour of Jesse Brown Contl bills 811:4:0
1780 Jany By Cash of Treasurer Lawrence recd by the hand of Jesse Brown in gold & Silver —— 50:0:0
Febry by cash in gold & silver recd of Treasurer Lawrence recd pr J. Brown 50:0:0
July 12th By an Order in my favour on M. Hillegas Esqr for 333 30/90 Specie charged to this State 40:0:0
Sepr 14th By an Order from the Comtee of pay table on Treasurer Lawrence for Specie: which remains unpaid 50:0:0
ruary 8th: 1780 Errors Excepted
pr Saml Huntington

Page two - Samuel Huntington accounting as a Delegate from Connecticut –
Courtesy of the Library of Congress

CHAPTER EIGHT

Portrait of Thomas McKean from
Appleton Cyclopedia of American Biography

THOMAS MCKEAN

2nd President of the United States
in Congress Assembled
July 10, 1781 to November 5, 1781

Thomas Mc Kean, signer of the Declaration of Independence, was born in New London, Chester County, Pennsylvania on March 19, 1734 and died in Philadelphia, Pennsylvania, June 24, 1817. Mc Kean's parents were both natives of Ireland. He studied with the Reverend Francis Allison, who was at that time, a renowned teacher of New Castle, Delaware. McKean was of Scots-Irish descent and was a man of energetic personality, *"with a thin face, hawk's nose and hot eyes."*

McKean had important family connections in Delaware and used them to his advantage to pursue a career in politics. He was admitted to the bar before he was twenty-one years old, appointed deputy attorney general of Sussex county a year later, and served as clerk of the assembly from 1757 to 1759. In 1762 McKean, along with Caesar Rodney became reviser of laws that had been passed previous to 1752. In October of that year he was elected to the Colonial General Assembly, holding office for seventeen successive years, during the last of which he resided in Philadelphia.

Mc Kean was a trustee of the loan-office of New Castle County for twelve years, and in 1765 he was elected to the Stamp Act Congress. Had the votes in this body been taken according to the population of the states that were represented, that of Delaware would have been insignificant, but, through the influence of McKean, each state was given an equal voice. He was one of the most influential members of the Stamp Act Congress, serving on the committee that drew the memorial to the House of Lords and Commons and, with John Rutledge and Philip Livingston, revised its proceedings. When business was concluded on the last day of its session, and Timothy Ruggles, the president of the body, as well as a few other timid members, refused to sign the memorial of rights and grievances, McKean arose, and insisted that the president give his reasons for his refusal. After a pause Ruggles remarked, "*it was against his conscience.*" McKean then rang the changes on the word "conscience" so loudly and so long that a challenge was given and accepted between himself and Ruggles in the presence of the congress. Ruggles hastily left the next morning at daybreak, so that the duel could not take place.

In July of the same year McKean was appointed sole notary of the lower counties of Delaware and judge of the court of common pleas, and of the orphans' court of New Castle. In November of 1765 he ordered that all the proceedings of this court be recorded on un-stamped paper; this was the first court in the colonies that established such a rule. He was collector of the port of New Castle in 1771, Speaker of the House of Representatives in 1772. In 1774 he was elected a member of the Continental Congress.

In September 1774, he had just married his second wife, Sarah Armitage of New Castle. His first wife, Mary Borden, the daughter of Joseph Borden of Bordentown, New Jersey, and sister of the wife of Francis Hopkinson, died in 1773, leaving him with six children. He would father five more children with his second wife.

He was the only member that served in Congress from its 1774 opening until the Treaty of Paris, representing Delaware until 1783. Mc Kean was chief justice of Pennsylvania from July 1777 until 1799; he also occupied a seat in the Delaware legislature until 1799. During Congressional session in 1776 he was a member of the committee to state the rights of the colonies, as well as a member of the secret committee to contract for the importation of arms. He was also selected to prepare and digest the draft of the Articles of Confederation to be entered into between the colonies, which he signed on behalf of Delaware in 1777. He superintended the finances and a variety of important measures in the Continental Congress.

At the Second Congress, McKean was a true fighter for independence. Since the Stamp Act of 1765, he had opposed British rule. He believed that the crown had *"no right to regulate American affairs in any way"*. In June 1776, McKean returned to Delaware and gained authority for its delegates to vote for independence. Although particularly active in procuring the Declaration to which his name is subscribed in the original instrument, he does not, through a mistake on the part of the printer, appear as a subscriber in the copy published in the Journal of The Continental Congress. A few days after McKean cast his vote, he left Congress to command a battalion of troops to assist Washington at Perth Amboy, New Jersey. He was not available when most Signers placed their signatures on the Declaration on August 2, 1776. There is considerable question as to when McKean actually signed the Declaration of Independence. He certainly did not do this in August, and although he claimed in old age that he attached his name some time in 1776, his name did not appear on the printed copy that was authenticated on January 17, 1777. It is assumed that he signed after that date while attending Congress in Philadelphia.

In July 1776, he was chairman of the delegates from New York, New Jersey and Pennsylvania, and in the same year chairman of the Pennsylvania committees of safety and inspection as well as the Philadelphia committee of observation. A few days after signing the Declaration of Independence he marched at the head of a battalion to Perth Amboy, New Jersey to re-enforce General Washington until the arrival of the flying camp. On his return to Dover he found a committee awaiting him to urge him to prepare the Constitution of Delaware, which he drew up on the night of his arrival, and which was unanimously adopted by the assembly the next day.

In 1777, while acting in the double capacity of president of Delaware and chief justice of Pennsylvania, he describes himself in a letter to his intimate friend, John Adams, as

> *"hunted like a fox by the enemy, compelled to remove my family five times in three months, and at last fixed them in a little log-house on the banks of the Susquehanna, but they were soon obliged to move again on account of the incursions of the Indians."*

As a delegate to the Continental Congress he was present when the Articles of Confederation were ratified on March 1, 1781. By virtue of this ratification the ever fluid Continental Congress ceased to exist and on March 2nd *"The United States in Congress Assembled"* was placed at the head of each page of the Official Journal of Congress. The United States of America, which was conceived on July 2, 1776, had finally been born in 1781 under the Presidency of Samuel Huntington.

By May of 1781, President Huntington's health began to fail. Huntington, despite the pleadings of the delegates, tendered his resignation as President on July 6, 1781. The United States in Congress Assembled Journals reported:

> *"The President having informed the United States in Congress assembled, that his ill state of health" ... not permit him to continue longer in the exercise of the duties of that office".*

Congress held off electing a new President until July 10th in the hope that Huntington would recover and reconsider. On July 10th Delegate Thomas McKean was elected as the second President of the United States in Congress Assembled and was first to be elected under the Articles of Confederation, as President Huntington assumed the position as the former President of the Continental Congress.

McKean was president of the United States in Congress Assembled in 1781, and in that capacity received Washington's dispatches announcing the surrender of Cornwallis.

So revered was this office by Thomas McKean that the Presidency was used to turn down his party's 1804 nomination for Vice President under Thomas Jefferson saying:

> *"... President of the United States in Congress Assembled in the year of 1781 (a proud year for Americans) equaled any merit or pretensions of mine and cannot now be increased by the office of Vice President."*

Although McKean's tenure as US President was quite brief, it was an eventful period in US History, beginning with Samuel Johnson the first President of the United States in Congress Assembled duly elected under the Articles of Confederation declining the office with the Journals recording July 10th:

> *Mr. [Samuel] Johnston having declined to accept the office of President, and offered such reasons as were satisfactory, the House proceeded to another election; and, the ballots being taken, the hon. Thomas McKean was elected.*

The reasons for Johnson's refusal to not serve are unclear but some historians claim the letter of July 30th 1781 clearly indicated he was in no position to accept an office which offered no salary:

> *Having no prospect of being relieved or supplied with money for my expenses and my disorder, which abated a little on the first approach of warm weather, returning so as to render me of little use in Congress I left Philadelphia the 14th, for which I hope I shall be held excusable by this state.*

North Carolina with this decline lost her opportunity to declare one of her sons held the Presidency of the United States in Congress Assembled.

McKean's Presidency is most curious because he was elected as a delegate of Delaware but was serving as Chief Justice of Pennsylvania. The opposition of many Pennsylvanians against his Presidency was vicious due to his affiliation with both States and maintaining that in Congress he represented Delaware. Born in Pennsylvania, he remained steadfast in his right to serve in both positions and did not resign the Presidency until it was time to take his seat on the bench. The October 23, 1781 Journals of the United States in Congress Assembled reports:

> *The secretary laid before Congress a letter from the President in the words following: Whereupon,*

Sir: I must beg you to remind Congress, that when they did me the honor of electing me President, and before I assumed the Chair, I informed them, that as Chief Justice of Pensylvania, I should be under the necessity of attending the Supreme Court of that State, the latter end of September, or at farthest in October. That court will be held to-day; I must therefore request, that they will be pleased to proceed to the choice of another President.

I am, sir, with much respect, your most obedient humble servant,

Thos. McKean.

This was at first accepted with the vote for a new President being postponed until the following day. Congress did not elect a new President on the 23rd instead they required McKean to continue his service as President until new Congress convened in November. The Summary of his Presidency is as follows:

1781 - July 9 Elects Samuel Johnston president of Congress. **July 10** Elects Thomas McKean President of Congress upon Samuel Johnston's declining the office; instructs Thomas Barclay, Vice-Consul to France. **July 11** Authorizes Robert Morris to negotiate loans in Spain and Portugal. **July 12** Revokes John Adams' commission to negotiate commercial treaty with Britain. **July 16** Reinstates General Lachlan McIntosh. **July 20** Receives report on claims to the New Hampshire Grants. **July 23** Endorses creation of a relief fund for South Carolina and Georgia refugees. **July 25** Commends General Nathanael Greene. **July 26** Appoints committee to confer with General Washington on troop arrangements "*for the ensuing year.*" **July 27** Receives plan for a consular convention from the minister of France. **July 31** Orders superintendent of finance and a member of the Board of War to headquarters to confer with General Washington; approves appropriation for the support of three Delaware Native American youths at the Princeton college.

August 1 Orders preparation of a plan to reform the Post Office. **August 3** Reads New York memorial on the New Hampshire Grants. **August 7** Requests Connecticut to revoke commissions authorizing the seizure of property on Long Island; authorizes committee to confer with Vermont agents on their claim to independence. **August 10** Elects Robert R. Livingston secretary for foreign affairs; rejects motion to cede the United States claim to navigation of the Mississippi. **August 14** Authorizes the importation of salt. **August 16** Adopts instructions to John Adams for negotiating a Dutch alliance. **August 17** Instructs committee to confer with Vermont agents despite credentials dispute. **August 20-21** Declares Vermont acceptance of prescribed boundaries as a condition to acceptance of Vermont independence. **August 21** Enlarges General Washington's prisoner exchange authority. **August 23** Exhorts states to maintain their representation in Congress. **August 24** Directs superintendent of finance "*to make provision for support of the civil list.*" **August 29** Debates motion to retaliate against the execution of Colonel Isaac Hayne; resolves to appoint an agent of marine to exercise the duties of a secretary of marine. **August 31** Authorizes recognition of Philippe de L'Etombe as French Consul to the New England states.

September 3 Receives account of John Laurens' mission to France. **September 4** Directs Washington to investigate British treatment of prisoners. **September 5** Orders inquiry into General Robert Howe's southern command. **September 7** Recognizes Philippe Letombe's appointment as French Consul to New England; appoints Robert Morris agent of marine. **September 10** Recognizes Jean Holker's appointment as French Consul to Mid-Atlantic states; orders New Jersey and Pennsylvania militia call. **September 11** Adopts new treasury ordinance. **September 12** Places control of US navy under the agent of marine. **September 13** Sets day of thanksgiving. **September 18** Orders retaliation for execution of Isaac Hayne; plans retaliation for enemy mistreatment of prisoners. **September 19** Orders Delaware militia call; appoints treasury officers. **September 20** Reorganizes hospital department. **September 21** Receives French Minister's report on mediation offers and peace overtures. **September 24** Appoints William Irvine to Fort Pitt command. **September 25** Receives memorial from Spanish Agent Rendon; issues reassurance to northern Native Americans.

October 1 Sets salaries for secretaries of war and marine. **October 5** Appoints Thomas Barclay Consul to France; discharges Delaware and Pennsylvania militia. **October 11-12** Debates Yorktown campaign plans. **October 16-17** Debates exercise of Continental jurisdiction over claims within Virginia's western lands. **October 19** Reforms Post Office department. **October 23** Accepts Thomas McKean's resignation as president (to remain until new Congress November 5). **October 24** Receives news of Yorktown victory; observes "*divine service (suitable to the occasion)*" conducted by Chaplain George Duffield. October 26 Adopts thanksgiving proclamation; rejects Virginia motion to curtail committee investigation of land companies' western claims. **October 29** Thanks American and French victors at Yorktown; thanks General Nathanael Greene and southern army. **October 30** Appoints General Benjamin Lincoln Secretary at War; sets $8 million fiscal quota for 1782.

November 1 Endorses General Greene's plans to treat with Cherokee and Chickasaw Native Americans. **November 2** Apportions states' 1782 fiscal quotas; authorizes acceptance of quartermaster certificates in payment of quotas.

McKean was also a member of the Pennsylvania Constitutional Convention of 1790, and from 1799 until 1808 was the governor of that state. His policy as a leader of the Republican Party paved the way for the accession of Thomas Jefferson to the presidency.

He became a member of the Pennsylvania Society of the Cincinnati in 1785, and was subsequently its vice-president. Princeton gave him the degree of L.L.D. in 1781;

Dartmouth presented the same honor in 1782, The University of Pennsylvania gave him the degree of A.M. in 1763, and L.L.D. in 1785. With Professor John Wilson he published "*Commentaries on the Constitution of the United States*" (London, 1790).

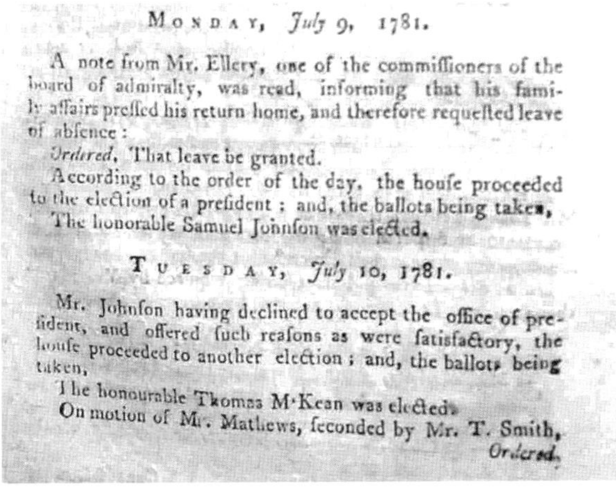

MONDAY, *July* 9, 1781.

A note from Mr. Ellery, one of the commiſſioners of the board of admiralty, was read, informing that his family affairs preſſed his return home, and therefore requeſted leave of abſence:

Ordered, That leave be granted.

According to the order of the day, the houſe proceeded to the election of a preſident; and, the ballots being taken,

The honorable Samuel Johnſon was elected.

TUESDAY, *July* 10, 1781.

Mr. Johnſon having declined to accept the office of preſident, and offered ſuch reaſons as were ſatisfactory, the houſe proceeded to another election; and, the ballots being taken,

The honourable Thomas M'Kean was elected.

On motion of Mr. Mathews, ſeconded by Mr. T. Smith,

Ordered,

18th Century Journal of the United States in Congress Assembled recording Samuel Johnson's election as President of the United States in Congress Assembled on July 9th, 1781. The Journal also records Mr. Johnson's decision to turn down the office and the election of Thomas McKean of Delaware as the Second President of the United States in Congress Assembled. – *Courtesy of the Klos Family*

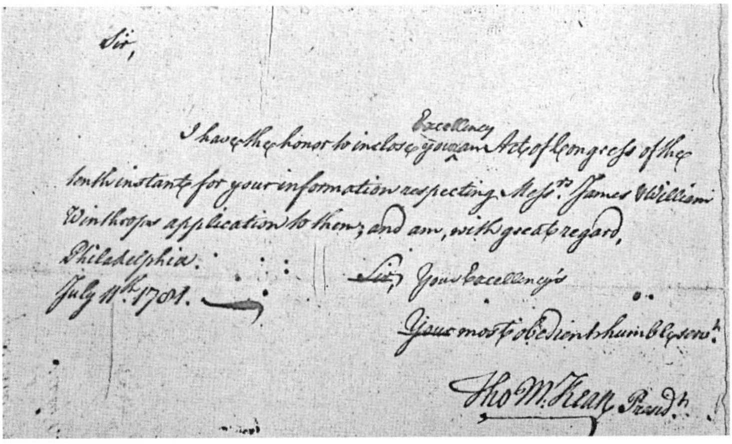

Sir,

I have the honor to inclose your Excellency an Act of Congress of the tenth instant for your information respecting Messrs. James & William Winthrops application to them, and am, with great regard,

Philadelphia:
July 11th 1781.

Sir, Your Excellency's
Your most obedient humble serv.t
Tho M:Kean Presid.t

July 11, 1781 Thomas Mc. Kean as President of the United States in Congress Assembled – *Courtesy of the Library of Congress*

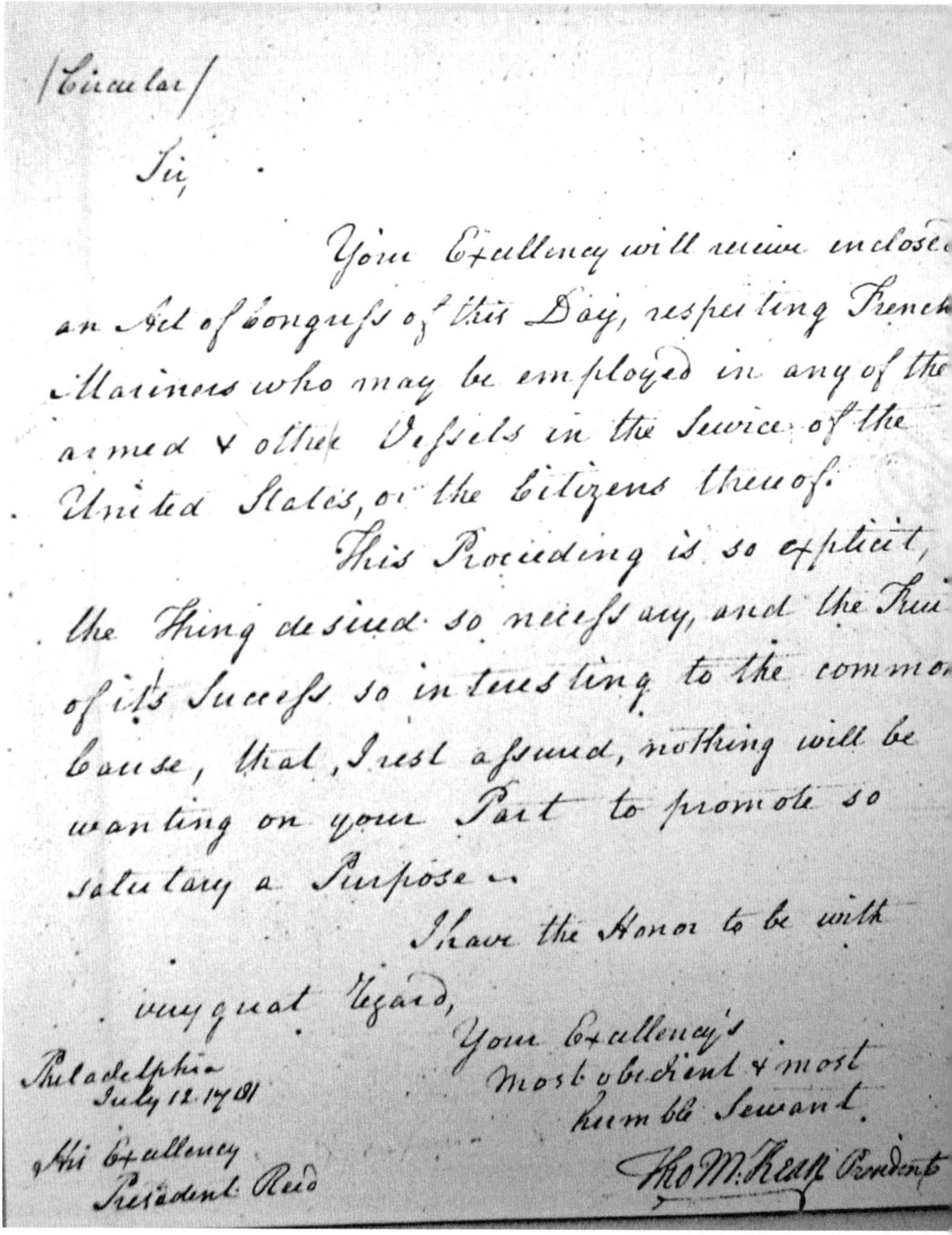
(Circular)

Sir,

Your Excellency will receive inclosed an Act of Congress of this Day, respecting French Mariners who may be employed in any of the armed & other Vessels in the Service of the United States, or the Citizens thereof.

This Proceeding is so explicit, the Thing desired so necessary, and the Pre[illegible] of its Success so interesting to the common Cause, that, I rest assured, nothing will be wanting on your Part to promote so salutary a Purpose.

I have the Honor to be with very great Regard,

Your Excellency's
most obedient & most
humble Servant.
Thos M:Kean President

Philadelphia
July 12. 1781

His Excellency
President Reed

July 12, 1781 Circular letter to Joseph Reed transmitting Acts of Congress as President of the United States in Congress Assembled – *Courtesy of the Library of Congress*

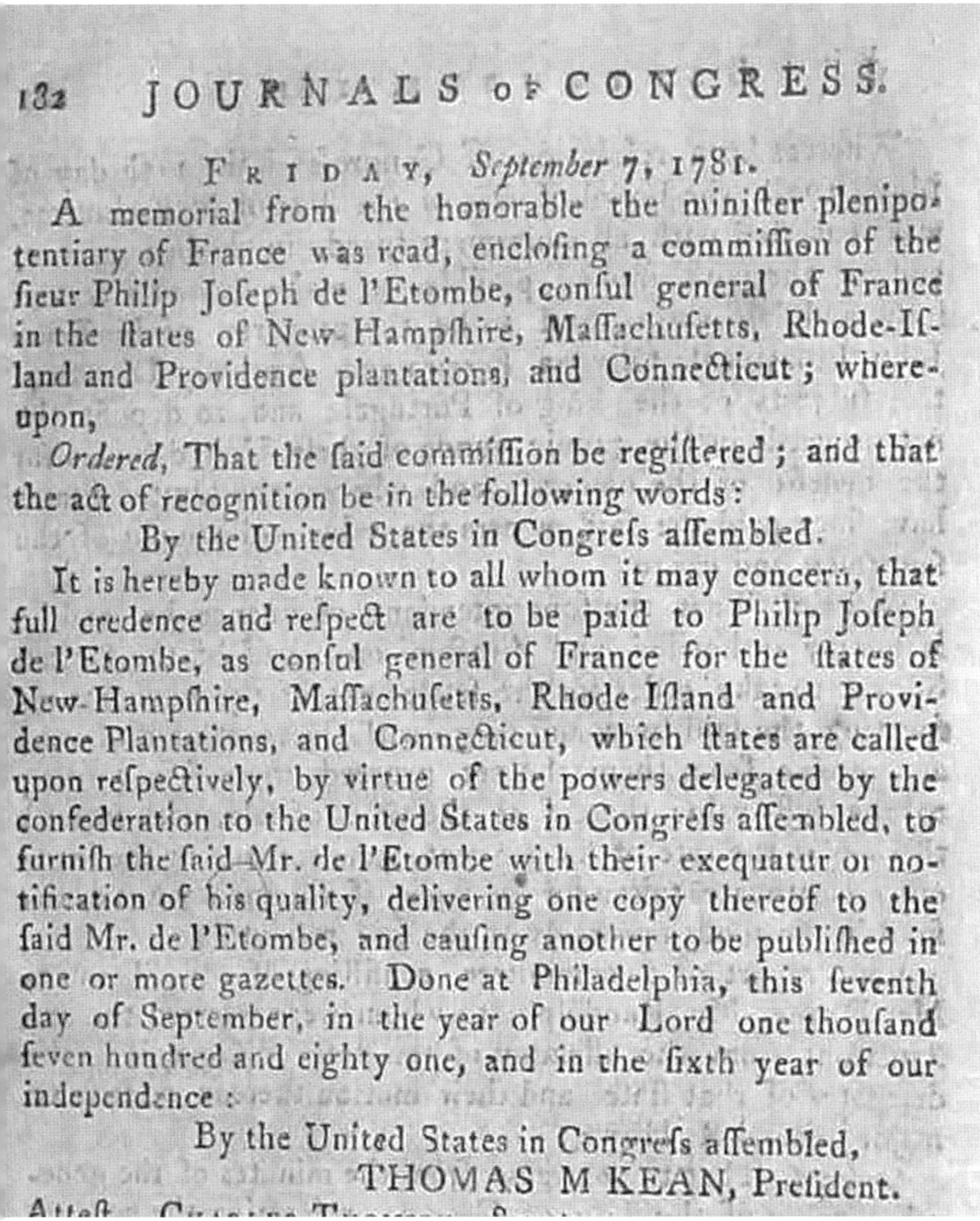
182 JOURNALS OF CONGRESS.

FRIDAY, *September* 7, 1781.

A memorial from the honorable the miniſter plenipotentiary of France was read, encloſing a commiſſion of the ſieur Philip Joſeph de l'Etombe, conſul general of France in the ſtates of New-Hampſhire, Maſſachuſetts, Rhode-Iſland and Providence plantations, and Connecticut; whereupon,

Ordered, That the ſaid commiſſion be regiſtered; and that the act of recognition be in the following words:

By the United States in Congreſs aſſembled.

It is hereby made known to all whom it may concern, that full credence and reſpect are to be paid to Philip Joſeph de l'Etombe, as conſul general of France for the ſtates of New-Hampſhire, Maſſachuſetts, Rhode Iſland and Providence Plantations, and Connecticut, which ſtates are called upon reſpectively, by virtue of the powers delegated by the confederation to the United States in Congreſs aſſembled, to furniſh the ſaid Mr. de l'Etombe with their exequatur or notification of his quality, delivering one copy thereof to the ſaid Mr. de l'Etombe, and cauſing another to be publiſhed in one or more gazettes. Done at Philadelphia, this ſeventh day of September, in the year of our Lord one thouſand ſeven hundred and eighty one, and in the ſixth year of our independence:

By the United States in Congreſs aſſembled,

THOMAS M'KEAN, Preſident.

18th Century Journal of the United States in Congress Assembled recording a September 7th, 1781 order by the United States in Congress Assembled
Thomas McKean, President. – *Courtesy of the Klos Family*

CHAPTER NINE

Portrait of John Hanson from
Maryland State Archives

JOHN HANSON

3rd President of the United States
in Congress Assembled
November 5, 1781 to November 4, 1782

John Hanson was born in Charles County, Maryland in 1715 and died in Oxen Hills, Prince George County, Maryland on November 22, 1783. He received an English education, and was a member of the Maryland House of Delegates nearly every year from 1757 until 1781. He moved to Frederick County in 1773 and was an energetic patriot, who in 1775 became treasurer of the county. About that time he was commissioned by the Maryland convention to establish a gun-lock factory at Frederick.

On October 9th, 1776 he was part of a committee empowered to call on the Maryland Troops in New Jersey, "*with power to appoint officers and to encourage the re-enlistment of the Maryland militia*" as General Washington's military losses in New York and New Jersey were substantial and desertion was rampant.

John Hanson was elected a delegate to the United States in Congress Assembled in 1781 and served until his death in 1783. Delegate Hanson was instrumental in persuading the Maryland Legislature to ratify the Articles of Confederation, which created the Perpetual Union of the United States. On November 5, 1781 Hanson was elected President of the United States in Congress Assembled:

> *The following members attended from the State of New Hampshire, Mr. [Samuel] Livermore,Massachusetts, Mr. [James] Lovell, [George] Partridge, [Samuel] Osgood,Rhode Island, Mr. [Daniel] Mowry, [James Mitchell] Varnum, Connecticut, Mr. [Richard] Law, New Jersey, Mr. [Abraham] Clark, [Elias] Boudinot, Pennsylvania, Mr. [Joseph] Montgomery, [Samuel John] Atlee, T[homas] Smith, Maryland, Mr. [John] Hanson, [Daniel of St. Thomas] Jenifer, [Daniel] Carroll, Virginia, Mr. [James] Madison, [Edmund] Randolph, Jo[seph] Jones, North Carolina, Mr. [Benjamin] Hawkins, South Carolina, Mr. [Arthur] Middletown, [John] Mathews, [Thomas] Bee, [Nicholas] Eveleigh, [Isaac] Motte, Georgia, Mr. [Edward] Telfair, N[oble] W[imberly] Jones.*
>
> *Their credentials being read, Congress proceeded to the election of a President; and the ballots being taken, the honble. John Hanson was elected.*

President Hanson served one year as US President, beginning November 5th of that year, and in that capacity gave General Washington the thanks of Congress for the victory at Yorktown. Due to this Victory and the rise of the Executive Departments under Huntington and McKean, his burdens were much more manageable.

President Hanson was the first to utilize the title President of the United States in Congress Assembled after his name in an official resolution of Congress. Thomas McKean signed his resolutions, United States in Congress Assembled, Thomas McKean President. The Journals of the United States in Congress Assembled report that on MONDAY, SEPTEMBER 16, 1782 the following resolution was enacted for the exchange of Prisoners with Great Britain, whereby John Hanson signed his name as President of the United States in Congress Assembled:

> *THE UNITED STATES IN CONGRESS ASSEMBLED.*
>
> *To all people who shall see these presents, send greeting.*
>
> *Whereas justice and humanity and the practice of civilized nations, require that the calamities and asperities [SEAL] John Hanson Chas. Thomson, Secy. of war should as far as possible be mitigated; and we being disposed for that benevolent purpose to accede to a general cartel between the United States of America and the British nation, for the exchange, subsistence and better treatment of all prisoners of war: ....*
>
> *In testimony whereof we have caused these our letters to be made patent, and the great seal of the United States of America to be thereunto affixed. Witness his Excellency John Hanson, President of the United States in Congress assembled, the 16th day of September, in the year of our Lord one thousand seven hundred and eighty-two, and of our sovereignty and independence the seventh.*

As President of United States in Congress Assembled, Hanson was responsible for initiating a number of programs that helped America gain a world position. During his tenure the first consular service was established, a post office department was initiated, a national bank was chartered, progress was made towards taking the first census and a uniform system of coinage was adopted. As "President", Hanson also signed a treaty with Holland affirming the indebtedness of the United States for a loan from that country. In addition, he signed all laws, regulations, official papers and letters. His presidency's chronology is as follows:

1781 - November 5 New Congress convenes; elects John Hanson president. **November 8** Authorizes Board of War to prosecute spies under the Articles of War. **November 9** Restricts travel of Yorktown prisoners on parole. **November 12** Repeals resolve accepting quartermaster certificates in payment of quotas. **November 14** Urges states to maintain representation; sets date for hearing Connecticut-Pennsylvania boundary dispute. **November 20** Augments authority of secretary of marine. **November 23** Recommends that states legislate to punish violations of international law. **November 28** Holds audience with General Washington.

December 4 Adopts ordinance on "*captures on water.*" **December 5** Receives New York protest against Congressional resolves on Vermont. **December 10** Exhorts states to complete troop quotas. **December 11** Calls states to take census "*of the white inhabitants thereof.*" **December 13** Observes day of thanksgiving. **December 17** Appeals to the states for men and money. **December 19** Orders placing supernumerary generals on half pay. **December 20** Authorizes exchange of Governor Thomas Burke. **December 31** Adopts ordinance incorporating Bank of North America.

1782 - January 2 Exhorts states to suppress trade with the enemy. **January 3** Reforms medical department. **January 8** Amends ordinance on captures on water; rejects motion to enlarge peace ultimatum. **January 9** Authorizes negotiation of consular convention with France. **January 10** Reforms inspector general's department. **January 17** Investigates suspicious Silas Deane letters on conciliating Britain. **January 22** Instructs peace commissioners to communicate informal demands on fisheries and boundaries. **January 25** Amends consular convention. **January 28** Enlarges duties of Secretary Charles Thomson to relieve president of Congress. **January 29** Advised of diminution of French aid.

February 1 Instructs Benjamin Franklin on repayment of Dutch loan obtained for United States by France. **February 8** Authorizes Franklin to borrow additional 12 million livres from France. **February 11** Authorizes export of tobacco to New York by Yorktown "*capitulants*"; rejects appeal to permit states to clothe own Continental troops. **February 18** Authorizes Washington to negotiate general prisoner exchange. **February 20** Seeks authorization to apportion war expenses in contravention of Articles of Confederation quota formula.

February 21 Authorizes establishment of a mint. **February 22** Reorganizes department of foreign affairs. **February 23** Authorizes exchange of Cornwallis for Henry Laurens. **February 26** Amends ordinance on captures on water. **February 27** Adopts plan for settlement of state accounts.

March 1 Sets conditions for recognizing Vermont independence. **March 7** Revises rules of Court of Appeals. **March 11** Orders settlement of Bon Home Richard prize claims; refers Native American petition to New York. **March 15** Drafts fiscal appeal to the states. **March 19** Adopts fast day proclamation. **March 21** Holds audience with General Washington. **March 27** Orders study of Continental Army staffing needs. **March 30** Adopts measures for curtailing prisoner-of-war escapes.

April 1 Rejects fiscal quota reduction appeal. **April 3-4** Debates Vermont compliance with independent statehood conditions. **April 8** Revises paymaster regulations. **April 9** Orders submission of comprehensive army returns. **April 15** Rejects motion to elect a vice-president upon the disability of the president; elects Daniel Carroll "*chairman*" during the illness of President Hanson. **April 18** Rejects motion to require delegates to disclose conflicts of interest on land claim issues. **April 20** Debates Vermont compliance with independent statehood conditions. **April 23** Recommends pensions for disabled troops; orders reduction of supernumerary officers. **April 29** Endorses Washington's proposals for retaliation against the death of Joshua Huddy. **April 30** Endorses John Jay's conduct of negotiations with the court of Madrid.

May 1 Warns states of British plans to divide their enemies with proposals of separate peace; debates western land cessions and motion to disclose delegates' conflicts of interest. **May 4** Orders measures for the protection of American shipping. **May 8** Opposes sending William Carmichael to the court of Portugal. **May 13** Holds audience with French minister to celebrate birth of a Dauphin. **May 14** Denies emissary of Sir Guy Carleton passport to Philadelphia. **May 21** Authorizes state authorities to curb trade with the enemy. **May 22** Sends delegations to states to solicit compliance with requisitions. **May 24** Reviews superintendent of finance report on status of US credit abroad. **May 27** Exhorts states to maintain representation in Congress; instructs Francis Dana to delay presenting his credentials to the court of Russia. **May 28** Receives French report on peace overtures. **May 31** Reaffirms opposition to separate peace negotiations.

June 5 Orders study of proposal to enlist German prisoners of war. **June 7** Rescinds work-release program for British prisoners of war. **June 12** Revises regulations for naval courts-martial. **June 14** Endorses proposals for return of South Carolina exiles. **June 17** Calls for biannual inspection of the operation of the executive departments. **June 20** Adopts great seal for the United States in

Congress assembled. **June 21** Exhorts states to curb trade with the enemy. **June 24-27** Debates proposals for resolution of the Connecticut-Pennsylvania boundary dispute. **June 27** Receives report from the congressional delegation to the southern states. **June 28** Endorses General Greene's rejection of truce proposal in South Carolina.

July 2 Endorses superintendent of finance's recommendation against appointing consuls in the West Indies. **July 3** Complains against Spanish release of British prisoners of war. **July 10** Adopts ordinance regulating distribution of prizes. **July 11** Places moratorium on promotion or appointment of Continental officers. **July 17** Adopts ordinance to prevent illicit trade with the enemy. **July 18** Receives report from the congressional delegation to the northern states; orders measures to stop mail robberies. **July 23** Revises hospital department regulations. **July 31** Debates recommendation for acceptance of western land cessions as a preliminary to restoring the public credit of the United States.

August 1 Reorganizes adjutant general's department. **August 5** Receives Robert Morris' funding plan. **August 6** Revises John Jay's diplomatic instructions. **August 7** Reorganizes Continental Army. **August 9** Receives British commissioners' announcement that peace negotiations have begun at Paris. **August 12** Authorizes Washington to negotiate prisoner exchange. **August 14** Suspends inquiry into General Gates' conduct at Camden. **August 15** Rejects move to repeal peace commissioners' instructions to be guided by French court. **August 16-20** Debates Massachusetts' petition to include fisheries claim in peace ultimatum. **August 23** Appoints judges to hear Connecticut-Pennsylvania boundary dispute. **August 27** Debates Kentucky statehood petition. **August 29** Orders purchase of ship for packet service to Europe.

September 3 Orders resumption of postal service to the Carolinas and Georgia; presents ship *America* to France. **September 4** Sets fiscal quota for the immediate payment of interest on the public debt. **September 6** Debates proposal to appeal to the states to cede western lands. **September 9** Suspends issuance of bills of exchange to pay loan office certificate interest; instructs Washington on prisoner cartel. **September 10** Sets state fiscal quotas. **September 12** Endorses Robert Aitken's proposal to print an American edition of the Bible. **September 14** Authorizes solicitation of $4 million in foreign loans. **September 16** Commissions Washington to negotiate prisoner exchange. **September 17** Refuses to accept Henry Laurens' resignation as peace commissioner. **September 19-20** Debates report that Henry Laurens improperly petitioned parliament while imprisoned. **September 24** Receives information from the Chevalier de La Luzerne on recent peace maneuvers in Europe. **September 28** Adopts plan of a treaty of amity and commerce with Sweden.

October 1 Rejects New Jersey's plan to retain Continental revenues for the payment of the state's Continental troops. **October 3** Reassures France on US commitment to military preparedness and to its no separate peace pledge. **October 10** Appeals to Rhode Island and Georgia to adopt impost amendment. **October 11** Sets day of thanksgiving and prayer. **October 14-15** Debates promotion of general officers. **October 16** Sets fiscal quota for 1783; instructs Washington on prisoner exchange negotiations. **October 18** Requests Washington to decide fate of Wyoming garrison; sets state fiscal quotas; adopts Post Office ordinance. **October 23** Reorganizes quartermaster department. **October 28** Adopts supplemental Post Office ordinance; recommends suspension of plans to execute Charles Asgill in retaliation for the death of Joshua Huddy. **October 29** Accepts New York's western land cession.

November 1 Refers investigation of Alexander Gillon to the superintendent of finance. **November 2** Committee on Native American affairs confers with Catawba Native American delegation.

After his eventful Presidency, Hanson's health failed and compelled him to retire from public life. Hanson died on November 15, 1783, at the age of 68 in Oxen Hills, Prince George County, Maryland. John Hanson's contributions to the government under the Articles of Confederation were absorbed by the new federal government.

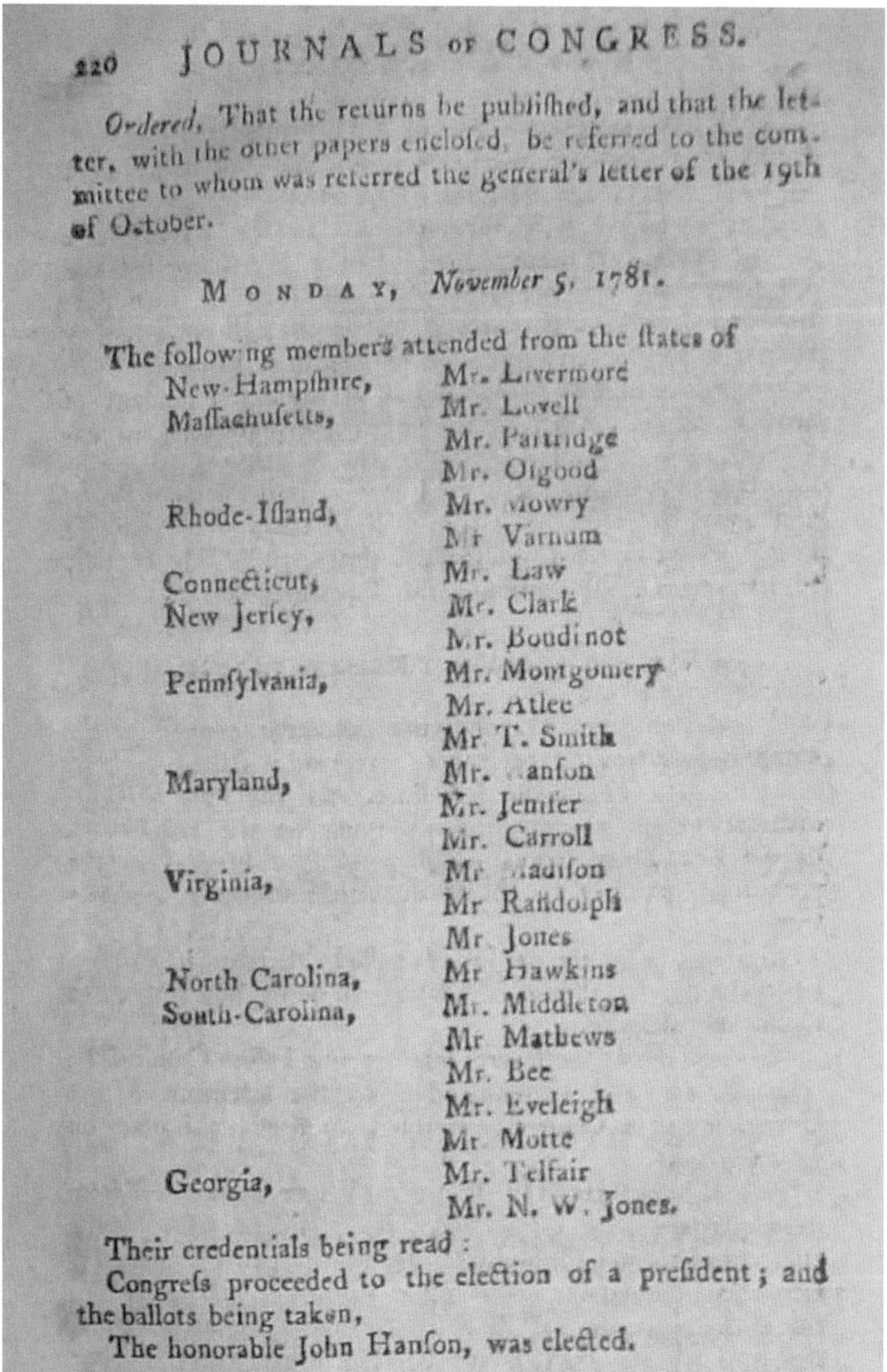

220 JOURNALS of CONGRESS.

Ordered, That the returns be publiſhed, and that the letter, with the other papers encloſed, be referred to the committee to whom was referred the general's letter of the 19th of October.

MONDAY, *November* 5, 1781.

The following members attended from the ſtates of

New-Hampſhire,	Mr. Livermore
Maſſachuſetts,	Mr. Lovell
	Mr. Partridge
	Mr. Oſgood
Rhode-Iſland,	Mr. Mowry
	Mr Varnum
Connecticut,	Mr. Law
New Jerſey,	Mr. Clark
	Mr. Boudinot
Pennſylvania,	Mr. Montgomery
	Mr. Atlee
	Mr T. Smith
Maryland,	Mr. Hanſon
	Mr. Jenifer
	Mr. Carroll
Virginia,	Mr Madiſon
	Mr Randolph
	Mr Jones
North Carolina,	Mr Hawkins
South-Carolina,	Mr. Middleton
	Mr Mathews
	Mr. Bee
	Mr. Eveleigh
	Mr Motte
Georgia,	Mr. Telfair
	Mr. N. W. Jones.

Their credentials being read:

Congreſs proceeded to the election of a preſident; and the ballots being taken,

The honorable John Hanſon, was elected.

18th Century Journal of the United States in Congress Assembled dated November 5th, 1781 of the Roll Call and election of John Hanson as the 3rd President of the United States in Congress Assembled. – *Courtesy of the Klos Family*

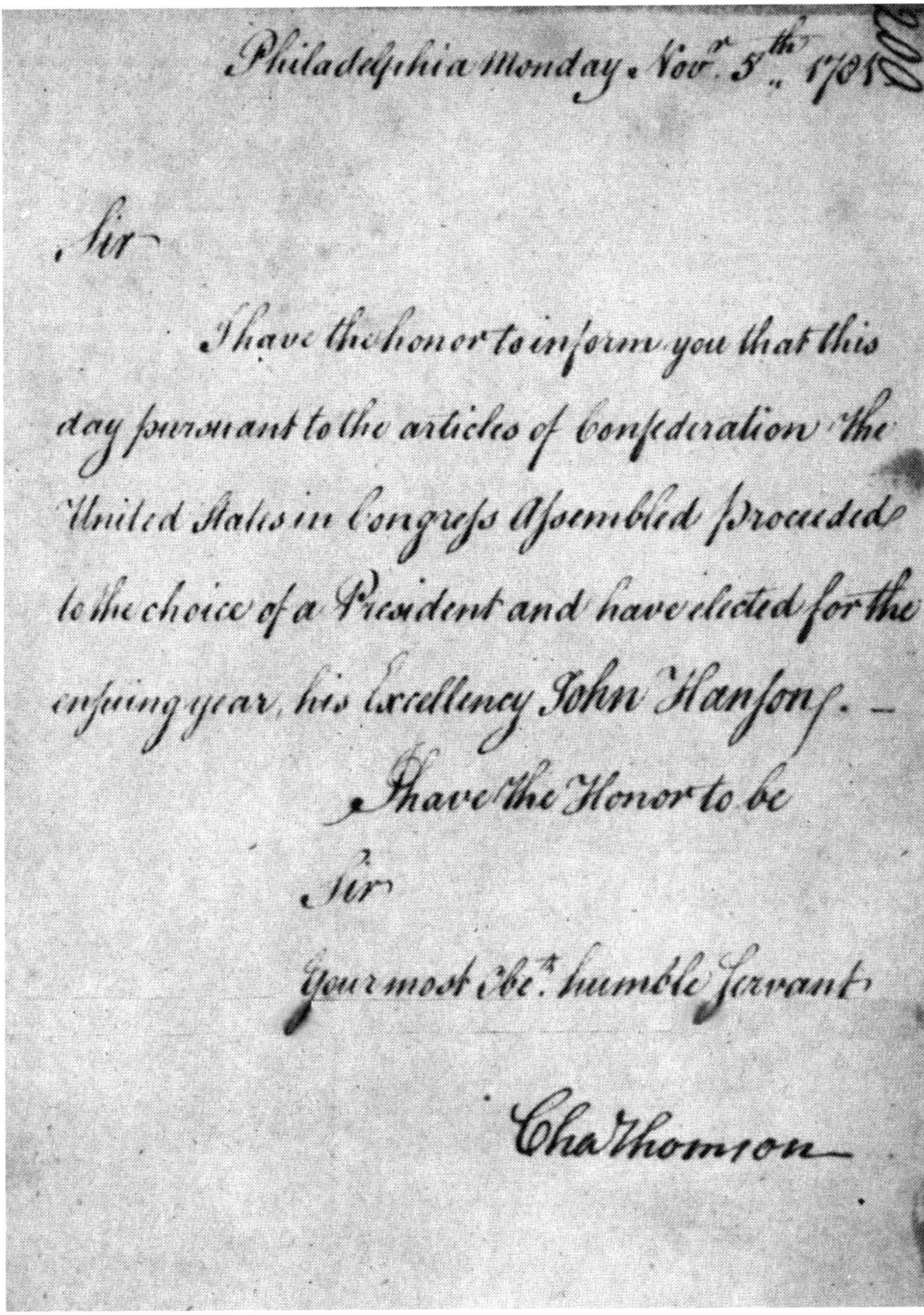

Philadelphia Monday Novr. 5th 1781

Sir

I have the honor to inform you that this day pursuant to the articles of Confederation the United States in Congress Assembled proceeded to the choice of a President and have elected for the ensuing year, his Excellency John Hanson. —

I have the Honor to be

Sir

Your most Obedt. humble Servant

Chas Thomson

November 5, 1781 Circular letter announcing the election of John Hanson as the 3rd President of the United States in Congress Assembled signed by Charles Thomson – *Courtesy of the Library of Congress*

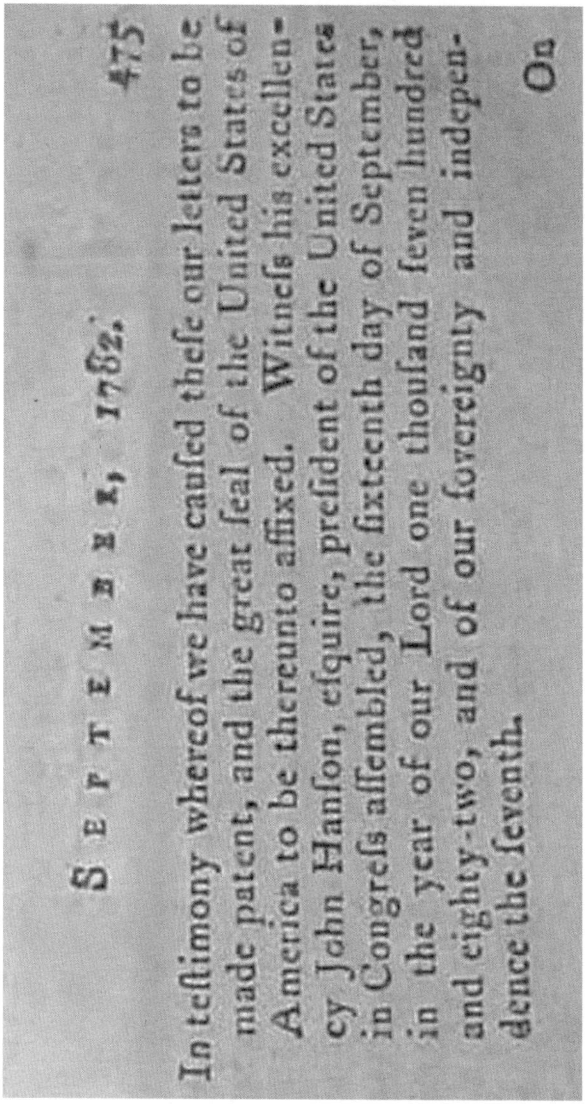
SEPTEMBER, 1782. 475

In teſtimony whereof we have cauſed theſe our letters to be made patent, and the great ſeal of the United States of America to be thereunto affixed. Witneſs his excellency John Hanſon, eſquire, preſident of the United States in Congreſs aſſembled, the ſixteenth day of September, in the year of our Lord one thouſand ſeven hundred and eighty-two, and of our ſovereignty and independence the ſeventh.

On

18th Century Journal of the United States in Congress Assembled dated September 16th, 1781 of a resolution authorizing George Washington to negotiate terms of Peace with Great Britain a month after his Victory at Yorktown "Witness his Excellency JohnHanson, esquire, President of the United States in Congress assembled". – *Courtesy of the Klos Family*

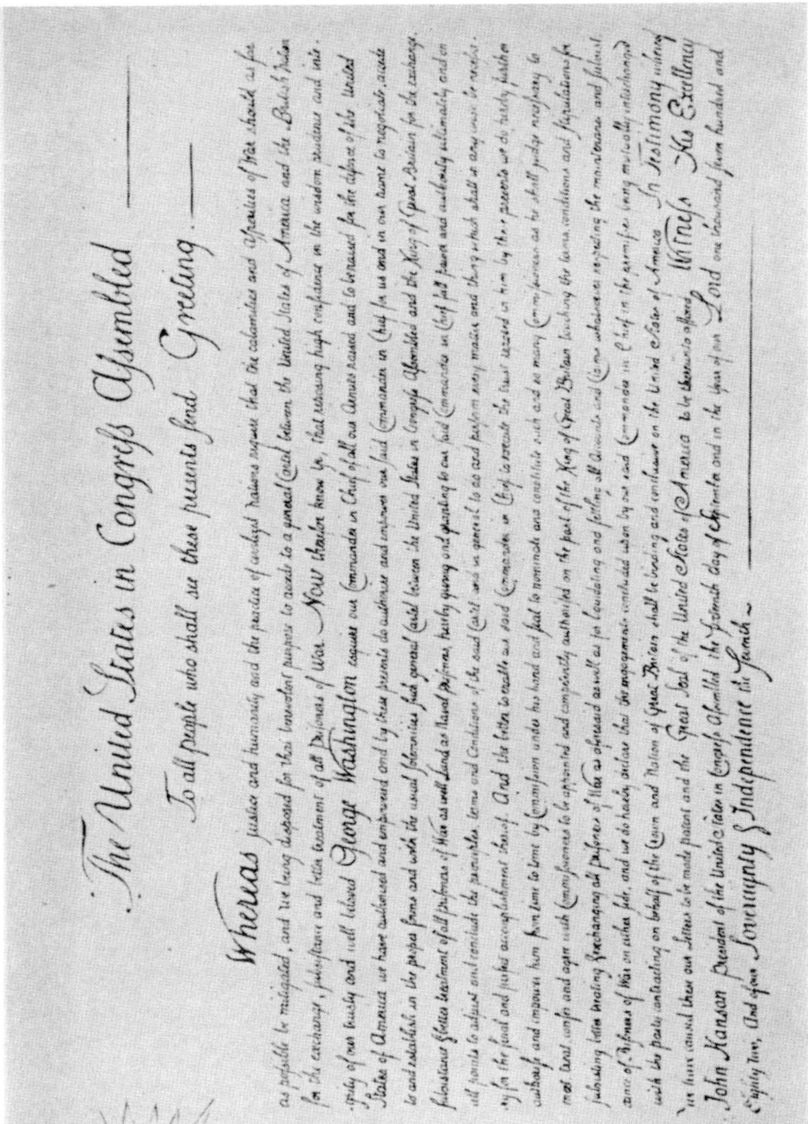

The United States in Congress Assembled

To all people who shall see these presents send Greeting.

Whereas justice and humanity and the practice of civilized Nations require that the calamities and Asperities of War should as far as possible be mitigated, and we being disposed for that benevolent purpose to accede to a general Cartel between the United States of America and the British Nation for the exchange, subsistance and better treatment of all Prisoners of War. Now therefore know ye, that reposing high confidence in the wisdom prudence and integrity of our trusty and well beloved George Washington esquire our Commander in Chief of all our Armies raised and to be raised for the defence of the United States of America we have authorised and empowered and by these presents do authorise and empower our said Commander in Chief for us and in our name to negotiate, accede to and establish in the proper forms and with the usual solemnities such general Cartel between the United States in Congress Assembled and the King of Great Britain for the exchange, subsistance & better treatment of all prisoners of War as well Land as Naval prisoners, hereby giving and granting to our said Commander in Chief full power and authority ultimately and on all points to adjust and conclude the principles, terms and Conditions of the said Cartel, and in general to do and perform every matter and thing which shall in any wise be necessary for the final and perfect accomplishment thereof. And the better to enable our said Commander in Chief to execute the trust reposed in him by these presents we do hereby further authorise and impower him from time to time by Commission under his hand and seal to nominate and constitute such and so many Commissioners as he shall judge necessary to meet, treat, confer and agree with Commissioners to be appointed and competently authorised on the part of the King of Great Britain touching the terms, conditions and stipulations for subsisting better treating & exchanging all prisoners of War as aforesaid as well as for liquidating and settling all Accounts and Claims whatsoever respecting the maintenance and subsistance of Prisoners of War on either side, and we do hereby declare that the engagements concluded upon by our said Commander in Chief in the premises being mutually interchanged with the party contracting on behalf of the Crown and Nation of Great Britain shall be binding and conclusive on the United States of America. In Testimony whereof we have caused these our Letters to be made patent and the Great Seal of the United States of America to be thereunto affixed. Witness His Excellency John Hanson President of the United States in Congress Assembled the Sixteenth day of September and in the Year of our Lord one thousand seven hundred and Eighty two, And of our Sovereignty & Independence the Seventh.

John Hanson

Chas Thomson Secy

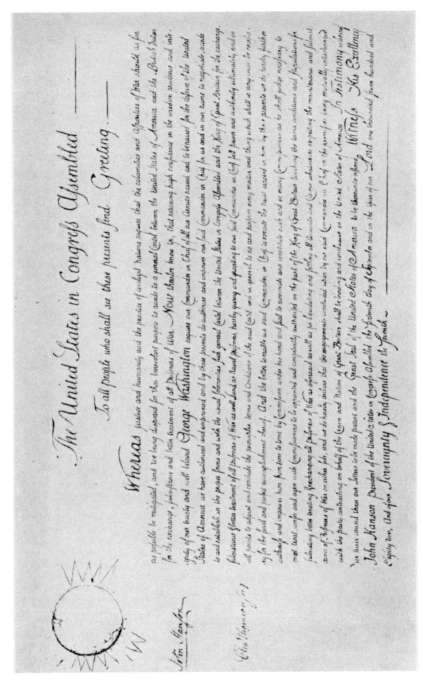

The actual Resolution of September 16th, 1781 authorizing George Washington to negotiate terms of Peace with Great Britain a month after his Victory at Yorktown "Witness his Excellency John Hanson, esquire, President of the United States in Congress assembled". – *Courtesy of "John Hanson Our First President"*

CHAPTER TEN

Portrait of Elias Boudinot from
Appleton Cyclopedia of American Biography

ELIAS BOUDINOT

4th President of the United States
in Congress Assembled|
November 4, 1782 to November 3, 1783

Elias Boudinot was born in Philadelphia, Pennsylvania on May 2nd 1740 and died in Burlington, New Jersey October 24th, 1821. His great-grandfather, Elias, was a French Huguenot, who fled to this country after the revocation of the decree of Nantes. After receiving a Liberal Arts education, Elias Boudinot studied law with Richard Stockton. He became distinguished in his profession, opening a practice in New Jersey. He was dutiful to the cause of independence in New Jersey, serving as a member of the Committee of Correspondence for Essex County. He often used his influence and great legal mind to persuade the New Jersey Provincial Congress to approve the actions of the

United States in Congress Assembled. He was appointed NJ Commissary-General of Prisoners in 1777. In the same year he was elected a delegate to Continental Congress from New Jersey, serving from 1778 until 1779. He also served in the United States in Congress Assembled from 1781 until 1784.

Boudinot, a wealthily New Jersey lawyer and leader of the Presbyterian Church, won the presidency by a narrow margin The delegate count was 16 to 11. The law however of One state One Vote ended the tally seven states to four and two states not voting.

The other four states cast their votes for three different southern delegates. Eliphalet Dyer wrote to Jonathan Trumbull, November 8, 1782:

> *Mr. Boudinot of the State of New Jersey, a gebtn of good carracter, virtuous, and decent behavior, was elected President of Congress on Monday last for the year ensuing; the choice was clear, no strift, as it is the prevailing inclination of Congress, to proceed in course through the States when it can be done with propriety, Jersey having none before.*

He was elected President of the United States in Congress Assembled on November 4th, 1782:

> *Journals of the United States in Congress Assembled, 1781-1789*
>
> *MONDAY, NOVEMBER 4, 1782*
>
> *The following members attended, from*
>
> *New Hampshire, Mr. John Taylor Gilman, Phillips White, Massachusetts, Mr. Samuel Osgood, Rhode Island, Mr. Jonathan Arnold, David Howell, Connecticut, Mr. Benjamin Huntington, Eliphalet Dyer, New York, Mr. James Duane, Ezra L'Hommedieu, New Jersey, Mr. Elias Boudinot, John Witherspoon, Pennsylvania, Mr. Thomas Smith, George Clymer, Henry Wynkoop, Delaware, Mr. Thomas McKean, Samuel Wharton, Maryland, Mr. John Hanson, Daniel Carroll, William Hemsley, Virginia, Mr. James Madison, Theodorick Bland, North Carolina, Mr. Abner Nash, Hugh Williamson, William Blount, South Carolina, Mr. John Rutledge, Ralph Izard, David Ramsay, John Lewis Gervais. Their credentials being read, the states proceeded to the election of a President; and the ballots being taken, the hon. Elias Boudinot was elected.*

Boudinot was a lifelong friend of Alexander Hamilton and very close to Robert Morris. He belonged to "the wealthy, wise, and the good" and had the ear of George Washington. As President, Boudinot and Congress expended a great deal of time and consideration to ending the war favorably with the Treaty of Peace with England. Thankfully his fellow conservative John Jay persuaded Benjamin Franklin and John Adams to ignore Boundinot's (Congress') instructions to include France in the negotiations of The Treaty of Paris which consequently ended the war with Great Britain. The violation of these instructions displeased a large majority of the Confederation Congress but President Boudinot, once realizing the outcome, sided with John Jay. Mr. Madison, who had voted for the instruction, wrote:

"In this business Jay has taken the lead, and proceeded to a length of which you can form little idea. Adams has followed with cordiality. Franklin has been dragged into it."

Mr. Sparks, in his *"Life of Franklin,"* contended that the violation of their instructions by the American commissioners in concluding and signing their treaty without the concurrence of the French government was "unjustifiable."

Spain also presented challenges to this emerging new nation; in June 1783 Boudinot signed this appointment as President of the United States in Congress Assembled:

The United States In Congress Assembled,

To Oliver Pollock Esquire Greeting:

We reposing special trust and confidence in your abilities and integrity have constituted and appointed, and by these presents do constitute and appoint you our commercial agent during our pleasure, at the city and port of Havannah, to manage the occasional concerns of Congress, to assist; the American traders with your advice, and to solicit their affairs with the Spanish Government, and to govern yourself according to the orders you may from time to time receive from the United States in Congress assembled. And that you may effectually execute the office to which you are appointed, we request the Governor, Judges and all other officers of his Catholic Majesty to afford you all countenance and assistance.

In Testimony whereof we have caused the Seal of the United States of America to be hereunto affixed. Witness his Excellency Elias Boudinot, President of the United States in Congress assembled, the second day of June in the Year of our Lord one thousand seven hundred and eighty three, and of our Sovereignty and Independence the seventh.

In July 1783, while President Boudinot and Congress struggled with the treaty, massive debt, a corrupt court system and a host of other ills, they were dealt a now unthinkable blow to the new democracy. On a sizzling Sunday afternoon, soldiers from Lancaster, Pennsylvania mutinied and marched for Philadelphia for the stated purpose of compelling Congress to relinquish to their demands of back pay, food and desperately needed supplies. Recruits from the barracks in Philadelphia reinforced the mutineers; as they surrounded the Independence Hall where Congress was in session, they numbered in excess of three hundred. Moreover, the Executive Council of Pennsylvania's State Government was meeting at the same very hall.

President Boundinot called out the Pennsylvania militia but they failed to come to the two-year old government's rescue. The President of the United States, the Unicameral Confederation Congress and Pennsylvania's Executive Council, in the midst of final negotiations with Great Britain for peace, were held captive in Philadelphia's famed Independence Hall. The mutineers demands were made in very dictatorial tones, that

"...unless their demand were com-plied with in twenty minutes, they would let in upon them the injured soldiery, the consequences of which they were to abide."

Word was immediately sent to Major General Arthur St. Clair requesting his presence. St. Clair rushed to the rescue and confronted the mutineers. He reported the facts and demands to the Confederation Congress. After lengthy debate Congress directed General St. Clair:

" ... to endeavor to march the mutineers to their barracks, and to announce to them that Congress would enter into no deliberation with them; that they must return to Lancaster, and that there, and only there, they would be paid.'

After this, Congress appointed a committee to confer with the executive of Pennsylvania and adjourned:

Saturday, June 21, 1783 – Journals of the Continental Congress: The mutinous soldiers presented themselves, drawn up in the street before the state-house, where Congress had assembled. The executive council of the state, sitting under the same roof, was called on for the proper interposition. President DICKINSON came in, and explained the difficulty, under actual circumstances, of bringing out the militia of the place for the suppression of the mutiny. He thought that, without some outrages on persons or property, the militia could not be relied on. General St. Clair, then in Philadelphia, was sent for, and desired to use his interposition, in order to prevail on the troops to return to the barracks. His report gave no encouragement.

In this posture of things, it was proposed by Mr. IZARD, that Congress should adjourn. It was proposed by Mr. HAMILTON, that General St. Clair, in concert with the executive council of the state, should take order for terminating the mutiny. Mr. REED moved, that the general should endeavor to withdraw the troops by assuring them of the disposition of Congress to do them justice. It was finally agreed, that Congress should remain till the usual hour of adjournment, but without taking any step in relation to the alleged grievances of the soldiers, or any other business whatever. In the mean time, the soldiers remained in their position, without offering any violence, individuals only, occasionally, uttering offensive words, and wantonly pointing their muskets to the windows of the hall of Congress. No danger from premeditated violence was apprehended, but it was observed that spirituous drink, from the tippling-houses adjoining, began to be liberally served out to the soldiers, and might lead to hasty excesses. None were committed, however, and, about three o'clock, the usual hour, Congress adjourned; the soldiers, though in some instances offering a mock obstruction, permitting the members to pass through their ranks. They soon afterwards retired themselves to the barracks.

Thanks to Arthur St. Clair's ability to reason with the men, President Boudinot and the Congressional members passed through the files of the mutineers without being molested. The committee, with Alexander Hamilton as chairman, waited on the State Executive Council to insure the Government of the United States protection when Congress was ready to convene the following day. Elias Boudinot, receiving no pledge of protection by the Pennsylvania militia, advised an adjournment of the United States in Congress Assembled on June 24th to Princeton, New Jersey.

President Elias Boudinot now in his home state of New Jersey, and protected by their militia, wasted no time in dealing harshly with the mutineers. On June 30th, the day after Congress's arrival in New Jersey, a resolution was passed ordering General Howe to march fifteen hundred troops to Philadelphia to disarm the mutineers and bring them to trial.

> *That Major General Howe be directed to march such part of the force under his command as he shall judge necessary to the State of Pennsylvania; and that the commanding officer in the said State he be instructed to apprehend and confine all such persons, belonging to the army, as there is reason to believe instigated the late mutiny; to disarm the remainder; to take, in conjunction with the civil authority, the proper measures to discover and secure all such persons as may have been instrumental therein; and in general to make full examination into all parts of the transaction, and when they have taken the proper steps to report to Congress*

Before this force could reach Philadelphia, General St. Clair and the Executive Council succeeded in quieting the disturbance without bloodshed. The principal leaders were arrested, obedience secured and a trial was set.

The Congressional resolution directing General Howe to move with the troops against the mutineers affronted General St. Clair. St. Clair regarded it as an attempt to supersede his command and undermine his negotiations. Arthur St. Clair took it upon himself to write Congress a scathing letter, which was answered by Elias Boudinot, President of the United States in Congress Assembled, from Princeton New Jersey:

> *Dear Sir,*
>
> *I duly recd your favor of yesterday but conceiving that you had mistaken the Resolution of Congress, I showed it to Mr. Fitzsimmons and we have agreed not to present it to Congress, till we hear again from you. Congress were so careful to interfere one way or the other in the military etiquette, that we recommitted the Resolution to have every thing struck out that should look towards any determination as to the Command, and it was left so that the Commanding officer be him who it might, was to carry the Resolution into Execution; and it can bear no other Construction.*
>
> *If on the second reading you choose your Letter should be read in Congress, it shall be done without delay …*
>
> *Elias Boudinot, President*
>
> *P. S., You may depend on Congress having been perfectly satisfied with your conduct.*

Boudinot undoubtedly trusted St. Clair's judgment and spared him the embarrassment of making his letter known to Congress. Peace once again reigned. As a result of the mutiny the accused ringleaders were sentenced to death, but were pardoned by Congress in September 1783.

Despite problems on many fronts, President Boudinot steered Congress through the final intricacies of the Treaty of Paris, which was finally ratified in January 1784 and signed by his successor President Thomas Mifflin. The Chronology of Boudinot's presidency is as follows:

1782 -- November 4 Convenes new Congress; elects Elias Boudinot president. **November 7** Orders Washington to free Charles Asgill. **November 8** Requests British officials to continue investigation of the death of Joshua Huddy. **November 12** Renews appointment of Thomas Jefferson as peace commissioner. **November 14** Debates report on Vermont's seizure of New York citizens. **November 18** Appoints Thomas Barclay commissioner to settle the accounts of Continental officials abroad. **November 19** Adopts new rules for carrying out the reorganization of the Continental Army. **November 20** Debates Pennsylvania petitions on providing for the state's public creditors. **November 21** Debates salaries of officials abroad. **November 25-26** Debates propriety of exchanging Henry Laurens for Earl Cornwallis. **November 27** Orders seizure of two Vermonters reported to be in correspondence with the enemy.

December 3 Accepts the resignation of secretary for foreign affairs. **December 4** Grants John Paul Jones' request to serve with French navy. **December 5** Censures Vermont officials; appoints appeals court judges. **December 6** Directs superintendent of finance to exhort states to comply with fiscal quotas; appoints deputation to go to Rhode Island to secure ratification of impost amendment. **December 11** Authorizes hiring out of prisoners of war. **December 12** Receives Rhode Island explanation of rejection of impost amendment. **December 13** David Howell acknowledges authorship of published letter violating Congressional secrecy rules. **December 16** Adopts response to Rhode Island's rejection of impost amendment. **December 17** Reaffirms determination to send deputation to Rhode Island. **December 21** Postpones resignation of secretary for foreign affairs; grants secretary leave of absence. **December 24** Amends Post Office ordinance to extend franking privilege. **December 25-26** Observes Christmas. **December 31** Instructs peace commissioners to seek commercial reciprocity with Britain.

1783 - January 1 & 2 Thanks France for military aid and naval protection. **January 3** Records Trenton trial decree in Connecticut-Pennsylvania boundary dispute *(first settlement of interstate dispute under Articles of Confederation)* **January 6** Receives army petition on pay arrears; appoints committees to inquire into the management of the executive departments. **January 7** Debates setting exchange rate for redeeming old Continental emissions. **January 10** Learns that superintendent of finance has over drawn bills of exchange on "*the known funds procured in Europe*"; army deputation meets with grand committee on Continental Army grievances. **January 13** Debates expediency of negotiating additional foreign loans. **January 14** Acquiesces in Rhode Island delegates' request to share intelligence from abroad with state's officials; debates land valuation formula in grand committee. **January 17** Thanks General Greene and the southern army; declares inexpediency of seeking additional foreign loans. **January 21** Receives US-Dutch treaty negotiated by John Adams.

January 22 Ratifies Franco-American contract negotiated by Benjamin Franklin. **January 23** Ratifies Dutch treaty. **January 24** Orders investigation of abuses of flag of truce by the Amazon; rejects report recommending establishment of a library for Congress. **January 25** Directs the superintendent of finance to pay the Continental Army. **January 27-31** Debates proposals for funding the public debt. **January 30** Rejects Pennsylvania proposal to pay interest due on Continental securities owned by its own citizens.

February 4 Receives Vermont remonstrance against threatened Continental intervention. **February 4-8** Debates proposals for funding the public debt and setting state quotas. **February 10-14** Debates proposals for funding the public debt and setting state quotas. **February 17** Adopts plan to appoint commissioners for estimating land values and setting state quotas. **February 18** Orders superintendent of finance to estimate the public debt, and each executive department to report a comprehensive civil list. **February 21** Exhorts states to maintain their representation in Congress. **February 25-28** Debates proposals for commutation of Continental officers' half pay.

March 4 Amends ordinance *"for establishing courts for the trial of piracies."* **March 6-7** Receives report on funding the public debt. **March 10** Debates commutation of Continental officers' half pay. **March 11** Debates revenue proposals. **March 12** Receives the preliminary treaty of peace. **March 12-15** Reads treaty and foreign dispatches. **March 17** Receives Washington's report on the army crisis at Newburgh. **March 18** Debates report on the public credit. **March 19** Debates proposal to censure ministers for ignoring negotiating instructions. **March 20-21** Debates report on the public credit. **March 22** Adopts resolve to commute Continental officers' half pay for life to full pay for five years. **March 24** Recalls all Continental ships on cruise. **March 27-28** Debates report on the public credit. **March 29** Rejects proposal for increasing congressional oversight of the office of finance. **March 31** Renews committee for overseeing the office of finance.

April 1 Recommends that states revise formula for setting Continental quotas; learns of call for an economic convention at Hartford; receives invitation to locate Continental capital in Kingston, New York. **April 4** Orders suspension of enlistments in Continental Army; debates report on the public credit. **April 7** Revises Continental quotas. **April 11** Adopts cease-fire proclamation. **April 15** Ratifies preliminary treaty of peace. **April 17** Orders sale of Continental horses. **April 18** Asks states for authority to levy revenue duties. **April 23** Authorizes Washington to discharge Continental troops. April 24 Directs Washington to confer with General Guy Carleton on the evacuation of New York. **April 26** Adopts Address to the States on new revenue plan. **April 28** Requests Robert Morris to continue as superintendent of finance until the reduction of the Continental Army. April 30 Rejects motion to hold debates in public.

May 1 Directs secretary at war to negotiate cease-fire with hostile Native American nations; authorizes American ministers to negotiate treaty of commerce with Great Britain. **May 2** Appeals to states for collection of taxes for payment of discharged troops; recommends that states adopt copyright laws for protection of authors. **May 9** Asks states to convene assemblies to adopt fiscal recommendations. **May 15** Revises rules to appoint committees by secret ballot. **May 19-20** Debates treaty article on restitution of confiscated loyalist property. **May 22** Instructs Francis Dana on negotiating treaty with Russia. **May 26** Instructs American ministers on peace terms concerning evacuation of American posts and carrying off of American slaves; instructs Washington on furloughing Continental troops. **May 29-30** Debates treaty articles on British debts and loyalist property.

June 2 Appoints Oliver Pollock Commercial Agent to Cuba. **June 4** Debates Virginia cession of western land claims; refers offers to locate the Continental capital at Kingston, New York or Annapolis, Maryland to the states (to be debated October 6). **June 10** Receives report of the mutiny of a troop of Virginia dragoons. **June 11** Directs furlough of Delaware, Maryland, Pennsylvania, and Virginia troops. **June 12** Instructs American ministers on avoiding treaties of armed neutrality. **June 13** Receives *"mutinous memorial"* from Continental Army sergeants. **June 17** Commends the conduct of business in the office of finance. **June 19** Receives notice of the mutiny of Continental troops at Carlisle; appoints committee to confer with Pennsylvania officials on the mutiny. **June 20** Debates Virginia cession of western land claims. **June 21** Confronts mutineers of the Pennsylvania Line; authorizes president to reconvene Congress at Trenton or Princeton, NJ. **June 21** President Boudinot issues proclamation, reconvening Congress at Princeton. **June 30** Reconvenes at Princeton, New Jersey.

July 1 Directs General Robert Howe to suppress mutiny; adopts report explaining congressional response to the mutiny. **July 2** Thanks New Jersey officials for their reception of Congress. **July 9-11** Debates proposals for paying arrears due Continental troops. **July 16** Orders recall of commissioners investigating British embarkations from New York; directs Secretary Thomson to maintain record of un-represented states. **July 23** Receives Philadelphia address inviting Congress' return. **July 28** Returns noncommittal response to Philadelphia address; directs General Washington to attend Congress; relieves General Howe's detachment ordered to suppress Pennsylvania mutiny. **July 29** Ratifies Treaty of Amity and Commerce with Sweden. **July 30** Directs superintendent of finance to publish regulations for receiving *"Morris notes"* in payment of taxes.

August 1 Rejects motion to adjourn to Philadelphia. **August 6** Authorizes distribution of "*necessities*" to Delaware Native Americans and friendly "*northern nations.*" **August 7** Orders preparation of "an equestrian statue of the Commander in Chief." **August 9** Authorizes furloughing additional Continental troops and continuation of subsistence for Hazen's Canadian regiment. **August 13-14** Debates motion for returning to Philadelphia. **August 15** Receives proceedings of the court-martial of the Philadelphia mutineers. **August 18** Directs superintendent of finance to report estimate of the Continental debt. **August 26** Conducts audience with General Washington. **August 28** Debates ordinance for prohibiting settlement of Native American lands.

September 1 Receives Pennsylvania Assembly resolves for re turning to Philadelphia. **September 10** Orders renewal of committees to oversee the executive departments. **September 13** Adopts stipulations concerning the cession of Virginia's western land claims; confirms acquittal of leaders of the Philadelphia mutiny. **September 16-19** Debates Massachusetts' call for retrenchment of Continental expenses. **September 22** Adopts proclamation regulating the purchase of Native American lands. **September 24** Adopts secret order authorizing Washington to discharge Continental troops "*as he shall deem proper and expedient.*" **September 25** Reaffirms commitment to commutation of half pay claims; proclaims treaty with Sweden; debates report on federal jurisdiction over site of congressional residence. **September 29** Lifts injunction of secrecy on most foreign dispatches. **September 30** Promotes Continental officers not promoted since 1777.

October 1 Debates instructions for ministers abroad. **October 3** Debates Native American affairs. **October 6-9** Debates location of the Continental capital. **October 8** Receives Quaker petition for suppression of the slave trade. **October 10** Resolves to leave Princeton; debates location of the capital. **October 15** Adopts resolves regulating Native American affairs. **October 17** Debates location of the capital. **October 18** Adopts Thanksgiving proclamation. **October 21** Adopts two capital locations-Congress to meet alternately "*on the banks of the Delaware and Potomac.*" **October 22** Orders distribution of the peace treaty to the states. **October 23-24** Debates peacetime military arrangements. **October 27-28** Fails to convene quorum. **October 29** Adopts instructions for negotiating commercial treaties. **October 30** Authorizes Pennsylvania to negotiate Native American lands purchase. **October 31** Ratifies fiscal contract with France; holds audience with Dutch Minister Van Berckel.

After the Presidency, Boudinot resumed his law practice. In 1788, after the ratification of the constitution, he was elected to the 1st, 2nd, and 3rd congresses, serving from March 3, 1789, until March 3, 1795. He was appointed by Washington in 1795 to succeed Rittenhouse as director of the mint at Philadelphia, and held the office for ten years, resigning in July 1805. Elias Boudinot passed the rest of his life at Burlington, New Jersey, and devoted his retirement years to the study of biblical literature. He had amassed a modest fortune and chose philanthropy in his later years as a permanent endeavor.

He was a trustee of Princeton College and in 1805 endowed it with a cabinet of natural history, valued at $3,000. In 1812 he was chosen a member of the American Board of Commissioners for Foreign Missions, to which he gave £100 in 1813. He assisted in founding the American Bible Society in 1816, was its first president, and gave that organization $10,000. He was interested in attempts to educate Native Americans, and when three Cherokee youth were brought to the foreign mission school in 1818, he allowed one of them to take his name. This boy became afterward a man of influence in his tribe, and at age 25, became the first editor of the bilingual English/Cherokee newspaper Cherokee Phoenix, which began publication in the Cherokee Nation East in 1828. Cherokee Boudinot was a signer of the Treaty of New Echota, which ceded Native American Lands to Georgia and was primarily responsible for the *Trail of Tears.* On June 10th, 1838 Cherokee Boudinot was assassinated along with two others by Native Americans west of the Mississippi for their support of the Treaty.

Dr. Boudinot was also interested in the instruction of deaf-mutes, the education of young men for the ministry, and efforts for the relief of the poor. He bequeathed his property to his only daughter, Mrs. Bradford, and to charitable uses. Among his bequests were one of $200 to buy spectacles for the aged poor, another of 13,000 acres of land to the mayor and corporation of Philadelphia, that the poor might be supplied with wood at low prices, and another of 3,000 acres to the Philadelphia hospital for the benefit of foreigners. Dr. Boudinot published "*The Age-of Revelation,*" a reply to Paine (1790); an oration before the Society of the Cincinnati (1793); "*Second Advent of the Messiah*" (Trenton, 1815); and "*Star in the West,* or *An Attempt to Discover the Long-lost Tribes of Israel*" (1816), in which he concurs with James Adair in the opinion that the Native Americans are the lost tribes. He also wrote, in "*The Evangelical Intelligencer*" of 1806, an anonymous memoir of the Rev. William Tennent.

In closing one should note that the US Mint, in 1999, began to release a redesigned quarter under The 50 State Quarter Program. The US Mint's website states:

> *The 50 State Quarters™ Program is 'changing' the 'state' of coin collecting. Approximately every 10 weeks, from 1999 to 2008, there will be a new state quarter to collect. Each quarter's reverse will celebrate one of the 50 states with a design honoring its unique history, traditions, and symbols. The quarters are released in the same order that the states joined the union.*

On January 1, 1999 the United States Mint, despite my protests, unveiled its first George Washington State Quarter with the mark of Delaware on its reverse. The Delaware Quarter was release first because the US Mint, by virtue of an Act of Congress, recognized Delaware as the first state due to its ratification of the US Constitution on December 7, 1787. The Constitutional Congress is on this particular fact quite mistaken.

The United States was formed by the Articles of Confederation; Delaware actually joined the Perpetual Union on its ratification date of February 1, 1779. Delaware was the 12th state to join the Union, ten years before its ratification of the US Constitution.

On July 4, 1861, eighty years after the formation of the Perpetual Union, President Abraham Lincoln used the Articles of Confederation's language against South Carolina, North Carolina, Georgia and Virginia's attempt to secede from the United States. It was the unanimous "Perpetual Union" verbiage in the Articles that provided President Lincoln with the legal authority, not granted in the US Constitution, to Preserve the Union.

> "*The express plighting of faith by each and all of the original thirteen in the Articles of Confederation, two years later, that the Union shall be perpetual is most conclusive.*" - Abraham Lincoln's Address to Congress in Special Session 4 July 1861.

It is incongruous that the US Mint was forced to serve as the official government agency to perpetuate the Delaware First State Myth (*the first state was actually Virginia - December 16, 1777*). The US Mint's third Director, Elias Boudinot, was the 4th President of the United States in Congress Assembled under the Articles of Confederation. One would think that a Government Institution once headed by a US President under the Articles would have objected vehemently to Congress' error of the historical facts behind statehood.

Virginia, has the "*bragging rights*" to being the first state in the US "*Perpetual Union*" and Congress must correct this glaring error memorialized in the new Washington Quarter. Perhaps after the last state is honored under the current minting, a new quarter could be started yearly honoring each of the forgotten Presidents. I am sure Washington wouldn't mind a 14-year rest on the head of the US quarter. The US Mint could start off with our first state Virginia on the verso with the First President of the United States, Samuel Huntington, on the head. Additionally, a special event at the US Mint would be most definitely in order when former President and Mint Director, Elias Boudinot of New Jersey, is rightfully honored as a temporary head of the familiar US Quarter, with his home State of New Jersey on the verso.

The correct order of US State ratification and entrance into the Union is as follows:

US Statehood Order

Articles of Confederation - 1 to 13 States
US Constitution - 37 to 50 States

	State	State Passes Ratification	Reported to Congress	Delegates Sign
1	Virginia	16 December 1777	25 June 1778	9 July 1778
2	South Carolina	5 February 1778	25 June 1778	9 July 1778
3	New York	6 February 1778	23 June 1778	9 July 1778
4	Rhode Island	16 February 1778	23 June 1778	9 July 1778
5	Georgia	26 February 1778	25 June 1778	9 July 1778
6	Connecticut	27 February 1778	23 June 1778	9 July 1778
7	New Hampshire	4 March 1778	23 June 1778	9 Jul 1778-8 Aug 1778
8	Pennsylvania	5 March 1778	25 June 1778	9 Jul 1778-22 Jul 1778
9	Massachusetts	10 March 1778	23 June 1778	9 July 1778
10	North Carolina	24 April 1778	25 June 1778	21 July 1778
11	New Jersey	20 November 1778	25-26 Nov. 1778	26 Nov 1778
12	Delaware	1 February 1779	16 February 1779	22 Feb 1779-5 May 1779
13	Maryland	2 February 1781	12 February 1781	1 March 1781

Sources: *The Documentary History of the Ratification of the Constitution:* Vol. 1: *Constitutional Documents and Records, 1776-1787,* ed. Merrill Jensen, Madison, Wis.: State Historical Society of Wisconsin, 1976; *Encyclopedia of American History: Bicentennial Edition,* ed. Richard Morris, New York; Harper & Row, 1976; *Documents of American History,* ed. Henry Steele Commanger, Englewood Cliffs, NJ; Prentice-Hall, 1973

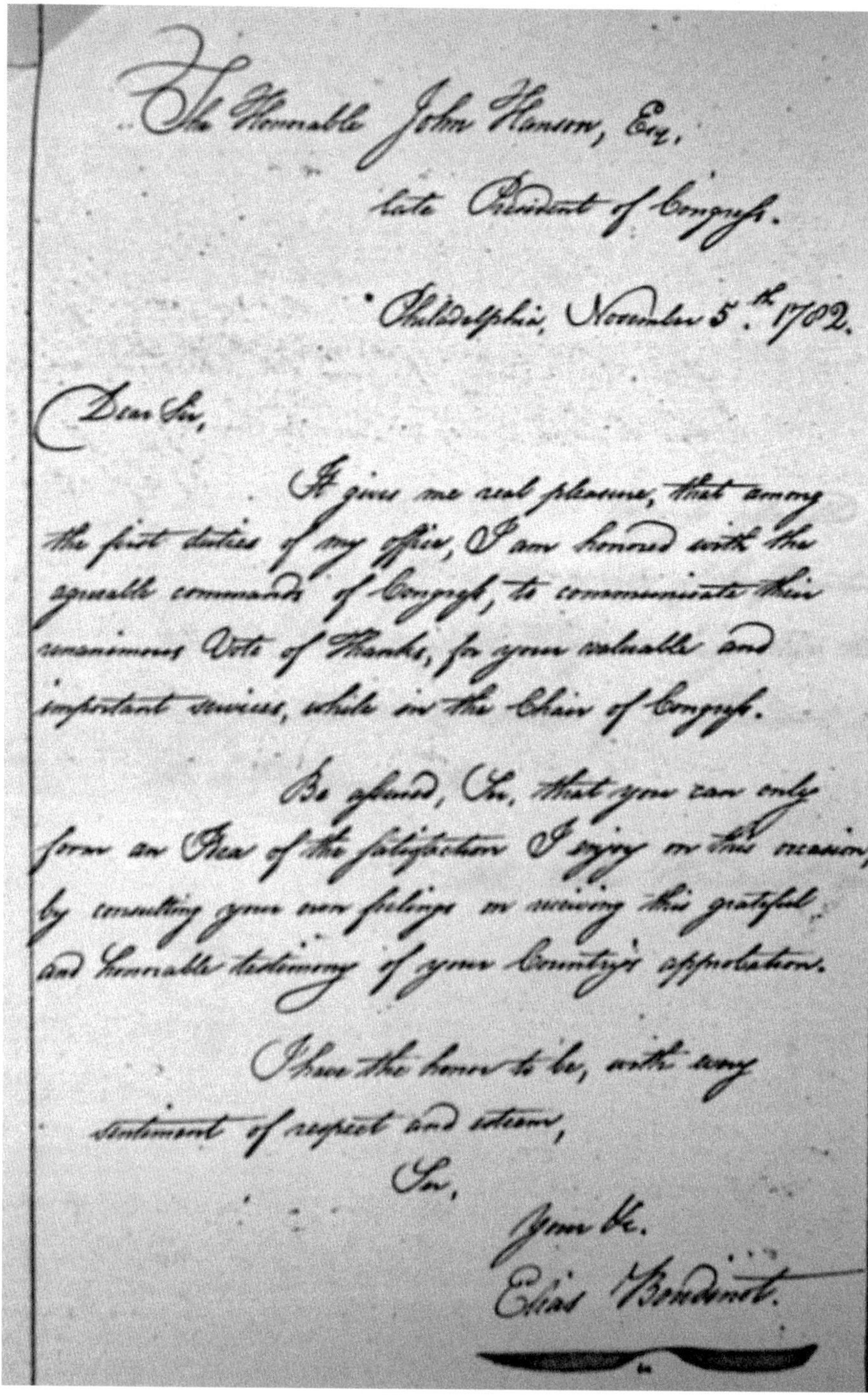
The Honorable John Hanson, Esq.

late President of Congress.

Philadelphia, November 5th 1782.

Dear Sir,

It gives me real pleasure, that among the first duties of my office, I am honored with the agreeable commands of Congress, to communicate their unanimous Vote of Thanks, for your valuable and important services, while in the Chair of Congress.

Be assured, Sir, that you can only form an Idea of the satisfaction I enjoy on this occasion, by consulting your own feelings on receiving this grateful and honorable testimony of your Country's approbation.

I have the honor to be, with every sentiment of respect and esteem,

Sir,

Your &c.

Elias Boudinot.

President of the United States in Congress Assembled Elias Boudinot letter to former President John Hanson transmitting Congress' official Vote of Thanks. – *Courtesy of the Library of Congress.*

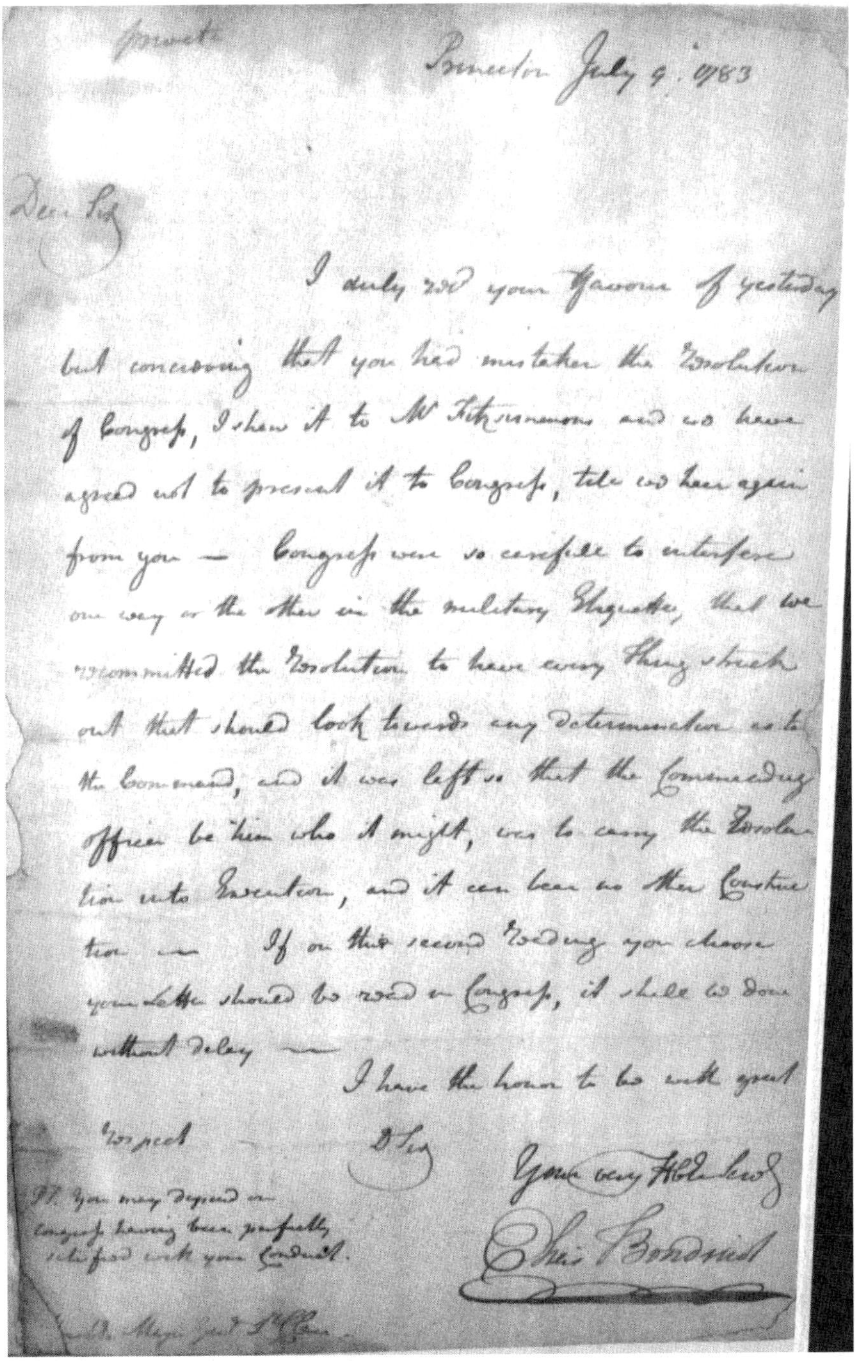
Private

Princeton July 9. 1783

Dear Sir

I duly rec'd your favour of yesterday but conceiving that you had mistaken the Resolution of Congress, I shew it to Mr Fitzsimmons and we have agreed not to present it to Congress, till we hear again from you — Congress were so careful to interfere one way or the other in the military Etiquette, that we recommitted the Resolution to have every thing struck out that should look towards any determination as to the command, and it was left so that the Commanding officer be him who it might, was to carry the Resolution into Execution, and it can bear no other Construction — If on this second reading you choose your letter should be read in Congress, it shall be done without delay —

I have the honor to be with great respect

D Sir

Your very Hble Servt

Elias Boudinot

PS. You may depend on Congress having been perfectly satisfied with your Conduct.

Hon. Major Genl St Clair

Arthur St. Clair took it upon himself to write Congress a scathing letter, which was not submitted to the United States in Congress Assembled by President Elias Boudinot. The from Princeton NJ on July 9th, 1783 responded to General St. Clair with this letter –

Courtesy of the Klos Family

CHAPTER ELEVEN

Portrait of Thomas Mifflin from
Appleton Cyclopedia of American Biography

THOMAS MIFFLIN

5th President of the United States
in Congress Assembled|
November 3, 1783 to June 3, 1784

Thomas Mifflin was born in Philadelphia, Pennsylvania sometime in 1744, with the exact date still to be established. Mifflin died in Lancaster, Pennsylvania on January 20, 1800. He was a 1760 graduate of Philadelphia College. In that same year he entered a counting-house, and in the course of this business traveled throughout Europe in 1765. In 1766 he returned to the colonies and left that position to engage in a commercial business in partnership with a brother.

In 1772 and 1773 he was a representative in the Colonial State Legislature of

Pennsylvania. His efforts there were rewarded in 1774 by being elected as was one of the distinguished Pennsylvania delegates sent to the Continental Congress. His business and patriotic fervor was instantly embraced and he was appointed to serve on important committees. When the news came of the fight at Lexington he eloquently advocated resolute action in the many Pennsylvania town-meetings. When troops were finally enlisted from Pennsylvania he was active in organizing and drilling one of the first regiments. He was made its major, thereby severing his connection with the Quaker society in which he was born and reared, as well as his role as a delegate.

General Washington chose, now Colonel Mifflin as his first aide-de-camp soon after the establishment of his headquarters at Cambridge. While there, he successfully led a force against a British detachment. In July 1775, he was promoted to quartermaster-general of the army; after the evacuation of Boston by the enemy, he was commissioned as brigadier-general on May 19th, 1776. He was assigned to the command of a part of the Pennsylvania troops when the army lay encamped before New York and enjoyed the fastidious confidence of George Washington.

His Pennsylvania brigade was described as the best disciplined of any in the Continental Army. Mifflin's First Continental Regiment covered the retreat of the American army. Through a military order gaffe General Mifflin received the word to retreat before all of the troops had embarked. At the ferry, upon learning of the error, Mifflin managed to regain the lines before the enemy discovered that the post was deserted. Mifflin's regiment was the last to leave Long Island.

Washington's error to defend Long Island against a superior enemy forced the Continental Army into a rapid retreat across the East River. The small number of boats and limited time meant that wagons containing most of the Continental Army's powder, baggage and critical supplies fell into to the hands of the British. In the aftermath soldier moral was low and the Continental Congress held a committee hearing. After a three-day investigation the committee recommended that quartermaster Moylan, who was given the impossible task to protect the waterways resign. In an effort to restore the morale of the soldiers, Mifflin was appointed this position. Against his wishes, by a special resolve of Congress, Mifflin resumed the duties of quarter-master-general. The Journal of Congress reported:

> *"Resolved, That Brigadier General Mifflin be authorized and requested to resume the said office, and that his rank and pay, as brigadier, be still continued to him:1[Note 1: 1 "We have obtained Colonel Moylan's resignation, and General Mifflin comes again into the office of Quartermaster General." Elbridge Gerry to Horatio Gates, 27 September 1776.]*
>
> *That a committee of three four be appointed to confer with Brigadier General Mifflin: The members chosen, Mr. Richard Henry Lee, Mr. Roger Sherman, Mr. John Adams, and Mr. Elbridge Gerry."*

In November 1776, General Mifflin was sent to Philadelphia to represent to the Continental Congress the critical condition of the army. Washington was fleeing the advancing British towards Philadelphia. He was out of supplies and money to pay the troops whose tours of duty were set to expire in 60 days. It was a wise move to send General Mifflin, as Congress in fear of losing Philadelphia, was preparing to take flight to Baltimore. As the Continental Army crossed the Delaware, the citizens of Philadelphia began to panic. Business was suspended, schools were closed and agitated Patriots and Tories gathered in the streets. As news of the Continental Army's plight filtered in, roads leading from the city were crowded with refugees leaving the city.

In the Pennsylvania Statehouse Yard a town meeting was called and Thomas Mifflin addressed the crowd and much of Congress. After listening to him, Congress formally appealed to the militia of Philadelphia and the nearest counties to join Washington's beleaguered Army in New Jersey. Congress also sent word to all parts of the country for re-enforcements and supplies, and then ordered Mifflin to remain in Philadelphia for consultation and advice. Mifflin organized and trained the three regiments of militia of the city and neighborhood, sending a body of 1,500 men to Trenton. After the successful win at Trenton, General Mifflin, accompanied by a Committee of the legislature, made the tour of the principal towns of Pennsylvania; by his stirring oratory he brought recruits to the ranks of the army. He came up with more re-enforcements before the Battle of Princeton was fought. In recognition of his services, Congress commissioned him as a major-general on February 19th, 1777 and made him a member of the Board of War.

On the Board of War, General Mifflin joined a growing number of delegates and generals who shared the dissatisfaction at the "Fabian policy" of General Washington. Clearly, at the very least, Thomas Mifflin sympathized with the views of General Horatio Gates and General Thomas Conway. Mifflin vehemently declared, after Washington overcame the Conway Cabal which was an effort to elevate General Gates to the supreme command, that he had not participated in their efforts to remove General Washington as commander-in-chief. The Conway Cabal and responsibilities of his various offices so impaired General Mifflin's health that he offered his resignation. Congress refused to accept it. However, General Mifflin, was replaced by General Nathanael Greene in the quartermaster's department in March, 1778, and in October of 1778 he and General Gates were discharged from their places on the Board of War.

More trouble followed from his "loosing side" affiliation. An investigation of his conduct was ordered by Congress resulting from charges that the distresses of the army at Valley Forge were due to the mismanagement of the quartermaster-general. When the decree was revoked, after he had himself demanded an examination, he resigned his commission. Congress once again refused to accept it, and placed in his hands $1,000,000 to settle outstanding claims. In January1780, he was appointed on a board to devise means for retrenching expenses. After the achievement of the Treaty of Paris he was elected as a delegate to the United States in Congress Assembled.

In a twist of fate, Thomas Mifflin was so respected by his fellow delegates that he was elected President of the United States in Congress Assembled, on November 3, 1783. George Washington never forgot the Conway Cabal. Mifflin was jealous of others who the Commander-in-Chief favored this did not affect his presidency. In fact, Mifflin was not present in Congress on the day of his election. His presidency lasted only six months, as Congress adjourned on June 3, 1784. On his presidential election the Journals of the United States in Congress Assembled reporting:

> *Pursuant to the Articles of Confederation, the following delegates attended:*
>
> *FROM THE STATE OF NEW HAMPSHIRE, Mr. A[biel] Foster, MASSACHUSETTS, Mr. E[lbridge] Gerry, who produced a certificate under the seal of the State, signed John Avery, Mr. S[amuel] Osgood, RHODE ISLAND AND PROVIDENCE PLANTATIONS, Mr. W[illiam] Ellery and Mr. D[avid] Howell, CONNECTICUT, Mr. S[amuel] Huntington and Mr. B[enjamin] Huntington, NEW YORK, Mr. James Duane, NEW JERSEY, Mr. E[lias] Boudinot, MARYLAND, Mr. D[aniel] Carroll,Mr. J[ames] McHenry, VIRGINIA.Mr. J[ohn] F[rancis], Mr. A[rthur] Lee, NORTH CAROLINA, Mr. [Benjamin] Hawkins, and Mr. [Hugh] Williamson, SOUTH CAROLINA, Mr. J[acob] Read, Mr. R[ichard] Beresford, Seven states being represented, they proceeded to the choice of a President; and, the ballots being taken, the honorable Thomas Mifflin was elected.*

One of the most remarkable events of United States history occurred the very next month under Mifflin's Presidency. In November of 1783 the British finally evacuated New York and Congress made the momentous decision to place the Continental Army on "*Peace Footing*". It was in Annapolis, where the US Government convened, that the last great act of the Revolutionary War occurred. George Washington was formally received by President Thomas Mifflin and Congress. Instead of declaring himself King, Washington resigned his commission as Commander-in-Chief to the President of the United States.

What made this action especially remarkable was that George Washington, at his pinnacle of his power and popularity, surrendered the commission to President Thomas Mifflin, who by all accounts, conspired to replace Washington as Commander-in-Chief with Horatio Gates in 1777. What follows is The United States in Congress Assembled Journal account of George Washington's December 23, 1783 resignation:

> *According to order, his Excellency the Commander in Chief was admitted to a public audience, and being seated, and silence ordered, the President, after a pause, informed him, that the United States in Congress assembled, were prepared to receive his communications; Whereupon, he arose and addressed Congress as follows:*

'Mr. President:

The great events on which my resignation depended, having at length taken place, I have now the honor of offering my sincere congratulations to Congress, and of presenting myself before them, to surrender into their hands the trust committed to me, and to claim the indulgence of retiring from the service of my country.

Happy in the confirmation of our independence and sovereignty, and pleased with the opportunity afforded the United States, of becoming a respectable nation, I resign with satisfaction the appointment I accepted with diffidence; a diffidence in my abilities to accomplish so arduous a task; which however was superseded by a confidence in the rectitude of our cause, the support of the supreme power of the Union, and the patronage of Heaven.

The successful termination of the war has verified the most sanguine expectations; and my gratitude for the interposition of Providence, and the assistance I have received from my countrymen, increases with every review of the momentous contest.

While I repeat my obligations to the army in general, I should do injustice to my own feelings not to acknowledge, in this place, the peculiar services and distinguished merits of the gentlemen who have been attached to my person during the war. It was impossible the choice of confidential officers to compose my family should have been more fortunate. Permit me, sir, to recommend in particular, those who have continued in the service to the present moment, as worthy of the favorable notice and patronage of Congress.

I consider it an indispensable duty to close this last act of my official life by commending the interests of our dearest country to the protection of Almighty God, and those who have the superintendence of them to his holy keeping. Having now finished the work assigned me, I retire from the great theatre of action, and bidding an affectionate farewell to this august body, under whose orders I have so long acted, I here offer my commission, and take my leave of all the employments of public life'

George Washington then advanced and delivered to President Mifflin his commission, with a copy of his address, and resumed his place, whereupon President Thomas Mifflin returned him the following answer:

Sir,

The United States in Congress assembled receive with emotions, too affecting for utterance, the solemn deposit resignation of the authorities under which you have led their troops with safety and triumph success through a long a perilous and a doubtful war. When called upon by your country to defend its invaded rights, you accepted the sacred charge, before they it had formed alliances, and whilst they were it was without funds or a government to support you. You have conducted the great military contest with wisdom and fortitude, through invariably regarding the fights of the civil government power through all disasters and changes. You have, by the love and confidence of your fellow-citizens, enabled them to display their martial genius, and transmit their fame to posterity. You have persevered, till these United States, aided by a magnanimous king and nation, have been enabled, under a just Providence, to close the war in freedom, safety and independence; on which happy event we sincerely join you in congratulations.

Having planted defended the standard of liberty in this new world: having taught an useful lesson a lesson useful to those who inflict and to those who feel oppression, you retire from the great theatre of action, loaded with the blessings of your fellow-citizens, but your fame the glory of your virtues will not terminate with your official life the glory of your many virtues will military command, it will continue to animate remotest posterity ages and this last act will not be among the least conspicuous

We feel with you our obligations to the army in general; and will particularly charge ourselves with the interests of those confidential officers, who have attended your person to this interesting affecting moment.

We join you in commending the interests of our dearest country to the protection of Almighty God, beseeching him to dispose the hearts and minds of its citizens, to improve the opportunity afforded them, of becoming a happy and respectable nation. And for you we address to him our earnest prayers, that a life so beloved may be fostered with all his care; that your days may be happy, as they have been illustrious; and that he will finally give you that reward which this world cannot give.

President Thomas Mifflin's third month in office was equally eventful as he presided over another great US event. On January 14, 1784 Congress finally assembled enough States to ratify the Definitive Treaty of Peace, which half-ended the War with Great Britain (*King George III did not ratify the treaty for Britain until April 9, 1784 which officially ending the War)*. On January 21st the following proclamation was published and appeared in the *Pennsylvania Gazette:*

PHILADELPHIA, January 21.

By the UNITED STATES in CONGRESS assembled.

A PROCLAMATION.

WHEREAS Definitive Articles of peace and friendship, between the United States of America and his Britannic Majesty, were concluded and signed at Paris on the 3d day of September, 1783, by the Plenipotentiaries of the said United States and of His said Britannic Majesty, duly and respectively authorized for that purpose, which definitive articles are in the words following:

And we, the United States in Congress assembled, having seen and duly considered the definitive articles aforesaid, did, by a certain article, under the seal of the United States, bearing date this 14th day of January, 1784, approve, ratify and confirm the same, and every part and clause thereof, engaging and promising that we would sincerely and faithfully perform and observe the same, and never to suffer them to be violated by any one, or transgressed in any manner, as far as should be in our power.

And being sincerely disposed to carry the said articles into execution, truly, honestly and with good faith, according to the intent and meaning thereof, We have thought proper, by these presents, to notify the premises to all the good citizens of these States, hereby enjoining all bodies of magistracy, legislative, executive and judiciary, all persons bearing office, civil or military, of whatever rank, degree or powers, and all others, the good citizens of these states, of every vocation and condition, that, reverencing those stipulations entered into on their behalf, under the authority of that federal bond, by which their existence as an independent people is bound up together, and is known and acknowledged by the nations of the world, and with that good faith, which is every man's surest guide, within their several offices, jurisdictions and vocations, they carry into effect the said definitive articles, and every clause and sentence thereof, strictly and completely.

Given under the seal of the United States. Witness his Excellency THOMAS MIFFLIN, our President, at Annapolis, this 14th day of January 1784, and of the sovereignty and independence of the United States of America, the eighth.

In March 1784, a congressional committee led by Thomas Jefferson proposed dividing up sprawling western territories into states, to be considered equal with the original 13.

Whereas the general Assembly of Virginia at their session, commencing on the 20 day of October, 1783, passed an act to authorize their delegates in Congress to convey to the United States in Congress assembled all the right of that Commonwealth, to the territory northwestward of the river Ohio: And whereas the delegates of the said Commonwealth, have presented to Congress the form of a deed proposed to be executed pursuant to the said Act, in the words following:

To all who shall see these presents, we Thomas Jefferson, Samuel Hardy, Arthur Lee and James Monroe, the underwritten delegates for the Commonwealth of Virginia, in the Congress of the United States of America, send greeting:

Known as the Ordinance of 1784, Jefferson's committee not only proposed a ban on slavery in these new states, but everywhere in the U.S. after 1800. This proposal was narrowly defeated by the Southern Contingent of Congress, despite President Thomas Mifflin's support. The chance of peacefully abolishing slavery nationally was lost with the invention of the cotton gin, which increased cotton production a thousand fold. It would not be until July 1787, under President Arthur St. Clair, that an ordinance would be passed to govern, free of slavery, the Northwest Territory, which later became the states of Ohio, Indiana, Illinois, Michigan and Wisconsin.

Earlier in 1784 Mifflin's Congress, through the efforts of James Monroe, granted the necessary ships papers to the *Empress of China:*

We the United States in Congress assembled, make known, that John Green, captain of the ship called the Empress of China, is a citizen of the United States of America, and that the ship which he commands belongs to citizens of the said United States, and as we wish to see the said John Green prosper in his lawful affairs, our prayer is to all the before mentioned, and to each of them separately, where the said John Green shall arrive with his vessel and cargo, that they may please to receive him with goodness, and treat him in a becoming manner, permitting him upon the usual tolls and expences in passing and repassing, to pass, navigate and frequent the ports, passes and territories, to the end, to transact his business where and in what manner he shall judge proper, whereof we shall be willingly indebted.

On August 30, 1784 The Empress of China reached Canton, China. It would return to New York City months later filled with a cargo of spices, silks, exotic plants, new metal alloys and tea, inspiring a host of US Merchants to enter into the Far East trade.

Mifflin chose not to serve his full one-year term as President of the United States in Congress Assembled, and resigned on June 3, 1784. The following motion was entered in to the Journals of the United States in Congress Assembled:

Resolved, That the thanks of Congress be given to his Excellency Thomas Mifflin, for his able and faithful discharge of the duties of President, whilst acting in that important station

The Chronology of Mifflin's presidency is as follows:

1783 - November 3 Convenes new Congress; elects Thomas Mifflin president (elects Daniel Carroll chairman in the president's absence). **November 4** Authorizes discharge of the Continental Army- "*except 500 men, with proper officers.*" Adjourns to Annapolis, to reconvene the 26th.

December 13 Reconvenes at Annapolis. **December 15** Fails to convene quorum. **December 16** Reads foreign dispatches. **December 17** Fails to convene quorum. **December 22** Holds public entertainment for General Washington. **December 23** Appeals to unrepresented states to maintain congressional attendance; receives Washington and accepts his resignation. **December 27** Receives report on capital location. **December 29**

January 1 Fails to convene quorum. 1784 **January 3** Resolves to receive Francis Dana, "*relative to his mission to the Court of Russia.*" **January 5** Rejects proposal to nominate knights to the Polish Order of Divine Providence. January 8 Debates Quaker petition for suppression of the slave trade. **January 10** Fails to convene quorum. **January 14** Ratifies definitive treaty of peace, "*nine states being present*"; recommends that the states "*provide for the restitution of*" confiscated loyalist property. **January 15** Acquiesces in public creditor demand that loan office certificate interest not be subject to depreciation. **January 17-20** Fails to convene quorum. **January 21** Rejects motion denying Continental jurisdiction in Lusannah admiralty appeal. **January 22** Halts plan to dispose of military stores. **January 23** Sets date for selecting judges to determine "*the private right of soil*" in the Wyoming Valley. **January 26** Narrows half-pay eligibility rules. **January 27-28** Fails to convene quorum. **January 30** Grants sea-letters for The Empress of China voyage to Canton.

February 3 Creates post of under secretary to revive office for foreign affairs.

February 4-5 Fails to convene quorum. **February 6** Issues brevet promotions for departing foreign officers. **February 7-9** Fails to convene quorum. **February 10** Plans general treaty with Native American nations of the northern department. **February 11** Registers commissions of five French consuls and five vice-consuls. **February 12** Fails to convene quorum. **February 16-23** Fails to convene quorum. **February 24** Postpones debate on garrisoning frontier posts for failure of nine-state representation. **February 27** Commends Marquis de la Rouerie; deadlocks over appointment of a secretary for foreign affairs.

March 1 Receives Indiana Company petition; accepts Virginia cession of western land claims; reads western land ordinance report. **March 2** Elects Henry Remsen under secretary for foreign affairs; deadlocks over appointment of a secretary. **March 4** Elects commissioners to negotiate with the Native Americans. **March 5** Debates plans for holding treaty with the Native Americans. **March 10** Fails to convene quorum. **March 12** Rejects Connecticut protest against half-pay plan. **March 13** Rejects Delaware delegate credentials, exceeding three-year limitation. **March 16** Bars appointment of aliens to consular and other foreign posts. **March 19** Adopts instructions for Native American commissioners. **March 22-25** Postpones debate on Lusannah admiralty appeal. **March 23** Rejects credentials of Massachusetts delegate Samuel Osgood. **March 26** Affirms that in negotiating commercial treaties these United States be considered . . . as one nation, upon the principles of the federal constitution." **March 30** Sets quotas and adopts fiscal appeal to the states; rejects motion denying Continental jurisdiction in Lusannah appeal.

April 1-2 Debates report on negotiating commercial treaties. **April 5** Adopts appeal to the states on arrears of interest payments on the public debt. **April 6** Reads report on maintaining frontier garrisons. **April 8** Instructs agent of marine on sale of Continental ships. **April 12** Debates public debt. **April 14** Debates motion to adjourn from Annapolis to various proposed sites. **April 16** Instructs "*commissioners for treating with the Native American nations.*" **April 19** Debates western land ordinance; deletes anti-slavery paragraph. **April 20-21** Debates western land ordinance. **April 23** Debates western land ordinance. **April 24** Receives New York memorial concerning the Vermont dispute. **April 26** Resolves to adjourn June 3, to reconvene at Trenton October 30; debates capital's location. **April 27-28** Debates public debt. **April 28** Orders arrest of Henry Carbery, leader of Pennsylvania mutiny. **April 29** Exhorts states to complete western land cessions. **April 30** Requests states to vest Congress with power to regulate trade "*for the term of fifteen years.*"

May 3 Reaffirms secrecy rule on foreign dispatches; receives French announcement on opening free ports to US trade. **May 5** Debates retrenchment of the civil list. **May 7** Sets diplomatic salaries; appoints John Jay secretary for foreign affairs. **May 11** Adopts instructions for negotiation of commercial treaties.

May 12 Resolves to request delivery of frontier posts to US troops. **May 15** Debates disqualification of Rhode Island delegates. **May 17** Receives announcement of French Minister La Luzerne's intention to return to France. **May 18** Orders troops for the protection of Native American commissioners. **May 19-24** Debates disqualification of Rhode Island delegates. **May 21-22** Fails to convene quorum. **May 25-27** Debates garrisoning frontier posts. **May 28** Adopts "*Ordinance for putting the department of finance into Commission*"; reads proposed land ordinance and report on Native American affairs. **May 29** Appoints Committee of the States "*to sit in the recess of Congress,*" and adopts resolutions defining its powers and rules. Offers reward for arrest of chevalier de Longchamps for assault on the French consul general, the marquis de Barbe-Marbois. **May 31** Debates garrisoning frontier posts.

June 1 Resolves to meet thrice daily until adjournment. **June 2** Orders discharge of Continental troops "*except 25 privates to guard the stores at Fort Pitt, and 55 to guard the stores at West Point.*" **June 3** Instructs ministers plenipotentiary not to relinquish navigation of the Mississippi; authorizes call of 700 militiamen to protect the northwestern frontiers; elects three treasury commissioners; adjourns "*to meet at Trenton on the 30th day of October.*"

Thomas Mifflin's interest in politics did not end with the Presidency. He was a member of the Pennsylvania Legislature and was elected speaker of that body in 1785. In 1787, Mifflin was elected as a delegate to the convention that framed the Constitution of the United States. Mifflin attended regularly, but made no speeches and did not play a substantial role in the Convention. He was one of the signers of the US Constitution on September 17, 1787.

He was elected a member of the supreme executive council of Pennsylvania in 1788, succeeded to its presidency, and filled that office until 1790. He presided over the convention that was called to devise a new constitution for Pennsylvania, was elected the first governor over Arthur St. Clair, and re-elected for the two successive terms of three years each. He raised Pennsylvania's quota of troops for the suppression of the Whiskey Insurrection, and served during the campaign under the orders of Governor Henry Lee, of Virginia. Governor Mifflin was a member of the American Philosophical Society from 1768 until his death.

Not being eligible under the constitution for a fourth term in the governor's chair, he was elected in 1799 to the assembly, during which time he affiliated himself with the emerging Republican Party. Thomas Mifflin, like his colleague Thomas Jefferson, was wealthy most of his life, but a copious spender. Demands from his creditors forced him to leave Philadelphia in 1799, and he died in Lancaster the following year at age 56. Pennsylvania remunerated his burial expenses at the local Trinity Lutheran Church.

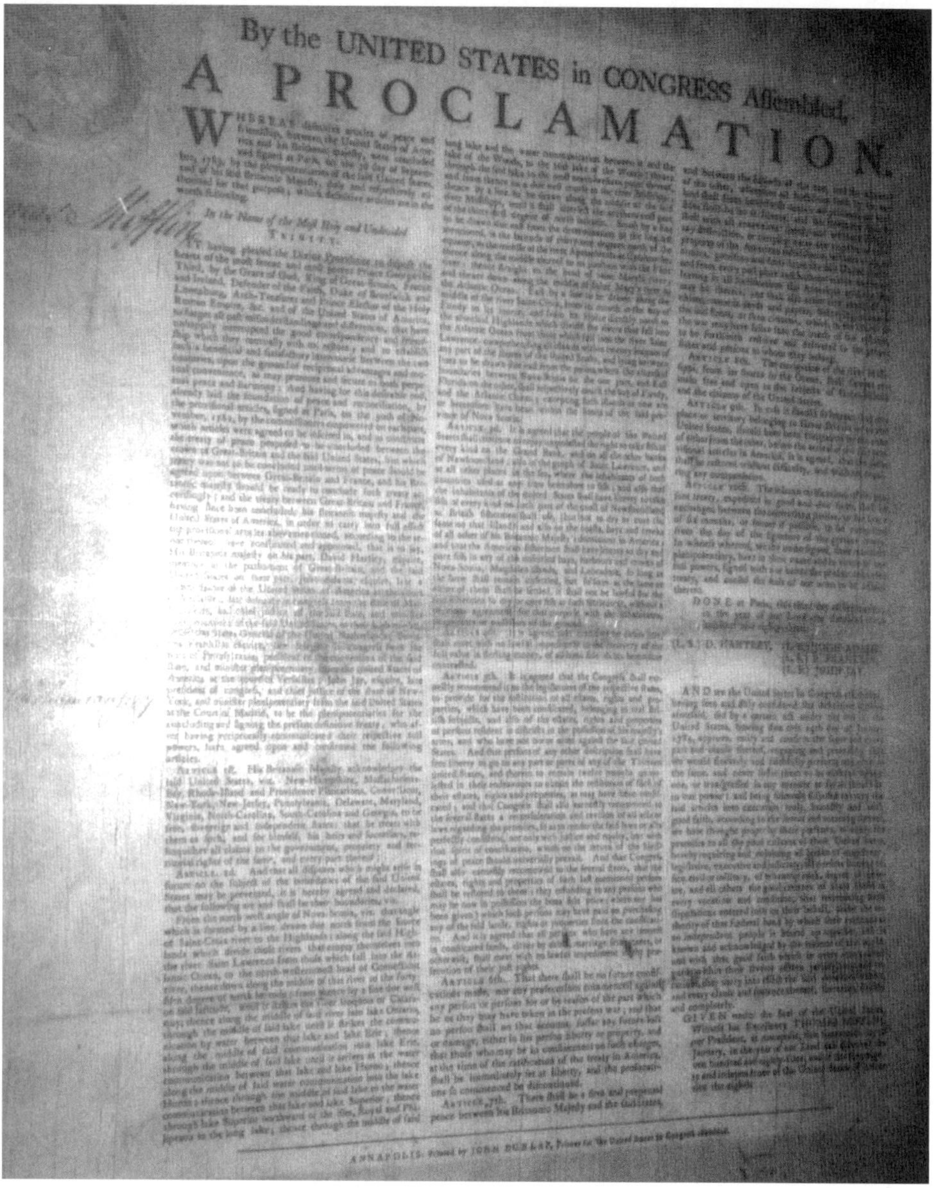
By the UNITED STATES in CONGRESS Assembled.

A PROCLAMATION.

A PROCLAMATION.

Definitive Treaty of Peace

<u>Given under the seal of the United States. Witness his Excellency THOMAS MIFFLIN, our President,</u> at Annapolis, this 14th day of January 1784, and of the sovereignty and independence of the United States of America, the eighth – *Courtesy of the National Archives*

CHAPTER TWELVE

Portrait of Richard Henry Lee from

Appleton Cyclopedia of American Biography

RICHARD HENRY LEE

6th President of the United States
in Congress Assembled
November 30, 1784 to November 23, 1785

Richard Henry Lee was born in Stratford, Westmoreland County, Virginia on January 20th, 1732 and died in Chantilly, Virginia on June 19th, 1794. He was the third son of a Thomas Lee, and at an early age was sent over to England for schooling at the academy of Wakefield in Yorkshire. The personal wealth of his family enabled Lee to choose any profession, including philanthropist. In 1752 he returned to Virginia and without any plans for a professional practice applied himself with great diligence to the study of law. Both English and Roman law occupied his attention; he was also an earnest student of history.

In 1757 he was appointed justice of the peace for Westmoreland County. In 1761 he was elected to the Virginia House of Burgesses, of which he remained a delegate until 1788. Extreme shyness prevented his taking any part in the debates for some time. His first speech was on a motion:

> *"to lay so heavy a duty on the importation of slaves as effectually to put an end to that iniquitous and disgraceful traffic within the colony of Virginia."*

On this occasion his hatred of slavery overcame his timidity and he made a powerful speech containing the proofs of the principal arguments used in later days by the northern Abolitionists.

He was an energetic opponent of the Stamp-Act, and in 1765 formed an association of citizens of Westmoreland County for the purpose of deterring all persons from undertaking to sell stamped paper. A Tory gentleman in the neighborhood accepted the office of Stamp-Collector and boasted that he would enforce the use of stamped paper upon the people in spite of all resistance. Mr. Lee, being then captain of a volunteer company of Light Horse, at once went with his men to this gentleman's house and made him deliver up his commission as collector and all the stamped paper in his possession. He also insisted the former collector bind himself by oath never again to meddle with such matters. The Stamp-Collector Commission and the obnoxious paper were thereupon burned with due ceremony in a bonfire on the lawn.

At the news of the Townshend Acts of 1767, Mr. Lee moved a petition to the king in the House of Burgesses, setting forth in pointed terms the grievances of the colonies. In July 1768, he wrote a letter to John Dickinson, suggesting that all the colonies should appoint select committees "*for mutual information and correspondence between the lovers of liberty in every province.*" The suggestion was in harmony with the views of the famous "*circular letter*" of the Massachusetts assembly, written by Samuel Adams and lately sent forth to all the colonies.

There has been some discussion as to whether Adams or Lee is to be credited with the first suggestion of those remarkable "*committees of correspondence*" which organized the American Revolution. The earliest suggestion of such a step, however, is to be found in a letter from the great Boston preacher, Jonathan Mayhew, to James Otis, in June 1766. This letter from Lee to Dickinson seems to have come next in point of date, and at the same time Christopher Gadsden appears to have received from Lee a letter of similar purport. Mr. Lee may or may not nave heard of Mayhew's suggestion. The idea was one that might naturally have occurred to several of these eminent men independently. The machinery of committees of correspondence was first actually set in motion by Samuel Adams in 1772 to be used between the towns of Massachusetts. The project of inter-colonial committees was first put into practical shape by the Virginia House of Burgesses, in the spring of 1773, on motion of the youthful Dabney Cart, brother-in-law of Thomas Jefferson.

Mr. Lee was a member of the Virginia committee and about this time he wrote to Samuel Adams a letter, which was the beginning of the lifelong friendship between the two great leaders. In August 1774, Mr. Lee was chosen as a delegate to the First Continental Congress just about to assemble at Philadelphia. He was a member of the committees for stating the rights of the colonies, for enforcing commercial non-intercourse with Great Britain, and for preparing suitable addresses to the king and to the colonies - Canada, New Brunswick, Nova Scotia, Georgia, and the Floridas - that had not sent delegates to the congress.

In the second Congress he drew up the address to the people of Great Britain, which along with a last petition to the king, was carried over to London by Richard Penn in August 1775. About this time Mr. Lee was chosen lieutenant of Westmoreland County, an office which, after the analogy of the lord-lieutenancy of a county in England, gave him command of the militia; hence he is often addressed or described, in writings of the time, as "*Colonel Lee.*"

For more than a year he openly and warmly advocated a declaration of independence. After the May 17, 1776 Virginia Convention instructed its delegates in congress to propose such a measure, it was Lee who took the foremost part. On June 7th, 1776 he moved

> "*that these united colonies are, and of right ought to be, free and independent states; and that all political connection between them and the state of Great Britain is, and ought to be, totally dissolved.*"

John Adams seconded the motion. Congress deferred action for three weeks, in order that more definite instructions might be received from the middle colonies. In an uncanny twist of fate Mr. Lee was called home by the illness of his wife. It was at this time that Thomas Jefferson was appointed in his place as chairman of the committee for preparing a draft of the proposed declaration. For the same reason, the task of defending the motion, when taken up for discussion, fell mainly upon John Adams, who had seconded it.

John Adams was successful in defending Mr. Lee's motion, and on July 2, 1776, the United Colonies of America officially became the United States of America. It was July 2, 1776 that John Adams thought would be celebrated by future generations of Americans.

> "*The Second Day of July 1776 will be the most memorable Epocha, in the History of America. . . . It ought to be solemnized with Pomp and Parade, with Shews, Games, Sports, Guns, Bells, Bonfires, and Illuminations from one End of this Continent to the other from this Time forward forever more.*" --John Adams to Abigail Adams, July 3, 1776

Thomas Jefferson, of course went on to author the formal Declaration of Independence, which was passed by Congress on July 4, 1776, immortalizing the young delegate forever.

During the next four years Mr. Lee served on more than a hundred committees; his labors in Congress were so arduous as to injure his health. He was several times obliged to go home and devote himself to recruiting his strength. From 1780 until 1782 he did not take his seat in Congress, inasmuch as the affairs of Virginia seemed to require his presence in the assembly of that state. Besides the business of defense against the British army then operating in the southern states, two questions of great importance were at that time debated in Virginia. One related to the propriety of making a depreciated paper currency a legal tender for debts, the other was brought up by a proposal to repudiate all debts to British merchants contracted by citizens of Virginia before the beginning of the war. In these debates Mr. Lee took strong ground against paper money, and he vehemently condemned the repudiation of debts, declaring that it were better to be "*the honest slaves of Great Britain than to become dishonest freemen.*"

After the peace he devoted much time to considering the best method of funding the public debt of the state and providing for the revival of public credit. In the hopes that Mr. Lee could duplicate his financial success with Virginia's debt, Congress elected him President on November 30, 1784:

> *The committee, to whom were referred the credentials produced by the delegates from the states of Massachusetts, Rhode Island, New Jersey, Pennsylvania, Virginia, North Carolina, South Carolina and Georgia, report, "That they have carefully examined the credentials to them referred, and are of opinion, that the honorable Samuel Holten and George Partridge, of the State of Massachusetts; the honorable David Howell, of the State of Rhode Island; the honorable William Churchill Houston and John Beatty, of the State of New Jersey; the honorable Joseph Gardner and William Henry, of Lancaster, of the State of Pennsylvania; the honorable Samuel Hardy, James Monroe and Richard Henry Lee, of the State of Virginia; the honorable Hugh Williamson and Richard Dobbs Spaight, of the State of North Carolina; the honorable Jacob Read, John Bull and Charles Pinckney, of the State of South Carolina; and the honorable William Houstoun and William Gibbons, of the State of Georgia, appear to be clearly and indisputably entitled to their seats, are authorized to sit and vote in the present Congress of the United States. Eight states being assembled, the United States in Congress assembled, proceeded to the election of a President, and, the ballots being taken, the honorable Richard Henry Lee was elected.*

Richard Henry Lee's Presidency was a busy one, attending to the needs of the new nation. Lee belonged to the Adams Republican faction of whose candor and straightforwardness bore few secrets. In a November 18, 1784 letter to Samuel Adams he wrote, "*I shall be extremely happy to be aided by tour counsels during my residence in Congress.*" Lee's letters are abundant and we know he favored low taxes by funding the debt with foreign loans. Lee despised taxes and Congress' willingness to tax the citizens at a Federal level. Lee wrote to Samuel Adams on March 14, 1785

> But I can never agree that this Body shall dictate the mode of Taxation, or the collection shall in any manner be subject to Congressional control.

The man who wrote the resolution for Independence distrusted the central government and in 1788 fought against the ratification of the new US Constitution. In an October 1787 letter to George Mason, Lee warned that the new Federal government would "... produce a coalition of monarchy of men, military men, aristocrats and drones, whose noise, impudence and zeal exceeds all belief". Lee summed up his philosophy to Samuel Adams in a March 14, 1785 letter two years earlier stating:

> *I think sir that the first maxim of a man who loves liberty should be, never to grant to Rulers an atom of power that is not most clearly and indispensable necessary for the safety and well being of Society.*

Lee was the only true "radical" to win the President of the United States in Congress Assembled but the new executive departments had weaned away the power of the office in this time of Peace to a shadow of Huntington's Presidency. The journals of the United States in Congress Assembled reported this of Lee's Congress:

> **1784 - December 3** Registers commission of Swedish Consul Charles Hellstedt; orders redeployment of Fort Stanwix troops to West Point. **December 7** Countermands redeployment of Fort Stanwix troops, who are ordered to Fort Rensselaer. **December 8** Receives Massachusetts and New York agents assembled to select judges for hearing land claim dispute between the two states. **December 11** Rejects motion to adjourn from Trenton; commends the Marquis de Lafayette. **December 14** Postpones election of treasury commissioners; directs Benjamin Franklin to delay signing consular convention with France. **December 15** Receives Spanish announcement closing Mississippi River. **December 17** Elects chaplain to Congress; resolves to appoint minister to Spain. **December 20** Overturns decision to create two capitals; appropriates $100,000 for capital buildings. **December 23** Adopts ordinance for fixing upon a place for the residence of Congress." **December 24** Certifies selection of judges for hearing Massachusetts-New York land claim dispute; adjourns to New York City.
>
> **1785 -January 11** Reconvenes, five states represented. **January 13** Achieves quorum, seven states represented. **January 18** Accepts offer of New York City Hall for the use of Congress. **January 20** Communicates to states intelligence on the precariousness of United States credit abroad. **January 24** Orders preparation of a requisition on the states for 1785. **January 25** Elects treasury commissioners; tables L'Enfant plan for establishing a corps of engineers. **January 27** Adopts ordinance "for ascertaining the powers and duties of the Secretary at War." **January 31** Resolves to appoint minister to Great Britain. February 1 Ratifies terms of a two-million-guilder Dutch loan.
>
> **February 2** Adopts proclamation urging states to penalize counterfeiting. **February 7** Approves lease of public buildings at Carlisle, Pennsylvania., to Dickinson College; orders removal of War Office, Post Office and Treasury

offices to New York. **February 10** Elects Philip Schuyler commissioner for planning federal capital. **February 11** Adopts regulations for the office for foreign affairs, conceding to Secretary Jay's demands. **February 18** Limits terms of ministers abroad. **February 21** Resolves to send commissioners to the Illinois Settlements. **February 24** Appoints John Adams minister to Great Britain. March 4 Opens debate on western land ordinance.

March 7 Authorizes Benjamin Franklin's return to America; resolves to appoint minister to the Netherlands. **March 8** Elects Henry Knox secretary at war. **March 10** Elects Thomas Jefferson minister to France. **March 11** Adopts instructions for negotiating with the Barbary States. **March 15** Adopts instructions for the southern Native American commissioners. **March 16** Rejects motion to limit slavery in the territories. **March 17** Imposes 12-month limit for submission of claims against the United States. **March 18** Adopts instructions for the western Native American commissioners. **March 21** Elects southern Native American commissioners; thanks king of Denmark for offer to ordain American candidates for holy orders. **March 28** Receives report on granting Congress commerce powers. **March 31** Adopts ordinance for regulating the office of secretary of Congress; receives report on 1785 requisition.

April 1 Debates Continental military needs. **April 7** Authorizes military establishment of 700 troops. **April 14** Reads revised western land ordinance. **April 18** Accepts Massachusetts western land cession. **April 22-28** Debates western land ordinance. **April 29** Appeals to states to maintain representation.

May 2-6 Debates western land ordinance. **May 9-10** Fails to achieve quorum (five states). **May 12** Fails to achieve quorum (six states). **May 13** Receives coinage report. **May 18-19** Debates western land ordinance. **May 20** Adopts western land ordinance; appeals to North Carolina to repeat western land cession. **May 24** Fails to achieve quorum (four states). **May 27** Renews appointment of geographer of the United States; appoints 13 continental surveyors.

June 1 Authorizes appointment of federal court to decide South Carolina-Georgia boundary dispute. **June 3** Publishes treaties with the Native Americans negotiated at Fort Stanwix and Fort McIntosh. **June 6** Authorizes negotiation of a Native American treaty at Vincennes. **June 7** Discharges Fort Pitt garrison. **June 14** Responds to French announcement of the birth of a second heir to the throne. **June 17** Orders John Jay to plan audience for the Spanish plenipotentiary Diego de Gardoqui. **June 20** Orders inquiry into the administration of the late superintendent of finance. **June 21** Orders annual inquiry into treasury administration. **June 23** Appoints William Livingston minister to the Netherlands (declines). **June 29** Asks Virginia to provide military support for Native American commissioners. **June 30** Orders a study of mail transportation.

July 1 Rejects motion to abolish court of appeals, but terminates salaries of the judges. **July 2** Receives Diego de Cardoqui. **July 4** Celebrates Independence Day. **July 5** Appoints John Rutledge minister to the Netherlands (declines). **July 6** Adopts the dollar as the money unit of the United States. **July 11** Continues rations for Canadian refugees. **July 12** Receives Post Office report. **July 13-14** Debates granting Congress commerce power. **July 18** Debates 1785 requisition. **July 20** Abolishes commissary of military stores. **July 22** Debates 1785 requisition. **July 25** Abolishes quartermaster department. **July 28-29** Debates 1785 requisition.

August 1-3 Debates 1785 requisition. **August 5** Orders removal of the treasurer's office to New York (by October 1). **August 10-13** Recesses. **August 15** Thanks king of Spain for sending Gardoqui mission. **August 17** Appoints Samuel Holten chairman in the absence of President Lee (through September 29 for the recovery of his health); Secretary Thomson to report delegate attendance monthly. **August 18** Endorses conduct of Massachusetts Governor James Bowdoin in controversy with British naval captain Henry Stanhope. **August 25** Grants John Jay greater latitude in negotiating with Gardoqui. **August 29** Abolishes committee of the week (duties transferred to secretary of Congress.

September 2-3 Fails to achieve quorum (five states and two states, respectively). **September 5** Receives John Jay report on British occupation of northwest posts. **September 7** Authorizes John Jay to inspect the mails when ever required by United States "safety or interest"; approves the conveyance of mails by stage carriages. **September 13-17** Debates 1785 requisition. **September 19-21** Debates appeal of Connecticut settlers in the Wyoming valley. **September 22-26** Debates 1785 requisition. **September 27** Adopts 1785 requisition. **September 29** Authorizes commission to settle Massachusetts-New York eastern boundary.

October 5 Orders postmaster general to extend system of posts. **October 7** Debates threat of western separatism. **October 12** Authorizes troops to attend western Native American negotiations; exhorts states to meet fiscal quotas. **October 17-18** Mourns death of Virginia delegate Samuel Hardy (age 27). **October 20** Receives John Jay's report on naval threat of Barbary States. **October 21-22** Fails to achieve quorum (six states and one state, respectively). **October 25** Fails to achieve quorum (four states). **October 27** Rejects proposal to create consular establishment. **October 28** Confers consular powers on ministers abroad.

November 2 Postpones convening of court to determine Massachusetts-New York western land claims dispute; suspends recruitment for 700-troop establishment. **November 4** Congressional session expires.

At the end of the presidential term of one year he returned to Virginia, but in 1787 was sent again to Congress. He was not a member of the convention at Philadelphia, which in the summer of that year framed our Federal constitution; when the new constitution was reported to congress, he earnestly opposed its adoption. He thought it provided for a consolidated national power that would ultimately destroy the state governments and end in a centralized despotism. His correspondence at this time with Samuel Adams, who was inclined to entertain the same fears, is very instructive.

These misgivings were also shared by Patrick Henry and many other patriotic Virginians. The first senators elected by their state were Lee and Grayson, in opposition to two Federalists, one of whom was James Madison, who had been foremost in the constructive work of the great convention. As senator, Mr. Lee proposed the tenth amendment to the Constitution in these words: "*The powers not delegated by the Constitution to the United States, nor prohibited by it to the states, are reserved to the states respectively.*" The amendment, as adopted, substituted the word "*granted*" for "*delegated*," and added at the end the words "*or to the people.*"

Though at first an Anti-Federalist, Mr. Lee came to be a warm supporter of Washington's administration, and especially approved of his course in the affair of "citizen" Genet. In 1792 he was obliged, by failing health, to resign his seat in the senate and retire to his estate at Chantilly, where he spent the last two years of his life

Mr. Lee was tall and graceful in person and striking in feature. His voice was clear and rich, and his oratory impressive. He did not waste time in rhetoric, but spoke briefly and to the point. His ideas were so lucid and his expression so forcible that when he sat down after a few weighty words it used to seem as if there were no more to be said on the subject. His capacity for work was great, though sometimes limited by poor health; as Dr. Rush said, "**His mind was like a sword too large for its scabbard.**"

He was twice married, and left, by his first wife, a Miss Aylett, two sons and two daughters; by his second, a Miss Pinkard, two daughters. His life has been written by his grandson, Richard Henry Lee, of Leesburg, Virginia, "*Memoir of the Life of Richard Henry Lee, and his Correspondence*" (2 vols., Philadelphia, 1825).

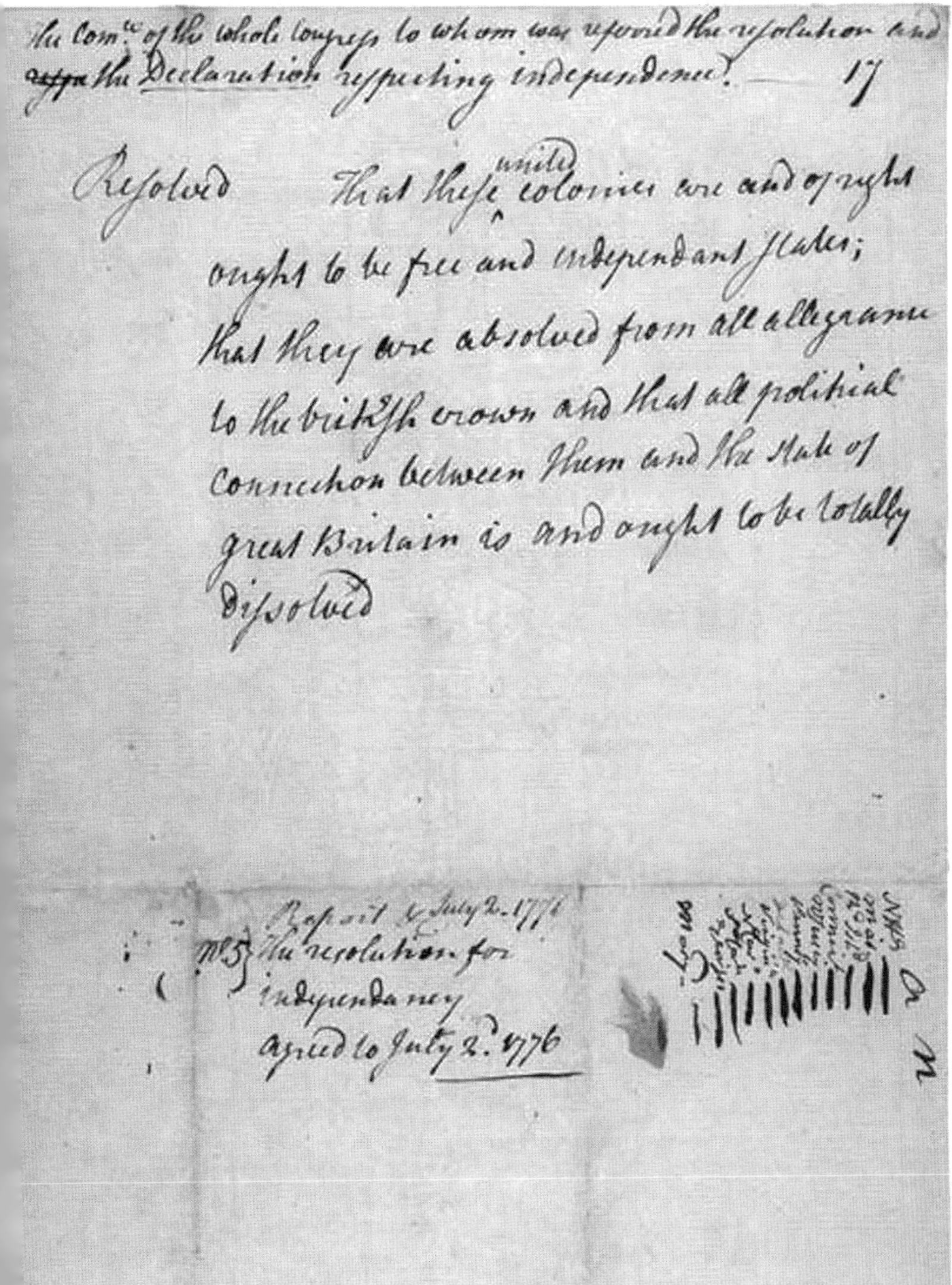
the Com.ee of the whole Congress to whom was referred the resolution and ~~resp~~ the Declaration respecting independence. 17

Resolved That these united colonies are and of right ought to be free and independant states; that they are absolved from all allegiance to the british crown and that all political connection between them and the state of great Britain is and ought to be totally dissolved

Report of July 2. 1776
No. 5 The resolution for independancy
agreed to July 2. 1776

Lee's Resolution -- Independence Day was actually July 2, 1776 -- *Courtesy of the National Archives*

CHAPTER THIRTEEN

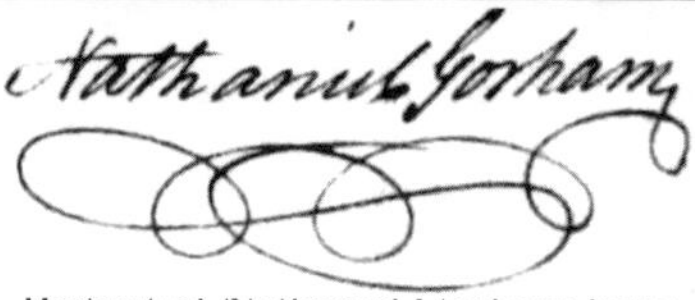

Portrait of Nathaniel Gorham from
Library of Congress

NATHANIEL GORHAM

8th President of the United States
in Congress Assembled
June 1786 - November 13, 1786

Nathaniel Gorham was born in Charlestown, Massachusetts on May 27th, 1738 and died there on June 11th, 1796. He was the son of a small boat operator, a family of modest means. After receiving a public school education, he engaged in mercantile pursuits in his native town. He was apprenticed in 1754 to Nathaniel Coffin, a merchant in New London, Connecticut. He left Coffin's employ in 1759 and returned to his hometown. Gorham established a small business there, which quickly succeeded. In 1763 he wed Rebecca Call, who was to bear nine children. In 1770, he launched his public career as a notary, soon winning election to the colonial legislature in 1771. He took an active part in public affairs at the beginning of the Revolution, where he supported the Whigs. He was elected delegate to the Massachusetts' Provincial Congress in 1774 and served throughout 1775. He was a member of the board of war from 1778 until its dissolution in 1781, which oversaw Massachusetts' military strategy, logistics and recruitment. He paid the price for the effective service in that office, as British troops ravaged much of his property.

In 1779 he served as a delegate in the Massachusetts' Constitutional Convention. He was elected to the new Massachusetts' Upper House in 1780. In 1781 he was elected to the Lower House and served until 1787. In 1782, Gorham was also elected delegate to the United States in Congress Assembled, serving through 1783. He was re-elected in 1785, serving until 1787.

On May 15, 1786 he assumed the Chair of Congress in the absence of President John Hancock. Gorham was the antithesis of his predecessor Richard Henry Lee as he was conservative in government and monarchly inclined. With Hancock's resignation as President he was a natural to serve out the term until the new President was elected in November. Rufus King supported his Presidency and mustered the support to have him elected On June 5th, 1786 President of the United States in Congress Assembled.

It turned-out that with the advent of Shays Rebellion his Presidency came at a most perilous time in US History, as the Articles of Confederation had failed to provide the Federal Government with the necessary authority and taxes to govern. Additionally, under his presidency the Annapolis Convention to revise the Articles of Confederation failed to offer Congress a direction to improve the crumbling federal government. The Chronology of his presidency is as follows:

1786 - May 15, 1786 Elects Nathaniel Gorham chairman of Congress to succeed David Ransay. **May 17** Ratifies Prussian-American treaty of commerce. **May 18** Postpones until September meeting of agents for Georgia-South Carolina boundary dispute. **May 22-25** Debates Connecticut cession. **May 26** Declares conditional acceptance of Connecticut cession. **May 29** Fails to achieve quorum. **May 31** Amends rules to war; receives John Jay request for a committee to confer with him on negotiations with Diego de Gardoqui.

June 5 Receives resignation of President John Hancock; receives report on military establishment. **June 6** Elects Chairman Nathaniel Gorham president of the United States in Congress Assembled. **June 13-14** Fails to achieve quorum. **June 15** Receives reports on prospects for Native American hostilities and on Continental arsenals and magazines. **June 16** Orders Native American commissioners to report on prospects for hostilities **June 19-20** Fails to achieve quorum. **June 21** Bans acceptance of paper money by post offices. **June 22** Orders troop reinforcements "*to the rapids of the Ohio.*" **June 27** Directs court of appeals judges to reconvene November 6 and reinstates salaries on per diem basis. **June 28** Receives draft ordinance for the Native American department. **June 30** Responds to Virginia appeal for protection against western Native Americans.

July 4 Celebrates anniversary of independence. **July 7** Requests revision of

Virginia cession to permit creation of "*not more than five nor less than three*" states from the Northwest Territory. **July 12** Revokes commissions of those appointed to negotiate treaties with the Native Americans. **July 13** Recommits draft territorial plan of government. **July 21** Debates Native American affairs ordinance. **July 24** Orders second reading of Native American affairs ordinance **July 27** Seeks revision of New York act authorizing Continental impost.

August 1 Receives report on arsenals and ordnance. **August 2** Adopts 1786 requisition. **August 3** Authorizes purchase of West Point; confers with secretary for foreign affairs on negotiation of treaty with Spain. **August 7** Adopts Native American affairs ordinance. **August 8** Adopts coinage standards; orders board of treasury to report an ordinance for establishment of a mint. **August 9** Appeals to North Carolina, South Carolina and Georgia for land cessions. **August 10** Debates John Jay's instructions for negotiating Spanish treaty. **August 14** Appoints committee to meet with Pennsylvania Assembly on revising act authorizing Continental impost. **August 16-23** Debates John Jay's instructions for negotiating Spanish treaty. **August 24** Orders relief for displaced Moravian Native Americans. **August 28** Debates John Jay's negotiating instructions. **August 29** Repeals John Jay's negotiating instructions by seven-to-five vote (which was contested on the ground that nine votes were constitutionally required). **August 30-31** Debates repeal of John Jay's instructions.

September 1-2 Debates repeal of John Jay's instructions. **September 4** Convenes agents for appointing a court to hear South Carolina-Georgia boundary dispute. **September 5** Authorizes settlement of Pennsylvania fiscal claim. **September 11** Receives South Carolina appeal for congressional intervention in hearing boundary dispute with Georgia. **September 12** Receives John Jay's report on consular convention with France. **September 13** Selects judges for hearing South Carolina- Georgia boundary dispute. **September 14** Accepts Connecticut land cession. **September 18** Bars payment of Continental requisitions in paper money. **September 20** Receives report on Annapolis Convention; orders postmasters "*to receive no other money in payment for postage than specie.*" **September 25** Receives report on conference of congressional committee with Pennsylvania Assembly. **September 28** Debates repeal of John Jay's negotiating instructions. **September 29** Debates ordinance for territorial government.

October 3 Instructs Thomas Jefferson on renegotiation of consular convention with France. **October 4** Debates Northwest ordinance. **October 6** Elects James White southern Native American superintendent. **October 10** Directs Native American superintendent to confer with southern states. **October 13** Adopts ordinance for settlement of the states' Continental accounts; receives report on British response to request for evacuation of frontier posts.

October 16 Adopts ordinance for establishment of a mint. **October 18** Receives secretary at war's report on Shays' Rebellion. **October 21** Increases military establishment - ostensibly for Native American defense but with an eye to the "*disorders*" in Massachusetts. **October 23** Appeals to states for authority to regulate trade; authorizes secretary for foreign affairs to inspect the mails for reasons of national security (excepting the mail of members of Congress). **October 26** Orders inquiry into postal service. **October 30** Authorizes suspension of interest credits on Rhode Island-held debt in retaliation for state paper money policy.

November 1-2 Debates postal reform. **November 3** Adjourns - referring "*the several matters now before Congress*" to the new Congress scheduled to meet "on Monday next." **November 6** Convenes - five states represented **November 7-24** Fails to achieve a quorum. **November 13** - Nathaniel Gorham's term as President ends.

For several years after his presidency, Gorham was judge of Middlesex County's court of common pleas. Most importantly he was elected to represent Massachusetts in the Philadelphia Convention that framed the National Constitution. When the convention was sitting as committee of the whole, he was called by George Washington to preside, and filled the chair for three of the four months. As chairman, he spoke often, wielded much influence and served on the Committee of Detail. In the final hours of the Constitution's preparation for vote, Nathaniel Gorham suggested the ratio of representation in the Lower House of Congress could amend from one for every forty-thousand inhabitants to one for every thirty-thousand. Gorham's proposal was unanimously passed:

It was moved to reconsider the clause declaring that "the number of representatives shall not exceed one for every forty thousand," in order to strike out "forty thousand," and insert "thirty thousand;" which passed in the affirmative.

On the question to agree to the Constitution, enrolled in order to be signed,--all the states answered, "Ay."

On the question to agree to the above form of signing, it passed in the affirmative.

Yeas: New Hampshire, Massachusetts, Connecticut, New Jersey, Pennsylvania, Delaware, Maryland, Virginia, North Carolina, Georgia, 10. Divided: South Carolina, 1.

-- The Debates in the Several State Conventions on the Adoption of the Federal Constitution

He afterward exerted a powerful influence in securing the ratification of the Constitution in the Massachusetts State Convention. Unfortunately, Gorham did not serve in the new government he helped to create.

In connection with Oliver Phelps, he purchased from the state of Massachusetts, in 1786, an immense tract of land on the Genesee River, for the sum of $1,000,000. This had been previously ceded to Massachusetts from the state of New York. They soon extinguished the Native American title to a part of this territory, surveyed it into tracts, laid out townships, and sold large parts to speculators and settlers. In 1788and 1789 Massachusetts scrip rose dramatically in value, enormously swelling the purchase price of the vast tract. In 1790, being unable to fulfill their contract in full to Massachusetts, Phelps and Gorham compromised and surrendered that portion of the land, which remained under the Native American title. Gorham never recovered from the insolvency and like Robert Morris in Philadelphia, he fell from a pinnacle of society and lost his political esteem. At the age of 58 on the 11th of June, 1796 he died a financially broken man and was buried at the Phipps Street Cemetery in Charlestown, MA.

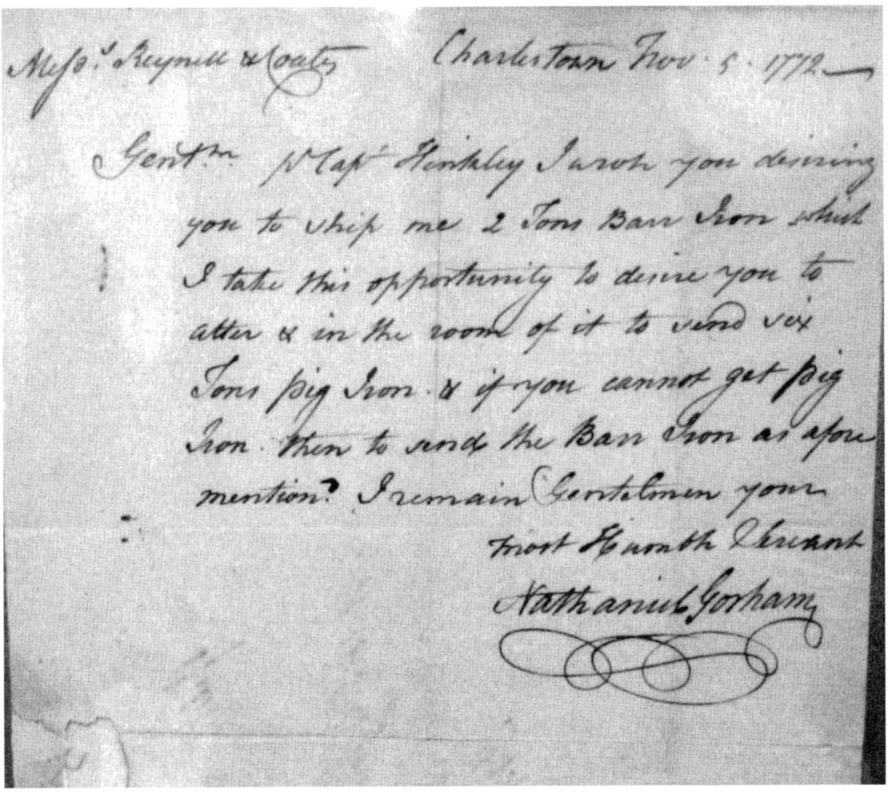

Mess.rs Reynell & Coates   Charlestown Nov. 5. 1772

Gent.m per Capt. Hinkley I wrote you desiring you to ship me 2 Tons Barr Iron which I take this opportunity to desire you to alter & in the room of it to send six Tons pig Iron & if you cannot get pig Iron then to send the Barr Iron as afore mention.d I remain Gentelmen your most Humble Servant

Nathaniel Gorham

November 9th, 1772 Autograph Letters Signed by Nathaniel Gorham –
Courtesy of the Klos Family

CHAPTER FOURTEEN

Portrait of Arthur St. Clair from
Appleton Cyclopedia of American Biography

ARTHUR ST. CLAIR

9th President of the United States
in Congress Assembled February 2, 1787 to October 29, 1787

Arthur St. Clair was born in Thurso, Scotland on March 23, 1734 and died in Greensburg, Pennsylvania on August 31, 1818. There is much debate over President St. Clair's Lineage and even his year of birth. Laurel Fechner, Historian Clan Sinclair USA, for instance maintains that St. Clair's actual name in Scotland was Sinclair born March 23, 1736.

St. Clair's life was a study in contrasts, enjoying a great family inheritance and then ending his life in desolate poverty; crossing the Delaware with Washington to capture Trenton while later loosing Fort Ticonderoga under his own command; presiding as President of the United States in the Congress Assembled that produced the US Constitution and Northwest Ordinance only to be removed by President Jefferson as Governor of the Northwest Territory for opposing Ohio Statehood.

St. Clair attended the University of Edinburgh and studied medicine, serving part of an apprenticeship with the renowned anatomist, William Hunter. In 1757, St. Clair changed his career path by purchasing a commission as ensign in the 60th Foot Infantry. He came to America with Admiral Edward Boscawen's fleet in that same year to exchange blows in the *French and Native American War.* He served under General Jeffrey Amherst at the capture of Louisburg on July 26th, 1758. On April 17, 1759 he received a lieutenant's commission and was assigned to the command of General James Wolfe. At the *Battle of the Plains,* which decided the fate of the French in America, St. Clair took a notable part:

> *"Then came the fatal struggle on the plains during which Lieutenant St. Clair seized the colors, which had fallen from the hand of a dying soldier, and bore them until the field was won by the British."*

One year later on duty in Boston, St. Clair married Phoebe Bayard in May of 1760 at the Trinity Episcopal Church. Phoebe was the daughter of Balthazar Bayard & Mary Bowdoin whose grandfather was James Bowdoin of Boston. In 1762 he resigned his commission and moved to Bedford, Pennsylvania to survey land for the Penn's. By 1764 the couple decided to settle permanently in Ligonier Valley, Pennsylvania. St. Clair purchased land and erected mills, becoming the largest landowner in western Pennsylvania and a quite prominent British subject.

In 1770 he was made surveyor of the district of Cumberland. He subsequently became a justice of the court, of quarter sessions and of common pleas, a member of the proprietary council, a justice, recorder, and clerk of the orphans' court, and prothonotary of Bedford and Westmoreland counties. In 1774 Virginia St. Clair as magistrate decided to reclaim Pittsburgh and a Dr. John Connolly, a native Pennsylvanian

> *"appeared on the ground, and having the authority and blessings of Lord Dunmore, Governor of Virginia, took possession of Fort Pitt."*

The Fort had recently been abandoned by the British government, and upon Connolly's seizure, it was renamed, calling it Fort Dunmore. At the Fort, in his official role of Captain Commandant of the Virginia Militia, he issued a proclamation, calling on the people of Western Pennsylvania to meet him, as a militia, on the 25th of January 1774.

Arthur St. Clair, then a magistrate of Westmoreland County was appalled by this action, and issued a warrant against John Connolly, having him committed to jail at Hannastown, the seat of justice of Westmoreland. In asserting the claims of Virginia, Lord Dumore insisted that Mr. St. Clair should be punished for his temerity in arresting his agent by dismissal from office. Governor Penn declined to remove St. Clair, who, he said, as a good magistrate, was bound to take legal notice of Mr. Connolly.

> *"Mr. St. Clair is a gentleman, who for a long time had the honor of serving his maj-esty in the regulars with reputation, and in every station of life has preserved the character of a very honest, worthy man; and though, perhaps, I should not, without first expostulating with you on the subject, have directed him to take that step, yet you must excuse my not complying with your Lordship's re1cttisition of stripping hire, on this occasion, of his offices and livelihood, which you will allow me to think not only unreasonable, but somewhat dic-tatorial."*

Counter arrests and much correspondence followed, but the controversy was soon obscured by the stirring events of Lord Dunmore's War. After this ended, disturbances were again received. Connolly was again arrested, but a counter arrest of three of the Pennsylvania justices caused his release. The Boundary Troubles between Virginia and Pennsylvania were finally settled while Arthur St. Clair was commissioned in the Revolutionary War.

On January 3rd, 1776, St. Clair became colonel of the 2nd Pennsylvania Regiment, and, being ordered to Canada, joined General John Sullivan after the disastrous affair at Three Rivers. St. Clair aided Sullivan by his counsel, saving the army from capture. In recognition of this service he was appointed Brigadier-General on August 9th, 1776, hav-ing resigned his civil offices in the previous January.

Joining General Washington in November 1776, he was appointed to organize the New Jersey militia and together with General Sullivan raised over 2000 new troops to support the Revolution. He and Sullivan joined Washington's beleaguered 400 troops in Pennsylvania and prepared for the Delaware Crossing. On Christmas night 1776 St. Clair's Continental troops, now under Washington's command, crossed into New Jersey and attacked the Hessians in Trenton at dawn on the 26th. Twenty-two Hessians were killed, 84 wounded and 918 taken prisoner.

Washington called a council of war on January 2, 1777 with his troops camped along Assunpink Creek. Many of St. Clair's Biographers, and even St. Clair himself, claim that he suggested the movement that culminated in the Victory at Princeton the following day. Biographers maintain that not only did St. Clair direct the details of the march but also his own brigade marched at the head of the advancing army. British losses were esti-mated at 400 to 600 killed, wounded or taken prisoner and Cornwallis was forced to withdraw into Northern New Jersey.

Arthur St. Clair's next call to action was by John Hancock who ordered him to defend Fort Ticonderoga. This upstate New York fort was built to control the strategic route between the St. Lawrence River in Canada and the Hudson River to the south. Overlooking the outlet of Lake George into Lake Champlain, it was considered a key to the continent. The fort was used in the French and Native American War and largely abandoned after that, but the British had military stores there at the beginning of the

Revolution. In 1775, Ethan Allen and Benedict Arnold surprised the British and captured the fort. The cannons and armaments were used in the siege of Boston, which drove the British out of Massachusetts. The fort was garrisoned with 12,000 troops to counter any invading force coming into America from Canada.

In 1776 with Washington's losses troops deserted and were moved to more pressing posts in Pennsylvania and New Jersey. By the spring of 1777 the fort had fallen in disrepair with only a handful of troops protecting the northern passage When it became clear that the British, under General Burgoyne, were marching south to retake the fort, Congress quickly ordered Major General Arthur St. Clair to command and defend Fort Ticonderoga, by this very letter:

Philadelphia, April 30, 1777,

> *Sir:*
>
> *The Congress having received intelligence of the approach of the enemy towards Ticonderoga have thought proper to direct you to repair thither without delay. I have it therefore in charge to transmit the enclosed resolve [not present] and to direct that you immediately set out on the receipt hereof.*
>
> *John Hancock, Presidt.*
>
> *To: Maj. Gen. Arthur St. Clair.*

He arrived in early June and set about preparations for defense.

However desirous Congress was of retaining Fort Ticonderoga, St. Clair was only spared some 2,500 men and scarce provisions to hold it. A minimum garrison of 10,000 men was required to check the British advance. Burgoyne's army consisted of 8,000 British regulars and 2,500 auxiliary troops. When they arrived in the area, the British placed artillery batteries atop nearby Mount Defiance, and were soon capable of bombarding the fort without fear of retaliation by the Americans.

St. Clair's force was too small to cover all exposed points. He neglected to fortify the steep assent to Sugar Loaf Mountain over which the British approached. St. Clair and his officers held a council of war, and decided to evacuate the fort. Matthias Alexis Roche de Fermoy was commander of Fort Independence, opposite Fort Ticonderoga. By orders of Congress, and against the protest of Washington made a grave military error that almost caused St. Clair the loss of a large number of his forces. Upon the retreat of St. Clair from Ticonderoga, Fermoy set fire to his quarters on Mount Independence at two o'clock on the morning of July 6th, 1777 thus revealing to Burgoyne St. Clair's evacuation of Ticonderoga. Had it not been for this, St. Clair would have made good his retreat.

St. Clair fled through the woods, leaving a part of his force at Hubbardto. These troops were attacked and defeated by General Fraser on July 7th, 1777, after a well-contested battle. On July 12th St. Clair reached Fort Edward with the remnant of his men. St. Clair reported:

"I know I could have saved my reputation by sacrificing the army; but were I to do so, I should forfeit that which the world could not restore, and which it cannot take away, the approbation of my own conscience".

St. Clair's action forced Burgoyne to divide his forces between pursuit of St. Clair and garrisoning Fort Ticonderoga. Burgoyne, after a long and arduous trek through the New York frontier, made an unsuccessful attempt to break through American Forces and Capture Saratoga. Burgoyne retreated and ordered his troops to entrench in the vicinity of the Freeman Farm. Here he decided to await support from Clinton, who was supposedly preparing to move north toward Albany from New York City. He waited for three weeks but Clinton never came. With his supply line cut and a growing Continental Army he decided to attack on October 7th ordering a reconnaissance-in-force to test the American left flank. This attack was unsuccessful and Burgoyne loss General Fraser primarily due to Benedict Arnold's direct counter-attack against the British Center.

That evening, following St. Clair's example, the British retreated but kept their campfires burning brightly to mask their withdrawal. Burgoyne's troops took refuge in a fortified camp on the heights of Saratoga. Clinton never arrived, the Continental Forces swelled to over 20,000. Faced with overwhelming numbers, Burgoyne surrendered on October 17, 1777 to General Horatio Gates without Gates firing a shot. This was one of the great American victories of the war and made the British retention of Fort Ticonderoga untenable. This surrender shocked the European Nations and foreign aid poured into US coffers from France and the Netherlands.

Despite this outcome General St. Clair was accused of cowardice. St. Clair remained with his army and was with Washington at Brandywine, September 11th, 1777, acting as voluntary aide. A court-martial was held in 1778, and he was acquitted, *"with the highest honor, of the charges against him,"* which verdict was approved by congress. The court inquiry concluded

"... the facts brought out by the court martial spoke eloquently in favor of St. Clair. Burgoyne's army, when he met St. Clair, numbered 7,863. St. Clair had less than 2200 men, all of whom were ill fed and half clad. Burgoyne surrounded him with 142 guns, while St. Clair had less than 100-second rate cannon of various sizes and these were served by inexperienced men. It is scarcely necessary to defend his retreat in this age of general intelligence."

Lafayette wrote to St. Clair,

"I cannot tell you how much my heart was interested in anything that happened to you and how I rejoiced, not that you were acquitted, but that your conduct was examined."

John Paul Jones wrote,

"I pray you be assured that no man has more respect for your character, talents, and greatness of mind than, dear General, your most humble servant."

Later St. Clair assisted General John Sullivan in preparing his expedition against the Six Nations, was a commissioner to arrange a cartel with the British at Amboy on March 9th, 1780. St Clair was appointed to command the corps of light infantry in the absence of Lafayette, but did not serve, owing to the return of General George Clinton. He was a member of the court-martial that condemned Major Andre, commanded at West Point in October 1780, and aided in suppressing the mutiny in the Pennsylvania line in January 1781.

St. Clair remained active during the 1780's Campaigns raising troops and forwarding them to the south. In the above Congress orders St. Clair's to round up his troops in preparation for his journey to Yorktown.

> *By the United States in Congress Assembled*
>
> *September 19, 1781*
>
> *Ordered that Major General St. Clair cause the levies of the Pennsylvania line now in Pennsylvania to rendezvous at or near Philadelphia with all possible exposition.*
>
> *Extract from the minutes*
>
> *Charles Thompson*

Specifically the Journals of the Continental Congress reported:

> *The report of the committee on the letter from Major General St. Clair was taken into consideration; Whereupon, The Committee to whom were referred the letter of the 28th. of August last from Major General St Clair, beg leave to report-- That they have conferred with the Financier on the subject of the advance of money requested by General St Clair for officers and privates of the Pennsylvania line, and that he informs your Committee that it is not in his power to make the said advances--*
>
> *That your Committee know of no means which enables Congress at present to make the advance requested by General St Clair: and they are therefore of opinion that his application ought to be transmitted to his Excellency the President and the Supreme Executive of the State of Pennsylvania with an earnest request that they will take the most effectual measures in their power to enable General St Clair to expedite the march of the troops mentioned in his letter.*
>
> *Ordered, That the application of Major General St. Clair be transmitted to his Excellency the president and the supreme executive council of the State of Pennsylvania and they be earnestly requested to take the most effectual measures in their power to enable General St. Clair to expedite the march of the troops mentioned in his letter.*

The result was that St. Clair joined Washington at Yorktown a few days before the surrender of Lord Cornwallis. In November he was placed in command of a body of troops to join General Nathanael Greene, and remained in the south until October 1782.

In 1783, while St. Clair was engaged in closing up the accounts and furloughing the veteran soldiers, new levies, stationed at Lancaster, refused to accept their discharges without immediate pay. The soldiers mutinied and marched for Philadelphia, for the stated purpose of compelling Congress to relinquish to their demands. The mutineers were reinforced by the recruits in the barracks of Philadelphia, and, as they marched to the hall where Congress was in session, they numbered three hundred.

Congress called out the Pennsylvania militia but it failed to come to the rescue. The Government of the United States of America, the Delegates of Congress Assembled, were held hostage in Philadelphia's famed Independence Hall. The mutineers demands were made in very dictatorial terms, that,

> *"unless their demand were com-plied with in twenty minutes, they would let in upon them the injured soldiery, the consequences of which they were to abide."*

Word was immediately sent to General St. Clair and his presence requested. Arthur St. Clair hurried to the rescue and confronted the mutineers. St. Clair reported to Congress and after hearing a report of the facts by him, Congress directed him

> *" ... to endeavor to march the mutineers to their barracks, and to announce to them that Congress would enter into no deliberation with them; that they must return to Lancaster, and that there, and only there, they would be paid."*

After this, Congress appointed a committee to confer with the executive of Pennsylvania, and adjourned:

> *Saturday, June 21, 1783 – Journals of the Continental Congress: The mutinous soldiers presented themselves, drawn up in the street before the state-house, where Congress had assembled. The executive council of the state, sitting under the same roof, was called on for the proper interposition. President DICKINSON came in, and explained the difficulty, under actual circumstances, of bringing out the militia of the place for the suppression of the mutiny. He thought that, without some outrages on persons or property, the militia could not be relied on. General St. Clair, then in Philadelphia, was sent for, and desired to use his interposition, in order to prevail on the troops to return to the barracks. His report gave no encouragement.*
>
> *In this posture of things, it was proposed by Mr. IZARD, that Congress should adjourn. It was proposed by Mr. HAMILTON, that General St. Clair, in concert with the executive council of the state, should take order for terminating the mutiny. Mr. REED moved, that the general should endeavor to withdraw the troops by assuring them of the disposition of Congress to do them justice. It was finally agreed, that Congress should remain till the usual hour of adjournment, but without taking any step in relation to the alleged grievances of the soldiers, or any other business whatever. In the mean time, the soldiers remained in their position, without offering any violence, individuals only, occasionally, uttering offensive words, and wantonly pointing their muskets to the windows of the hall of Congress. No danger from premeditated violence was apprehended, but it was observed that spirituous drink, from the tippling-houses adjoining, began to be liberally served out to the soldiers, and might lead to hasty excesses. None were committed, however, and, about three o'clock, the usual hour, Congress adjourned; the soldiers, though in some instances offering a mock obstruction, permitting the members to pass through their ranks. They soon afterwards retired themselves to the barracks.*

Thanks to Arthur St. Clair's ability to reason with the men, President Boudinot and the Congressional members passed through the files of the mutineers, without being molested. The committee, with Alexander Hamilton as chairman, waited on the State Executive Council to insure the Government of the United States protection when Congress was ready to convene the following day. Elias Boudinot, receiving no pledge of protection by the Pennsylvania militia advised an adjournment of the United States in Congress Assembled on June 24th to Princeton, New Jersey.

President Elias Boudinot now in his home state of New Jersey and protected by their militia wasted no time in dealing harshly with the mutineers. On June 30th, the day after Congress's arrival in New Jersey, a resolution was passed ordering General Howe to march fifteen hundred troops to Philadelphia to disarm the mutineers and bring them to trial.

> *That Major General Howe be directed to march such part of the force under his command as he shall judge necessary to the State of Pennsylvania; and that the commanding officer in the said State he be instructed to apprehend and confine all such persons, belonging to the army, as there is reason to believe instigated the late mutiny; to disarm the remainder; to take, in conjunction with the civil authority, the proper measures to discover and secure all such persons as may have been instrumental therein; and in general to make full examination into all parts of the transaction, and when they have taken the proper steps to report to Congress*

Before this force could reach Philadelphia, General St. Clair and the Executive Council had succeeded in quieting the disturbance without bloodshed. The principal leaders were arrested, obedience secured, and a trial was set.

The Congressional resolution directing General Howe to move with the troops against the mutineers affronted General St. Clair. The General regarded it as an attempt to supersede his command and undermined his negotiations. Arthur St. Clair took it upon himself to write Congress a scathing letter, which was answered by Elias Boudinot, President of the United States in Congress Assembled from Princeton NJ in the July 9, 1783 letter:

> *Dear Sir,*
>
> *I duly recd your favor of yesterday but conceiving that you had mistaken the Resolution of Congress, I showed it to Mr. Fitzsimmons and we have agreed not to present it to Congress, till we hear again from you. Congress were so careful to interfere one way or the other in the military etiquette, that we recommitted the Resolution to have every thing struck out that should look towards any determination as to the Command, and it was left so that the Commanding officer be him who it might, was to carry the Resolution into Execution; and it can bear no other Construction.*
>
> *If on the second reading you choose your Letter should be read in Congress, it shall be done without delay …*
>
> *Elias Boudinot, President*
>
> *P. S., You may depend on Congress having been perfectly satisfied with your conduct.*

Boudinot, undoubtedly, trusted St. Clair's judgment and spared him the embarrassment of making his letter known to Congress. Peace once again reigned. As a result of the mutiny the accused ringleaders were sentenced to death, but were pardoned by Congress in September 1783.

After the war General St. Clair returned to his neglected Ligonier estate finding the mill, which he had opened for communal use, to be in ruins. He was financially ruined by Native American depredations, which were antagonized by the British on his frontier holdings in Western Pennsylvania during the Revolutionary War. In 1785 St. Clair wrote his friend and mentor George Washington, *"I am poor, indeed a very poor man."*

St. Clair was of an *"imposing appearance"* bearing a tall and graceful carriage with blue eyes and graying chestnut hair. He was known to be intelligent and well-educated, *"of great uprightness of purpose, as well as suavity of manners."* He was a devoted husband to Phoebe who became mentally ill in 1777, as well as a caring father to his seven children. He personally suffered from gout, which prevented him from riding a horse or in later years from leaving his bed.

St. Clair seemed to prefer the calling of public service, finding it to be more engaging and meaningful than handling his private investments. He remained a member of the Pennsylvania Council of Censors. In 1785 he was elected Pennsylvania delegate to the United States in Congress Assembled and served until November 28th, 1787.

These were turbulent years and the United States Government was in chaos. Shay's Rebellion, led by Daniel Shays a former Revolutionary Army captain exemplified the mood of the nation. His followers, who were primarily New England farmers, rebelled against unsettled economic conditions, corrupt politicians and laws which were revoltingly unfair to working people in general. They protested against excessive taxes on property, polling taxes which prohibited the underprivileged from voting, inequitable actions by the court of common pleas, the excessive cost of lawsuits, and the lack of a stable currency.

On August 29, 1786, rebel mobs stormed the courthouse in Northampton to prevent the trial and imprisonment of debtors. In September 1786, Shays and about 600-armed farmers stormed the courthouse in Springfield. On January 25, 1787, Shays led 2000 rebels to Springfield, Massachusetts to storm the arsenal and in the midst of this bedlam Congress needed to elect a President of the United States to lead the unicameral government.

> *"...The Rebels formed and fired on our people, killed a Mr. Gleason of Stockbridge, a Mr. Porter of Barrington, and wounded three others. The fire was returned, which killed two and wounded five, among whom was their commander. At this instant, our troops in sleighs came up; but before the men could form, the Rebels broke and took to the woods. We have made prisoners of 25 of them, retook all our friends and their property...We have been very much harassed since out troops left this point. The malice of the Rebels can be equaled only by no order of beings but Devils." - CONNECTICUT COURANT 1787*

In 1787, the most eventful legislative year in US History, eight states assembled at New York City and elected Arthur St. Clair, President of the United States in Congress Assembled on February 2, 1787 only 9 days after Shay's attack on the Massachusetts Arsenal. Two days later, General Benjamin Lincoln's troops successfully defeated Shays' rebels at Petersham, Massachusetts. Despite the desperately needed victory St. Clair, as well as many other delegates, knew the Articles of Confederation were not sufficient enough to hold the Union together. His influence in Congress, however, reached new heights with the government constantly threatened by citizen rebellion and his close personal ties to retired George Washington.

In an earlier attempt to revise the Articles an Annapolis Constitutional Convention was held in September 1786. The convention only attracted Delegates from five of the 13 states, Maryland, New York, New Jersey, Delaware, Pennsylvania, and Virginia and was called *"Proceedings Of Commissioners To Remedy Defects Of The Federal Government"*. This gathering in Annapolis issued a report on September 11, 1786 that called upon the thirteen states to send representatives:

> *... to meet at Philadelphia on the second Monday in May next, to take into consideration the situation of the United States, to devise such further provisions as shall appear to them necessary to render the constitution of the Federal Government adequate to the exigencies of the Union; and to report such an Act for that purpose to the United States in Congress assembled, as when agreed to, by them, and afterwards confirmed by the Legislatures of every State, will effectually provide for the same.*

Five months later, unlike his predecessor Nathaniel Gorham, President Arthur St. Clair brought the Annapolis motion before Congress. On February 21, 1787 St. Clair's Confederation Congress formally approved the resolution for a Philadelphia Convention at now "Historic" Independence Hall to revise the Articles of Confederation beginning in the 2nd week of May 1787.

> *Resolved that in the opinion of Congress it is expedient that on the second Monday in May next a Convention of delegates who shall have been appointed by the several States be held at Philadelphia for the sole and express purpose of revising the Articles of Confederation and reporting to Congress and the several legislatures such alterations and provisions therein as shall when agreed to in Congress and confirmed by the States render the federal Constitution adequate to the exigencies of Government3 and the preservation of the Union. - Journals of the Confederation Congress WEDNESDAY, FEBRUARY 21, 1787*

On May 25, 1787 a quorum of delegates from seven states arrived in Philadelphia to start the meeting that is now known as the Constitutional Convention. The Constitutional Convention began the work on the New Plan for The Federal Government on June 19. St Clair's Congress, meanwhile, turned to the pressing matters of governing a nation that was splintering apart.

In June, St. Clair decided to recycle Jefferson's Ordinance of 1784 as the blueprint for national expansion to the West. This ordinance had failed enactment for nearly three years. The lack of a body of laws to govern the vast territory north and west of the Ohio River ceded to the United States in the Treaty of Paris stifled the westward expansion. It was a combination of the dire need for federal money and St. Clair's leadership that the Confederation Congress, on July 13, 1787, passed one the most far-reaching acts in American history, the Northwest Ordinance.

> *"An Ordinance for the government of the Territory of the United States northwest of the River Ohio. Section 1. Be it ordained by the United States in Congress assembled, That the said territory, for the purposes of temporary government, be one district, subject, however, to be divided into two districts, as future circumstances may, in the opinion of Congress, make it expedient. ..." (see the end of the chapter for the full text of the Northwest Ordinance)."*

The world was now put on notice that the land north and west of the Ohio River and east of the Mississippi would be settled and utilized for the creation of *"... not less than three nor more than five territories."* Additionally, this plan for governing the Northwest Territory included freedom of religion, right to trial by jury, the banishment of slavery, and public education as asserted rights granted to the people in the territory. This ordinance was and still remains one of the most important laws ever enacted by the government of the United States.

Specifically, this ordinance was an exceptional piece of legislation because *Article 5* permitted the people North and West of the Ohio River to settle their land, form their own territorial government, and take their place as a full fledged state, equal to the original 13. *The Northwest Ordinance's Article 5* became the principle that enabled the United States rapid westward expansion, which ended with the inclusion of Alaska and Hawaii as our 49th and 50th states. This ordinance guaranteed that inhabitants of the Territory would have the same rights and privileges that citizens of the first thirteen States enjoyed. Equally important *Article 6* provided that slavery and involuntary servitude were outlawed in the Northwest Territory. This was a law that finally gave some merit to the Declaration of Independence's "*... all men are created equal...*" It took 3 years and a Congress led by Arthur St. Clair to pass the ordinance making the Northwest Ordinance one of the great documents in American History. In the words of Daniel Webster:

> *"We are accustomed to praise lawgivers of antiquity ... but I doubt whether one single law of any lawgiver, ancient or modern, has produced the effects of more distinct, marked, and lasting character than the Ordinance of 1787"*

It wasn't until two months later that the most important body of laws ever proposed in the United States was placed on President Arthur St. Clair's desk. On September 17, 1787 that Philadelphia Convention of 12 states called to revise the Articles of Confederation voted to approve and send an entirely New Plan For the Federal Government the U. S. Constitution:

Present The States of New Hampshire, Massachusetts, Connecticut, Mr. Hamilton from New York, New Jersey, Pennsylvania, Delaware, Maryland, Virginia, North Carolina, South Carolina, and Georgia.

Resolved, That the preceeding Constitution be laid before the United States in Congress assembled, and that it is the Opinion of this Convention, that it should afterwards be submitted to a Convention of Delegates, chosen in each State by the People thereof, under the Recommendation of its Legislature, for their Assent and Ratification; and that each Convention assenting to, and ratifying the Same, should give Notice thereof to the United States in Congress assembled.

Resolved, That it is the Opinion of this Convention, that as soon as the Conventions of nine States shall have ratified this Constitution, the United States in Congress assembled should fix a Day on which the Electors should be appointed by the States which shall have ratified the same, and a Day on which the Electors should assemble to vote for the President, and the Time and Place for commencing Proceedings under this Constitution. That after such Publication the Electors should be appointed, and the Senators and Representatives elected: That the Electors should meet on the Day fixed for the Election of the President, and should transmit their Votes certified, signed, sealed and directed, as the Constitution requires, to the Secretary of the United States in Congress assembled, that the Senators and Representatives should convene at the Time and Place assigned; that the Senators should appoint a President of the Senate, for the sole Purpose of receiving, opening and counting the Votes for President; and, that after he shall be chosen, the Congress, together with the President, should, without Delay, proceed to execute this Constitution.

By the Unanimous Order of the Convention

Go. Washington Presidt.

W. Jackson Secretary.

George Washington, who had been virtually dragged to the Convention by Virginia's Governor Edmund Randolph, served as President and wrote the following cover letter to Arthur St. Clair:

Sir. We have now the honor to submit to the consideration of the United States in Congress Assembled, that Constitution which has appeared to us the most adviseable.

The friends of our Country have long seen and desired, that the power of making war, peace and treaties, that of levying money and regulating commerce, and the correspondent executive and judicial authorities should be fully and effectually vested in the general government of the Union: but the impropriety of delegating such extensive trust to one body of men is evident. Hence results the necessity of a different organization.

It is obviously impracticable in the federal government of these States, to secure all rights of independent sovereignty to each, and yet provide for the interest and safety of all. Individuals entering into society must give up a share of liberty to preserve the rest. The magnitude of the sacrifice must depend as well on situation and circumstance, as on the object to be obtained. It is at all times difficult to draw with precision the line between those rights which must be surrendered, and those which may be reserved; and on the present occasion this difficulty was increased by a difference among the several States as to their situation, extent, habits, and particular interests.

In all our deliberations on this subject we kept steadily in our view, that which appears to us the greatest interest of every true American, the consolidation of our Union, in which is involved our prosperity, felicity, safety, perhaps our national existence. This important consideration, seriously and deeply impressed on our minds, led each State in the Convention to be less rigid on points of inferior magnitude, than might have been otherwise expected; and thus the Constitution, which we now present, is the result of a spirit of amity, and of that mutual deference and concession which the peculiarity of our political situation rendered indispensable.

That it will meet the full and entire approbation of every State is not perhaps to be expected, but each will doubtless consider, that had her interests been alone consulted, the consequences might have been particularly disagreeable or injurious to others; that it is as liable to as few exceptions as could reasonably have been expected, we hope and believe; that it may promote the lasting welfare of that country so dear to us all, and secure her freedom and happiness, is our most ardent wish

With great respect

We have the honor to be

Sir

Your Excellency's
Most Obedient and humble servts.
George Washington, President.

By Unanimous Order of the Convention.

The "New Plan for the Federal Government" arrived in New York on September 20th and its fate was subject to the vote of the United States in Congress Assembled, the very body that would be disassembled should they vote to send it to the states for ratification. The great debate that must have ensued is forever lost due to the veil of secrecy that surrounded Congress. We do know however that the same Congress that passed the most important legislation in its 6 year history voted, only eight days later, to send the Constitution to the legislature of each state. St. Clair's legislation asked each state hold a special convention that would either ratify or reject the new Constitution. The Journals of the United States in Congress Assembled reported on September 28, 1787:

Congress having received the report1 of the Convention lately assembled in Philadelphia

[Note 1: 1 The report of the Convention, including the Constitution, the resolution of the Convention and Washington's letter, together with the resolve of Congress of September 28, 1787, were entered by Benjamin Bankson, in Ratifications of the Constitution, pp. 45--74. A copy of the Continental Congress imprint of the foregoing documents, signed by Charles Thomson, is wafered in between pages 98 and 99 of Papers of the Continental Congress,

No. 122, which is deposited in the Department of State. This imprint is apparently from the shop of J. McLean, since most of the report of the Convention appears printed from the same type form as was used in the supplement to the Independent Journal of September 22, 1787. Copies of this imprint were transmitted by Thomson to the executives of several States with his circular letter of September 28, 1787, a copy of which is in Papers of the Continental Congress, No. 18 B., p. 129. See September 20, and 27, 1787.]

Resolved Unanimously that the said Report with the resolutions and letter accompanying the same be transmitted to the several legislatures in Order to be submitted to a convention of Delegates chosen in each state by the people thereof in conformity to the resolves of the Convention made and provided in that case.

President St. Clair, *in less than one year,* presided over the United States Government that not only enacted the Northwest Ordinance, but enacted legislation that created and provided for the ratification of the most important law in US History, The Constitution of the United States of America (see the end of this Chapter for a complete printing of the 1787 US Constitution).

The last major act of President Arthur St. Clair's Congress was on October 5, 1787 when they selected a governor and other officers for the Northwest Territory according to the terms of the Ordinance of 1787. General St. Clair was overwhelmingly appointed governor of what is now Ohio, Indiana, Illinois, Michigan, and Minnesota whose lands, at that time, comprised more than one half of the United States. The Journals of the United States in Congress Assembled report

Congress proceeded to the election of a governor for the western territory pursuant to the Ordinance of the 13th. of July last and the ballots being taken

The honble Arthur St Clair was elected.

[Note 2: 2 The proceedings regarding the election of governor and secretary of the Western territory, were also entered, by John Fisher, in Western Territory, Papers of the Continental Congress, No. 176, p. 14--15.]

Congress proceeded to the election of a secretary pursuant to the said Ordinance and the ballots being taken

Mr Winthrop Sargent was elected

Governor St. Clair went right to work in 1788 and began negotiations on a treaty with the Native Americans in Ohio, Pennsylvania and Indiana. On January 9th, 1789, St. Clair signed a treaty with the Sachems and Warriors of the Six Nations, the Mohawks excepted; and with the Sachems and Warriors of the Wyandot, Delaware, Ottawa, Chippewa, Pattiwatima, and Sac nations, inhabiting part of the country northwest of the Ohio, at Fort Hamar. Since the Continental Congress was unable to obtain a quorum in 1789, the Treaty was never ratified under the Articles of Confederation.

When George Washington took office the treaty was waiting for him on his desk; when ratified it would be the first US Treaty under the US Constitution and an important one at that, as it opened a large area in the Northwest Territory for expansion. Washington submitted the treaties (there were two - executed by St. Clair) to the US Senate on May 25, 1789 with this letter

Gentlemen of the Senate:

In pursuance of the order of the late Congress, treaties between the United States and several nations of Native Americans have been negotiated and signed. These treaties; with sundry papers respecting them, i now lay before you, for your consideration and advice, by the hands of General Knox, under whose official superintendence the business was transacted; and who will be ready to communicate to you any information on such points as may appear to require it.

Go. WASHINGTON.

The Senate turned over the treaties to a committee on June 10 and did not report in the affirmative on ratification until August 24, 1789. The Journals of the US Senate: WEDNESDAY, August 26, 1789 report

Proceeded to consider the report of a Committee, appointed June the10th, on Native American treaties made at Fort Harmar, the 9th day of January,1789, viz: The Committee to whom was referred the message of the President of the United States, of the 25th of May, 1789, with the Native American treaties and papers accompanying the same--

Report: That the Governor of the Western Territory, on the 9th day of January, 1789, at Fort Harmar, entered into two treaties, one with the sachems and warriors of the Six Nations, the Mohawks excepted, the other with the sachems and warriors of the Wyandot, Delaware, Ottawa, Chippewa, Pattawattima, and Sacs nations--that those treaties were made in pursuance of the powers and instructions heretofore given to the said Governor by the late Congress, and are a confirmation of the treaties of Fort Stanwix, in October, 1784, and of Fort McIntosh, in January, 1785, and contain a more formal anti regular conveyance to the United States of the Native American claims to the lands yielded to these States by the said treaties of 1784and 1785.

Your Committee, therefore, submit the following resolution, viz:

That the treaties concluded at Fort Harmar, on the 9th day of January, 1789, between Arthur St. Clair, Esq. Governor of the Western Territory, on the part of the United States, and the sachems and warriors of the Six Nations, (the Mohawks excepted,) and the sachems and warriors of the Wyandot, Delaware, Ottawa, Chippewa, Pattawattima, and Sacs nations, be accepted; and that the President of the United States be advised to execute and enjoin an observance of the same.

The US Senate ordered, that the consideration thereof be postponed.

On August 30th Washington, thinking that by virtue of the Senate taking-up up the matter meant the treaty was ratified, began to execute transmittal letters enclosing a copy of the treaties to all the governors. This letter to Samuel Huntington was the one sent to Connecticut.

New York August 30th 1789

Sir,

I have the honor to transmit to your Excellency a Resolution of Congress for carrying into effect a Survey directed to be made by an Act of the late Congress -- and requesting the President of the United Sates to appoint a proper person to compleat[sic] the same. -- Also the duplicate of an Act relative to negotiations and Treaties with the Native American Tribes. -

I have the honor to be With due consideration Your Excellency's Most Obt. and Most Humble Sevt.

Go: Washington

His Excellency

Samuel Huntington

George Washington, with this transmittal letter to Samuel Huntington, failed to obtain the advice and consent of the US Senate before proclaiming a US Treaty valid. Realizing his error Washington wrote the US Senate on September 17th:

September 17, 1789.

Gentlemen of the Senate.

It doubtless is important that all treaties and compacts formed by the United States with other nations, whether civilized or not, should be made with caution and executed with fidelity.

It is said to be the general understanding and practice of nations, as a check on the mistakes and indiscretions of ministers or commissioners, not to consider any treaty negotiated and signed by such officers as final and conclusive until ratified by the sovereign or government from whom they derive their powers. This practice has been adopted by the United States respecting their treaties with European nations, and I am inclined to think it would be advisable to observe it in the conduct of our treaties with the Indians; for though such treaties, being on their part made by their chiefs or rulers, need not be ratified by them, yet, being formed on our part by the agency of subordinate officers, it seems to be both prudent and reasonable that their acts should not be binding on the nation until approved and ratified by the Government. It strikes me that this point should be well considered and settled, so that our national proceedings in this respect may become uniform and be directed by fixed and stable principles.

The treaties with certain Native American nations, which were laid before you with my message of the 25th May last, suggested two questions to my mind, viz: First, whether those treaties were to be considered as perfected and consequently as obligatory without being ratified. If not, then secondly, whether both or either, and which, of them ought to be ratified. On these questions I request your opinion and advice.

You have, indeed, advised me "to execute and enjoin an observance of" the treaty with the Wyandottes, etc. You, gentlemen, doubtless intended to be clear and explicit, and yet, without *further explanation, I fear I may misunderstand your meaning, for if by my executing that treaty you mean that I should make it (in a more particular and immediate manner than it now is) the act of Government, then it follows that I am to ratify it. If you mean by my executing it that I am to see that it be carried into effect and operation, then I am led to conclude either that you consider it as being perfect and obligatory in its present state, and therefore to be executed and observed, or that you consider it as to derive its completion and obligation from the silent approbation and ratification which my proclamation may be construed to imply. Although I am inclined to think that the latter is your intention, yet it certainly is best that all doubts respecting it be removed.*

Permit me to observe that it will be proper for me to be informed of your sentiments relative to the treaty with the Six Nations previous to the departure of the governor of the Western territory, and therefore I recommend it to your early consideration.

Go WASHINGTON

The US Senate received the letter the 17th of September and postponed the decision once again on the 18th. The US Senate finally ratified the First US Treaty under the Constitution on the 22nd. The US Senate Journals for that day reported:

On motion to postpone the report, to substitute the following, to wit: Resolved, That the Senate do advise and consent that the President of the United States ratify the treaty concluded at Fort Harmar, on the 9th day of January, 1789, between Arthur St. Clair, Governor of the Western Territory on the part of the United States, and the sachems and warriors of the Wyandot, Delaware, Ottawa, Chippewa, Pattawattima, and Sac nations: It passed in the affirmative.

In 1790 Arthur St. Clair fixed the seat of justice of this territory, which he named Cincinnati, in honor of the Society of the Cincinnati. St. Clair was President of Pennsylvania's Society of the Cincinnati from 1783 until 1789. St. Clair's accomplishments as governor were many, but once again a disastrous military campaign all but obliterated his early work as the *Territorial Governor.*

After the American Revolution, the militia was disbanded due to worries over how much power a government should have as well as lack of funds. During a time of relative peace a small army of 600 regulars was maintained, called the First American Regiment. This group plus militia under the supervision of Josiah Harmar, protected settlers in the vast new territory. After the treaty was ratified, General Harmar set off into the Northwest Territory with some 1400 men to deter Native American raids, skirmishes, and kidnappings.

Receiving information that the Wabash Native Americans failed to agree to a treaty, Governor St. Clair hastily returned to Ohio and ordered Major Hamtramck and Colonel Sargent to organize the militia for an attack upon the Native Americans on the Wabash River. The Native Americans were encouraged by Chief Brandt and the British to ignore the treaty and be belligerent and hostile. A Kickapoo chief said; "*You invite us to stop our young men. It is impossible to do it, being constantly encouraged by the British.*"

Governor St. Clair directed General Harmar to gather militia from various counties to rendezvous at Fort Washington. General Harmar exclaimed with dismay when the men arrived that they, "*were raw and unused to the gun or woods.*" In addition to the inexperience of the militia, many of the muskets and rifles were unfit for use. There were quarrels between the men and the officers, some preferring Colonel Trotter's leadership to Colonel Hardin's.

When the march began there were 320 regulars and 1,133 militia, under the command of Colonel Hardin. They captured a Shawanese Native American who told them that a group of Native Americans were leaving their village, 30 miles away as fast as possible. Colonel Hardin detached 600 troops and one company of regulars to travel to the Native American village at the junction of the St. Joseph and St. Mary's rivers. When he arrived he found it deserted, so he rejoined the main body of militia and gave the orders to burn and destroy the buildings and vast fields of corn.

The following day Colonel Trotter with a body of men marched out from camp to see if he could see any trace of the Native Americans. He returned at nightfall reporting no trace of the Native Americans. The next day Colonel Hardin marched with about 300 militia and 30 regulars about 10 miles from the camp. Suddenly about 100 Native Americans appeared. At the first attack by the Native Americans nearly all the militia fled without returning a shot. The regulars stood firm as usual, but were decimated. About 70 men were killed.

After that unfortunate and humiliating defeat by the Native Americans, the rest of the army continued on to accomplish their goal of burning villages and corn fields. In all they destroyed the Native American capital and five villages before marching back to Fort Washington. The army camped approximately 8 miles away from the ruins of the village. At 9:00pm Colonel Hardin and General Harmar sent 400 men under the direction of Major Wyllys to return to the village to see if there were any more Native American parties roaming the area. Early in the morning they came upon a large body of Native Americans following their leader Little Turtle, who later became more famous with his encounter with Governor St. Clair's ill-fated troops. The American troop fought desperately but sustained great losses, 48 regulars and two officers, Major Wyllys and Lieutenant Frothingham. The Native American braves had hit the jugular.

Little Turtle faced General Harmar with a force of Miami, Shawnee, Patawatomi, and Chippewa warriors. Little Turtle skillfully drew General Harmar into the Maumee Valley by convincing the troops Native Americans were fleeing in terror. Harmar was caught off guard, flanked, and lost 183 soldiers to Little Turtle's warriors. General Harmar wisely retreated and thankfully Little Turtle did not follow.

Upon learning of Harmar's defeat, President Washington decided to appoint St. Clair commander-in-chief of the army that was operating against the Native Americans on March 4th, 1791. Harmar resigned his post, and predicted continued struggle and military failure for the governor.

At 55 and suffering from gout St. Clair was reluctant to take command of an army comprised of short term soldiers who had no formal training in military matters. The men who arrived as reinforcements to defend and fight for the American presence in the new territory were from, "*the prisons, wheelbarrows and brothels of the nation.*" Lieutenant John Armstrong observed that the gathering troops were "*the worst and most dissatisfied troops I ever served with.*" The men who were finally recruited were "*badly clothed, badly paid, and badly fed.*"

Despite this, St. Clair accepted the command, followed Secretary of War Knox's orders comprising of over 4500 words and moved toward the Native Americans on the Miami and Wabash Rivers, suffering so severely from gout that he needed to be carried on a litter. He was surprised near the Miami villages on 4 November, and his force was defeated by a horde of Native Americans led by Blue Jacket, Little Turtle, and Simon Girty, the renegade.

Little Turtle had organized alliances with the Shawnees of Chief Blue Jacket and the Delawares of Chief Buckongahelas, to create a very disciplined offensive unit. A young Shawnee warrior named Tecumseh acted as a scout to report movement of the American troops as well as the best time and place for attack. The place turned out to be at the headwaters of the Wabash River on the cold, wet morning of November 4, 1791. General St. Clair had not ordered any fortifications built that night, nor had he sent out any scouts. Little Turtle's warriors surprised the unsuspecting army on three sides, and instructed his men to shoot officers and artillerymen first. In less than an hour nearly half of the troops had been killed or wounded, with most of the horses shot. By the middle of the morning, the rest of the panicked soldiers hastily retreated, and were easily shot as they ran away. All told, from a fighting force of about 1400, men St. Clair lost 700 men and most of the rest were wounded. The Native Americans captures eight abandoned pieces of artillery, 200 oxen and approximately 100 women. Three quarters of the Second United States Regiment were lost with nearly $33,000 of war supplies abandoned. Little Turtle, in contrast, with 1040 warriors walked away from the battle losing only 21 warriors with forty wounded. St. Clair's loss of men was the greatest number ever killed or wounded in a battle with Native American warriors. The battlefield "*was literally covered with the dead.*"

Later it was revealed that profiteering by the Chief Quartermaster supplied the ill-fated troops with defective powder. Another possible reason for the carnage was the strained relations between St. Clair and his deputy, General Richard Butler. The night before the massacre, Butler was warned that a large body of Native American warriors was gathering nearby, which he failed to relay to his superior. He paid dearly for his miscommunication by not living to see the next night. Washington refused a court of inquiry, and St. Clair resigned his general's commission on March 5th, 1792. Despite this Congress appointed a committee of investigation of St. Clair's defeat at Wabash River.

St. Clair did make several tactical mistakes. Twenty Chickasaw scouts who were at his disposal for retrieving vital information concerning the location of the adversary were dispatched on October 29th on a distant assignment to seize prisoners. St. Clair also made a geographical error in the location of his November 4th camp, thinking it was close to Kekionga. In reality they were 20 miles south of the settlement. In addition, he chose to direct his most able soldiers, 300 officers and men of the First American Regiment, to attend to deserters and guard incoming supplies, rather than to prepare for battle. They undoubtedly were looking for 60 deserters who had fled four days before the battle due to low morale, poor supplies and inclement weather. The First American Regiment never made it back in time to the battle, but were ordered to guard Fort Jefferson when they heard cannon fire in the distance. The supplies were never located.

St. Clair also erroneously chose not to entrench the camp the night before even though his "*men are much fatigued.*" Simple earth or wood fences would have given the troops at least a crude barrier, as well as relay the unspoken message to the Native Americans that they were on their guard.

To his merit, St. Clair was observed to be, "*cool, deliberate and calm during the battle.*" A bullet grazed his face shoring off a lock of hair, eight bullet holes were found in his coat and hat, and several of his horses were killed even as he sat on them. When there were no mounts, St. Clair ignored his gouty leg and fought on foot, directing bayonet attacks and remaining to cover for his retreating troops until the last had fled. Unfortunately, St. Clair was in no condition to personally fight a battle, but his sense of duty was rallied to obey the request of his long-time friend George Washington, Lieutenant-Colonel Wiliam Drake sarcastically observed, "*A general, enrapped ten-fold in flannel robes, unable to walk, placed on his car, bolstered on all sides with pillows and medicines, and thus moving to attack the most active enemy in the world, was...tragi-comical indeed.*"

The House of Representatives established an investigative committee on March 27 1792,:

> "*to call for such persons, papers and records, as may be necessary to assist their inquiries.*" *(20 5 Annals of Congress* (1796), 771, 782-783.)

The investigating committee requested from President Washington the testimony and documents regarding St. Clair's failed expedition. This was the first time Congress tested what is now known as executive privilege and Washington set the benchmark for all future presidents.

So remarkable was this inquiry that President Washington deemed it compulsory to convene his cabinet to determine how to respond to this maiden request for presidential materials by a congressional committee. The president wanted to discuss whether he could legally refuse to submit documents to Congress and whether such public disclosure would jeopardize the national security of his office. On April 2, 1792 the cabinet, consisting of Alexander Hamilton Secretary of the Treasury; Thomas Jefferson, Secretary of State; Henry Knox, Secretary of War; and Edmund Randolph, Attorney General met, and Washington noted the group's determination:

> *We had all considered, and were of one mind, first, that the House was an inquest, and therefore might institute inquiries. Second, that it might call for papers generally. Third, that the Executive ought to communicate such papers as the public good would permit, and ought to refuse those, the disclosure of which would injure the public: consequently were to exercise a discretion. Fourth, that neither the committees nor House has a right to call on the Head of a Department, who and whose papers were under the President alone; but that the committee should instruct their chairman to move the House to address the President. (20 5 Annals of Congress* (1796), 773.)

Upon careful deliberation Washington realized that:

- Such disclosure of Presidential papers and reports was necessary to vindicate Arthur St. Clair.
- Such public disclosure under the condition of a closed session of Congress would not harm the national interest.
- Most importantly his office established the right of the executive branch of government to withhold information from Congress.

Once again the greatness of Washington shone through, as he refused to claim executive privilege to hide his administration's part in the military defeat at Wabash River and was determined to exonerate his Governor, Arthur St. Clair. Congress did exonerate St. Clair and he served as Governor for an additional ten years while General Anthony Wayne took the field against the Indians.

Retaining the position of governor after the inquest, St. Clair was confronted with many challenges in this newly formed territory. Many settlers emigrated into the vast Northwest before the Ordinance of 1787 and had established small farms and cabins. These citizens maintained that they were entitled to the land upon which they had settled. This "*squatter problem*" was one of the challenges of this new territory, which would linger until the turn of the century. It was through William Henry Harrison, who rose to prominence as a representative delegate to Congress, and by the passing the Land Act of 1800 legislation, which finally settled the problem. The Act granted "*squatters rights*" giving the land holders a chance to obtain a clear title with low minimal purchase opportunities. Financing was also provided in four equal payments.

With General Wayne's success in eliminating Native American hostilities, Arthur St Clair was faced with a large flux of immigrants requiring the construction, maintenance, and repair of wilderness roads. In 1792 St. Clair adopted a highway transportation act. This act required that all able-bodied men above sixteen years of age must work ten days out of the year to construct the highways. St. Clair also had numerous ferries constructed, which allowed the new settlers to easily cross the Ohio River and its tributaries. The question of County borders and seats became the topic of heated debate in the growing territory. In this letter to Colonel Massei dated June 9th, 1798, St. Clair writes:

> *"The Commissions for the Officers to whom you have given temporary Appointments shall be forwarded soon by some convenient Opportunity, but, as to the request of the People for a division of the County of Adams, I am not sufficiently informed of their present numbers, nor how they would stand relatively to each other after a division, to determine upon it immediately. Correct Returns of the Militia would assist me much, and I shall be very glad to receive them from you as soon as you can have them made out with accuracy, for, it is both my duty, and my inclination to render the Situation of the Inhabitants as easy as Circumstances will admit of."*
>
> *In a postscript, St. Clair continues, "I would wish you to add to the Returns by way of annotation the part of the County in which the bulk of the Companies, respectively, reside."*

In 1790 St. Clair's struggle with Virginians (specifically the Chillicothe regime) resurfaced and plagued him throughout his remaining tenure as Governor of the Northwest Territory. Specifically, Governor St. Clair and Territorial Judges Parson, Symmes, and Varnum adopted the laws from Pennsylvania for the Territory virtually ignoring laws from Virginia. These laws re-opened the not so ancient Virginia wounds over their border losses to Pennsylvania. In the minds of many Virginian settlers in the Ohio Territory, Governor St. Clair was still detested as the official who brazenly arrested John Connolly, only 16 years earlier, reclaiming Fort Pitt and Washington County for Pennsylvania.

This Virginia-Pennsylvania struggle entered a turning point of control when the population exceeded five thousand inhabitants. This new population threshold required Governor St. Clair to hold elections for a new House of Representatives. The migration into the Ohio Territory was overwhelmingly Virginian due to its long border along the Ohio River. The inevitable elections, which were finally held in Cincinnati on February 4, 1799, resulted in Virginian Edward Tiffin being chosen president of the new House of Representatives. Ironically Tiffin, St. Clair's future nemesis, was made known to the governor by a letter of introduction from General Washington who spoke of Dr. Tiffin as being "*very familiar with law.*" Tiffin, along with fellow Virginian and brother-in-law Thomas Worthington who was born in Charleston, Virginia (now West Virginia), were Jeffersonians who held great contempt for the federalists, especially President John Adams. Together they out maneuvered St. Clair to make Chillicothe preeminent in territorial affairs.

It was only St. Clair's veto power that held their "*Virginian*" House at bay. The frequent use of the veto by St. Clair became the Jeffersonian mantra of autocratic Federalist rule. These vetoes proved, according to his opponents, that St. Clair and other Federalists believed the people of Ohio could not properly govern themselves. Tiffin and Worthington judiciously positioned themselves as men of the people akin to their mentor Republican Thomas Jefferson.

In the election of 1800 Arthur St. Clair strappingly backed John Adams against Thomas Jefferson for President of the United States. It was a political catastrophe for Arthur St. Clair as Adams came in third behind Jefferson and Aaron Burr. Even Western Pennsylvania voted overwhelmingly against the Federalists and John Adams. Thomas Jefferson eventually won the Presidency in the House of Representatives in opposition to Aaron Burr. In what some scholars claim to be the first bloodless revolution in history, President Jefferson now governed the United States of America with a majority of republicans in the US House and Senate. Despite only being recently re-appointed Northwest Territory Governor by John Adams, Arthur St. Clair must have realized his days were numbered unless he conformed to Jeffersonian reasoning.

With complete disregard of the election results and Thomas Jefferson's new presidency, St. Clair's tactics became more autocratic. He foolishly opposed Ohio Statehood in a misguided attempt to hold onto to the Federalist reigns of power in the Northwest Territory. Despite St. Clair's defiance, Ohio's first constitutional convention convened in Chillicothe in November 1802.

The now 68 year old Governor, instead of towing the overwhelmingly popular Jeffersonian plan, took a strong Federalist position against Ohio Statehood at the Constitutional Convention. He opposed statehood for various reasons but most notably he argued that the Ohio Territory had not reached the required 60,000 population mandated in the Ordinance of 1787. This was a purposeful political pronouncement against the Ordinance's primary author, President Thomas Jefferson.

St. Clair's legal challenges were weak and in April 1802, President Thomas Jefferson usurped the Ordinance of 1787's power by signing into law the Enabling Act, which "*enabled*" the Ohio Territory to become a state. It established the state boundaries and gave its people the right to institute a constitution. Thomas Worthington and his forces wasted no time in orchestrating the ousting Governor St. Clair.

At the conclusion of the Ohio Constitutional Convention, less then 18 months after Jefferson's inauguration, Worthington petitioned President Jefferson with a letter apprising him of St. Clair's outburst against statehood at the Convention. On November 22, 1802 the President chose to ignore St. Clair's letters of protest and dismissed St. Clair from his position as Northwest Territorial Governor. Worthington was hailed the hero of the Ohio Constitutional Convention. The last words St. Clair uttered on his departure from his Governor's post were: "*Beware of a surprise.*"

It only took thirty-five men 29 days to write the Ohio Constitution in Chillicothe. One reason for the vigorous pace was that all but one founder favored statehood and St. Clair was no longer an impediment. The new constitution set the first state election for January 1803. Offices to be elected included: state senators and representatives, governor, sheriffs, township trustees, justices of the peace and coroners.

Worthington was chosen to hand-deliver the new Ohio Constitution to Congress. After a three-week journey, he arrived December 22, 1802 in Washington, D.C., where he met with Jefferson before delivering the document to Congress. With this trip, Worthington usurped forever the moniker: "*The Father of Ohio's Statehood*" from Arthur St. Clair and on February 19, 1803, the Republican US Congress approved Ohio's constitution and admitted Ohio as the 17th state.

Out of power and with virtually no income, Arthur St. Clair made repeated requests for compensation from the government for reimbursement of his many personal expenses during the revolution, years of traveling and governing as a public servant. The fledgling nation with the Virginians Jefferson, Madison, and then Monroe as presidents insured that he was always denied. Despite this St. Clair tried to capitalize on what land he had left in Western Pennsylvania. In a letter to his son Daniel at Penn Square, Montgomery County, Pennsylvania St. Clair discusses the iron ore on their property, matters related to the early iron industry and a lawsuit against an employee of his iron furnace which produced castings and stoves on his estate.

Finally, in 1810 St. Clair's credit was depleted and a creditor secured a judgment for $10,000. St. Clair was forced to sell most of his property including his beloved Hermitage, his mill and iron furnace. Despite the value being estimated near $60,000, St. Clair only received $4,000 due to the judgment's expediency requirements.

His dire poverty forced him to retire to a small log-house on the summit of Chestnut Ridge, 5 miles west of Ligonier on land owned by his son Daniel. St. Clair. He spent the rest of his life in poverty, vainly endeavoring to effect a settlement of his claims against the government.

In his "*fall from grace*" and retirement St. Clair's Northwest Territory continued to have positive effects on the lives of thousands settlers and more importantly many Black Americans. The Slave Emancipation in the appendix is just one example of the St. Clair's legacy in the State of Indiana. This emancipation was signed with the mark of David Enlow, and dated in the same year St. Clair lost his home and vast land holdings, 1810. In this simple Harrison County, Indiana Territory manuscript Enlow is forced to free a Negro woman named Sara:

> *"... a my right, title, and interest in and to the said Negro woman Sarah ... in consequence of her voluntarily bound herself to serve me and during the term of four years commencing from the first day of January in the year Eighteen hundred and Seven..."*

Despite the final language in Article Six in St. Clair's Northwest Ordinance excepting fugitive slaves, many Black Americans swam or walked into the Northwest Territory with the Ordinance protecting their claim to freedom until proven a fugitive. Beginning with Ohio, all the territories became Free States and the exportation of fugitives from the Northwest became quite impossible and illegal as new laws were enacted to protect all former slaves. This trek north and west became so popular that by the 1830's it was named the Underground Railroad.

In addition to the Underground Railroad many slaves, such as Sarah, gained their freedom through their "*masters*" north and westward migration as this virgin territory provided settlers with unprecedented advantages of inexpensive land and government incentives to migrate. Those citizens with slaves were forced to emancipate them to comply with Article Six of the Ordinance which not only forbade slavery but involuntary servitude. Consequently, Sarah's emancipation states that she "*voluntarily bound herself to serve me and during the term of four years*".

St. Clair, now in his seventies, deepened poverty forcing him to seek an annuity, not from the Jeffersonians, but his home State of Pennsylvania. In these state petitions word of his dire circumstances became public knowledge and a few citizens of Pennsylvania came personally to his aide. In this March 4th, 1813 letter, Arthur St. Clair thanks several women for sending him money in his poverty while reminding his benefactors that he "*... made the people happy and laid a foundation for the continuance of the happinefs to millions yet unknown...*" In part he states:

> "*... My Heart Is not yet so cold as to be insensible to female Praife (Praise) --- it conveyed a Balm to my wounded spirit. Wounded not by the loss of fortune and the need of pecuniary aid, but by confine obloquy and contumely whom I thought (and now since I have their approbation I say it boldly), I thought that I had least merited thanks, for to say nothing of my military services which they have so kindly eulogized. I had, in a great meafsive (massive) therefore at my own expense, raised up for the United States in fifteen years a colony from thirty men to upwards of sixty thousand --- amalgamation the most heterogeneous mafs -- Mafs of population --- carried Laws, Religion, Mounts and Manner to the extreme limits of New Territory --- made the people happy and laid a foundation for the continuance of the happinefs to millions yet unknown and in which every faculty of mind and Body has been overwhelmingly employed. ...* "

Several months later the legislature of Pennsylvania finally granted St. Clair an annuity of $8400, and shortly before his death he received from congress $2,000 in discharge of his claims, and a pension of $60 a month.

In August, 1818 at the age of 84 Arthur St. Clair decided to visit his family in Youngstown, Ohio. His buggy was jolted and overturned. St. Clair fell to the ground and was knocked unconscious. He died a few days later on August 31, 1818 in Westmoreland County, Pennsylvania. Phoebe died a mere 18 days later and was interned with her husband at Old St. Clair Cemetery, Greensburg, Pennsylvania. In 1858 his heirs were finally awarded a fair compensation for his service as a Revolutionary War Major General, Northwest Territory Governor, and President of the United States in Congress Assembled.

St. Clair County, Alabama; St. Clair County, Illinois; St. Clair County, Michigan; St. Clair County, Missouri; St. Clair Lake, Michigan; St. Clairsville, Ohio, and Upper St. Clair, Pennsylvania are all named for him. St. Clair published "*A Narrative of the Manner in which the Campaign against the Native Americans in the Year 1791 was conducted under the Command of Major-General St. Clair, with his Observations on the Statements of the Secretary of War*" (Philadelphia, 1812). See "*The Life and Public Services of Arthur St. Clair,*" with his correspondence and other papers, arranged by William H. Smith (Cincinnati, 1882).

Regrettably, St. Clair's Revolutionary War career is not remembered for his great successes at Trenton and Princeton or his recruitment of troops for Washington's crucial 1780-1 campaigns. Ironically, it is his tactful retreat from Fort Ticonderoga and his exoneration at the inevitable court marshal that are consistently summarized into the historic one liner;

> "*Arthur St. Clair revolutionary Major General who loss Fort Ticonderoga to the British in 1777 and suffered the greatest Native American Defeat in 1791*"

The mention of Arthur St. Clair's 1783 role in freeing the United States Congress from Independence Hall from the mutinous military is not even a footnote in contemporary history books. Astoundingly, Arthur St. Clair's accomplishments as President of the United States under the Articles of Confederation are completely forgotten despite his 1787 administration being responsible for the passage of the Northwest Ordinance and US Constitution. Here is a Chronology of the Proceedings in St. Clair's Congress:

> **1787 - February 2** Achieves quorum; elects Arthur St. Clair president, Samuel Provost and John Rodgers chaplains. **February 3** Reads correspondence received since early November **February 5** Orders report on 1787 fiscal estimates. **February 6-9** Fails to achieve a quorum. **February 12** Adopts report of committee on qualifications; reads accumulated treasury and war office reports. **February 14** Nine states represented for first time; reads draft Post Office ordinance. **February 15** Authorizes postmaster general to contract for mail delivery. **February 19** Elects Lambert Cadwalader chairman in absence of President St. Clair. **February 21** Receives report on Annapolis Convention; endorses Philadelphia convention called to "*render the federal Constitution adequate to the exigencies of Government and the preservation of the Union.*" **February 22-23** Fails to achieve a quorum **February 26** Receives Virginia call for an interstate commercial convention.
>
> **March 5-7** Fails to achieve quorum **March 8** Reaffirms specie requirement for quota payments. **March 9** Receives Massachusetts report on Shays' Rebellion; adopts report on western posts. **March 13** Receives report on military stores; authorizes appointment of unsalaried commercial agent at Lisbon. **March 23** Adopts reduction of the Continental civil list. **March 28** Debates motions on the loan or sale of Continental property. **March 30** Receives report of seizure of American property at Natchez.
>
> **April 2** Receives 1787 fiscal estimates. **April 4** Orders John Jay to report on Spanish negotiations: receives report on the military establishment. **April 5** Receives report on land sales plan. **April 9** Orders discharge of troops enlisted

against Shays' Rebellion except two artillery companies; receives treasury report on copper coinage. **April 10** Debates location of federal capital. **April 13** Adopts letter to the states recommending repeal of all state acts repugnant to the treaty of peace; receives John Jay reports on Spanish negotiations. **April 16-17** Fails to achieve quorum (three and six states attending). **April 18** Receives draft ordinance on settlement of state accounts; debates sending commissioner to Spain to negotiate Mississippi question. **April 20** Receives John Jay report on sending commissioner to Spain; receives committee report on copper coinage. **April 21** Adopts copper coinage plan; adopts western land sales plan. **April 23** Extends franking privilege to Philadelphia Convention delegates. **April 24** Orders recapture of Fort Vinncennes; receives notification of the settlement of the Massachusetts-New York land dispute **April 25** Receives North Carolina protest against federal Native American treaties; receives report on western land ordinance. **April 27** Fails to achieve quorum.

May 1 Fails to achieve quorum **May 2** Authorizes sale of surplus Continental arms. **May 3** Receives British Consul Phinease Bond; receives report on the military establishment. **May 7** Appoints commissioners for settling departmental accounts; adopts ordinance for settlement of state accounts. **May 8** Debates proposal concerning interstate commercial conventions. **May 9** Debates Northwest Ordinance. **May 10** Debates Northwest Ordinance; debates location of federal capital. **May 11** Debates Mississippi negotiations with Spain. **May 12-31** Fails to achieve quorum.

June 1-29 Fails to achieves quorum

July 2-3 Fails to achieve quorum. **July 4** Achieves quorum; elects William Grayson chairman in absence of President St. Clair; receives report on Spanish negotiations. **July 5** Fails to achieve quorum. **July 10** Receives report on sale of western lands to land companies. **July 11** Reads Northwest Ordinance; receives report on issuance of indents for Continental quotas; receives report on Native American hostilities. **July 13** Adopts Northwest Ordinance. **July 14** Orders report on 1787 requisition. **July 18** Ratifies commercial treaty with Morrocco; receives report on southern Native American land claims. **July 19-21** Debates measures for Native American pacification **July 20** Instructs John Adams on a convention with Britain on violations of the treaty of peace. **July 23** Approves appointments of commercial agents to Morocco. **July 25** Debates measures for pacification of western Native Americans. **July 26** Debates measures for pacification of southern Indians; authorizes postal contracts; receives report on foreign loans. **July 27** Orders report on formation of "*a Confederacy with the powers of Europe*" against the Barbary States; instructs Jefferson on consular convention with France.

August 3 Debates southern Native American affairs. **August 6-8** Fails to achieve quorum. **August 9** Accepts South Carolina land cession; receives report on northern Native American affairs. **August 10-31** Fails to achieve quorum.

September 3-19 Fails to achieve quorum **September 20** Receives report of the Philadelphia Constitutional Convention. **September 21** Reelects treasury commissioners Arthur Lee, Walter Livingston, and Samuel Osgood; reduces civil list. **September 24** Accepts John Adams' retirement (post February 24, 1788); receives report on Netherlands protest. **September 26-27** Debates Constitution submitted by Philadelphia Convention.. **September 28** Resolves to submit Constitution to the states. **September 29** Receives report on prize money received by John Paul Jones; receives report on 1787 requisition.

October 2 Receives report on foreign debt. **October 3** Sets civil list and military establishment for Northwest Territory. **October 5 Elects Arthur St. Clair governor of the Northwest Territory**, Winthrop Sargent, secretary; resolves that a treaty be held with the western Native Americans; receives report on U.W. embassy at London. **October 8** Terminates federal proceedings in Massachusetts-New York land dispute. **October 11** Ratifies John Adams' contract for Dutch loan; authorizes indents for loan office interest in payment of Continental quotas; directs payment of prize monies received by John Paul Jones. **October 12** Authorizes ransom of American captives at Algiers; reelects Thomas Jefferson minister to France; receives Postmaster General report. **October 13** Orders arrest of Lt. John Sullivan for jeopardizing American-Spanish relations; debates Virginia infringement of U.S. treaty obligations. **October 15** Authorizes postal contracts. **October 16** Elects John Armstrong, Jr., Samuel Holden Parsons, and James Mitchell Varnum judges of the Northwest Territory, commends John Paul Jones. **October 17** Authorizes sale of the Carlisle barracks. **October 18-19** Fails to achieve quorum. **October 20** Appeals for North Carolina and Georgia land cessions; reduces postal rates. **October 21** Authorizes sale of one million acres to the Ohio Company. **October 22** Sets aside military bounty lands; authorizes treaty with the western Native Americans. **October 26** Adopts instructions for holding Native American negotiations. **October 29-31** Fails to achieve quorum

November 1-2 Fails to achieve quorum. **November 5** New Congress assembles; five delegates attend, two states represented. **November 6-30** Fails to achieve quorum.

Finally Arthur St. Clair's 15-year record as an honorable and effective Northwest Territory Governor was obliterated due to his military defeat at Wabash River and his opposition of the Tiffin and Worthington Jeffersonian plan for Ohio's statehood. Arthur St. Clair remains a sleeping giant among our founding fathers. It is the hope of this author that America one day recognizes the Herculean accomplishments of the 8th US President of the United States in Congress Assembled, Arthur St. Clair.

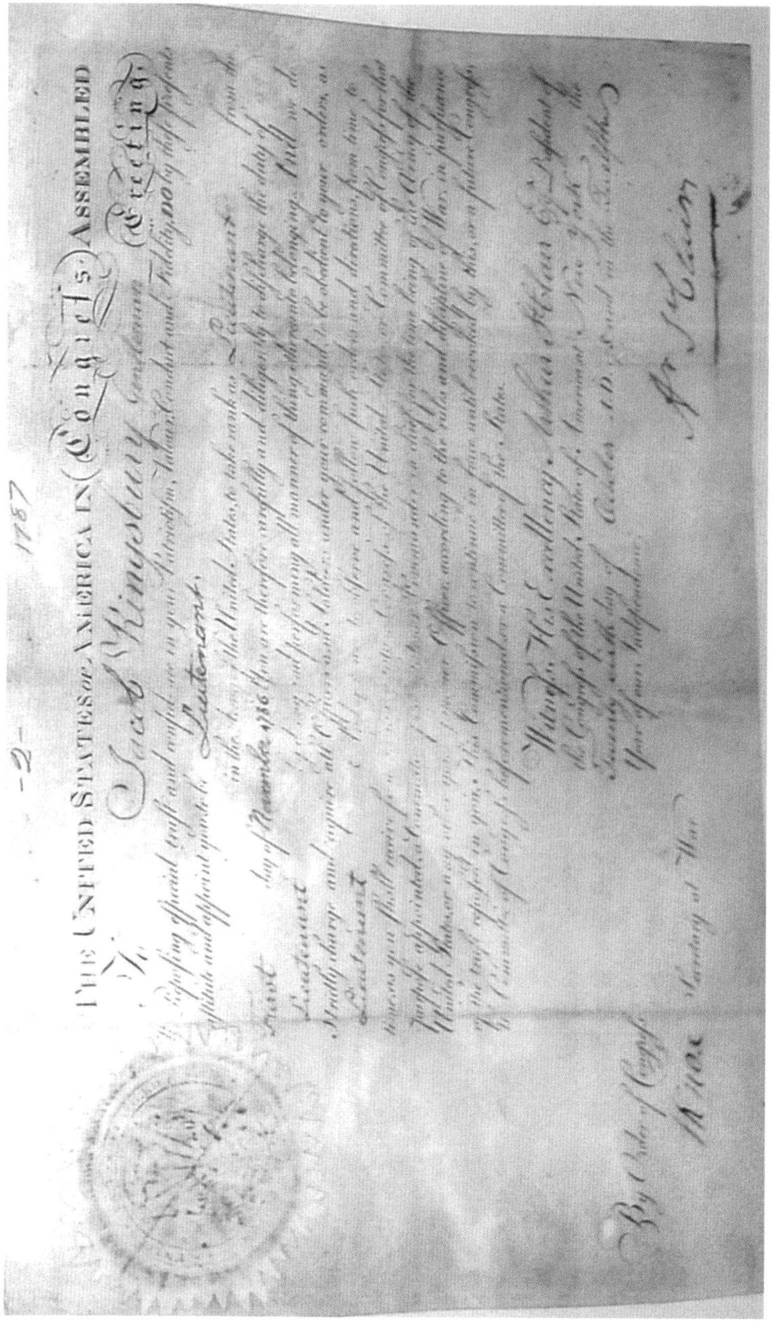

THE UNITED STATES OF AMERICA IN CONGRESS ASSEMBLED

Military Commission Signed By Arthur St. Clair as President and Henry Knox as Secretary of War of the United States in Congress Assembled – *Courtesy of the Klos Family*

CHAPTER FIFTEEN

Portrait of Cyrus Griffin by Lawrence Sully
The Documentary History of the Supreme Court
of the United States, 1789-1800

CYRUS GRIFFIN

10th President of the United States
in Congress Assembled
January 22, 1788 to March 4, 1789

Cyrus Griffin was born in Farnham, Richmond County, Virginia in 1749 and died in Yorktown, Virginia on December 14th, 1810. He was educated in Britain, studying law at the University of Edinburgh and at the Temple in London. While in England Griffin courted nobility and married a Lady Christhena, daughter of John Stuart, sixth Earl of Traquair. He returned to Virginia and as a young lawyer was a staunch supporter of the patriot cause. In 1777, 1778, 1786, and 1787 Griffin was elected a member of the State House of Delegates. He was also a member of the Virginia legislature.

Cyrus Griffin was elected a delegate to the Continental Congress in 1778 and served until 1761. He was elected as a delegate to the United States in Congress Assembled in

1787. On January 22, 1788 Griffin was elected President of the United States in Congress Assembled serving until the government's demise in 1789. The influence of the Articles of Confederation Presidency once again with St. Clair's departure and the pending ratification of the new US Constitution. The Chronology of his presidency is as follows:

1788 -- January 21 Convenes seven states represented. **January 22 Elects Cyrus Griffin president. January 23-31** Fails to achieve quorum

February 1 Reviews backlog of reports and letters. **February 5** Receives report on Massachusetts-New York boundary survey. **February 6-9** Fails to achieve quorum. **February 12** Authorizes secretary for foreign affairs to issue sea letters. **February 14** Sets date for reception of new French minister, Comte de Moustier. **February 19** Elects John Cleves Symmes judge of the Northwest Territory. **February 25** Debates appointment job superintendent of Native American affairs for the southern department. **February 26** Holds audience for comte de Moustier. **February 28** Receives treasury report on foreign debt. **February 29** Appoints Samuel Provost and John Rodgers chaplains of Congress, and Richard Winn superintendent of Native American affairs for the southern department; debates Kentucky statehood motion.

March 4 Debates Kentucky statehood in committee of the whole. **March 6** Receives reports on the claims of French settlers in the Illinois country and on the survey of western lands. **March 10-11** Fails to achieve quorum. **March 12** Receives report on military bounty lands. **March 18** Receives communications on Native American affairs. **March 19** Debates western land ordinance amendment. **March 24-27** Debates western land ordinance amendment. **March 31** Fails to achieve quorum.

April 1-30 Fails to achieve quorum.

May 1 Fails to achieve quorum. **May 2** Receives treasury report on proposed new Dutch loan, three war office reports on Native American affairs, and ten communications from the secretary for foreign affairs. **May 5** Receives reports on western land issues. **May 8** Elects Jonathan Burrall and Benjamin Walker commissioners for settling the accounts of the five wartime departments. **May 20** Authorizes fortnightly posts between Philadelphia and Pittsburgh. **May 21** Receives treasury report on coinage. **May 22** Orders institution of suits to collect outstanding Continental accounts. **May 26** Receives treasury report on western land contracts and war department report on settler violations of Cherokee treaty rights. **May 27-29** Debates western land ordinance amendment.

May 30 Debates Kentucky statehood in committee of the whole.

June 2 Receives committee of the whole report recommending Kentucky statehood. **June 3** Elects grand committee on Kentucky statehood. **June 5** Fails to achieve quorum. **June 6** Authorizes survey of New York; Pennsylvania boundary preparatory to granting Pennsylvania greater access to Lake Erie. **June 9** Directs treasury to submit 1788-1789 fiscal estimates. **June 12** Receives report on land reserve for French settlers in the Illinois country. **June 13** Responds to French protest against Virginia's harboring a French pirate. **June 17** Receives war office report on manpower and recruitment. **June 18** Receives report opposing state inspection of the mails. **June 19** Debates western land ordinance amendment. **June 20** Elects Joseph Martin Continental agent to the Cherokees; authorizes negotiation of western land contract with George Morgan associates. **June 24** Authorizes three-month extension of Continental claims. **June 25** Abolishes office of inspector of Continental troops. **June 27** Debates report on Georgia; Creek Native American affairs.

July 2 Debates western land ordinance amendment; receives notification of the ratification of the Constitution by the ninth state (New Hampshire); appoints committee "for putting the said constitution into operation." **July 3** Postpones action on Kentucky statehood until proceedings shall commence under the new Constitution. **July 7-8** Debates western land ordinance amendment. **July 9** Refers fiscal estimates to committee; adopts "supplement" to western land ordinance. **July 14** Debates report on implementing the Constitution. **July 15** Rejects terms of Georgia's western land cession, but accepts responsibility for southwestern frontier defense. **July 17** Directs resumption of western land surveys; rejects proposed Virginia western land reserve for military bounties. **July 21** Receives report on Continental Army manpower needs. **July 25** Orders deployment of Continental troops to pacify Luzerne County, Pennsylvania. **July 28** Debates report on implementing the Constitution; rejects motion to establish capital at Philadelphia. **July 30** Rejects motion to establish capital at New York.

August 1 Extends term of northern superintendent of Native American affairs. **August 4** Extends term of southern superintendent of Native American affairs. **August 5-6** Debates motions on the location of the capital. **August 7** Debates status of delegates from states that have not ratified the Constitution. **August 12** Plans mobilization of frontier militia against western Native Americans. **August 13** Debates report on implementing the Constitution. **August 20** Adopts 1788 requisition. **August 26** Debates report on implementing the Constitution; seeks Spanish cooperation for apprehending fugitive slaves fleeing to Florida. **August 28** Revises George Morgan associates western land contract. **August 29** Confirms land titles of French settlers in the Illinois country.

September 1 Condemns settler encroachments on Cherokee lands. **September 2** Debates report on implementing the Constitution. **September 3**

Reserves Ohio lands of Christian Delaware Indians; rejects motion to establish capital at Annapolis. **September 4** Debates report on implementing the Constitution; confirms land contract giving Pennsylvania large tract bordering Lake Erie. **September 8** Receives John Jay's report on negotiations with Spain concerning the Mississippi question. **September 13** Adopts plan for implementing the Constitution. **September 16** Recommends that states ban importation of felons; directs suspension of negotiations concerning the Mississippi question. **September 18-24** Fails to achieve quorum. **September 26-29** Fails to achieve quorum. **September 30** Receives report on treasury department inquiry.

October 1 Rejects Silas Deane settlement of Beaumarchais' accounts. **October 2** Receives report on war department inquiry. **October 6-7** Fails to achieve quorum. **October 8** Receives communications on Native American relations in the western territory. **October 10** Suspends the work of the commissioners appointed to settle the states' Continental accounts; adjourns what proves to be its final session under the Articles of Confederation. **October 13-16** Fails to achieve quorum.

November 1 Fails to achieve quorum. **November 3** Assembles for the new federal year with only two delegates attending.

1789 - March 2 Secretary Charles Thomson records occasional attendance of 17 additional delegates.

July 25 Secretary Thomson delivers papers and records of the Confederation to new federal government.

President's Griffin social status as US President in New York was second to none under the Articles of Confederation. His office, English education, and marriage to nobility solidified his status as the pinnacle of society among his nation's legal elite. Lady Christhena's state parties for foreign dignitaries were legendary. The Griffin's set the benchmark for Presidential entertaining that wasn't surpassed until well into the next century.

Some authors on Griffin, who was the US President during the ratification process, maintain that he was an anti-federalist. In this April 7th, 1788 letter to he congratulate James Madison, Father of the US Constitution, on his election to Virginia's delegation, he requests that Madison consider ratification of the Constitution:

> *My dear Sir,*
>
> *... Rhode Island have in fact rejected the constitution; so that only eight states can have adopted the system before the Session of Virginia. We all much rejoiced to hear of your election, especially as your being present, we are told, was absolutely necessary to counter- act some unwarrantable proceedings ...*

At some convenient hour I hope you will give me your opinion upon the prospect of the new-Constitution; the Elections now finished.

News papers enclosed. I am, my dear Sir, with the highest respect & friendship, your obedient Servant,

C Griffin, President

On May 5th he writes Madison again stating:

Maryland has acceded to the proposed Constitution by a great majority. Chase, Paca, Martin, and Mercer opposed it with their utmost vigor and abilities, but with decency. South Carolina will adopt the system very soon. The opposition in Virginia is much to be lamented and in New York also; however from the present appearance of things I rather incline to believe that in the course of 12 months we shall have the Government in operation ...

Finally, on May 26th, with the Constitution's passage hanging in the balance over New York and Virginia's indecisiveness Griffin writes to Madison:

The Courtiers are ridiculing our situation very much, and say upon all occasions in a laughing manner that when the united states shall assume some sort of Government then England will speak out.

Gentlemen are perpetually calling to know what will be the event of the Constitution in Virginia---;do, my kind friend, at this particular crisis write to me from time to time that I may give the best information upon the subject.

Clearly Griffin, a Virginian, in the 1788 pivotal role of President of the United States in Congress Assembled not only supported the Constitution's passage, but feared for the nation's survival if the New Plan for The Federal Government was not ratified. The Constitution was finally ratified well into 1789 and President Griffin help eased the nation into this new form of government as evidenced by this letter to Beverley Randolph:

March 9th. 1789.

I am honored by your excellency's letter of the 13th of Feby(1) only this morning. I did not understand that any person was appointed to come forward with the accounts of the State against the united States, or most certainly myself would not have been mentioned.(2) Colonel Davies is a man very proper to answer the purpose, and I think will be found extremely useful. The Board of Commissioners met on the 17th of January, and are now ready to act upon the business of their destination.

I am favored also with the Returns of nine of the Representatives of Virginia enclosed by your excellency, which I shall deliver to Colonel White, the only member at present from that State. There are only eight Senators and 18 Representatives assembled---;a very unfortunate thing.

Be so kind to accept the enclosed papers, and to believe me with sincere respect and attachment, Your excellency's most obedient Servant,

C Griffin

After the presidency Griffin was appointed president of the supreme court of admiralty from its creation until its abolition, was commissioner to the Creek Nation in 1789, and was judge of the First Federal Appeals Court for the district of Virginia from December, 1789, until his death in Yorktown on December 14, 1810. He is interred with his wife, Lady Christhena, in Bruton Churchyard, Williamsburg, Virginia.

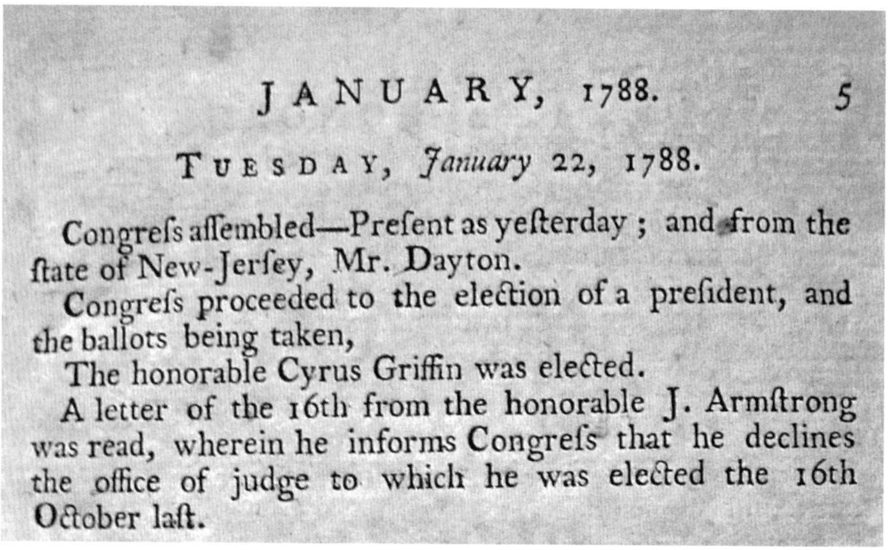

JANUARY, 1788. 5

TUESDAY, *January* 22, 1788.

Congreſs aſſembled—Preſent as yeſterday ; and from the ſtate of New-Jerſey, Mr. Dayton.

Congreſs proceeded to the election of a preſident, and the ballots being taken,

The honorable Cyrus Griffin was elected.

A letter of the 16th from the honorable J. Armſtrong was read, wherein he informs Congreſs that he declines the office of judge to which he was elected the 16th October laſt.

The Election of Cyrus Griffin -- JOURNALS OF THE UNITED STATES IN CONGRESS ASSEMBLED containing the proceedings from the 5th day of November, 1787 to the 3rd day of November 1788, Volume XIII, Published by order of the United States in Congress Assembled, [Philadelphia] Printed by John Dunlap, 1788. –
Courtesy of the Klos Family

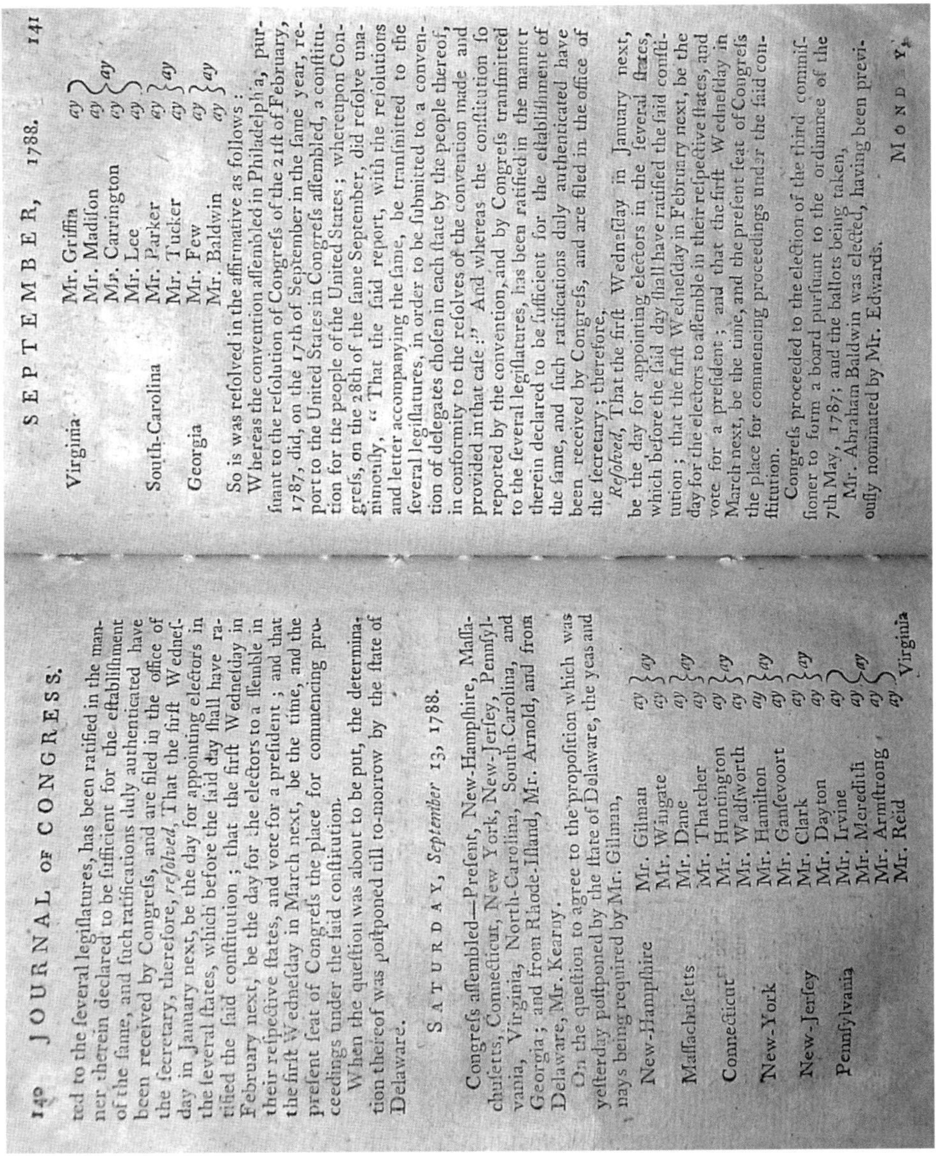

140 JOURNAL OF CONGRESS.

ted to the ſeveral legiſlatures, has been ratified in the manner therein declared to be ſufficient for the eſtabliſhment of the ſame, and ſuch ratifications duly authenticated have been received by Congreſs, and are filed in the office of the ſecretary, therefore, *reſolved*, That the firſt Wedneſday in January next, be the day for appointing electors in the ſeveral ſtates, which before the ſaid day ſhall have ratified the ſaid conſtitution; that the firſt Wedneſday in February next, be the day for the electors to aſſemble in their reſpective ſtates, and vote for a preſident; and that the firſt Wedneſday in March next, be the time, and the preſent ſeat of Congreſs the place for commencing proceedings under the ſaid conſtitution.

When the queſtion was about to be put, the determination thereof was poſtponed till to-morrow by the ſtate of Delaware.

SATURDAY, *September* 13, 1788.

Congreſs aſſembled—Preſent, New-Hampſhire, Maſſachuſetts, Connecticut, New York, New-Jerſey, Pennſylvania, Virginia, North-Carolina, South-Carolina, and Georgia; and from Rhode-Iſland, Mr. Arnold, and from Delaware, Mr. Kearny.

On the queſtion to agree to the propoſition which was yeſterday poſtponed by the ſtate of Delaware, the yeas and nays being required by Mr. Gilman,

New-Hampſhire	Mr. Gilman	*ay*	*ay*
	Mr. Wingate	*ay*	
Maſſachuſetts	Mr. Dane	*ay*	*ay*
	Mr. Thatcher	*ay*	
Connecticut	Mr. Huntington	*ay*	*ay*
	Mr. Wadſworth	*ay*	
New-York	Mr. Hamilton	*ay*	*ay*
	Mr. Ganſevoort	*ay*	
New-Jerſey	Mr. Clark	*ay*	*ay*
	Mr. Dayton	*ay*	
Pennſylvania	Mr. Irvine	*ay*	*ay*
	Mr. Meredith	*ay*	
	Mr. Armſtrong	*ay*	
	Mr. Reid	*ay*	

Virginia

SEPTEMBER, 1788. 141

Virginia	Mr. Griffin	*ay*	*ay*
	Mr. Madiſon	*ay*	
	Mr. Carrington	*ay*	
	Mr. Lee	*ay*	
South-Carolina	Mr. Parker	*ay*	*ay*
	Mr. Tucker	*ay*	
Georgia	Mr. Few	*ay*	*ay*
	Mr. Baldwin	*ay*	

So is was reſolved in the affirmative as follows:

Whereas the convention aſſembled in Philadelphia, purſuant to the reſolution of Congreſs of the 21ſt of February, 1787, did, on the 17th of September in the ſame year, report to the United States in Congreſs aſſembled, a conſtitution for the people of the United States; whereupon Congreſs, on the 28th of the ſame September, did reſolve unanimouſly, "That the ſaid report, with the reſolutions and letter accompanying the ſame, be tranſmitted to the ſeveral legiſlatures, in order to be ſubmitted to a convention of delegates choſen in each ſtate by the people thereof, in conformity to the reſolves of the convention made and provided in that caſe:" And whereas the conſtitution ſo reported by the convention, and by Congreſs tranſmitted to the ſeveral legiſlatures, has been ratified in the manner therein declared to be ſufficient for the eſtabliſhment of the ſame, and ſuch ratifications duly authenticated have been received by Congreſs, and are filed in the office of the ſecretary; therefore,

Reſolved, That the firſt Wedneſday in January next, be the day for appointing electors in the ſeveral ſtates, which before the ſaid day ſhall have ratified the ſaid conſtitution; that the firſt Wedneſday in February next, be the day for the electors to aſſemble in their reſpective ſtates, and vote for a preſident; and that the firſt Wedneſday in March next, be the time, and the preſent ſeat of Congreſs the place for commencing proceedings under the ſaid conſtitution.

Congreſs proceeded to the election of the third commiſſioner to form a board purſuant to the ordinance of the 7th May, 1787; and the ballots being taken,

Mr. Abraham Baldwin was elected, having been previouſly nominated by Mr. Edwards.

MOND Y,

Resolution to approve the 1787 Constitution and how to implement the transfer of power --JOURNALS OF THE UNITED STATES IN CONGRESS ASSEMBLED containing the proceedings from the 5th day of November, 1787 to the 3rd day of November 1788, Volume XIII, Published by order of the United States in Congress Assembled, [Philadelphia] Printed by John Dunlap, 1788. – *Courtesy of the Klos Family*

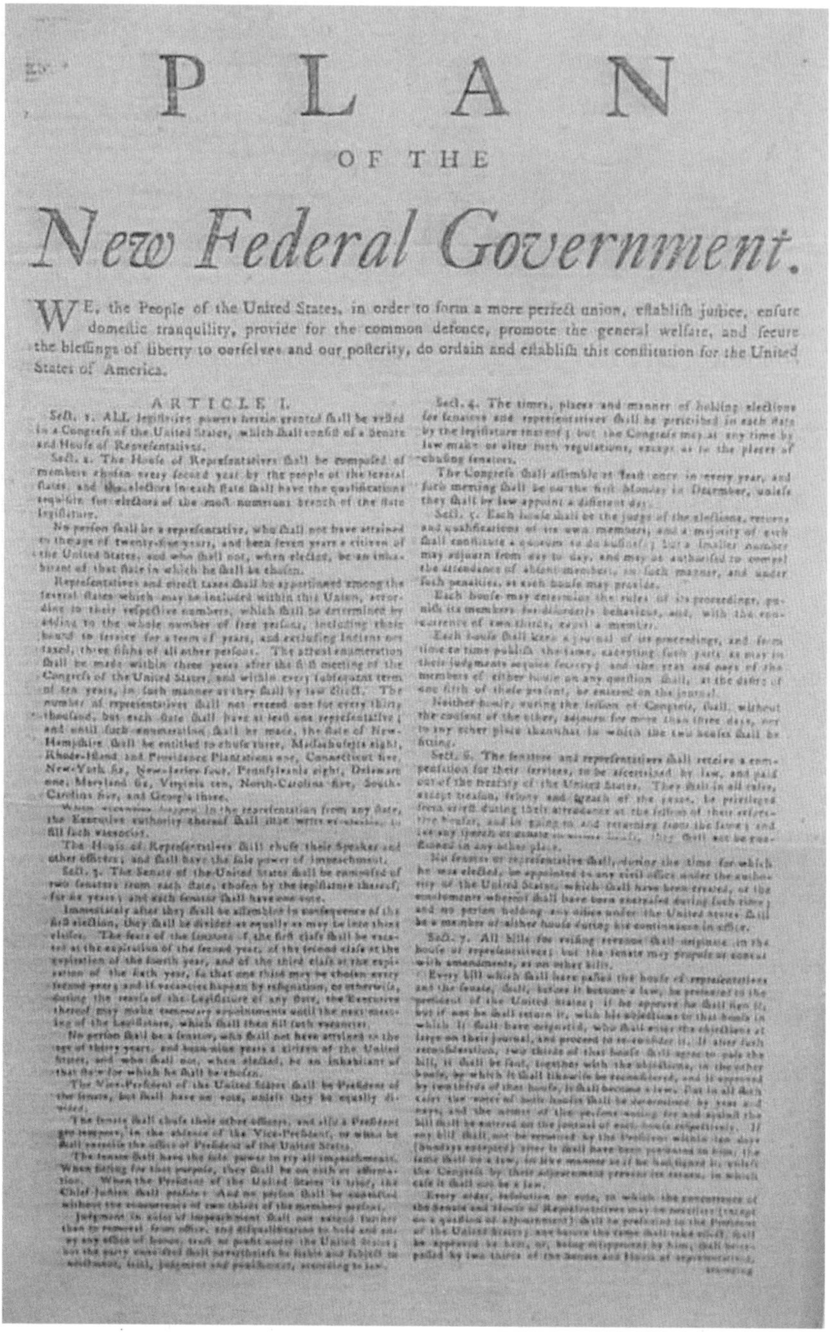

PLAN
OF THE
New Federal Government.

WE, the People of the United States, in order to form a more perfect union, establish justice, ensure domestic tranquility, provide for the common defence, promote the general welfare, and secure the blessings of liberty to ourselves and our posterity, do ordain and establish this constitution for the United States of America.

ARTICLE I.

Someone Leaked the Constitution?

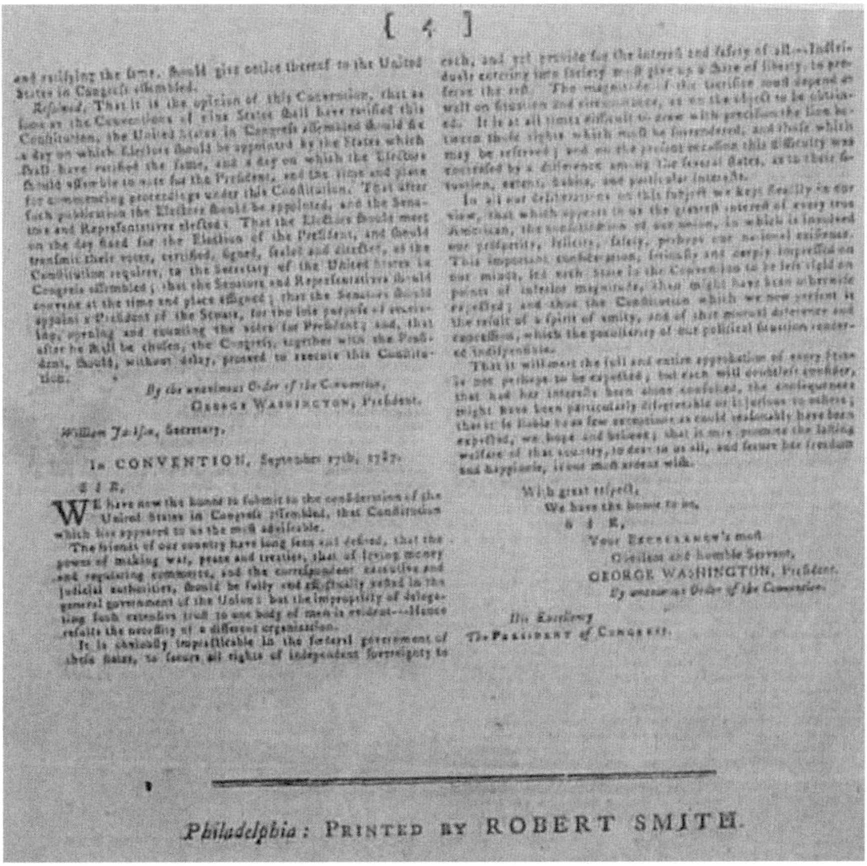

[4]

and ratifying the same, should give notice thereof to the United States in Congress assembled.

Resolved, That it is the opinion of this Convention, that as soon as the Conventions of nine States shall have ratified this Constitution, the United States in Congress assembled should fix a day on which Electors should be appointed by the States which shall have ratified the same, and a day on which the Electors should assemble to vote for the President, and the time and place for commencing proceedings under this Constitution. That after such publication the Electors should be appointed, and the Senators and Representatives elected: That the Electors should meet on the day fixed for the Election of the President, and should transmit their votes, certified, signed, sealed and directed, as the Constitution requires, to the Secretary of the United States in Congress assembled; that the Senators and Representatives should convene at the time and place assigned; that the Senators should appoint a President of the Senate, for the sole purpose of receiving, opening and counting the votes for President; and, that after he shall be chosen, the Congress, together with the President, should, without delay, proceed to execute this Constitution.

By the unanimous Order of the Convention,

GEORGE WASHINGTON, President.

William Jackson, Secretary.

In CONVENTION, September 17th, 1787.

SIR,

WE have now the honor to submit to the consideration of the United States in Congress assembled, that Constitution which has appeared to us the most adviseable.

The friends of our country have long seen and desired, that the power of making war, peace and treaties, that of levying money and regulating commerce, and the correspondent executive and judicial authorities, should be fully and effectually vested in the general government of the Union: but the impropriety of delegating such extensive trust to one body of men is evident---Hence results the necessity of a different organization.

It is obviously impracticable in the federal government of these states, to secure all rights of independent sovereignty to each, and yet provide for the interest and safety of all---Individuals entering into society must give up a share of liberty to preserve the rest. The magnitude of the sacrifice must depend as well on situation and circumstance, as on the object to be obtained. It is at all times difficult to draw with precision the line between those rights which must be surrendered, and those which may be reserved; and on the present occasion this difficulty was encreased by a difference among the several states, as to their situation, extent, habits, and particular interests.

In all our deliberations on this subject we kept steadily in our view, that which appears to us the greatest interest of every true American, the consolidation of our union, in which is involved our prosperity, felicity, safety, perhaps our national existence. This important consideration, seriously and deeply impressed on our minds, led each State in the Convention to be less rigid on points of inferior magnitude, than might have been otherwise expected; and thus the Constitution which we now present is the result of a spirit of amity, and of that mutual deference and concession, which the peculiarity of our political situation rendered indispensible.

That it will meet the full and entire approbation of every State is not perhaps to be expected; but each will doubtless consider, that had her interests been alone consulted, the consequences might have been particularly disagreeable or injurious to others; that it is liable to as few exceptions as could reasonably have been expected, we hope and believe; that it may promote the lasting welfare of that country so dear to us all, and secure her freedom and happiness, is our most ardent wish.

With great respect,

We have the honor to be,

SIR,

Your EXCELLENCY's most

Obedient and humble Servants,

GEORGE WASHINGTON, President.

By unanimous Order of the Convention.

His Excellency

The PRESIDENT *of* CONGRESS.

Philadelphia: PRINTED BY ROBERT SMITH.

Someone Leaked the Constitution? Philadelphia Printer Robert Smith, former employee of John Dunlap, trumped all competitors with 1st Public Printing of the US Constitution which was circulated this hastily printed broadsheet and inserted into his regularly scheduled September 18th Evening Chronicle under the headline *"New Plan for The Federal Government"*. Several other Philadelphia Newspapers, including Dunlap's, followed his lead printing the US Constitution on the 19th. This is the only known example of the Smith Printing currently on Display at the Heinz History Center's Smithsonian Exhibit "*The American Presidency, A Glorious Burden*" until May 2004. – Courtesy of the Klos Family

CHAPTER SIXTEEN

"FIRST"

The offices of President of the Continental Congress and the United States in Congress Assembled are a complex part of American History. Their duties, titles, and terms were undefined, fluid, and relatively brief. Additionally, both forms of government required their delegates, ministers, and Presidents to bind themselves to an oath of secrecy. The Journals of the two unicameral governments, therefore, leave us with a terribly incomplete picture of the legislative debates and workings of the executive functions of the Confederation. We do know that this period, from 1774 to 1789, was divided into three distinct and different entities; The Continental Congress of the United Colonies, the Continental Congress of the United States, by virtue of the July 2nd resolution and, finally, the United States in Congress Assembled, by virtue of the ratification of the Articles of Confederation. We also know that the First President of the Continental Congress of the United Colonies was Peyton Randolph, The First President of Continental Congress of the United States was John Hancock and the First President of the United States in Congress Assembled was Samuel Huntington. So why has the later title and creation of the Perpetual Union of the United States under the Articles of Confederation created such a fuss?

Striving to be recognized as *"First"* or number "1" is a national pastime of the United States of America. To even suggest George Washington was not the first US President raises a sundry of questions foreign to any Patriotic American. To make a clear, concise and scholarly case of ten US Presidents serving before George Washington is dismissed by most browsers as a topic so outrageous that few will get beyond the title page. If this is the first time you have seriously diverged into this historical record, I know how you feel.

On a recent visit to the Library of Congress and the National Archives, I stumbled onto the remnants of the amassed and catalogued Letters of the Delegates of the Continental Congress. In this 20-year project very bright men and women worked diligently to compile these letters to provide researchers with insight into some of the workings of the Continental Congress and the United States in Congress Assembled. When I discovered on this task was accomplished by first organizing copies of these letters into groups with handwritten notes, I requested to see the facsimiles. *Which ones the Librarian said? All of them I replied?* He looked at me quite oddly and said, *"You know there are 22,000 files"*. It was impossible to review all 22,000 so I selected files based on key dates in US History. The one thing that stood out in their correspondence and resolutions is that the signors used their titles, *President of Congress, President of the United States in Congress Assembled, United States* – President, and just President quite often. The exception was letters directed to George Washington, where most of the Presidents just signed their name. Conversely, George Washington almost always addressed them as President of Congress or your Excellency. The Presidents, even during the Conway Cabal, held Commander-in-Chief Washington in the highest esteem.

Please understand that few people in this country admire George Washington more than I. My decision to qualify *"First"* as *"under the US Constitution"* was not taken lightly. I am such a fan that I requested from Congress that they reinstitute February 22nd as a national holiday dedicated only to President Washington. We can just leave that *"floating"* Monday as a reflective day for all the other Presidents. February 22nd, I maintain, should be the day all High School Juniors put the final touches on a pre-assigned paper on George Washington. On February 23rd the papers should be submitted to the teachers and they pick the best one to send onto the County. Each County then selects one winner and submits it to the State. Each State then selects one outstanding paper and submits them for consideration by the White House, Congress, and the Supreme Court. Each Branch selects a winner and they are awarded a full scholarship to the college or technical school of their choice. The three winners are announced on February 22nd of their senior year and the process repeats for a new class of juniors. If you think the process is too complicated, just visit the website of the James Monroe Foundation, JamesMonroe.org for a working example of this proposal. Last year I was honored to attend their ceremonies at the Virginia State Capital where a young Lady from Alexandria Virginia read a most magnificent account of James Monroe's role in the Louisiana Purchase. Wouldn't it be a wonderful to tune-in to a nationally televised hour of the three young minds revealing some aspect of the life of George Washington that taught us something about our heritage?

I understand being recognized as *"First"*, especially in a noble endeavor, is prized by all who take the causes of liberty, and the pursuit of happiness seriously. More importantly, I know just how ingrained the idea of Washington being our *"First"* President is in our national consciousness. I am not alone. Certainly the people of Norwich, Connecticut have embraced the fact that their native son was the first US President, but the debate continues. I have heard via fax, email, telephone and in person from many Marylanders who insist that John Hanson was the First President of the United States in Congress Assembled. I certainly hope the evidence in this book and John Hanson's letter thanking Thomas McKean for his services as President of the United States in Congress Assembled puts this claim to rest once and for all. President Hanson was the 3rd President of the United States in Congress Assembled.

To those of you who still insist that Hanson was *"First"* because he took office after George Washington won the Battle of Yorktown as well as those of you who claim Elias Boudinot is "First" because he presided when John Jay, Benjamin Franklin, Henry Laurens, and John Adams signed the Treaty that ended the Revolutionary War and finally to those of you who claim Thomas Mifflin *"First"* because it was he, who signed and formally ratified the Definitive Treaty of Peace as "Our President" truly ending the war I say, reflect on the words of our 53rd US President George Bush:

"America will never seek a permission slip to defend the security of our people."

The only permission slip we required when the 1777 Continental Congress proposed the Perpetual Union of the United States of America under the Articles of Confederation was the ratification of the 13 States. Virginia was the *"First"* to ratify and by that fact has the claim, not Delaware, to being the *"First State"*. On March 1st, 1781, the Continental Congress inspected the reports of each of the states, and deemed the Articles of Confederation fully ratified. On March 2, 1781 the Secretary entered the named of United States in Congress Assembled on the top of the Journal, role call was taken, Samuel Huntington was entered into the records as President and then a celebration ensued. Samuel Huntington, a farmer's son, signer of the Declaration of Independence and a gifted lawyer was and is still the *"First"* President of the United States in Congress Assembled.

In recent weeks, thanks to the re-entombment of Samuel and Martha Huntington, the intensity of *"Who are you to raise this issue and proclaim Samuel Huntington the First President of the United States?"* has increased, I say,

Samuel Huntington was the First President of the United States in Congress Assembled under the ratified 1781 Articles of Confederation, our First Constitution. George Washington was the First President of the United States under the ratified 1788 US Constitution. It just so happens that 1781 came before 1788.

As for who is Stan Klos?

I was fortunate enough to be born in the United States of America, whose founders' deeds and laws circle above like majestic eagles. I have merely taken the time to look-up and point.

PRESIDENTIAL DEBATE 2004

"What luck for the rulers that men do not think" -- A Tyrannical Despot

As I researched and read the many letters of the Delegates of the United States in Congress Assembled in this presidential year I couldn't help but wonder what they would think of our Republic. Perhaps they would be amazed that the Federal Government, under the US Constitution, has become the center of American Life. The scenario that Richard Henry Lee painted 220 years ago, a massive constitutional government overtaxing the people, is a 21st Century reality. What would the 14 Founding Presidents, George Washington, James Madison, or Citizen Thomas Jefferson in election of 2004? I am convinced that these Founding Fathers would do three things in Campaign 2004–write articles, makes speeches, and vote. They have inspired me to do all three in 2004 and my opinions are published below.

After a recent Discovery Channel documentary filmed at the Library of Congress I went to lunch with a gifted historian, a veteran director, an insightful producer, the film crew. In the restaurant John Hancock's *"No Taxation Without Representation"* broadside was prominently displayed. Almost predictable our conversation centered on DC residents having no representatives in Congress and still having to pay federal taxes. The conversation then turned to the second amendment with a vigor I hadn't experienced in years. Talk about a power lunch, we also discussed such issues as term limits, when life begins, God's proper place in classrooms, among other topics. For example we discussed the fact that lewd photographs and movies of sodomy, bestiality and hardcore sexuality can readily be found on the internet under the guise of *"Free Speech."*

Being the father of eight children I was asked, *"What do you think?"* After a moment of reflection I replied, *"I can tell you what our nation's Founding Fathers would think. They would be shocked that we still haven't used the most important provision in the Constitution to address these and many other issues raised during this lunch --- a Second Constitutional Convention!"* I went on to explain that our Founders surely would have expected that a Constitutional Convention comprised of learned and well intentioned representatives from each state would have revisited the 1787 Constitution by now. The ultimate authority to our form of government, I explained, lies with the States; one state one vote to change anything or everything. To my amazement the group was actually surprised that a constitutional mechanism has always been in place for the States to convene such a convention without the interference of Congress, the President, Supreme Court or individual State Governors.

With this provision State Legislatures are empowered to convene a National Convention comprised of delegates who (behind closed doors) could study, debate, and deliberate on all aspects of the current Constitution. This synergy, which happened at our first Constitutional Convention, could form an improved foundation for our federal government.

Obviously the work would be colossal. It was argued that we presently don't have the great minds of Madison, Hamilton, Franklin, or Ellsworth to insure constitutional modifications worthy of consideration. I disagreed noting that we DO have the great legal, ethical and social minds with 280 million inhabits and a 21st Century knowledge base from which to draw. This mastermind, I maintained, could be just as insightful today as they were then. Admittedly our country is divided on many issues, however, men and women, liberals and conservatives, whites and blacks, could find common ground for meaningful change. Would not everyone agree that our present Federal Government is too large, intrusive, and not what our founders originally envisioned?

The Founders, realized the Constitution would require more then just amendments for change and deliberately provided us with the Article V provision for only 2/3rd of the States (34) to call a Constitutional Convention:

> "... *on the application of the legislatures of two thirds of the several states, shall call a convention for proposing amendments, which, in either case, shall be valid to all intents and purposes, as part of this Constitution, when ratified by the legislatures of three fourths of the several states, or by conventions in three fourths thereof...*"

The rhetorical situation couldn't be better in these times of plenty and mass communication to hold a Constitutional Convention. Our Citizens know so much more then the 18th Century Delegates did in all aspects of understanding and certainly our new 21st Century Patriots would recognize the gravity of their obligation. Wouldn't it be wonderful if each State would carefully chose representatives, three from each state, of which at least one must be of a different political party, one a different gender, and one a different race but all overflowing with devotion to their country and a burning desire to improve the laws by which we are governed?

Our original Constitution is, by any measure, a document to be admired, cherished, and revered. It is, however, time for meaningful deliberation and constructive change. The original Constitution was designed by white men of property over 200 years ago for only 4 million citizens. Today that same Constitution governs 280 million and has saddled us with an extravagant Federal Government. This condition is stifling our economic, social, and religious freedoms. The debate should begin as soon as possible in the public forum. Such a debate could include such issues as; the overburdened federal justice system, freedom of speech, the right to bear arms, the separation of church and state, line item veto, term limits, when life begins, and restoring states rights at the federal level as benchmarks but all aspects of the language are open for consideration in a Constitutional Convention.

Finally, it is important to understand that should a Convention be called the Constitution provides us with a safeguard in the form of a check and balance system. The balance is the constitutional delegates must build a consensus before amending or re-crafting the language in the constitution. The check is that changed language (no matter how small) would require 4/5th ratification by the states to become law. At the very least a 21st Century Constitutional Convention would result in a ratification debate that would inspire and educate our citizenry on the importance of the precise written word which is the glue which binds this nation together.

RE-INSTITUTE A "MANHATTAN PROJECT" OF ENERGY

Our national rate of fossil fuel consumption in this century will exceed world supply unless we put politics aside and assemble our best scientific minds to discover safe and virtually limitless energy sources. A new *"Manhattan Project"* of Energy, not geared solely towards the harnessing of the nuclear atom, could be convened by our government. All aspects of power -- solar, wind, hydrogen, water etc. should be investigated with collaborative openness with our present scientific masterminds of energy.

Breeder Reactor Research (A nuclear reactor that manufactures more fissionable isotopes than it consumes) which was halted in the 1970's should be immediately re-instituted. Most of the supposedly nuclear *"waste"* about to be buried under Yucca Mountain could give the US an almost immediate relief from the power shortages gripping the nation. Most importantly, a new generation of 21st Century breeder reactors could release us from the fossil fuel stranglehold, while the research marches on for an alternative and improved energy source by 2010.

If we pull together now and provide our diverse vast national scientific mastermind with the capital, organization, and a clearly defined objective (as was done in the 1940's at Los Alamos or in the 1960's to safely land and return a Man from the Moon) surely new energy sources and systems could be in place by the end of this decade. The goal would be to discover (or re-discover) innovative, safe, and vastly inexpensive energy methods that would propel a 21st Century *"Quality of Life"* far beyond the 20th Century's benchmark of inventions.

THE FORMATION OF CITY-STATES

This formation would require the mutual cooperation of United States financial and political resources. September 11th has taught America that the United States is not immune to foreign attack from even a small enemy who firmly believes (rightly or wrongly) that US culture directly threatens their way of life. Fundamental Muslims are abhorred by our culture that blankets their television, the world wide internet, and radio broadcasts with epideictic visions of sex, violence, and a secular way of life so vile (to them) that it justifies our complete and utter destruction. There is a legal and moral difference, but in their eyes these Muslims, and many other fundamental spiritual leaders, think the United States is just as despicable as other foreign governments who mass murder in the name of ethnic cleansing or cross international borders to subjugate neighboring nations. The saying that, *"It is much better to understand then to be understood"* is obviously a failed diplomatic position on our part to prevent misguided terrorism. America's true nature can only be revealed through the insightful education of others. This would help to overcome zealots who weave and exaggerate our supposed hedonistic philosophy (born from the misuse of free speech liberties) to eager minds seeking escape from unfathomable poverty and oppression.

In the past America has embraced the old adage "*Give a man a fish and he will eat for a day, teach him to fish and he will eat for a lifetime*". The United States has done the first part by providing many nations with vast amounts of funding for food programs, medical relief, and infrastructure on their home soil. We also provide visas for foreign citizens to attend a variety of public as well private educational institutions. No country on earth has given away more "fish" to help his fellow man than the United States of America. Despite all this generosity and genuine good will an unfortunate Bull's Eye of retribution has been painted on the heart of our Republic by many rouge nations and misguided segments of their citizenry. The United States needs to substitute a greater percentage of our distribution of "fish" with "teaching our neighbors HOW to fish". This will require long term commitments especially with emerging nations.

To implement prosperous models of instruction, I am suggesting that the United States should acquire real estate or long term leases (much like Hong Kong) via treaty and form *"City-States"* within the emerging nations who sincerely seek our aid. Such a City-State would eliminate most of the problems associated with operating on foreign soil because the land (which should be undeveloped real estate) becomes a flourishing zone of the United States. These City-States would be designed to become economic and educational zones providing financial, educational, and political stability for merging nations. These zones would underwrite and safeguard the public and private capital that would predictably pour into these territories of economic development. Ideally, these "*hands-on*" City-States would evolve into mutually beneficial free trade and educational districts which would inspire, instruct, and consequently lead the host nations into a new era of enlightenment and prosperity.

****

As the Presidential debate heats-up I ask you, wherever and whenever possible, to interject these issues into the campaigns. We must be geared up for the inevitable and omnipresent catalyst of civilization, change. We are all the benefactors of a 18th Century free enterprise system in what General Charles Cornwallis described as "*a world turned upside down.*" The United States financial system is a modern day economic paradigm of how our astonishing republic continues to stand the world on its head.

In my lifetime there have been some interesting trade issues that are a direct result of our dollar based world economy. In the 1970's the United States stood in lines to pay what was then soaring prices for gasoline while Arabia utilized these profits, among other things, to drive the price of gold to $1,000 an ounce. In the 1980's the United States consumer demand for more dependable cars, new VHS recorders, and sleeker television sets resulted in Japan being flush with US currency, which was ardently reinvested in real estate all across America including NYC's Rockefeller Center. In the 1990's the United States appetite for computers, designer clothes, SUV's, gasoline and a host of overseas goods flooded our foreign neighbors with so many dollars our trade partners invested heavily in Wall Street stocks creating unprecedented P/E Ratios (price to earnings ratios). At one point in the 90's a Dotcom CEO spelled profit - "*Prophet*" when asked to justify his stock's artificial value. Like the gold and silver of the 70's and the real estate of the 80's our millennium artificial stock market values collapsed. All that currency sent oversees to purchase foreign goods and natural resources evaporated via Wall Street as the world lost trillions in the dollar based marketplace.

Today the current tax cut and low interest rates has sent the economy surging again to another consumer spending cycle draining the goods and natural resources of Arabia, Mexico, Venezuela, China, Russia and a host of other foreign nations in exchange for PAPER currency. Once again this dollar world economy, due to its very nature, offers very few options other then to recycle the cash back into the United States market. Predictably, this new flood of trade dollars into foreign markets will once again drive-up artificial value in our nation's commodities, products, and or land (looks like real estate for the 00's) ending once again with a marketplace correction in value. This foreseeable 2010's correction, like the others before it, should return the incredible paper back to our economy only to start the cycle once again for another generation of consumers. I forecast, however, the contrary will occur.

The world, or at least part of it, has already rejected this model of preserving United States natural resources while depleting theirs in exchange for our miraculous paper. The Euro has arrived and the oil producing nations are seriously considering a change in their monetary trading base. This could be the beginning of the end of the world based dollar economy. When this economic epiphany becomes a reality the world once again will "*turn upside down*" to Europe unless we take the lead as a producer nation (renewable energy, biogenetics, nanotechnology, and robotics to name a few).

The United States needs to discover a new energy resource to thwart the fossil fuel stranglehold that will surely strangle us once the dollar basis is lost. We the people need to distribute this new energy source as an export if our nation expects to satisfy the voracious natural resource and foreign goods appetites of the American consumer. The federal bureaucracy must be streamlined to compete with these state-owned foreign forces by returning power to the states who were the true power structure of government until the17th Amendment was ratified in 1913. US Senators, to achieve office, were for 125 years elected by their state legislatures. The 17th Amendment enabled US Senators to be elected directly from the vote of the people. From 1913 to the 1960 Constitutional change seemed to work fine as candidates were still answerable to their political parties. Today with the advent of a TV electorate these US Senators are now only answerable to the almighty fund raising dollar unless of course the Senator is a multi-millionaire who can fund their own election then they are answerable to virtually no one (the top four are John Kerry of Massachusetts, with a net worth of at least $164 million; Herb Kohl of Wisconsin, with a net worth of at least $111 million, John "Jay" Rockefeller of West Virginia, with an estimated net worth of at least $82 million and Jon Corzine of New Jersey with a net worth of at least $71 million). It was in the 17th Amendment one can mark the beginning of the end of a check and balance between the States and the Federal Government. Now in the name of the people's will we have citizens calling for the popular election of the US President which strips the last vestige of state check and balance on the present federal government. Alexander Hamilton once said:

> *The voice of the people has been said to be the voice of God; and, however generally this maxim has been quoted and believed, it is not true to fact. The people are turbulent and changing, they seldom judge or determine right.*

Only the States can force the downsizing of the federal government. A smaller and more efficient federal government would free-up capital for consumers to invest and private enterprise to compete in the blossoming international free trade economy.

To add to the disintegration of the dollar basis woes many Americans are calling for the curbing of free trade, the reestablishment of industrial revolution jobs, and the return to heavily mining American resources to supply the voracious appetites of American Consumers. Intriguingly, these calls for "*Made in America*" products confuse our foreign trade partners and dupe them to increase production as well as their exports of natural resources to the United States accepting dollars in exchange. The "*Made in America*" is a noble pursuit but it is quite premature. We are not ready to compete. Time is needed to develop innovated tradable products. Most importantly we need a low cost and remarkably efficient new energy source to offset the capital disparity brought on by the absurdly low employee wages of the developing nations.

The question is, how long will the world stand on its dollar trade head empting its dwindling natural resources for pretty green and peach paper? If we are going to continue on this road of unprecedented consumption and ignore the issues then the United States, at the very least, should enter into negotiations with Denmark to acquire Greenland to forestall the collapse of our natural resources in the next century. In the 1990's Microsoft's eloquent taunt to IBM was - "*It's the software stupid*". Combining this expression with the 19th Century Alaskan Taunt "*Seward's Icebox*"; I generate -
"*It's the natural resources Mr. President*".

The exchange of our almost paranormal paper for foreign goods has, for decades, strengthened our nation's wealth while preserving natural resources that will be direly needed by future generations of Americans. It is entirely possible, unless we make a start on the issues outlined above, that our junkyards of foreign products and untapped natural resources will be our Century's greatest legacy to 22nd Century Americans.

In summary our leaders need to recover the states' rights foundation of the federal government with a Constitutional Convention. We need to adapt the historic model of City-States to United States aid policy which will help us establish free trade zones all over the world insuring the survival of the dollar based international economy. Most importantly in the name of preserving the world's natural resources we need immediately to establish a *Manhattan Project of Energy* to discover and implement an inexhaustible energy source. Mars is important, but America needs to zero in on energy knowing full well that once the United States focuses on this challenge a new power source is just around the corner.

APPENDIX

ARTICLES OF CONFEDERATION

NORTHWEST ORDINANCE

US CONSTITUTION

As reported in the Journals of Congress

Courtesy of the Library of Congress

Articles of Confederation

According to the order of the day, the honble John Hanson and Daniel Carroll, two of the delegates for the State of Maryland, in pursuance of the act of the legislature of that State, entitled "An act to empower the delegates of this State in Congress to subscribe and ratify the Articles of Confederation," which was read in Congress the 12 of February last, and a copy thereof entered on the minutes, did, in behalf of the said State of Maryland, sign and ratify the said articles, by which act the Confederation of the United States of America was completed, each and every of the Thirteen United States, from New Hampshire to Georgia, both included, having adopted and confirmed, and by their delegates in Congress, ratified the same, [which is in the words following:]

[Note 1: 1 The words in brackets are in the Papers of the Continental Congress, No. 9 (History of the Confederation) but not in the Journal.]

To all to whom these Presents shall come, we the under signed Delegates of the States affixed to our Names, send greeting.

Whereas the Delegates of the United States of America, in Congress assembled, did, on the 15th day of November, in the Year of our Lord One thousand Seven Hundred and Seventy seven, and in the Second Year of the Independence of America, agree to certain articles of Confederation and perpetual Union between the States of Newhampshire, Massachusetts-bay, Rhodeisland and Providence Plantations, Connecticut, New York, New Jersey, Pennsylvania, Delaware, Maryland, Virginia, North-Carolina, South-Carolina and Georgia in the words following, viz. "Articles of Confederation and perpetual Union between the states of Newhampshire, Massachusetts-bay, Rhodeisland and Providence Plantations, Connecticut, New-York, New-Jersey, Pennsylvania, Delaware, Maryland, Virginia, North-Carolina, South-Carolina and Georgia.

Article I. The Stile of this confederacy shall be "The United States of America."

Article II. Each state retains its sovereignty, freedom, and independence, and every Power, Jurisdiction and right, which is not by this confederation expressly delegated to the United States, in Congress assembled.

Article III. The said states hereby severally enter into a firm league of friendship with each other, for their common defence, the security of their Liberties, and their mutual and general welfare, binding themselves to assist each other, against all force offered to, or attacks made upon them, or any of them, on account of religion, sovereignty, trade, or any other pretence whatsoever.

Article IV. The better to secure and perpetuate mutual friendship and intercourse among the people of the different states in this union, the free inhabitants of each of these states, paupers, vagabonds and fugitives from justice excepted, shall be entitled to all privileges and immunities of free citizens in the several states; and the people of each state shall have free ingress and regress to and from any other state, and shall enjoy therein all the privileges of trade and commerce, subject to the same duties, impositions and restrictions as the inhabitants thereof respectively, provided that such restriction shall not extend so far as to prevent the removal of property imported into any state, to any other state, of which the Owner is an inhabitant; provided also that no imposition, duties or restriction shall be laid by any state, on the property of the united states, or either of them.

If any Person guilty of, or charged with treason, felony, or other high misdemeanor in any state, shall flee from Justice, and be found in any of the united states, he shall, upon demand of the Governor or executive power, of the state from which he fled, be delivered up and removed to the state having jurisdiction of his offence.

Full faith and credit shall he given in each of these states to the records, acts and judicial proceedings of the courts and magistrates of every other state.

Article V. For the more convenient management of the general interests of the united states, delegates shall be annually appointed in such manner as the legislature of each state shall direct, to meet in Congress on the first Monday in November, in every year, with a power reserved to each state, to recal its delegates, or any of them, at any time within the year, and to send others in their stead, for the remainder of the Year.

No state shall be represented in Congress by less than two, nor by more than seven Members; and no person shall be capable of being a delegate for more than three years in any term of six years; nor shall any person, being a delegate, be capable of holding any office under the united states, for which he, or another for his benefit receives any salary, fees or emolument of any kind.

Each state shall maintain its own delegates in a meeting of the states, and while they act as members of the committee of the states.

In determining questions in the united states in Congress assembled, each state shall have one vote.

Freedom of speech and debate in Congress shall not be impeached or questioned in any

Court, or place out of Congress, and the members of congress shall be protected in their persons from arrests and imprisonments, during the time of their going to and from, and attendance on congress, except for treason, felony, or breach of the peace.

Article VI. No state, without the Consent of the united states in congress assembled, shall send any embassy to, or receive any embassy from, or enter into any conference, agreement, alliance or treaty with any King prince or state; nor shall any person holding any office of profit or trust under the united states, or any of them, accept of any present, emolument, office or title of ally kind whatever from any king, prince or foreign state; nor shall the united states in congress assembled, or any of them, grant any title of nobility.

No two or more states shall enter into any treaty, confederation or alliance whatever between them, without the consent of the united states in congress assembled, specifying accurately the purposes for which the same is to be entered into, and how long it shall continue.

No state shall lay any imposts or duties, which may interfere with any stipulations in treaties, entered into by the united states in congress assembled, with any king, prince or state, in pursuance of any treaties already proposed by congress, to the courts of France and Spain.

No vessels of war shall be kept up in time of peace by any state, except such number only, as shall be deemed necessary by the united states in congress assembled, for the defence of such state, or its trade; nor shall any body of forces be kept up by any state, in time of peace, except such number only, as in the judgment of the united states, in congress assembled, shall be deemed requisite to garrison the forts necessary for the defence of such state; but every state shall always keep up a well regulated and disciplined militia, sufficiently armed and accoutred, and shall provide and constantly have ready for use, in public stores, a due number of field pieces and tents, and a proper quantity of arms, ammunition and camp equipage.

No state shall engage in any war without the consent of the united states in congress assembled, unless such state be actually invaded by enemies, or shall have received certain advice of a resolution being formed by some nation of Indians to invade such state, and the danger is so imminent as not to admit of a delay till the united states in congress assembled can be consulted: nor shall any state grant commissions to any ships or vessels of war, nor letters of marque or reprisal, except it be after a declaration of war by the united states in congress assembled, and then only against the kingdom or state and the subjects thereof, against which war has been so declared, and under such regulations as shall be established by the united states in congress assembled, unless such state be infested by pirates, in which case vessels of war may be fitted out for that occasion, and kept so long as the danger shall continue, or until the united states in congress assembled, shall determine otherwise.

Article VII. When land-forces are raised by any state for the common defence, all officers of or under the rank of colonel, shall be appointed by the legislature of each state respectively, by whom such forces shall be raised, or in such manner as such state shall direct, and all vacancies shall be filled up by the State which first made the appointment.

Article VIII. All charges of war, and all other expences that shall be incurred for the common defence or general welfare, and allowed by the united states in congress assembled, shall be defrayed out of a common treasury, which shall be supplied by the several states in proportion to the value of all land within each state, granted to or surveyed for any Person, as such land and the buildings and improvements thereon shall be estimated according to such mode as the united states in congress assembled, shall from time to time direct and appoint. The taxes for paying that proportion shall be laid and levied by the authority and direction of the legislatures of the several states within the time agreed upon by the united states in congress assembled.

Article IX. The united states in congress assembled, shall have the sole and exclusive right and power of determining on peace and war, except in the cases mentioned in the sixth article--of sending and receiving ambassadors--entering into treaties and alliances, provided that no treaty of commerce shall be made whereby the legislative power of the respective states shall be restrained from imposing such imposts and duties on foreigners, as their own people are subjected to, or from prohibiting the exportation or importation of any species of goods or commodities whatsoever--of establishing rules for deciding in all cases, what captures on land or water shall be legal, and in what manner prizes taken by land or naval forces in the service of the united states shall be divided or appropriated--of granting letters of marque and reprisal in times of peace--appointing courts for the trim of piracies and felonies committed on the high seas and establishing courts for receiving and determining finally appeals in all cases of captures, provided that no member of congress shall be appointed a judge of any of the said courts.

The united states in congress assembled shall also be the last resort on appeal in all disputes and differences now subsisting or that hereafter may arise between two or more states concerning boundary, jurisdiction or any other cause whatever; which authority shall always be exercised in the manner following. Whenever the legislative or executive authority or lawful agent of any state in controversy with another shall present a petition to congress stating the matter in question and praying for a hearing, notice thereof shall be given by order of congress to the legislative or executive authority of the other state in controversy, and a day assigned for the appearance of the parties by their lawful agents, who shall then be directed to appoint by joint consent, commissioners or judges to constitute a court for hearing and determining the matter in question: but if they cannot agree, congress shall name three persons out of each of the united states, and from the list of such persons each party shall alternately strike out one, the petitioners beginning, until the number shall be reduced to thirteen; and from that number not less than seven, nor more than nine names as congress shall direct, shall in the presence of congress be drawn out by lot, and the persons whose names shall be so drawn or any five of them, shall be commissioners or judges, to hear and finally determine the controversy, so always as a major part of the judges who shall hear the cause shall agree in the determination: and if either party shall neglect to attend at the day appointed, without showing reasons, which congress shall judge sufficient, or being present shall refuse to strike, the congress shall proceed to nominate three persons out of each state, and the secretary of congress shall strike in behalf of such party absent or refusing; and the judgment and sentence of the court to be appointed, in the manner before prescribed, shall be final and conclusive; and if any of the parties shall refuse to submit to the authority of such court, or to appear or defend their claim or cause, the court shall nevertheless proceed to pronounce sentence, or judgment, which shall in like manner be final and decisive, the judgment or sentence and other proceedings being in either case transmitted to congress, and lodged among the acts of congress for the security of the parties concerned: provided that every commissioner, before he sits in judgment, shall take an oath to be administred by one of the judges of the supreme or superior court of the state, where the cause shall be tried, "well and truly to hear and determine the matter in question, according to the best of his judgment, without favour, affection or hope of reward:" provided also, that no state shall be deprived of territory for the benefit of the united states.

All controversies concerning the private right of soil claimed under different grants of two or more states, whose jurisdictions as they may respect such lands, and the states which passed such grants are adjusted, the said grants or either of them being at the same time claimed to have originated antecedent to such settlement of jurisdiction, shall on the petition of either party to the congress of the united states, be finally determined as near as may be in the same manner as is before prescribed for deciding disputes respecting territorial jurisdiction between different states.

The united states in congress assembled shall also have the sole and exclusive right and power of regulating the alloy and value of coin struck by their own authority, or by that of the respective states--fixing the standard of weights and measures throughout the united states--regulating the trade and managing all affairs with the Indians, not members of any of the states, provided that the legislative right of any state within its own limits be not infringed or violated--establishing or regulating post-offices from one state to another, throughout all the united states, and exacting such postage on the papers passing thro' the same as may be requisite to defray the expences of the said office--appointing all officers of the land forces, in the service of the united states, excepting regimental officers--appointing all the officers of the naval forces, and commissioning all officers whatever in the service of the united states--making rules for the government and regulation of the said land and naval forces, and directing their operations.

The united states in congress assembled shall have authority to appoint a committee, to sit in the recess of congress, to be denominated "A Committee of the States," and to consist of one delegate from each state; and to appoint such other committees and civil officers as may be necessary for managing the general affairs of the united states under their direction--to appoint one of their number to preside, provided that no person be allowed to serve in the office of president more than one year in any term of three years; to ascertain the necessary sums of Money to be raised for the service of the united states, and to appropriate mid apply the same for defraying the public expences--to borrow money, or emit bills on the credit of the united states, transmitting every half year to the respective states an account of the sums of money so borrowed or emitted,--to build and equip a navy--to agree upon the number of land forces, and to make requisitions from each state for its quota, in proportion to the number of white inhabitants in such state; which requisition shall be binding, and thereupon the legislature of each state shall appoint the regimental officers, raise the men and cloath, arm and equip them in a soldier like manner, at the expence of the united states; and the officers and men so cloathed, armed and equipped shall **march** to the place appointed, and within the time agreed on by the united states in congress assembled: But if the united states in congress assembled shall, on consideration of circumstances judge proper that any state should not raise men, or should raise a smaller number than its quota, and that any other state should raise a greater number of men than the quota thereof, such extra number shall be raised, officered, cloathed, armed and equipped in the same manner as the quota of such state, unless the legislature of such state shall judge that such extra number cannot be safely spared out of the same, in which case they shall raise officer, cloath, arm and equip as many of such extra number as they judge can be sagely spared. And the officers and men so cloathed, armed and equipped, shall **march** to the place appointed, and within the time agreed on by the united states in congress assembled.

The united states in congress assembled shall never engage in a war, nor grant letters of marque and reprisal in time of peace, nor enter into any treaties or alliances, nor coin money, nor regulate the value thereof, nor ascertain the sums and expences necessary for the defence and welfare of the united states, or any of them, nor emit bills, nor borrow money on the credit of the united states, nor appropriate money, nor agree upon the number of vessels of war, to be built or purchased, or the number of land or sea forces to be raised, nor appoint a commander in chief of the army or navy, unless nine states assent to the same: nor shall a question on any other point, except for adjourning from day to day be determined, unless by the votes of a majority of the united states in congress assembled.

The congress of the united states shall have power to adjourn to any time within the year, and to any place within the united states, so that no period of adjournment be for a longer duration than the space of six Months, and shall publish the Journal of their proceedings monthly, except such parts thereof relating to treaties, alliances or military operations, as in their judgment require secrecy; and the yeas and nays of the delegates of each state on any question shall be entered on the Journal, when it is desired by any delegate; and the delegates of a state, or any of them, at his or their request shall be furnished with a transcript of the said Journal, except such parts as are above excepted, to lay before the legislatures of the several states.

Article X. The committee of the states, or any nine of them, shall be authorized to execute, in the recess of congress, such of the powers of congress as the united states in congress assembled, by the consent of nine states, shall from time to time think expedient to vest them with; provided that no power be delegated to the said committee, for the exercise of which, by the articles of confederation, the voice of nine states in the congress of the united states assembled is requisite.

Article XI. Canada acceding to this confederation, and joining in the measures of the united states, shall be admitted into, and entitled to all the advantages of this union: but no other colony shall be admitted into the same, unless such admission be agreed to by nine states.

Article XII. All bills of credit emitted, monies borrowed and debts contracted by, or under the authority of congress, before the assembling of the united states, in pursuance of the present confederation, shall be deemed and considered as a charge against the united states, for payment and satisfaction whereof the said united states, and the public faith are hereby solemnly pledged.

Article XIII. Every state shall abide by the determinations of the united states in congress assembled, on all questions which by this confederation are submitted to them. And the Articles of this confederation shall be inviolably observed by every state, and the union shall be perpetual; nor shall any alteration at any time hereinafter be made in any of them; unless such alteration be agreed to in a congress of the united states, and be afterwards confirmed by the legislatures of every state.

And Whereas it hath pleased the Great Governor of the World t incline the hearts of the legislatures we respectively represent in congress, to approve of, and to authorize us to ratify the said articles of confederation and perpetual union. Know Ye that we the undersigned delegates; by virtue of the power and authority to us given for that purpose, do by these presents, in the name and in behalf of our respective constituents, fully and entirely ratify and confirm each and every of the said articles of confederation and perpetual union, and all and singular the matters and things therein contained: And we do further solemnly plight and engage the faith of our respective constituents, that they shall abide by the determinations of the united states in congress assembled, on all questions, which by the said confederation are submitted to them. And that the articles thereof shall be inviolably observed by the states we respectively represent, and that the union shall be perpetual. In Witness whereof we have hereunto set our hands in Congress. Done at Philadelphia in the state of Pennsylvania the ninth day of July, in the Year of our Lord one Thousand seven Hundred and Seventy-eight, and in the third year of the independence of America.

On the part & behalf of the State of New Hampshire.

- Josiah Bartlett,
- John Wentworth, junr August 8th, 1778,

On the part and behalf of the State of Massachusetts Bay.

- John Hancock,
- Samuel Adams,
- Elbridge Gerry,
- Francis Dana,
- James Lovell,
- Samuel Holten,

On the part and behalf of the State of Rhode-Island and Providence Plantations.

- William Ellery,
- Henry Marchant,
- John Collins,

On the part and behalf of the State of Connecticut.

- Roger Sherman,
- Samuel Huntington,
- Oliver Wolcott,
- Titus Hosmer,
- Andrew Adams,

On the part and behalf of the State of New York.

- Jas Duane,
- Fra: Lewis,
- Wm Duer,
- Gouvr Morris,

On the Part and in Behalf of the State of New Jersey, November 26th, 1778.

- Jno Witherspoon,
- Nathl Scudder,

On the part and behalf of the State of Pennsylvania.

- Robert Morris,
- Daniel Roberdeau,
- Jon. Bayard Smith,
- William Clingar,
- Joseph Reed, 22d July, 1778,

On the part & behalf of the State of Delaware.

- Thos McKean, Feby 22d, 1779,
- John Dickinson, May 5th, 1779,
- Nicholas Van Dyke,

On the part and behalf of the State of Maryland.

- John Hanson, March 1, 1781,
- Daniel Carroll, do

On the Part and Behalf of the State of Virginia.

- Richard Henry Lee,
- John Banister,
- Thomas Adams,
- Jno. Harvie,
- Francis Lightfoot Lee,

On the part and behalf of the State of North Carolina.

- John Penn, July 21st, 1778,
- Corns Harnett,
- Jno. Williams,

On the part and on behalf of the State of South Carolina.

- Henry Laurens,
- William Henry Drayton,
- Jno Mathews,
- Richd Hutson,
- Thoo Heyward, junr.

On the part and behalf of the State of Georgia.

- Jno Walton, 24th July, 1778,
- Edwd Telfair,
- Edwd Langworthy,

[Note 1: 1 The proceedings of this day with respect to the signing of the Articles of Confederation, the Articles themselves and the signers are entered in the Papers of the Continental Congress, No. 9 (History of the Confederation), but not in the Journal itself. The Articles are printed here from the original roll in the Bureau of Rolls and Library, Department of State.]

Northwest Ordinance

An Ordinance for the government of the Territory of the United States northwest of the River Ohio.

Section 1. *Be it ordained by the United States in Congress assembled,* That the said territory, for the purposes of temporary government, be one district, subject, however, to be divided into two districts, as future circumstances may, in the opinion of Congress, make it expedient.

Sec 2. *Be it ordained by the authority aforesaid,* That the estates, both of resident and nonresident proprietors in the said territory, dying intestate, shall descent to, and be distributed among their children, and the descendants of a deceased child, in equal parts; the descendants of a deceased child or grandchild to take the share of their deceased parent in equal parts among them: And where there shall be no children or descendants, then in equal parts to the next of kin in equal degree; and among collaterals, the children of a deceased brother or sister of the intestate shall have, in equal parts among them, their deceased parents' share; and there shall in no case be a distinction between kindred of the whole and half blood; saving, in all cases, to the widow of the intestate her third part of the real estate for life, and one third part of the personal estate; and this law relative to descents and dower, shall remain in full force until altered by the legislature of the district. And until the governor and judges shall adopt laws as hereinafter mentioned, estates in the said territory may be devised or bequeathed by wills in writing, signed and sealed by him or her in whom the estate may be (being of full age), and attested by three witnesses; and real estates may be conveyed by lease and release, or bargain and sale, signed, sealed and delivered by the person being of full age, in whom the estate may be, and attested by two witnesses, provided such wills be duly proved, and such conveyances be acknowledged, or the execution thereof duly proved, and be recorded within one year after proper magistrates, courts, and registers shall be appointed for that purpose; and personal property may be transferred by delivery; saving, however to the French and Canadian inhabitants, and other settlers of the Kaskaskies, St. Vincents and the neighboring villages who have heretofore professed themselves citizens of Virginia, their laws and customs now in force among them, relative to the descent and conveyance, of property.

Sec. 3. *Be it ordained by the authority aforesaid,* That there shall be appointed from time to time by Congress, a governor, whose commission shall continue in force for the term of three years, unless sooner revoked by Congress; he shall reside in the district, and have a freehold estate therein in 1,000 acres of land, while in the exercise of his office.

Sec. 4. There shall be appointed from time to time by Congress, a secretary, whose commission shall continue in force for four years unless sooner revoked; he shall reside in the district, and have a freehold estate therein in 500 acres of land, while in the exercise of his office. It shall be his duty to keep and preserve the acts and laws passed by the legislature, and the public records of the district, and the proceedings of the governor in his executive department, and transmit authentic copies of such acts and proceedings, every six months, to the Secretary of Congress: There shall also be appointed a court to consist of three judges, any two of whom to form a court, who shall have a common law jurisdiction, and reside in the district, and have each therein a freehold estate in 500 acres of land while in the exercise of their offices; and their commissions shall continue in force during good behavior.

Sec. 5. The governor and judges, or a majority of them, shall adopt and publish in the district such laws of the original States, criminal and civil, as may be necessary and best suited to the circumstances of the district, and report them to Congress from time to time: which laws shall be in force in the district until the organization of the General Assembly therein, unless disapproved of by Congress; but afterwards the Legislature shall have authority to alter them as they shall think fit.

Sec. 6. The governor, for the time being, shall be commander in chief of the militia, appoint and commission all officers in the same below the rank of general officers; all general officers shall be appointed and commissioned by Congress.

Sec. 7. Previous to the organization of the general assembly, the governor shall appoint such magistrates and other civil officers in each county or township, as he shall find necessary for the preservation of the peace and good order in the same: After the general assembly shall be organized, the powers and duties of the magistrates and other civil officers shall be regulated and defined by the said assembly; but all magistrates and other civil officers not herein otherwise directed, shall during the continuance of this temporary government, be appointed by the governor.

Sec. 8. For the prevention of crimes and injuries, the laws to be adopted or made shall have force in all parts of the district, and for the execution of process, criminal and civil, the governor shall make proper divisions thereof; and he shall proceed from time to time as circumstances may require, to lay out the parts of the district in which the Native American titles shall have been extinguished, into counties and townships, subject, however, to such alterations as may thereafter be made by the legislature.

Sec. 9. So soon as there shall be five thousand free male inhabitants of full age in the district, upon giving proof thereof to the governor, they shall receive authority, with time and place, to elect a representative from their counties or townships to represent them in the general assembly: Provided, That, for every five hundred free male inhabitants, there shall be one representative, and so on progressively with the number of free male inhabitants shall the right of representation increase, until the number of representatives shall amount to twenty five; after which, the number and proportion of representatives shall be regulated by the legislature: Provided, That no person be eligible or qualified to act as a representative unless he shall have been a citizen of one of the United States three years, and be a resident in the district, or unless he shall have resided in the district three years; and, in either case, shall likewise hold in his own right, in fee simple, two hundred acres of land within the same; Provided, also, That a freehold in fifty acres of land in the district, having been a citizen of one of the states, and being resident in the district, or the like freehold and two years residence in the district, shall be necessary to qualify a man as an elector of a representative.

Sec. 10. The representatives thus elected, shall serve for the term of two years; and, in case of the death of a representative, or removal from office, the governor shall issue a writ to the county or township for which he was a member, to elect another in his stead, to serve for the residue of the term.

Sec. 11. The general assembly or legislature shall consist of the governor, legislative council, and a house of representatives. The Legislative Council shall consist of five members, to continue in office five years, unless sooner removed by Congress; any three of whom to be a quorum: and the members of the Council shall be nominated and appointed in the following manner, to wit: As soon as representatives shall be elected, the Governor shall appoint a time and place for them to meet together; and, when met, they shall nominate ten persons, residents in the district, and each possessed of a freehold in five hundred acres of land, and return their names to Congress; five of whom Congress shall appoint and commission to serve as aforesaid; and, whenever a vacancy shall happen in the council, by death or removal from office, the house of representatives shall nominate two persons, qualified as aforesaid, for each vacancy, and return their names to Congress; one of whom congress shall appoint and commission for the residue of the term. And every five years, four months at least before the expiration of the time of service of the members of council, the said house shall nominate ten persons, qualified as aforesaid, and return their names to Congress; five of whom Congress shall appoint and commission to serve as members of the council five years, unless sooner removed. And the governor, legislative council, and house of representatives, shall have authority to make laws in all cases, for the good government of the district, not repugnant to the principles and articles in this ordinance established and declared. And all bills, having passed by a majority in the house, and by a majority in the council, shall be referred to the governor for his assent; but no bill, or legislative act whatever, shall be of any force without his assent. The governor shall have power to convene, prorogue, and dissolve the general assembly, when, in his opinion, it shall be expedient.

Sec. 12. The governor, judges, legislative council, secretary, and such other officers as Congress shall appoint in the district, shall take an oath or affirmation of fidelity and of office; the governor before the president of congress, and all other officers before the Governor. As soon as a legislature shall be formed in the district, the council and house assembled in one room, shall have authority, by joint ballot, to elect a delegate to Congress, who shall have a seat in Congress, with a right of debating but not voting during this temporary government.

Sec. 13. And, for extending the fundamental principles of civil and religious liberty, which form the basis whereon these republics, their laws and constitutions are erected; to fix and establish those principles as the basis of all laws, constitutions, and governments, which forever hereafter shall be formed in the said territory: to provide also for the establishment of States, and permanent government therein, and for their admission to a share in the federal councils on an equal footing with the original States, at as early periods as may be consistent with the general interest:

Sec. 14. It is hereby ordained and declared by the authority aforesaid, That the following articles shall be considered as articles of compact between the original States and the people and States in the said territory and forever remain unalterable, unless by common consent, to wit:

Art. 1. No person, demeaning himself in a peaceable and orderly manner, shall ever be molested on account of his mode of worship or religious sentiments, in the said territory.

Art. 2. The inhabitants of the said territory shall always be entitled to the benefits of the writ of *habeas corpus*, and of the trial by jury; of a proportionate representation of the people in the legislature; and of judicial proceedings according to the course of the common law. All persons shall be bailable, unless for capital offenses, where the proof shall be evident or the presumption great. All fines shall be moderate; and no cruel or unusual punishments shall be inflicted. No man shall be deprived of his liberty or property, but by the judgment of his peers or the law of the land; and, should the public exigencies make it necessary, for the common preservation, to take any person's property, or to demand his particular services, full compensation shall be made for the same. And, in the just preservation of rights and property, it is understood and declared, that no law ought ever to be made, or have force in the said territory, that shall, in any manner whatever, interfere with or affect private contracts or engagements, *bona fide,* and without fraud, previously formed.

Art. 3. Religion, morality, and knowledge, being necessary to good government and the happiness of mankind, schools and the means of education shall forever be encouraged. The utmost good faith shall always be observed towards the Indians; their lands and property shall never be taken from them without their consent; and, in their property, rights, and liberty, they shall never be invaded or disturbed, unless in just and lawful wars authorized by Congress; but laws founded in justice and humanity, shall from time to time be made for preventing wrongs being done to them, and for preserving peace and friendship with them.

Art. 4. The said territory, and the States which may be formed therein, shall forever remain a part of this Confederacy of the United States of America, subject to the Articles of Confederation, and to such alterations therein as shall be constitutionally made; and to all the acts and ordinances of the United States in Congress assembled, conformable thereto. The inhabitants and settlers in the said territory shall be subject to pay a part of the federal debts contracted or to be contracted, and a proportional part of the expenses of government, to be apportioned on them by Congress according to the same common rule and measure by which apportionments thereof shall be made on the other States; and the taxes for paying their proportion shall be laid and levied by the authority and direction of the legislatures of the district or districts, or new States, as in the original States, within the time agreed upon by the United States in Congress assembled. The legislatures of those districts or new States, shall never interfere with the primary disposal of the soil by the United States in Congress assembled, nor with any regulations Congress may find necessary for securing the title in such soil to the *bona fide* purchasers. No tax shall be imposed on lands the property of the United States; and, in no case, shall nonresident proprietors be taxed higher than residents. The navigable waters leading into the Mississippi and St. Lawrence, and the carrying places between the same, shall be common highways and forever free, as well to the inhabitants of the said territory as to the citizens of the United States, and those of any other States that may be admitted into the confederacy, without any tax, impost, or duty therefore.

Art. 5. There shall be formed in the said territory, not less than three nor more than five States; and the boundaries of the States, as soon as Virginia shall alter her act of cession, and consent to the same, shall become fixed and established as follows, to wit: The western State in the said territory, shall be bounded by the Mississippi, the Ohio, and Wabash Rivers; a direct line drawn from the Wabash and Post Vincents, due North, to the territorial line between the United States and Canada; and, by the said territorial line, to the Lake of the Woods and Mississippi. The middle State shall be bounded by the said direct line, the Wabash from Post Vincents to the Ohio, by the Ohio, by a direct line, drawn due north from the mouth of the Great Miami, to the said territorial line, and by the said territorial line. The eastern State shall be bounded by the last mentioned direct line, the Ohio, Pennsylvania, and the said territorial line: Provided, however, and it is further understood and declared, that the boundaries of these three States shall be subject so far to be altered, that, if Congress shall hereafter find it expedient, they shall have authority to form one or two States in that part of the said territory which lies north of an east and west line drawn through the southerly bend or extreme of Lake Michigan. And, whenever any of the said States shall have sixty thousand free inhabitants therein, such State shall be admitted, by its delegates, into the Congress of the United States, on an equal footing with the original States in all respects whatever, and shall be at liberty to form a permanent constitution and State government: *Provided*, the constitution and government so to be formed, shall be republican, and in conformity to the principles contained in these articles; and, so far as it can be consistent with the general interest of the confederacy, such admission shall be allowed at an earlier period, and when there may be a less number of free inhabitants in the State than sixty thousand.

Art. 6. There shall be neither slavery nor involuntary servitude in the said territory, otherwise than in the punishment of crimes whereof the party shall have been duly convicted: *Provided, always,* That any person escaping into the same, from whom labor or service is lawfully claimed in any one of the original States, such fugitive may be lawfully reclaimed and conveyed to the person claiming his or her labor or service as aforesaid.

Be it ordained by the authority aforesaid, That the resolutions of the 23rd of April, 1784, relative to the subject of this ordinance, be, and the same are hereby repealed and declared null and void.

Done by the United States, in Congress assembled, the 13th day of July, in the year of our Lord 1787, and of their sovereignty and **independence the twelfth.**

US CONSTITUTION

The US Constitution as reported in the Journals of the United States in Congress Assembled on September 20th, 1787:

We the **People** of the United States, in Order to form a more perfect Union, establish Justice, insure domestic Tranquility, provide for the common defense, promote the general Welfare, and secure the Blessings of Liberty to ourselves and our Posterity, do ordain and establish this Constitution for the United States of America.

ARTICLE. I.

- Section. 1. All legislative Powers herein granted shall be vested in a Congress of the United States, which shall consist of a Senate and House of Representatives.
- Section. 2. The House of Representatives shall be composed of Members chosen every second Year by the **People** of the several States, and the Electors in each State shall have the Qualifications requisite for Electors of the most numerous Branch of the State Legislature.

No Person shall be a Representative who shall not have attained to the Age of twenty five Years, and been seven Years a Citizen of the United States, and who shall not, when elected, be an Inhabitant of that State in which he shall be chosen.

Representatives and direct Taxes shall be apportioned among the several States which may be included within this Union, according to their respective Numbers, which shall be determined by adding to the whole Number of free Persons, including those bound to Service for a Term of Years, and excluding Native Americans not taxed, three fifths of all other Persons. The actual Enumeration shall be made within three Years after the first Meeting of the Congress of the United States, and within every subsequent Term of ten Years, in such Manner as they shall by Law direct. The Number of Representatives shall not exceed one for every thirty Thousand, but each State shall have at Least one Representative; and until such enumeration shall be made, the State of New Hampshire shall be entitled to chuse three, Massachusetts eight, Rhode Island and Providence Plantations one, Connecticut five, New York six, New Jersey four, Pennsylvania eight, Delaware one, Maryland six, Virginia ten, North Carolina five, South Carolina five, and Georgia three.

When vacancies happen in the Representation from any State, the Executive Authority thereof shall issue Writs of Election to fill such Vacancies.

The House of Representatives shall chuse their Speaker and other Officers; and shall have the sole Power of Impeachment.

- Section. 3. The Senate of the United States shall be composed of two Senators from each State, chosen by the Legislature thereof, for six Years; and each Senator shall have one Vote.

Immediately after they shall be assembled in Consequence of the first Election, they shall be divided as equally as may be into three Classes. The Seats of the Senators of the first Class shall be vacated at the Expiration of the second Year, of the second Class at the Expiration of the fourth Year, and of the third Class at the Expiration of the sixth Year, so that one third may be chosen every second Year; and if Vacancies happen by Resignation, or otherwise, during the Recess of the Legislature of any State, the Executive thereof may make temporary Appointments until the next Meeting of the Legislature, which shall then fill such Vacancies.

No Person shall be a Senator who shall not have attained to the Age of Thirty Years, and been nine Years a Citizen of the United States, and who shall not, when elected, be an Inhabitant of that State for which he shall be chosen.

The Vice President of the United States shall be President of the Senate, but shall have no Vote, unless they be equally divided.

The Senate shall chuse their other Officers, and also a President pro tempore, in the Absence of the Vice President, or when he shall exercise the Office of President of the United States.

The Senate shall have the sole Power to try all Impeachments. When sitting for that Purpose, they shall be on Oath or Affirmation. When the President of the United States is tried, the Chief Justice shall preside: And no Person shall be convicted without the Concurrence of two thirds of the Members present.

Judgment in Cases of Impeachment shall not extend further than to removal from Office, and disqualification to hold and enjoy any Office of honor, Trust or Profit under the United States: but the Party convicted shall nevertheless be liable and subject to Indictment, Trial, Judgment and Punishment, according to Law.

- Section. 4. The Times, Places and Manner of holding Elections for Senators and Representatives, shall be prescribed in each State by the Legislature thereof; but the Congress may at any time by Law make or alter such Regulations, except as to the Places of chusing Senators.

The Congress shall assemble at least once in every Year, and such Meeting shall be on the first Monday in December, unless they shall by Law appoint a different Day.

- Section. 5. Each House shall be the Judge of the Elections, Returns and Qualifications of its own Members, and a Majority of each shall constitute a Quorum to do Business; but a smaller Number may adjourn from day to day, and may be authorized to compel the Attendance of absent Members, in such Manner, and under such Penalties as each House may provide.

Each House may determine the Rules of its Proceedings, punish its Members for disorderly Behaviour, and, with the Concurrence of two thirds, expel a Member.

Each House shall keep a Journal of its Proceedings, and from time to time publish the same, excepting such Parts as may in their Judgment require Secrecy; and the Yeas and Nays of the Members of either House on any question shall, at the Desire of one fifth of those Present, be entered on the Journal.

Neither House, during the Session of Congress, shall, without the Consent of the other, adjourn for more than three days, nor to any other Place than that in which the two Houses shall be sitting.

- Section. 6. The Senators and Representatives shall receive a Compensation for their Services, to be ascertained by Law, and paid out of the Treasury of the United States. They shall in all Cases, except Treason, Felony and Breach of the Peace, be privileged from Arrest during their Attendance at the Session of their respective Houses, and in going to and returning from the same; and for any Speech or Debate in either House, they shall not be ques tioned in any other Place.

No Senator or Representative shall, during the Time for which he was elected, be appointed to any civil Office under the Authority of the United States, which shall have been created, or the Emoluments whereof shall have been encreased during such time, and no Person holding any Office under the United States, shall be a Member of either House during his Continuance in Office.

- Section. 7. All Bills for raising Revenue shall originate in the House of Representatives; but the Senate may propose or concur with Amendments as on other Bills.

Every Bill which shall have passed the House of Representatives and the Senate shall, before it become a Law, be presented to the President of the United States; If he approve he shall sign it, but if not he shall return it, with his Objections to that House in which it shall have originated, who shall enter the Objections at large on their Journal, and proceed to reconsider it. If after such Reconsideration two thirds of that House shall agree to pass the Bill, it shall be sent, together with the Objections, to the other House, by which it shall likewise be reconsidered, and if approved by two thirds of that House, it shall become a Law. But in all such Cases the Votes of both Houses shall be determined by yeas and Nays, and the Names of the Persons voting for and against the Bill shall be entered on the Journal of each House respectively. If any Bill shall not be returned by the President within ten Days (Sundays excepted) after it shall have been presented to him, the same shall be a Law, in like manner as if he had signed it, unless the Congress by their Adjournment prevent its Return, in which Case it shall not be a Law.

Every Order, Resolution, or Vote to which the Concurrence of the Senate and House of Representatives may be necessary (except on a Question of Adjournment) shall be presented to the President of the United States; and before the same shall take Effect, shall be approved by him, or being disapproved by him, shall be repassed by two thirds of the Senate and House of Representatives, according to the Rules and Limitations prescribed in the Case of a Bill.

- Section. 8. The Congress shall have Power To lay and collect Taxes, Duties, Imposts and Excises, to pay the Debts and provide for the common Defence and general Welfare of the United States; but all Duties, Imposts and Excises shall be uniform throughout the United States;

To borrow Money on the credit of the United States;

To regulate Commerce with foreign Nations, and among the several States, and with the Native American Tribes;

To establish an uniform Rule of Naturalization, and uniform Laws on the subject of Bankruptcies throughout the United States;

To coin Money, regulate the Value thereof, and of foreign Coin, and fix the Standard of Weights and Measures;

To provide for the Punishment of counterfeiting the Securities and current Coin of the United States;

To establish Post Offices and post Roads;

To promote the Progress of Science and useful Arts, by securing for limited Times to Authors and Inventors the exclusive Right to their respective Writings and Discoveries;

To constitute Tribunals inferior to the Supreme Court;

To define and punish Piracies and Felonies committed on the high Seas, and Offences against the Law of Nations;

To declare War, grant Letters of Marque and Reprisal, and make Rules concerning Captures on Land and Water;

To raise and support Armies, but no Appropriation of Money to that Use shall be for a longer Term than two Years;

To provide and maintain a Navy;

To make Rules for the Government and Regulation of the land and naval Forces;

To provide for calling forth the Militia to execute the Laws of the Union, suppress Insurrections and repel Invasions;

To provide for organizing, arming, and disciplining, the Militia, and for governing such Part of them as may be employed in the Service of the United States, reserving to the States respectively, the Appointment of the Officers, and the Authority of training the Militia according to the discipline prescribed by Congress;

To exercise exclusive Legislation in all Cases whatsoever, over such District (not exceeding ten Miles square) as may, by Cession of particular States, and the Acceptance of Congress, become the Seat of Government of the United States, and to exercise like Authority over all Places purchased by the Consent of the Legislature of the State in which the same shall be, for the Erection of Forts, Magazines, Arsenals, dock-Yards, and other needful Buildings;--And

To make all Laws which shall be necessary and proper for carrying into Execution the foregoing Powers, and all other Powers vested by this Constitution in the Government of the United States, or in any Department or Officer thereof.

- Section. 9. The Migration or Importation of such Persons as any of the States now existing shall think proper to admit, shall not be prohibited by the Congress prior to the Year one thousand eight hundred and eight, but a Tax or duty may be imposed on such Importation, not exceeding ten dollars for each Person.

The Privilege of the Writ of Habeas Corpus shall not be suspended, unless when in Cases of Rebellion or Invasion the public Safety may require it.

No Bill of Attainder or ex post facto Law shall be passed.

No Capitation, or other direct, Tax shall be laid, unless in Proportion to the Census or Enumeration herein before directed to be taken.

No Tax or Duty shall be laid on Articles exported from any State.

No Preference shall be given by any Regulation of Commerce or Revenue to the Ports of one State over those of another: nor shall Vessels bound to, or from, one State, be obliged to enter, clear, or pay Duties in another.

No Money shall be drawn from the Treasury, but in Consequence of Appropriations made by Law; and a regular Statement and Account of the Receipts and Expenditures of all public Money shall be published from time to time.

No Title of Nobility shall be granted by the United States: And no Person holding any Office of Profit or Trust under them, shall, without the Consent of the Congress, accept of any present, Emolument, Office, or Title, of any kind whatever, from any King, Prince, or foreign State.

- Section. 10. No State shall enter into any Treaty, Alliance, or Confederation; grant Letters of Marque and Reprisal; coin Money; emit Bills of Credit; make any Thing but gold and silver Coin a Tender in Payment of Debts; pass any Bill of Attainder, ex post facto Law, or Law impairing the Obligation of Contracts, or grant any Title of Nobility.

No State shall, without the Consent of the Congress, lay any Imposts or Duties on Imports or Exports, except what may be absolutely necessary for executing its inspection Laws: and the net Produce of all Duties and Imposts, laid by any State on Imports or Exports, shall be for the Use of the Treasury of the United States; and all such Laws shall be subject to the Revision and Controul of the Congress.

No State shall, without the Consent of Congress, lay any Duty of Tonnage, keep Troops, or Ships of War in time of Peace, enter into any Agreement or Compact with another State, or with a foreign Power, or engage in War, unless actually invaded, or in such imminent Danger as will not admit of delay.

Article. II.

- Section. 1. The executive Power shall be vested in a President of the United States of America. He shall hold his Office during the Term of four Years, and, together with the Vice President, chosen for the same Term, be elected, as follows

Each State shall appoint, in such Manner as the Legislature thereof may direct, a Number of Electors, equal to the whole Number of Senators and Representatives to which the State may be entitled in the Congress: but no Senator or Representative, or Person holding an Office of Trust or Profit under the United States, shall be appointed an Elector.

The Electors shall meet in their respective States, and vote by Ballot for two Persons, of whom one at least shall not be an Inhabitant of the same State with themselves. And they shall make a List of all the Persons voted for, and of the Number of Votes for each; which List they shall sign and certify, and transmit sealed to the Seat of the Government of the United States, directed to the President of the Senate. The President of the Senate shall, in the Presence of the Senate and House of Representatives, open all the Certificates, and the Votes shall then be counted. The Person having the greatest Number of Votes shall be the President, if such Number be a Majority of the whole Number of Electors appointed; and if there be more than one who have such Majority, and have an equal Number of Votes, then the House of Representatives shall immediately chuse by Ballot one of them for President; and if no Person have a Majority, then from the five highest on the List the said House shall in like Manner chuse the President. But in chusing the President, the Votes shall be taken by States, the Representation from each State having one Vote; A quorum for this Purpose shall consist of a Member or Members from two thirds of the States, and a Majority of all the States shall be necessary to a Choice. In every Case, after the Choice of the President, the Person having the greatest Number of Votes of the Electors shall be the Vice President. But if there should remain two or more who have equal Votes, the Senate shall chuse from them by Ballot the Vice President.

The Congress may determine the Time of chusing the Electors, and the Day on which they shall give their Votes; which Day shall be the same throughout the United States.

No Person except a natural born Citizen, or a Citizen of the United States, at the time of the Adoption of this Constitution, shall be eligible to the Office of President; neither shall any Person be eligible to that Office who shall not have attained to the Age of thirty five Years, and been fourteen Years a Resident within the United States.

In Case of the Removal of the President from Office, or of his Death, Resignation, or Inability to discharge the Powers and Duties of the said Office, the Same shall devolve on the Vice President, and the Congress may by Law provide for the Case of Removal, Death, Resignation or Inability, both of the President and Vice President declaring what Officer shall then act as President, and such Officer shall act accordingly, until the Disability be removed, or a President shall be elected.

The President shall, at stated Times, receive for Iris Services, a Compensation, which shall neither be encreased nor diminished during the Period for which he shall have been elected, and he shall not receive within that Period any other Emolument from the United States, or any of them.

Before he enter on the Execution of his Office, he shall take the following Oath or Affirmation:--"I do solemnly swear (or affirm) that I will faithfully execute the Office of President of the United States, and will to the best of my Ability, preserve, protect and defend the Constitution of the United States."

- Section. 2. The President shall be Commander in Chief of the Army and Navy of the United States, and of the Militia of the several States, when called into the actual Service of the United States; he may require the Opinion, in writing, of the principal Officer in each of the executive Departments, upon any Subject relating to the Duties of their respective

Offices, and he shall have Power to grant Reprieves and Pardons for Offences against the United States, except in Cases of Impeachment.

He shall have Power, by and with the Advice and Consent of the Senate, to make Treaties, provided two thirds of the Senators present concur; and he shall nominate, and by and with the Advice and Consent of the Senate, shall appoint Ambassadors, other public Ministers and Consuls, Judges of the supreme Court, and all other Officers of the United States, whose Appointments are not herein otherwise provided for, and which shall be established by Law: but the Congress may by Law vest the Appointment of such inferior Officers, as they think proper, in the President alone, in the Courts of Law, or in the Heads of Departments.

The President shall have Power to fill up all Vacancies that may happen during the Recess of the Senate, by granting Commissions which shall expire at the End of their next Session.

- Section. 3. He shall from time to time give to the Congress Information of the State of the Union, and recommend to their Consideration such Measures as he shall judge necessary and expedient; he may, on extraordinary Occasions, convene both Houses, or either of them, and in Case of Disagreement between them, with Respect to the Time of

Adjournment, he may adjourn them to such Time as he shall think proper; he shall receive Ambassadors and other public Ministers; he shall take Care that the Laws be faithfully executed, and shall Commission all the Officers of the United States.

- Section. 4. The President, Vice President and all civil Officers of the United States, shall be removed from Office on Impeachment for, and Conviction of, Treason, Bribery, or other high Crimes and Misdemeanors.

Article III.

- Section. 1. The judicial Power of the United States, shall be vested in one supreme Court, and in such inferior Courts as the Congress may from time to time ordain and establish. The Judges, both of the supreme and inferior Courts, shall hold their Offices during good Behaviour, and shall, at stated Times, receive for their Services, a Compensation, which shall not be diminished during their Continuance in Office.
- Section. 2. The judicial Power shall extend to all Cases, in Law and Equity, arising under this Constitution, the Laws of the United States, and Treaties made, or which shall be made, under their Authority;--to all Cases affecting Ambassadors, other public Ministers and Consuls;--to all Cases of admiralty and maritime Jurisdiction;--to Controversies to which the United States shall be a Party;--to Controversies between two or more States;--between a State

and Citizens of another State;--between Citizens of different States;--between Citizens of the same State claiming Lands under Grants of different States, and between a State, or the Citizens thereof, and foreign States, Citizens or Subjects.

In all Cases affecting Ambassadors, other public Ministers and Consuls, and those in which a State shall be Party, the Supreme Court shall have original Jurisdiction. In all the other Cases before mentioned, the Supreme Court shall have appellate Jurisdiction, both as to Law and Fact, with such Exceptions, and under such Regulations as the Congress shall make.

The Trial of all Crimes, except in Cases of Impeachment, shall be by Jury; and such Trial shall be held in the State where the said Crimes shall have been committed; but when not committed within any State, the Trial shall be at such Place or Places as the Congress may by Law have directed.

- Section. 3. Treason against the United States shall consist only in levying War against them, or in adhering to their Enemies, giving them Aid and Comfort. No Person shall be convicted of Treason unless on the Testimony of two Witnesses to the same overt Act, or on Confession in open Court.

The Congress shall have Power to declare the Punishment of Treason, but no Attainder of Treason shall work Corruption of Blood, or Forfeiture except during the Life of the Person attainted.

Article IV.

- Section. 1. Full Faith and Credit shall be given in each State to the public Acts, Records, and judicial Proceedings of every other State. And the Congress may by general Laws prescribe the Manner in which such Acts, Records and Proceedings shall be proved, and the Effect thereof.
- Section. 2. The Citizens of each State shall be entitled to all Privileges and Immunities of Citizens in the several States.

A Person charged in any State with Treason, Felony, or other Crime, who shall flee from Justice, and be found in another State, shall on Demand of the executive Authority of the State from which he fled, be delivered up, to be removed to the State having Jurisdiction of the Crime.

No Person held to Service or Labour in one State, under the Laws thereof, escaping into another, shall, in Consequence of any Law or Regulation therein, be discharged from such Service or Labour, but shall be delivered up on Claim of the Party to whom such Service or Labour may be due.

- Section. 3. New States may be admitted by the Congress into this Union; but no new State shall be formed or erected within the Jurisdiction of any other State; nor any State be formed by the Junction of two or more States, or Parts of States, without the Consent of the Legislatures of the States concerned as well as of the Congress.

The Congress shall have Power to dispose of and make all needful Rules and Regulations respecting the Territory or other Property belonging to the United States; and nothing in this Constitution shall be so construed as to Prejudice any Claims of the United States, or of any particular State.

- Section. 4. The United States shall guarantee to every State in this Union a Republican Form of Government, and shall protect each of them against Invasion; and on Application of the Legislature, or of the Executive (when the Legislature cannot be convened) against domestic Violence.

Article. V.

The Congress, whenever two thirds of both Houses shall deem it necessary, shall propose Amendments to this Constitution, or, on the Application of the Legislatures of two thirds of the several States, shall call a Convention for proposing Amendments, which, in either Case, shall be valid to all Intents and Purposes, as Part of this Constitution, when ratified by the Legislatures of three fourths of the several States, or by Conventions in three fourths thereof, as the one or the other Mode of Ratification may be proposed by the Congress; Provided that no Amendment which may be made prior to the Year One thousand eight hundred and eight shall in any Manner affect the first and fourth Clauses in the Ninth Section of the first Article; and that no State, without its Consent, shall be deprived of its equal Suffrage in the Senate.

Article. VI.

All Debts contracted and Engagements entered into, before the Adoption of this Constitution, shall be as valid against the United States under this Constitution, as under the Confederation.

This Constitution, and the Laws of the United States which shall be made in Pursuance thereof; and all Treaties made, or which shall be made, under the Authority of the United States, shall be the supreme Law of the Land; and the Judges in every State shall be bound thereby, any Thing in the Constitution or Laws of any State to the Contrary notwithstanding.

The Senators and Representatives before mentioned, and the Members of the several State Legislatures, and all executive and judicial Officers, both of the United States and of the several States, shall be bound by Oath or Affirmation, to support this Constitution; but no religious Test shall ever be required as a Qualification to any Office or public Trust under the United States.

Article. VII.

The Ratification of the Conventions of nine States shall be sufficient for the

Establishment of this Constitution between the States so ratifying the Same. The Word, "the", being interlined between the seventh and eighth Lines of the first Page, The Word "Thirty" being partly written on an Erazure in the fifteenth Line of the first; Page, The Words "is tried" being interlined between the thirty second and thirty third Lines of the first Page and the Word "the" being interlined between the forty third and forty fourth Lines of the second Page.

Attest William Jackson

Secretary

done in Convention by the Unanimous Consent of the States present the Seventeenth Day of September in the Year of our Lord one thousand seven hundred and Eighty seven and of the Independence of the United States of America the Twelfth

In witness whereof

We have hereunto subscribed our Names.

Go. Washington Presidt.

and deputy from Virginia

Delaware

Geo: Read

Gunning Bedford junr.

John Dickinson

Richard Bassett

Jaco: Broom

Maryland

James McHenry

Dan of St Thos. Jenifer Danl. Carroll

Virginia

John Blair

James Madison Jr.

North Carolina

Wm. Blount

Richd. Dobbs Spaight

Hu Williamson

South Carolina

J. Rutledge

Charles Cotesworth Pinckney

Charles Pinckney

Pierce Butler

Georgia

William Few

Abr Baldwin

New Hampshire

John Langdon

Nicholas Gilman

Massachusetts

Nathaniel Gorham

Rufus King

Connecticut

Wm. Saml. Johnson

Roger Sherman

New York

Alexander Hamilton

New Jersey

Wil: Livingston

David Brearley

Wm. Paterson

Jona: Dayton

Pennsylvania

B Franklin

Thomas Mifflin

Robt. Morris

Geo. Clymer

Thos. Fitzsimons

Jared Ingersoll

James Wilson

Gouv. Morris

BIBLIOGRAPHY

Allan, Herbert S, JOHN HANCOCK PATRIOT IN PURPLE, Macmillan Co - New York 1948

ANNUAL REGISTER OR A VIEW OF THE HISTORY, POLITICS, AND LITERATURE (The), London: J. Dodsley, Various 18th Century Printings.

APPLETON'S CYCLOPEDIA OF AMERICAN BIOGRAPHY, edited by James Grant Wilson and John Fiske. Six volumes, New York: D. Appleton and Company, 1887-1889

THE ARTICLES OF CONFEDERATION; the Declaration of Rights; The Constitution of this Commonwealth, and the Articles of the Definitive Treaty between Great-Britain and the United States of America. Published by Order of the General Assembly. Richmond: Printed by Dixon and Holt, [1785].

Billias, George (ed). GEORGE WASHINGTON'S OPPONENTS: BRITISH GENERALS & ADMIRALS IN THE AMERICAN REVOLUTION, Morrow, 1969.

Boudinot, J. J., THE LIFE OF ELIAS BOUDINOT, Boston and New York, Houghton, Mifflin and Company 1896

Boyd, George Adams, ELIAS BOUDINOT - PATRIOT AND STATESMAN 1740-1821, Princeton, NJ: Princeton University Press, 1952.

Bradford, M. E. , Editor, Jonathan Elliot's Debates in the Several State Conventions on the Adoption of the Federal Constitution, Richmond, James River, 1989.

Brown, Abram English. JOHN HANCOCK, HIS BOOK, Lee & Shepard Boston 1898.

Burnett, Edmund C. LETTERS OF MEMBERS OF THE CONTINENTAL CONGRESS, Carnegie Institution of Washington, Washington, D. C. 1923

Butler, John P. (Ed.), INDEX: THE PAPERS OF THE CONTINENTAL CONGRESS, 1774-1789 Washington, DC Government Printing Office 1978.

Collins, Varnum Lansing, CONTINENTAL CONGRESS AT PRINCETON, The Princeton, 1908

THE CONNECTICUT COURANT AND WEEKLY INTELLIGENCER, Various 18th Century Issues, Hartford: Hudson and Goodwin, 1782

Continental Congress, EXTRACTS FROM THE VOTES AND PROCEEDINGS OF THE AMERICAN CONTINENTAL CONGRESS, HELD AT PHILADELPHIA ON THE 5TH OF SEPTEMBER 1774, CONTAINING THE BILL OF

RIGHTS. Timothy Green. New London, 1774.

Continental Congress, JOURNALS OF THE CONTINENTAL CONGRESS, 1774-1789; 1904, Edited from the Original Records in the Library of Congress by Worthington Chauncey Ford, Washington: Government Printing Office, 1904-22

Continental Congress and United States in Congress Assembled, JOURNALS OF THE CONTINENTAL CONGRESS, FARRAND'S RECORDS, ELLIOT'S DEBATES, & LETTERS OF THE DELEGATES - ON-LINE, http://memory.loc.gov/ammem/amlaw/lwjc.html

Daniels, Jonathan, THE RANDOLPHS OF VIRGINIA-AMERICA'S FOREMOST FAMILY, N.Y. Doubleday & Co. 1972.

Dictionary, Illustrated, AMERICAN DICTIONARY OF PRINTING AND BOOK-MAKING CONTAINING A HISTORY OF THESE ARTS IN EUROPE AND AMERICA, WITH DEFINITIONS OF TECHNICAL TERMS AND BIOGRAPHICAL SKETCHES, New York: Howard Lockwood & Co. 1894.

DUNLAP John & CLAYPOOLE David C (Publishers): The Pennsylvania Packet, and Daily Advertiser. Various 18th Century Issues.

Dreher, George Kelsey(Ed), SAMUEL HUNTINGTON, PRESIDENT OF CONGRESS:LONGER THAN EXPECTED:A NARRATIVE ESSAYS ON THE LETTERS OF SAMUEL HUTINGTON 1779-1781, Horse Free Press Midland, TX 1996.

ENYART, O.M., BIOGRAPHICAL CONGRESSIONAL DIRECTORY: 1774-1903, WASHINGTON D.C.: WASHINGTON PTINTING OFFICE, 1903.

Fitzpatrick, John C. , CALENDAR OF THE CORRESPONDENCE OF GEORGE WASHINGTON, Commander in Chief of the Continental Army (Correspondence with the Continental Congress; Correspondence with the Officers, 1775-1784) 5 Volume Set Washington, DC: Government Printing Office 1906 & 1915.

FORCE, Peter, compiler, AMERICAN ARCHIVES: CONSISTING OF A COLLECTION OF AUTHENTICK RECORDS, STATE PAPERS, DEBATES, AND LETTERS AND OTHER NOTICES OF PUBLICK AFFAIRS, THE WHOLE FORMING A DOCUMENTARY HISTORY OF THE ORIGIN AND PROGRESS OF THE NORTH AMERICAN COLONIES; VOLS I-IV. Washington: Published by M. St. Clair Clarke and Peter Force, 1837-43.

Force, Peter, AMERICAN ARCHIVES: FIFTH SERIES. CONTAINING A DOCUMENTARY HISTORY OF THE UNITED STATES OF AMERICA, M. St. Clair Clarke and Peter Force under the authority of Acts of Congress; Washington, D.C.: 1851

Garland, Hugh A., LIFE OF JOHN RANDOLPH OF ROANOKE, 2 volumes. NY: Appleton, 1850.

Giunta, Mary A. [editor-in-chief]; THE EMERGING NATION: A DOCUMENTARY HISTORY OF FOREIGN RELATIONS OF THE UNITED STATES UNDER THE ARTICLES OF CONFEDERATION, 1780-1789 [3 volumes]

Hamilton, Alexander, John Jay, and James Madison. THE FEDERALIST, ON THE NEW CONSTITUTION; WRITTEN IN 1788, BY MR. HAMILTON, MR. JAY, AND MR. MADISON. [The Federalist Papers by Alexander Hamilton, John Jay, and James Madison.] Philadelphia: Published by Benjamin Warner, No. 147 Market Street, and sold at his stores, Richmond, Virginia, and Charleston, South Carolina, 1818.

Harkey, Lewis R., LIFE OF CHARLES THOMSON, SECRETARY OF THE CONTINENTAL CONGRESS, Philadelphia, 1900.

Jay, William, THE LIFE OF JOHN JAY: WITH SELECTIONS FROM HIS CORRESPONDENCE AND MISCELLANEOUS PAPERS, New York: J & J Harper, 1833.

Knollenberg, Bernhard, WASHINGTON AND THE REVOLUTION A REAPPRAISAL: GATES, CONWAY, AND THE CONTINENTAL CONGRESS, Macmillan 1940

LEE, Richard H., MEMOIR OF THE LIFE OF RICHARD HENRY LEE, AND HIS CORRESPONDENCE WITH THE MOST DISTINGUISHED MEN IN AMERICA AND EUROPE.AND OF THE EVENTS OF THE AMERICAN REVOLUTION. 2 vols. Phila.: H. C. Carey & I. Lea,1825

Lord, Clifford, ed, THE CONTINENTAL CONGRESSES AND THE CONGRESS OF CONFEDERATION 1777-1789 New York St Historical Society, Cooperstown 1943

Matthews, John Carter, RICHARD HENRY LEE, Williamsburg, Va.: Virginia Independence Bicentennial Commission, 1978

Monaghan, Frank - JOHN JAY: DEFENDER OF LIBERTY AGAINST KINGS & PEOPLES, author of the constitution & Governor of New York, President of the Continental Congress, co-author of the Federalist, negotiator of the peace of 1783 & the Jay Treaty of 1794, first Chief Justice of the United States. Bobbs-Merrill, NY, 1935

Morgan, David, with Wm Schmidt, NORTH CAROLINA IN THE CONTINENTAL CONGRESS, NC; Blair, 1976

Robins, Sally Nelson, LOVE STORIES OF FAMOUS VIRGINIANS. Published Under The Auspices Of The National Society Colonial Dames Of America In The State Of Virginia. Richmond: Press of the Dietz Printing Co. 1923.

Rogers, Thomas J. A NEW AMERICAN BIOGRAPHICAL DICTIONARY; OR, REMEMBRANCER OF THE DEPARTED HEROES, SAGES, AND STATES-

MEN OF AMERICA. Easton, Penn: Printed and Published By Thomas J. Rogers, 1824

Rossman, Kenneth R., THOMAS MIFFLIN AND THE POLITICS OF THE AMERICAN REVOLUTION, Chapel Hill: University of North Carolina Press, 1952

Rowe, G. S. , THOMAS MCKEAN. THE SHAPING OF AN AMERICAN REPUBLICANISM Boulder: Colorado Associated University 1978.

Sanders, Jennings B., EVOLUTION OF EXECUTIVE DEPARTMENTS OF THE CONTINENTAL CONGRESS, 1774-1789., The University of North Carolina Press Chapel Hill 1935

Sanders, Jennings B., THE PRESIDENCY OF THE CONTINENTAL CONGRESS 1774-1789; A Study in American Institutional History, Gloucester, MA Peter Smith 1971

Smith, Paul H., LETTERS OF DELEGATES TO CONGRESS, 1774-1789, Washington, D.C.: Library of Congress 1976-1987. Very good. 14 vols.

Smith, Seymour Wemyss, JOHN HANSON - OUR FIRST PRESIDENT, New York, NY: Brewer et al, 1932.

Smith, William Henry, ST. CLAIR PAPERS: THE LIFE AND PUBLIC SERVICES OF ARTHUR ST. CLAIR, SOLDIER OF THE REVOLUTIONARY WAR, PRESIDENT OF THE CONTINENTAL CONGRESS, AND GOVERNOR OF THE NORTH-WESTERN TERRITORY; WITH HIS CORRESPONDENCE AND OTHER PAPERS., The Cincinnati, (OH): Robert Clarke, 1882. 8vo. 2 volumes: xii

Souder, Casper, CARPENTERS' HALL: THE MEETING PLACE OF THE FIRST CONTINENTAL CONGRESS. Full Sketch of Its History From 1724; With Views and Sketches of Carpenters' Hall, Clarke's hall, Benezet's House, And Chestnut Street Bridge, Duche's House, etc. Prepared For the Soldier and Sailors Home Fair. Philadelphia, 1865.

Staples, William R., RHODE ISLAND IN THE CONTINENTAL CONGRESS, Providence Press Co. 1870

United States in Congress Assembled, JOURNALS OF CONGRESS, AND OF THE UNITED STATES IN CONGRESS ASSEMBLED, 1787. Continental Congress: JOURNALS OF CONGRESS, AND OF THE UNITED STATES IN CONGRESS ASSEMBLED, FOR THE YEAR 1781. PUBLISHED BY ORDER OF CONGRESS, VOLUME VII. NEW YORK: Printed by John Patterson. 1787.

Urban, Sylvanius, GENTLEMEN'S MAGAZINE AND HISTORICAL CHRONICAL, Various 18th Century Issues, St. Johns Gate, London D. Henry & R. Cave 1757

Ver Steeg, Clarence L., ROBERT MORRIS REVOLUTIONARY FINANCIER with an Analysis of his Earlier..., Philadelphia: Univ. of Pennsylvania Press, 1954

Wallace, David Duncan, THE LIFE OF HENRY LAURENS: WITH A SKETCH OF THE LIFE OF LIEUTENANT-COLONEL JOHN LAURENS, NY: G. P. Putnam's, 1915.

William, Allen, THE AMERICAN BIOGRAPHICAL DICTIONARY: CONTAINING AN ACCOUNT OF THE LIVES CHARACTERS AND WRITINGS OF THE MOST EMINENT PERSONS DECEASED IN NORTH AMERICA FROM ITS FIRST SETTLEMENT. Book-On-Demand Reprint from: Boston J. P. Jewett; Cleveland, O. H. P. B. Jewett 1857.

Young, Eleanor, FORGOTTEN PATRIOT ROBERT MORRIS, New York: Macmillan, 1950

AUTHORS BIOGRAPHY

Stan Klos launched his rhetorical career in 1999 after 20 years of historic real estate and rare manuscript acquisition. During that period Stan purchased a fledgling RE/MAX Pennsylvania regional franchise of two offices and expanded it to 61 offices in 12 years. The company's yearly sales in real estate topped $1.2 billion dollars in 1999 when it was sold back to RE/MAX International. Stan was one of a select group of Regional Owners who helped mastermind RE/MAX into the world's largest real estate company with sales nearly exceeding the combined volume of real estate giants C-21 and Coldwell Banker.

Stan's lectures and historical document exhibits have been featured at the 2000 GOP Convention Philadelphia's PoliticalFest, American Philatelic Museum, Capitol of the United States - United States Senate, Carnegie Institute, Carnegie Historical Society, Carnegie Library, Clara Barton National Historic Site, Fairmont State College, Fort Pitt Museum, James Madison's Montpelier, MGM Grand Hotel in Las Vegas, NASA Classroom of the Future, Ohio University, Patrick Henry College, Smithsonian Institution, Heinz Pittsburgh Regional History Center, Virginia State Capitol – James Monroe Foundation, West Virginia State Capitol and Wheeling Jesuit University. He currently houses his collections at the Skibo Centre where he speaks regularly before local K-12 schools, Universities, Pittsburgh Area Conventions and Special events. Most recently, Stan had the distinct honor to serve as keynote speaker for the tomb rededication and reburial of 1st US President Samuel Huntington and First Lady Martha Huntington in Norwich, Connecticut.

Stan's ideas about history, its implications on politics, business, education and real estate have been quoted in newspapers and magazines throughout the country as well as on both local and National Radio, Cable-TV and Network TV affiliates. On top of his consulting practice, Stan has been an MBA Adjunct Professor and Lecturer - MBA BUSINESS AND THE MEDIA, MBA EXECUTIVE LEADERSHIP AND MBA ENTREPRENEURSHIP - at Wheeling Jesuit University, MARKETING & FINANCE, Georgian Court College, New Jersey; MARKETING & COMMUNICATIONS, The Pennsylvania State University; BUSINESS AND PROFESSIONAL SPEAKING, Idaho State University.

As the father of eight children, Stan is committed to K-12 education. He is the Founder of Virtualology.com that has 1.5 million unique visitors a month. Virtualology is internationally ranked 29th in the TOP 100 Online Educational Sites and has been herald as one of USA Today's Hot Sites.

Stan also served as the Finance Chairman for the West Virginia Republican Party in 1992-93. In 1994 Stan won the Republican Nominee for the US Senate with a mission to compel his opponent, Robert C. Byrd, to campaign rigorously in West Virginia. As a "*Sacrificial Lamb*" Stan's candidacy persuaded both Senator Byrd, the DNC and WV Democratic State Committee to utilize personnel resources and millions of dollars in West Virginia while the RNC focused assets on winnable races capturing the majority in the US Senate. Stan, the father of 8 children, retired from politics in 1996 after turning down a political appointment by then newly elected Governor Cecil Underwood because *"the children just didn't understand why my political commitments often trumped my parenting responsibilities."*

Stan, as a consultant, is currently working with several municipalities and counties on Economic Development. Stan's "*Share The Vision Campaign*" took First Place in the State winning the 2003 "*Pennsylvania Downtown Center's Townie Award*". Stan also participated in the inception and development of the Fort Henry Project in Ohio County West Virginia.

When you hear Stan speak you will discover a unique perspective on how the United States was formed with a special emphasis on the trials and tribulations of those who succeeded against all odds. Most importantly Stan artistically applies the US Founders' Vision and accomplishments to 21st Century business, politics and education awakening a voluntary inclination in your audience to act and seize the moment.